MULTI-LEVEL & HILLSIDE HOMES

312 Designs
For Split-Levels, Bi-Levels, Multi-Levels and Walkout Basements

1,250 to 6,800 square feet

HOME PLANNERS, INC.

Contents

	Page
How To Read Floor Plans and Blueprints	3
How To Shop For Mortgage Money	4
The Cost of a Mortgage	5
How To Choose a Contractor	6
A Checklist For Plan Selection	7
How to Recognize Multi-Levels and Hillsides	13
Contemporary Split-Levels	15
Traditional Split-Levels	63
Split-Foyer Plans	101
Hillside Homes	139
One-Story Homes With Walkout Basements	215
Two-Story Homes With Walkout Basements	235
One-Story Homes With Open Staircases	262
Two-Story Homes With Open Staircases	279
The Landscape Blueprint Package	302
The Deck Blueprint Package	306
The Home Blueprint Package	310
The Home Blueprint Order Form	317
Additional Plans Books	318

Note: Many of the homes featured in this book have a matching or corresponding Landscape or Deck plan available from Home Planners, Inc. Some have both. These plans have a **L** or a **D** following their design number and square-footage notations. For information on how to order plans for landscapes and decks, see pages 302-309.

Published by Home Planners, Inc.
3275 West Ina Road, Suite 110
Tucson, Arizona 85741
Chairman: Charles W. Talcott
President and Publisher: Rickard D. Bailey
Publications Manager: Cindy J. Coatsworth
Editor: Paulette Mulvin
Front Cover Graphic Design: Paul Fitzgerald

First Printing December 1990
10 9 8 7 6 5 4 3 2 1

Library of Congress Number: 90-084446
ISBN: 0-918894-87-5

ON THE COVER: Plans for this grand Contemporary With Walkout Basement, Design V32894, can be found on page 134.
Home owned and built by Gretchen Kay Carlson & Kent Richard Hulet, Parker, Colorado.
Photographer: Roger Whitacre

How To Read Floor Plans and Blueprints

Selecting the most suitable house plan for your family is a matter of matching your needs, tastes, and lifestyle against the many designs we offer. When you study the floor plans in this book, and the blueprints that you may subsequently order, remember that they are a two-dimensional representation of what will be a three-dimensional reality.

Floor plans are easy to read. Rooms are clearly labeled, with dimensions given in feet and inches. Most symbols are logical and self-explanatory: The location of bathroom fixtures, fireplaces, planters, tile floors, cabinets and counters, sinks, appliances, closets, and sloped or beamed ceilings will be obvious.

A blueprint, although much more detailed, is also easy to read; all it demands is concentration. The blueprints that we offer come in many large sheets, each one of which contains a different kind of information. One sheet contains foundation and excavation drawings, another has a precise plot plan. An elevations sheet deals with the exterior walls of the house; section drawings show precise dimensions, fittings, doors, windows, and roof structures. This provides all the construction information needed by your contractor. Also available is a helpful materials list with size and quantities of all necessary components. Using this list, your contractor and suppliers can make a start at calculating costs for you.

When you first study a floor plan or blueprint, imagine that you are walking through the house. By mentally visualizing each room in three dimensions, you can transform the technical data and symbols into something more real. Interior space should be organized in a logical way, based on the intended use of such space. Usually the space is divided into rooms which fall into one of three categories. The sleeping area includes bedrooms and bathrooms; the work area includes the kitchen, laundry, utility room, garage and other functional rooms; the living area includes the living and dining rooms, family room, and other gathering areas as well as entrance ways.

To begin a mental tour of the home, start at the front door. It's preferable to have a foyer or entrance hall in which to receive guests. A closet here is desirable; a powder room is a plus.

Look for good traffic circulation as you study the floor plan. You should not have to pass all the way through one main room to reach another. From the entrance area you should have direct access to the three principal areas of a house—the living, work, and sleeping zones. For example, a foyer might provide separate entrances to the living room, kitchen, patio, and a hallway or staircase leading to the bedrooms.

Study the layout of each zone. Most people expect the living room to be protected from cross traffic. The kitchen, on the other hand, should connect with the dining room—and perhaps also the utility room, basement, garage, patio or deck, or a secondary entrance. A homemaker whose workday centers in the kitchen may have special

requirements: a window that faces the backyard; a clear view of the family room where children play; a garage or driveway entrance that allows for a short trip with groceries; laundry facilities close at hand. Check for efficient placement of kitchen cabinets, counter, and appliances. Is there enough room in the kitchen for additional appliances, for eating in? Is there a dining nook?

Perhaps this part of the house contains a family room or a den/bedroom/office. It's advantageous to have a bathroom or powder room in this section.

As you study the plan, you may encounter a staircase, indicated by a group of parallel lines, the number of lines equaling the number of steps. Arrows labeled "up" mean that the staircase leads to a higher level, and those pointing down mean it leads to a lower one. Staircases in a split-level will have both up and down arrows on one staircase because two levels are depicted in one drawing and an extra level in another.

Notice the location of the stairways. Is too much floor space lost to them? Will you find yourself making too many trips?

Study the sleeping quarters. Are the bedrooms situated as you like? You may want the master bedroom near the kids, or you may want it as far away as possible. Is there at least one closet per person in each bedroom or a double one for a couple? Bathrooms should be convenient to each bedroom—if not adjoining, then with hallway access and on the same floor.

Once you are familiar with the relative positions of the rooms, look for such structural details as:
- Sufficient uninterrupted wall space for furniture arrangement.
- Adequate room dimensions.
- Potential heating or cooling problems—i.e., a room over a garage or next to the laundry.
- Window and door placement for good ventilation and natural light.
- Location of doorways—avoid having a basement staircase or a bathroom in view of the dining room.
- Adequate auxiliary space—closets, storage, bathrooms, countertops.
- Separation of activity areas (will noise from the recreation room disturb sleeping children or a parent at work?).

As you complete your mental walk through the house, bear in mind your family's long-range needs. A good house plan will allow for some adjustments now and additions in the future.

Take time to notice special amenities: fireplaces and raised hearths, work islands in the kitchen, pass-through countertops between kitchen and breakfast nook, whirlpool baths. Note the placement of decks and balconies. Your family may find the listing of favorite features a most helpful exercise. Why not try it?

How To Shop For Mortgage Money

Most people who are in the market for a new home spend months searching for the right house plan and building site. Ironically, these same people often invest very little time shopping for the money to finance their new home, though the majority will have to live with the terms of their mortgage for as long as they live in the home.

The fact is that not all lending institutions are alike, nor are the loans that they offer.

- Lending practices vary from one city and state to another. If you are a first-time builder or are new to an area, it is wise to hire a real estate (not divorce or general practice) attorney to help you unravel the maze of your area's laws and customs.
- Before talking with a lender, write down all your questions and take notes so you can make accurate comparisons.
- Do not be intimidated by financial officers. Do not hesitate to reveal what other institutions are offering; they may be challenged to meet or better the terms.

A GUIDE TO LENDERS

Where can you turn for home financing? Here is a list of sources for you to contact:

Savings and Loan Associations
Savings Banks/Mutual Savings Banks
Commercial Banks
Mortgage Banking Companies
Some Credit Unions

Each of the above institutions generally offers a variety of loan types, interest rates, and fees. It is recommended that you survey each type of institution in your area to determine exactly what type of financing is available so that you can make an intelligent and informed decision.

A GUIDE TO LOAN TYPES

Conventional Loans

These types of loans usually require a minimum down payment of 10% of the lower of the purchase price or appraised value of the property. However, in many cases, this down payment requirement has been increased to 15% to 20% depending on the type of loan and the requirements of the lending institution. Often, the minimum down payment requirement is applied to owner-occupied residences and is usually increased if the property is purchased as a vacation home or investment.

The most common type of conventional loan is the **fixed-rate loan** which has a fixed interest rate and fixed monthly payments. The term of the loan may vary, but such loans generally are available in fifteen- and thirty-year terms. The obvious advantage of a fifteen-year term is an earlier loan payoff as well as reduced interest charges.

Other types of conventional loans are called **adjustable rate mortgages (ARM's)**. This type of loan usually has a lower initial interest rate than the fixed-rate loan, but the interest rate of payment may change depending on the loan terms and economic conditions. The frequency of these interest/payment adjustments depends on the individual loan, but they usually occur every twelve months.

Some key terms to understanding ARM loans are listed below:

Adjustment Period - The period between one rate change and the next. Therefore, a loan with an adjustment period of one year is known as a One Year ARM.

Index - The interest rate change is tied to an index rate. These indexes usually go up and down with the general movement of interest rates. If the index rate moves up, so does your monthly payment. If the index rate goes down, your monthly payment may also go down. There are a variety of indexes. Among the most common is the weekly average yield on U.S. Treasury securities adjusted to a constant maturity of one, three, or five years.

Margin - To determine the interest rate on an ARM, lenders add a few percentage points to the index rate. These percentage points are called the margin. The amount of the margin can differ from one lender to the next, but is usually constant through the life of the loan.

Caps - Most ARM loans limit the amount that the interest rate can increase. There are periodic caps which limit the increase from one adjustment period to the next and overall caps which limit the interest rate increase over the life of the loan.

Negative Amortization - Several ARM loans contain negative amortization which means that your mortgage balance can increase even though you are making regular monthly payments. This happens when the interest rate of the loan increases while your monthly payment remains the same.

Convertibility or Conversion Option - This is a clause in your agreement that allows you to convert the ARM to a fixed-rate mortgage at designated times. Not all ARM loans contain this option.

There are other types of less-common conventional loans which are offered by many institutions: Graduated Payment Mortgages, Reverse Annuity Mortgages, and Bi-Weekly Mortgages. Consult with a financial officer of a lending institution for details on these other loan types.

Government Loans

FHA loans are government insured and have substantially lower down payments than conventional loans; however, there are maximum allowable loan amounts for these loans depending on the location of the property.

Another type of government loan is through the Veteran's Administration (VA). Like the FHA, the VA guarantees loans for eligible veterans and the spouses of those veterans who died while in the service. Down payment requirements are also extremely low on these types of loans.

There are a variety of loan types available under these government programs including fixed rate, ARM's and graduated payment mortgages. The financial officer of the lending institution will be able to explain these various loan types and the qualification standards.

The Cost of a Mortgage

Monthly principal and interest per $1,000 of mortgage

Mortgage rate	15-year loan	20-year loan	25-year loan	30-year loan
9.00%	10.15	9.00	8.40	8.05
9.10%	10.21	9.07	8.47	8.12
9.20%	10.27	9.13	8.53	8.20
9.30%	10.33	9.20	8.60	8.27
9.40%	10.39	9.26	8.67	8.34
9.50%	10.45	9.33	8.74	8.41
9.60%	10.51	9.39	8.81	8.49
9.70%	10.57	9.46	8.88	8.56
9.80%	10.63	9.52	8.95	8.63
9.90%	10.69	9.59	9.02	8.71
10.00%	10.75	9.66	9.09	8.78
10.10%	10.81	9.72	9.16	8.85
10.20%	10.87	9.79	9.23	8.93
10.30%	10.94	9.85	9.30	9.00
10.40%	11.00	9.92	9.38	9.08
10.50%	11.06	9.99	9.45	9.15
10.60%	11.12	10.06	9.52	9.23
10.70%	11.18	10.12	9.59	9.30
10.80%	11.25	10.19	9.66	9.38
10.90%	11.31	10.26	9.73	9.45
11.00%	11.37	10.33	9.81	9.53
11.10%	11.43	10.40	9.88	9.60
11.20%	11.50	10.46	9.95	9.68
11.30%	11.56	10.53	10.02	9.76
11.40%	11.62	10.60	10.10	9.83
11.50%	11.69	10.67	10.17	9.91
11.60%	11.75	10.74	10.24	9.98
11.70%	11.81	10.81	10.32	10.06
11.80%	11.88	10.88	10.39	10.14
11.90%	11.94	10.95	10.46	10.21

Note: Multiply the cost per $1,000 by the size of the mortgage (in thousands). The result is the monthly payment, including principal and interest. For example, for an $80,000 mortgage for 30 years at 10 percent, multiply 80 x 8.78 = $702.40.

How To Choose
A Contractor

Contractors are part craftsmen, part businessmen, and part magicians. Transforming your dreams and drawings into a finished house, they are responsible for the final cost of the structure, for the quality of the workmanship, and for the solving of all problems that occur quite naturally in the course of construction.

There are two types of residential contractors: the construction company and the carpenter-builder, often called a general contractor. Each of these has its advantages and disadvantages.

Carpenter-builders work directly on the job as field foremen. Because their background is that of a craftsman, their workmanship is probably good—but their paperwork may be slow or sloppy. Their overhead—which you pay for—is less than that of a large construction company. However, if the job drags on for any reason, their interest may flag because your project is overlapping their next job and eroding profits.

Construction companies that handle several projects concurrently have an office staff to keep the paperwork moving and an army of reliable subcontractors. Though you can be confident that they will meet deadlines, they may sacrifice workmanship in order to do so. Emphasizing efficiency, they are less personal to work with than a general contractor and many will not work with an individual unless there is representation by an architect.

To find a reliable contractor, start by asking friends who have built homes for recommendations. Check with local lumberyards and building supply outlets for names of possible candidates and call departments of consumer affairs. Keep in mind that these watchdog organizations can give only the number of complaints filed; they cannot tell you what percent of those claims were valid. Remember, too, that a large-volume operation is logically going to have more registered complaints against it than will an independent contractor.

Interview each of the potential candidates. Find out about specialties—custom houses, development houses, remodeling, or office buildings. Ask each to take you into—not just to the site of—current projects. Ask to see projects that are complete as well as work in progress, emphasizing that you are interested in projects comparable to yours. A $300,000 dentist's office will give you little insight into a contractor's craftsmanship.

Ask each contractor for bank references from both a commercial bank and any other appropriate lender. If in good financial standing, the contractor should have no qualms about giving you this information. Also ask about warranties. Most will give you a one-year warranty on the structure; some offer as much as a ten-year warranty.

Ask for references, even though no contractor will give you the name of a dissatisfied customer. Ask about follow-through. Was the building site cleaned up or did the owner have to dispose of the refuse? Ask about the organization of business. Did the paperwork go smoothly, or was there a delay in hooking up the sewer because of a failure to apply for a permit?

Talk to each of the candidates about fees. Most work on a "cost plus" basis; that is, the basic cost of the project—materials, subcontractors' services, wages of those working directly on the project, but not office help—plus a fee. Some have a fixed fee; others work on a percentage of the basic cost. A fixed fee is usually better for you if you can get one. If a contractor works on a percentage, ask for a cost breakdown of the best estimate and keep very careful track as the work progresses. A crafty contractor can always use a cost overrun to good advantage when working on a percentage.

Do not be overly suspicious of a contractor who won't work on a fixed fee. One who is very good and in great demand may not be willing to do so and may also be reluctant to submit a competitive bid.

Give the top two or three candidates each copies of the plans and your specifications for materials. If they are not each working from the same guidelines, the competitive bids will be of little value. Give each the same deadline for turning in a bid; two or three weeks is a reasonable period of time. Make an appointment with each of them and open the envelopes at this time.

If one bid is remarkably low, the contractor may have made an honest error in the estimate. Don't insist that the contractor hold to a bid if it is in error. Forcing a building price that is too low could be disastrous for both of you. You may want to review the bids with your architect, if you have one, or with your lender to discuss which to accept. They may not recommend the lowest. A low bid does not necessarily mean that you will get the best quality with economy.

If the bids are relatively close, the most important consideration may not be money at all. A bid from a contractor who is easy to talk to and inspires confidence may be the best choice. Any sign of a personality conflict between you and a contractor should be weighed when making a decision.

Once you have financing, you can sign a contract with the builder. Most have their own contract forms, but it is advisable to have a lawyer draw one up or, at the very least, review the standard contract. This usually costs a small flat fee.

A good contract should include:

- Plans and sketches of the work to be done, subject to your approval.
- A list of materials, including quantity, brand names, style or serial numbers. (Do not permit any "or equal" clause that will allow the contractor to make substitutions.)
- The terms—who (you or the lender) pays whom and when.
- A production schedule.
- The contractor's certification of insurance for workmen's compensation, damage, and liability.
- A rider stating that all changes, whether or not they increase the cost, must be submitted and approved in writing.

Of course, this list represents the least a contract should include. Once you have signed it, your plans are on the way to becoming a home.

A Checklist
For Plan Selection

Developing an architectural plan from the various wants and needs of an individual or family that fits into lifestyle demands and design elegance is the most efficient way to assure a livable plan. It is not only possible but highly desirable to design a plan around such requirements as separate bedrooms for each member of the family, guest suites, a quiet study area, an oversized entertainment area, a two-car garage, a completely private master suite, and a living room fireplace. Incorporated into this can be such wants as Tudor styling, 1½-stories, a large entry hall, decks and balconies, and a basement.

While it is obviously best to begin with wants and needs and then design a home to fit these criteria, this is not always practical or even possible. A very effective way around this problem is to select a professionally prepared home plan which meets all needs and incorporates as many wants as possible. With careful selection, it will be possible to modify sizes and make other design adjustments to make the home as close to custom as can be. It is important to remember that some wants may have to be compromised in the interest of meeting budgetary limitations. The trick is to build the best possible home for the available money while satisfying all absolute needs.

Following are some cost-controlling ideas that can make a big difference in the overall price of a home:

1. Square or rectangular homes are less expensive to build than irregularly shaped homes.
2. It is less expensive to build on a flat lot than on a sloping or hillside lot.
3. The use of locally manufactured or produced materials cuts costs greatly.
4. Using stock materials and stock sizes of components takes advantage of mass production cost reductions.
5. The use of materials that can be quickly installed cuts labor costs. Prefabricating large sections or panels eliminates much time on the site.
6. The use of prefinished materials saves significantly on labor costs.
7. Investigating existing building codes before beginning construction eliminates unnecessary changes as construction proceeds.
8. Refraining from changing the design or any aspect of the plan after construction begins will help to hold down cost escalation.
9. Minimizing special jobs or custom-built items keeps costs from increasing.
10. Designing the house for short plumbing lines saves on piping and other materials.
11. Proper insulation saves heating and cooling costs.
12. Utilizing passive solar features, such as correct orientation, reduces future maintenance costs.

To help you consider all the important factors in evaluating a plan, the following checklist should be reviewed carefully. By comparing its various points to any plan and a wants-and-needs list, it will be possible to easily recognize the deficiencies of a plan or determine its appropriateness. Be sure to include family members in the decision-making process. Their ideas and desires will help in finding exactly the right plan.

CHECKLIST

The Neighborhood

1. _____ Reasonable weather conditions
2. No excess
   _____ a. wind
   _____ b. smog or fog
   _____ c. odors
   _____ d. soot or dust
3. _____ The area is residential
4. There are no
   _____ a. factories
   _____ b. dumps
   _____ c. highways
   _____ d. railroads
   _____ e. airports
   _____ f. apartments
   _____ g. commercial buildings
5. _____ City-maintained streets
6. No hazards in the area
   _____ a. quarries
   _____ b. storage tanks
   _____ c. power stations
   _____ d. unprotected swimming pools

7. Reasonably close to
   _____ a. work
   _____ b. schools
   _____ c. churches
   _____ d. hospital
   _____ e. shopping
   _____ f. recreation
   _____ g. public transportation
   _____ h. library
   _____ i. police protection
   _____ j. fire protection
   _____ k. parks
   _____ l. cultural activities
8. _____ Streets are curved
9. _____ Traffic is slow
10. _____ Intersections are at right angles
11. _____ Street lighting
12. _____ Light traffic
13. _____ Visitor parking
14. _____ Good design in street
15. _____ Paved streets and curbs
16. _____ Area is not deteriorating
17. _____ Desirable expansion
18. _____ Has some open spaces

19. _____ Numerous and healthy trees
20. _____ Pleasant-looking homes
21. _____ Space between homes
22. _____ Water drains off
23. _____ Near sewerage line
24. _____ Storm sewers nearby
25. _____ Mail delivery
26. _____ Garbage pickup
27. _____ Trash pickup
28. _____ No city assessments

The Lot

1. _____ Title is clear
2. _____ No judgments against the seller
3. _____ No restrictions as to the use of the land or the deed
4. _____ No unpaid taxes or assessments
5. _____ Minimum of 70 feet of frontage
6. _____ House does not crowd the lot
7. _____ Possible to build on
8. _____ Few future assessments (sewers, lights, and so forth)
9. _____ Good top soil and soil percolation
10. _____ Good view
11. _____ No low spots to hold water
12. _____ Water drains off land away from the house
13. _____ No fill
14. _____ No water runoff from high ground
15. _____ If cut or graded there is substantial retaining wall
16. _____ Permanent boundary markers
17. _____ Utilities available at property line
18. _____ Utility hookup is reasonable
19. _____ Utility rates are reasonable
20. _____ Taxes are reasonable
21. _____ Water supply is adequate
22. _____ Regular, simply shaped lot
23. _____ Trees
24. _____ Do not have to cut trees
25. _____ Privacy for outside activities
26. _____ Attractive front yard
27. _____ Front and rear yards are adequate
28. _____ Front yard is not divided up by walks and driveway
29. _____ Outdoor walks have stairs grouped

The Floor Plan

1. _____ Designed by licensed architect
2. _____ Purchased from a reputable stock plan company
3. _____ Supervised by skilled contractor
4. Orientation
  _____ *a.* sun
  _____ *b.* view
  _____ *c.* noise
  _____ *d.* breeze
  _____ *e.* contour of land
5. _____ Entry
6. _____ Planned for exterior expansion
7. Planned for interior expansion
  _____ *a.* attic
  _____ *b.* garage
  _____ *c.* basement
8. _____ Simple but functional plan
9. _____ Indoor recreation area
10. _____ Wall space for furniture in each room
11. Well-designed hall
  _____ *a.* leads to all areas
  _____ *b.* no congestions

  _____ *c.* no wasted space
  _____ *d.* 3' minimum widths
12. _____ Easy to clean
13. _____ Easy to keep orderly
14. _____ Plan meets family's needs
15. _____ All rooms have direct emergency escape
16. Doorways functional
  _____ *a.* no unnecessary doors
  _____ *b.* wide enough for moving furniture through
  _____ *c.* can see visitors through locked front door
  _____ *d.* do not swing out into halls
  _____ *e.* swing open against a blank wall
  _____ *f.* do not bump other subjects
  _____ *g.* exterior doors are solid
17. Windows are functional
  _____ *a.* not too small
  _____ *b.* enough but not too many
  _____ *c.* glare-free
  _____ *d.* roof overhang protection where needed
  _____ *e.* large ones have the best view
  _____ *f.* easy to clean
  _____ *g.* no interference with furniture placement
  _____ *h.* over kitchen sink
  _____ *i.* open easily
18. _____ No fancy gadgets
19. _____ Room sizes are adequate
20. _____ Well-designed stairs
  _____ *a.* treads are 9" minimum
  _____ *b.* risers are 8" maximum
  _____ *c.* 36" minimum width
  _____ *d.* 3' minimum landings
  _____ *e.* attractive
  _____ *f.* easily reached
21. _____ Overall plan "fits" family requirements
22. _____ Good traffic patterns
23. _____ Noisy areas separated from quiet areas
24. _____ Rooms have adequate wall space for furniture
25. _____ Halls are 3'6" minimum

The Living Area

1. _____ Minimum space 12' x 16'
2. _____ Front door traffic does not enter
3. _____ Not in a traffic pattern
4. _____ Windows on two sides
5. _____ Has a view
6. _____ Storage for books and music materials
7. _____ Decorative lighting
8. _____ Whole family plus guests can be seated
9. _____ Desk area
10. _____ Fireplace
11. _____ Wood storage
12. _____ No street noises
13. _____ Privacy from street
14. _____ Acoustical ceiling
15. _____ Cannot see or hear bathroom
16. _____ Powder room
17. _____ Comfortable for conversation
18. Dining room
  _____ *a.* used enough to justify
  _____ *b.* minimum of 3' clearance around table
  _____ *c.* can be opened or closed to kitchen and patio
  _____ *d.* can be opened or closed to living room
  _____ *e.* electrical outlets for table appliances

19. Family room
    _____ *a.* minimum space 10' x 12'
    _____ *b.* room for family activities
    _____ *c.* room for noisy activities
    _____ *d.* room for messy activities
    _____ *e.* activities will not disturb sleeping area
    _____ *f.* finish materials are easy to clean and durable
    _____ *g.* room for expansion
    _____ *h.* separate from living room
    _____ *i.* near kitchen
    _____ *j.* fireplace
    _____ *k.* adequate storage
20. _____ Dead-end circulation
21. _____ Adequate furniture arrangements

The Entry

1. _____ The entry is a focal point
2. _____ The outside is inviting
3. _____ The landing has a minimum depth of 5'
4. _____ Protected from the weather
5. _____ Has an approach walk
6. _____ Well planted
7. _____ Coat closet
8. _____ Leads to living, sleeping, and service areas
9. _____ Floor material attractive and easy to clean
10. _____ Decorative lighting
11. _____ Space for table
12. _____ Space to hang mirror
13. _____ Does not have direct view into any room

The Bedrooms

1. _____ Adequate number of bedrooms
2. _____ Adequate size—10' x 12' minimum
3. _____ Open into a hall
4. _____ Living space
5. _____ Children's bedroom has study and play area
6. _____ Oriented to north side
7. In quiet area
    _____ *a.* soundproofing
    _____ *b.* acoustical ceiling
    _____ *c.* insulation in walls
    _____ *d.* thermal glass
    _____ *e.* double doors
    _____ *f.* closet walls
8. _____ Privacy
9. _____ 4' minimum wardrobe rod space per person
10. Master bedroom
    _____ *a.* bath
    _____ *b.* dressing area
    _____ *c.* full-length mirror
    _____ *d.* 12' x 12' minimum
11. Adequate windows
    _____ *a.* natural light
    _____ *b.* cross-ventilation
    _____ *c.* windows on two walls
12. _____ Room for overnight guests
13. _____ Bathroom nearby
14. _____ Wall space for bed, nightstands, and dresser
15. _____ Quiet reading area

The Bathroom

1. _____ Well designed
2. _____ Plumbing lines are grouped
3. _____ Fixtures have space around them for proper use
4. _____ Doors do not interfere with fixtures
5. _____ Noises are insulated from other rooms
6. _____ Convenient to bedrooms
7. _____ Convenient to guests
8. _____ Ventilation
9. _____ Heating
10. _____ Attractive fixtures
11. _____ No windows over tub or shower
12. _____ Wall area around tub and shower
13. _____ Light fixtures are water tight
14. _____ Large medicine cabinet
15. _____ Children cannot open medicine cabinet
16. _____ No bathroom tie-ups
17. _____ Good lighting
18. _____ Accessible electrical outlets
19. _____ No electric appliance or switch near water supply
20. _____ Towel and linen storage
21. _____ Dirty clothes hamper
22. _____ Steamproof mirrors
23. _____ Wall and floor materials are waterproof
24. _____ All finishes are easy to maintain
25. _____ Curtain and towel rods securely fastened
26. _____ Grab bar by tub
27. _____ Mixing faucets
28. _____ Bath in service area
29. _____ No public view into open bathroom door
30. _____ Clean-up area for outdoor jobs and children's play

The Kitchen

1. _____ Centrally located
2. _____ The family can eat informally in the kitchen
3. _____ At least 20' of cabinet space
    _____ *a.* counter space on each side of major appliances
    _____ *b.* minimum of 8' counter work area
    _____ *c.* round storage in corners
    _____ *d.* no shelf is higher than 72"
    _____ *e.* floor cabinets 24" deep and 36" high
    _____ *f.* wall cabinets 15" deep
    _____ *g.* 15" clearance between wall and floor cabinets
4. _____ Work triangle is formed between appliances
    _____ *a.* between 12' and 20'
    _____ *b.* no traffic through the work triangle
    _____ *c.* refrigerator opens into the work triangle
    _____ *d.* at least six electric outlets in work triangle
    _____ *e.* no door between appliances
5. _____ No space between appliances and counters
6. _____ Window over sink
7. _____ No wasted space in kitchen
8. _____ Can close off kitchen from dining area
9. _____ Snack bar in kitchen
10. _____ Kitchen drawers are divided
11. _____ Built-in chopping block
12. _____ Writing and telephone desk
13. _____ Indoor play area visible from kitchen
14. _____ Outdoor play area visible from kitchen
15. _____ Exhaust fan
16. _____ Natural light
17. _____ Good lighting for each work area
18. _____ Convenient access to service area and garage
19. _____ Durable surfaces
20. _____ Dishwasher
21. _____ Disposal
22. _____ Built-in appliances
23. _____ Bathroom nearby

24. _____ Room for freezer
25. _____ Pantry storage

The Utility Room

1. _____ Adequate laundry area
2. _____ Well-lighted work areas
3. _____ 240-volt outlet
4. _____ Gas outlet
5. _____ Sorting area
6. _____ Ironing area
7. _____ Drip-drying area
8. _____ Sewing and mending area
9. _____ On least desirable side of lot
10. _____ Exit to outdoor service area
11. _____ Exit near garage
12. _____ Sufficient cabinet space
13. _____ Bathroom in area
14. _____ Accessible from kitchen
15. _____ Adequate space for washer and dryer
16. _____ Laundry tray
17. _____ Outdoor exit is protected from the weather
18. _____ Window

Working Areas

1. _____ Home repair area
2. _____ Work area for hobbies
3. _____ Storage for paints and tools
4. _____ Garage storage
5. _____ Incinerator area
6. _____ Refuse area
7. _____ Delivery area
8. _____ Near parking
9. _____ 240-volt outlet for power tools

Storage

1. _____ General storage space for each person
2. _____ 4' of rod space for each person
3. _____ Closet doors are sealed to keep out dust
4. _____ Minimum wardrobe closet size is 40" x 22"
5. _____ Cedar closet storage for seasonal clothing
6. _____ Bulk storage area for seasonal paraphernalia
7. _____ Closets are lighted
8. _____ Walk-in closets have adequate turnaround area
9. Storage for:
    _____ a. linen and towels
    _____ b. cleaning materials
    _____ c. foods
    _____ d. bedding
    _____ e. outdoor furniture
    _____ f. sports equipment
    _____ g. toys—indoor
    _____ h. toys—outdoor
    _____ i. bicycles
    _____ j. luggage
    _____ k. out-of-season clothes
    _____ l. storm windows and doors
    _____ m. garden tools
    _____ n. tools and paints
    _____ o. hats
    _____ p. shoes
    _____ q. belts
    _____ r. ties
    _____ s. bridge tables and chairs
    _____ t. camping equipment
    _____ u. china
    _____ v. silver
    _____ w. minor appliances
    _____ x. books
10. _____ Closets are ventilated
11. _____ Closets do not project into room
12. _____ Toothbrush holders in bathrooms
13. _____ Soap holders in bathrooms
14. _____ Adequate built-in storage
15. _____ Drawers cannot pull out of cabinet
16. _____ Drawers slide easily
17. _____ Drawers have divided partitions
18. _____ Adult storage areas easy to reach
19. _____ Children storage areas easy to reach
20. _____ Guest storage near entry
21. _____ Heavy storage areas have reinforced floors
22. _____ Sides of closets easy to reach
23. _____ Tops of closets easy to reach
24. _____ No wasted spaces around stored articles
25. _____ Sloping roof or stairs do not render closet useless
26. _____ Entry closet

The Exterior

1. _____ The design looks "right" for the lot
2. _____ Design varies from other homes nearby
3. _____ Design fits with unity on its site
4. _____ Definite style architecture—not mixed
5. _____ Simple, honest design
6. _____ Garage design goes with the house
7. _____ Attractive on all four sides
8. _____ Colors in good taste
9. _____ Finish materials in good taste
10. _____ Has charm and warmth
11. _____ Materials are consistent on all sides
12. _____ No false building effects
13. _____ Well-designed roof lines—not chopped up
14. _____ Window tops line up
15. _____ Bathroom windows are not obvious
16. _____ Does not look like a box
17. _____ Easy maintenance of finish materials
18. _____ Windows are protected from pedestrian view
19. _____ Attractive roof covering
20. _____ Gutters on roof
21. _____ Downspouts that drain into storm sewer
22. _____ Glass area protected with overhang or trees
23. _____ Dry around the house
24. _____ Several waterproof electric outlets
25. _____ Hose bib on each side
26. _____ Style will look good in the future

Outdoor Service Area

1. _____ Clothes hanging area
2. _____ Garbage storage
3. _____ Can storage
4. _____ On least desirable side of site
5. _____ Next to indoor service area
6. _____ Near garage
7. _____ Delivery area for trucks
8. _____ Fenced off from rest of site

Outdoor Living Area

1. _____ Area for dining
2. _____ Area for games
3. _____ Area for lounging
4. _____ Area for gardening
5. _____ Fenced for privacy
6. _____ Partly shaded
7. _____ Concrete deck at convenient places
8. _____ Garden walks

9. _____ Easy access to house
10. _____ Paved area for bikes and wagons
11. _____ Easy maintenance

Landscaping

1. _____ Planting at foundation ties
2. _____ Garden area
3. _____ Well-located trees
4. _____ Healthy trees
5. _____ Plants of slow-growing variety
6. _____ Landscaping professionally advised
7. _____ Garden walks
8. _____ Easy maintenance
9. _____ Extras as trellis or gazebo

Construction

1. _____ Sound construction
2. _____ All work complies to code
3. _____ Efficient contractor and supervision
4. _____ Honest builders
5. _____ Skilled builders
6. _____ Constructed to plans
7. Floors are well constructed
   _____ a. resilient
   _____ b. subfloor diagonal to joints
   _____ c. flat and even
   _____ d. slab is not cold
   _____ e. floor joists rest on 2" of sill—minimum
   _____ f. girder lengths are joined under points of support
8. Foundation is well constructed
   _____ a. level
   _____ b. sill protected from termites
   _____ c. vapor barrier
   _____ d. no cracks
   _____ e. no water seepage
   _____ f. no dryrot in sills
   _____ g. garage slab drains
   _____ h. waterproofed
   _____ i. walls are 8" thick
   _____ j. basement height 7'6" minimum
   _____ k. sills bolted to foundation
   _____ l. adequate vents
9. Walls are well constructed
   _____ a. plumb
   _____ b. no waves
   _____ c. insulation
   _____ d. flashing at all exterior joints
   _____ e. solid sheathing
   _____ f. siding is neat and tight
   _____ g. drywall joints are invisible
10. Windows are properly installed
   _____ a. move freely
   _____ b. weatherstripped
   _____ c. caulked and sealed
   _____ d. good-quality glass
11. Doors properly hung
   _____ a. move freely
   _____ b. exterior doors weatherstripped
   _____ c. exterior doors are solid-core
   _____ d. interior doors are hollow-core
12. Roof is well constructed
   _____ a. rafters are straight
   _____ b. all corners are flashed
   _____ c. adequate vents in attic
   _____ d. no leaks
   _____ e. building paper under shingles
13. _____ Tile work is tight

14. _____ Hot water lines are insulated
15. _____ Mortar joints are neat
16. _____ Mortar joints do not form shelf to hold water
17. _____ Ceiling is 8'0" minimum
18. _____ No exposed pipes
19. _____ No exposed wires
20. _____ Tight joints at cabinets and appliances
21. _____ Stairs have railings
22. _____ Neat trim application
23. _____ Builder responsible for new home flaws

The Fireplace

1. _____ There is a fireplace
2. _____ Wood storage near the fireplace
3. _____ Draws smoke
4. _____ Hearth in front (minimum 10" on sides; 20" in front)
5. _____ Does not project out into the room
6. _____ Has a clean-out
7. _____ Chimney top 2' higher than roof ridge
8. _____ No leaks around chimney in roof
9. _____ No wood touches the chimney
10. _____ 2" minimum air space between framing members and masonry
11. _____ No loose mortar
12. _____ Has a damper
13. _____ Space for furniture opposite fireplace
14. _____ Doors minimum of 6' from fireplace
15. _____ Windows minimum of 3' from fireplace
16. _____ On a long wall
17. _____ Install "heatilator"
18. _____ Install glass doors to minimize heat loss

Equipment

1. _____ All equipment listed in specifications and plans
2. _____ All new equipment has warranty
3. _____ All equipment is up to code standards
4. _____ All equipment is functional and not a fad
5. _____ Owner's choice of equipment meets builder's allowance
6. _____ Public system for utilities
7. _____ Private well is deep; adequate and healthy water
8. Electrical equipment is adequate
   _____ a. inspected and guaranteed
   _____ b. 240 voltage
   _____ c. 120 voltage
   _____ d. sufficient electric outlets
   _____ e. sufficient electric circuits—minimum of six
   _____ f. circuit breakers
   _____ g. television aerial outlet
   _____ h. telephone outlets
   _____ i. outlets in convenient places
9. Adequate lighting
   _____ a. all rooms have general lighting
   _____ b. all rooms have specific lighting for specific tasks
   _____ c. silent switches
   _____ d. some decorative lighting
   _____ e. light at front door
   _____ f. outdoor lighting
10. Plumbing equipment is adequate
   _____ a. inspected and guaranteed
   _____ b. adequate water pressure
   _____ c. hot water heater—50-gallon minimum
   _____ d. shut-off valves at fixtures

_____ e. satisfactory city sewer or septic tank

_____ f. septic tank disposal field is adequate

_____ g. septic tank is large enough for house (1000 gallons for three-bedroom house, plus 250 gallons for each additional bedroom)

_____ h. water softener for hard water

_____ i. siphon vertex or siphon reverse-trap water closet

_____ j. clean-out plugs at all corners of waste lines

_____ k. water lines will not rust

_____ l. water pipes do not hammer

_____ m. waste lines drain freely

_____ n. cast iron with vitreous enamel bathtub

11. _____ Good ventilation through house and attic

12. Heating and cooling systems are adequate

_____ a. insulation in roof, ceiling, walls

_____ b. air conditioning system

_____ c. heating and cooling outlets under windows

_____ d. air purifier

_____ e. thermostatic control

_____ f. walls are clean over heat outlets

_____ g. comfortable in hot or cold weather

_____ h. automatic humidifier

_____ i. furnace blower is belt-driven

_____ j. quiet-heating plant

_____ k. ducts are tight

13. _____ Windows are of good quality

_____ a. storm windows

_____ b. secure locks

_____ c. screened

_____ d. double glazed in extreme weather (thermal)

_____ e. glass is ripple-free

_____ f. safety or safe thickness of glass

_____ g. moisture-free

_____ h. frost-free

14. Doors are of good quality

_____ a. secure locks on exterior doors

_____ b. attractive hardware

_____ c. hardware is solid brass or bronze

15. All meters easily accessible to meter readers

16. _____ Fire extinguisher in house and garage

17. _____ Acoustical ceiling

18. _____ Facilities to lock mail box

19. _____ Facilities to receive large packages

20. _____ Gas or electric incinerator

21. Adequate small hardware

_____ a. soap dishes

_____ b. toilet-paper holders

_____ c. toothbrush holders

_____ d. towel holders

_____ e. bathtub grab bars

_____ f. door and drawer pulls

The Garage

1. _____ Same style as the house

2. _____ Fits with house

3. _____ Single garage 12' x 22' minimum

4. _____ Double garage 22' x 22' minimum

5. _____ Larger than minimum size if used for storage or workshop

6. _____ Protected passage to house

7. _____ Doors are safe

8. _____ Access to overhead storage

Financial Checklist

1. _____ Do you understand conveyancing fees (closing costs)?

2. _____ Is the house a good investment?

3. _____ Is the total cost approximately three times your annual income?

4. _____ Have you shopped for the best loan?

5. _____ Do you have a constant payment plan (sliding principal and interest)?

6. _____ Is there a prepayment penalty?

7. _____ Will a week's salary cover the total housing expense for one month?

8. _____ Are all the costs itemized in the contract?

9. Do you understand the following closing costs?

_____ a. title search

_____ b. lawyer

_____ c. plot survey

_____ d. insurance, fire, and public liability

_____ e. mortgage tax

_____ f. recording mortgage

_____ g. recording deed

_____ h. bank's commitment fee

_____ i. state and county taxes

_____ j. state and government revenue stamps

_____ k. title insurance (protects lender)

_____ l. homeowner's policy (protects owner)

_____ m. transferring ownership

_____ n. mortgage service charge

_____ o. appraisal

_____ p. notarizing documents

_____ q. attendant fee (paying off previous mortgage)

_____ r. personal credit check

10. _____ Do you have extra cash to cover unforeseen expenses?

11. Can you afford to pay the following?

_____ a. closing costs

_____ b. old assessments or bonds

_____ c. new assessments or bonds

_____ d. downpayment

_____ e. immediate repairs

_____ f. immediate purchases (furniture, appliances, landscape, tools, fences, carpets, drapes, patio)

_____ g. adequate insurance

_____ h. mortgage payments

_____ i. general maintenance

_____ j. utilities (water, heat, electricity, phone, gas, trash pickup)

_____ k. special design features wanted

_____ l. extras not covered in plans and contract

_____ m. prepayment of interest and taxes for first month of transition

_____ n. moving

_____ o. gardener

_____ p. travel to work

_____ q. interest on construction loan

_____ r. advances to contractors

12. _____ Who will pay for the following?

_____ a. supervision costs of architect or contractor

_____ b. inspection fees

_____ c. increased costs during building

_____ d. building permits

_____ e. difficulties in excavation

_____ f. dry wells

_____ g. extra features the building inspector insists upon

The above Checklist is used with permission. It is taken from Home Planners' Guide to Residential Design _by Charles Talcott, Don Hepler, and Paul Wallach; 1986; McGraw-Hill, Inc._

Types of Multi-Level Homes

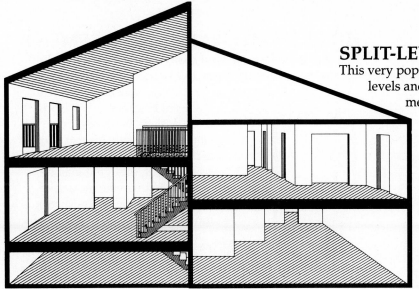

SPLIT-LEVEL HOMES

This very popular housing type has three living levels and an optional fourth-level base ment. All are connected by sets of stairs that combine to make one full-stair flight. Providing distinct separation for different living functions, this type of multi-level allows for activity planning with unlimited variety. Split-levels work and look better on rolling sites where lower-level living areas can have full-story height exposure to outdoor living.

SPLIT-FOYER HOMES

The split-foyer home can be identified as a sunken two-story house without basement or a raised one-story home with an optional finished basement. The split-foyer divides functional areas in a variety of ways. There may be complete living areas on the upper level with flexible use of space on the lower level. Or some split-foyer designs may allow living areas between two floors in various combinations. In any configuration, this housing type enjoys a maximum use of space and efficient use of construction dollars.

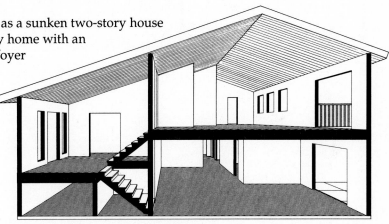

HILLSIDES

Houses of good design, properly oriented to sloping land, are often more interesting than any other type. Hillsides are characterized by the full-story stairs between living levels with the main en- trance on either the upper or lower grade, as deter- mined by the site. This type of housing is extremely flexible. Exteriors offer a chal- lenging variety of design possi- bilities with the exterior wall exposure usually determining the amount of living space in the lower level. Remaining space may be used for utility rooms, storage, hobby rooms or play rooms, as needs dictate.

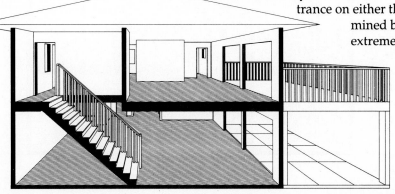
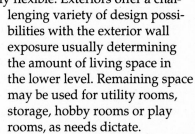

continued on next page

HOMES WITH WALKOUT BASEMENTS

This may be one of the most easily achieved of the multi-level housing types. In essence, just about any plan that can be built with a basement can be a walk-out basement plan. Naturally, these designs work best on a sloping or hillside lot that allows exposure of the lower level to full-story height, though it may be possible to excavate in such a manner as to allow exposure on a more level site. Homes with walk out basements allow a perfect blend of indoor/outdoor living arrangements and work well as expandables if the basement is left partially or fully unfinished until needed. Common use of the lower level includes play rooms, activity areas, guest bedrooms and in-law suites.

OPEN-STAIRCASE PLANS

Homes with floor plans that include open staircases have a spacious and roomy quality that invites casual lifestyles. The open staircase may be one that reaches an upper-level lounge near the master suite or descends to a lower-level family room or guest suite. These kind of plans may be found in one-story homes with finished basements, two-story or multi-level homes and are often accented with atriums, balconies, vaulted ceilings, skylights and other favorite amenities.

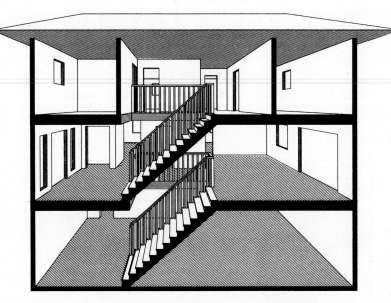

CONTEMPORARY SPLIT LEVELS . . . *offer the*

livability feature of separation of functions on main, upper and lower levels. Special highlights of these family homes are indoor and outdoor balconies, functional terraces, sloping ceilings and dramatic glass areas.

Design V34128

Upper Level: 1,664 square feet
Lower Level: 740 square feet
Total: 2,404 square feet

D

LIFESTYLE HOME PLANS

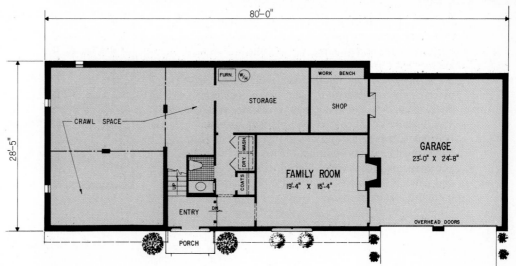

80'-0"

28'-5"

FURN. (W/H)

STORAGE

WORK BENCH

SHOP

CRAWL SPACE

DRY WASH

COATS

FAMILY ROOM
19'-4" X 15'-4"

GARAGE
23'-0" X 24'-8"

UP

DN

ENTRY

OVERHEAD DOORS

PORCH

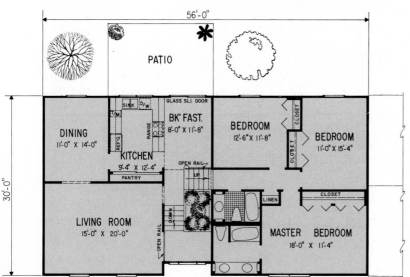

56'-0"

30'-0"

PATIO

DINING
11'-0" X 14'-0"

SINK D/W

RANGE

REF'G

GLASS SLI. DOOR

BK' FAST.
8'-0" X 11'-8"

BEDROOM
12'-6" X 11'-8"

CLOSET

CLOSET

BEDROOM
11'-0" X 15'-4"

KITCHEN
9'-4" X 12'-4"

PANTRY

OPEN RAIL

UP

LINEN

CLOSET

LIVING ROOM
15'-0" X 20'-0"

OPEN RAIL

DOWN

MASTER BEDROOM
18'-0" X 11'-4"

● Split-level design makes this an efficiently planned home. The lower level features a comfortable family room with fireplace. Tucked in back is a large storage area and workshop. The upper level contains the main living area. There's a spacious living room and connecting dining room. The ample, U-shaped kitchen is conveniently placed between the formal dining room and cheery breakfast room. A sliding glass door leads to a quiet patio. Up a few steps is the sleeping area with three nice-sized bedrooms and two full baths.

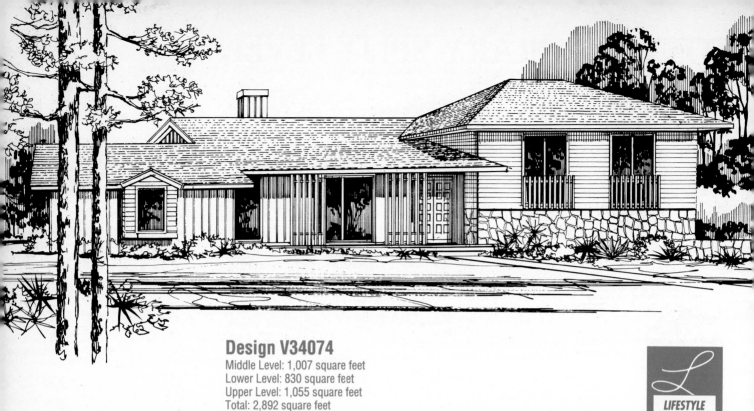

Design V34074

Middle Level: 1,007 square feet
Lower Level: 830 square feet
Upper Level: 1,055 square feet
Total: 2,892 square feet

● This handsome contemporary has three levels of livability. Just off the entry foyer is a sunken living room and adjoining dining room — a perfect arrangement for entertaining. To the rear is a large kitchen with breakfast area, built-in desk, and pantry. Nearby is a cozy family room with corner fireplace. A sliding glass door leads onto a redwood deck, expanding the living area in warmer weather. The upstairs sleeping area features four spacious bedrooms, two baths, and lots of closet space. The lower level contains additional living space with an enormous playroom with adjacent covered terrace and patio. Also downstairs: a spare bedroom with bath and a storage room.

Design V34105

Upper Level: 672 square feet
Lower Level: 1,023 square feet
Total: 1,695 square feet

● Vertical wood siding and stonework lend this split-level a warm, rustic appearance. Its rectangular shape makes this an economical, easy-to-build design. The well-planned interior includes a family room with fireplace off the entry foyer. Also on this level are a utility room and powder room. Up a few steps are a spacious living room and adjacent dining room and kitchen. A pass-through to the dining room saves steps when serving and clearing. Off the dining room is a stone terrace — a perfect spot for dining alfresco. On the upper level are three bedrooms and two baths.

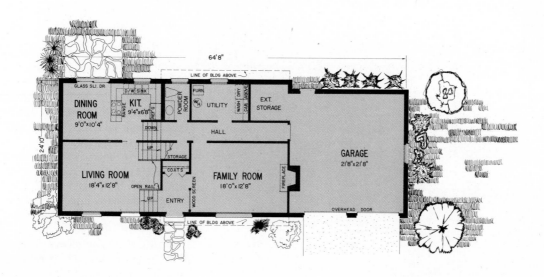

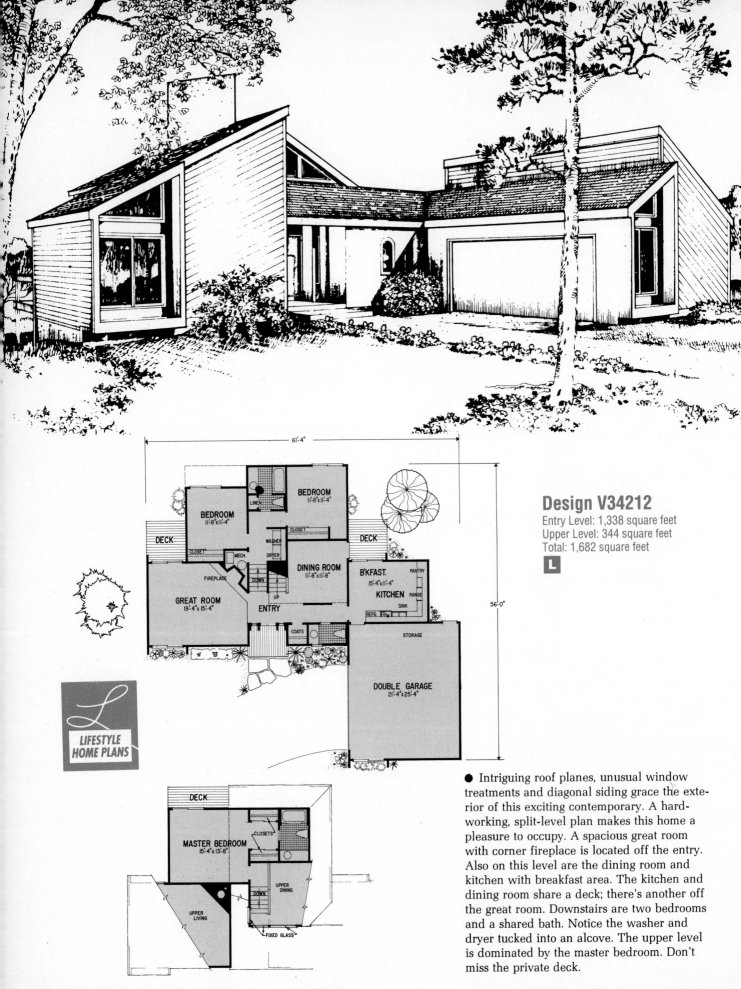

Design V34212

Entry Level: 1,338 square feet
Upper Level: 344 square feet
Total: 1,682 square feet

L

● Intriguing roof planes, unusual window treatments and diagonal siding grace the exterior of this exciting contemporary. A hardworking, split-level plan makes this home a pleasure to occupy. A spacious great room with corner fireplace is located off the entry. Also on this level are the dining room and kitchen with breakfast area. The kitchen and dining room share a deck; there's another off the great room. Downstairs are two bedrooms and a shared bath. Notice the washer and dryer tucked into an alcove. The upper level is dominated by the master bedroom. Don't miss the private deck.

L
LIFESTYLE HOME PLANS

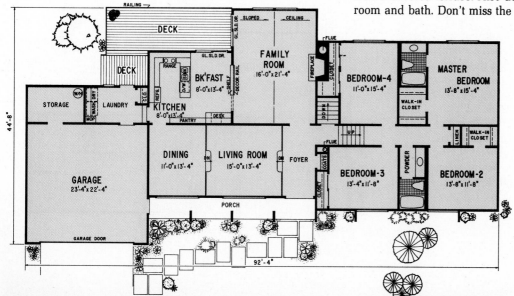

Design V34327

Middle Level: 1,122 square feet
Upper Level: 1,152 square feet
Lower Level: 985 square feet
Total: 3,259 square feet

D

● This spacious contemporary will meet all the demands of today's active family. There's a sunken living room and adjoining dining room for entertaining and formal occasions. The enormous family room with its sloped ceiling and fireplace will be a favorite spot to gather and relax. Next door is a large kitchen with breakfast room. Upstairs are four good-sized bedrooms and two baths. The lower level features a sizable playroom. Sliding glass doors open onto a covered terrace. Also downstairs is an extra bedroom and bath. Don't miss the deck off the family room.

LIFESTYLE
HOME PLANS

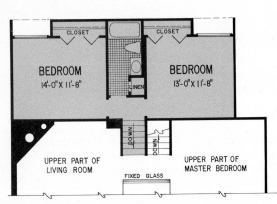

CLOSET   CLOSET

BEDROOM
14'-0" X 11'-8"

BEDROOM
13'-0" X 11'-8"

LINEN

DOWN

DOWN

UPPER PART OF
LIVING ROOM

UPPER PART OF
MASTER BEDROOM

FIXED GLASS

Design V34117

Entry Level: 1,251 square feet
Upper Level: 454 square feet
Total: 1,705 square feet

LIFESTYLE
HOME PLANS

● The convenience and practicality of split-level planning make this attractive contemporary a delight to live in. Flanking the entry are the master bedroom suite and the living room. The latter boasts a corner fireplace and overlooks the large dining room. Adjacent to the dining room, the well-equipped kitchen has plenty of counter space for working. A spacious family room rounds out this level. Sliding glass doors here and in the dining room lead to a large deck with a built-in barbecue grill. Two more bedrooms and full bath are found on the upper level.

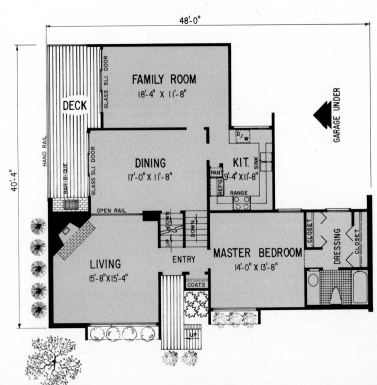

48'-0"

40'-4"

HAND RAIL

BAR-B-QUE

DECK

GLASS SLI. DOOR

FAMILY ROOM
18'-4" X 11'-8"

GARAGE UNDER

D/W

SINK

DINING
17'-0" X 11'-8"

KIT.
9'-4" X 11'-8"

PANT

REFG

RANGE

GLASS SLI. DOOR

OPEN RAIL

LIVING
15'-8" X 15'-4"

UP

DOWN

DOWN

UP

ENTRY

CLOSET

MASTER BEDROOM
14'-0" X 13'-8"

CLOSET

DRESSING

COATS

UP

Design V34213

First Floor: 1,427 square feet
Second Floor: 487 square feet
Total: 1,914 square feet

L

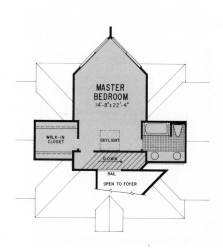

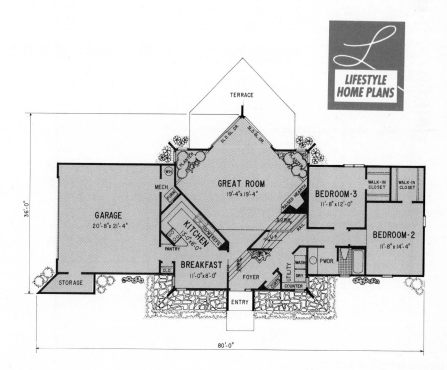

● Interesting angles and shapes define the exterior and interior of this design. The diagonally placed foyer features angled staircases leading to different areas of the house. Down a few steps is the dramatic great room with raised-hearth fireplace. Triangular projections contain planters and sliding glass doors onto the terrace. Also on this level are the U-shaped kitchen and breakfast room. To the right of the entry foyer are two bedrooms and a shared bath. Notice the walk-in closets in both rooms. The upper-level master suite is a cozy haven away from the bustle and noise of the rest of the house. Notice the large windows and skylight.

Design V34184

Middle Level: 1,102 square feet
Upper Level: 1,197 square feet
Lower Level: 584 square feet
Total: 2,883 square feet

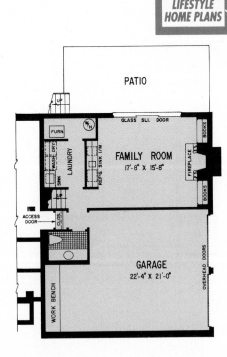

● This spacious contemporary has plenty of room for today's active family. The large entry hall leads to the living room and adjoining dining room — both have sloped ceilings with beams. The well-equipped kitchen has plenty of counter space for working and a pass-through to the breakfast room. The upper level has three large bedrooms and two baths. Notice the abundant closet space. The lower-level family room features a large, stone fireplace, built-in bookshelves, and a wet bar. The adjacent patio connects with the deck, located off the breakfast room.

Design V34103

Upper Level: 1,101 square feet
Lower Level: 1,437 square feet
Total: 2,538 square feet

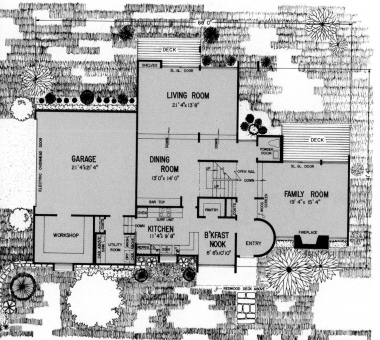

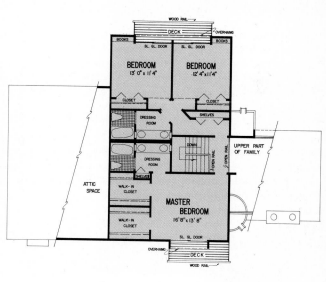

LIFESTYLE HOME PLANS

● This plan was designed with indoor-outdoor living in mind. Located off the entry is a step-down family room with fireplace. Access to a deck is through sliding glass doors to the rear. The open dining room and living room provide a large entertaining space. A sliding glass door leads to another deck off the living room. An efficient kitchen and breakfast nook round out this level. Don't miss the large pantry. Upstairs are three sizable bedrooms; the master suite boasts His and Hers walk-in closets. Two more decks provide additional outdoor living space.

Design V34283

Entry Level: 2,340 square feet
Lower Level: 578 square feet
Total: 2,918 square feet

● This impressive contemporary boasts the increased living space that's in demand in today's housing market. Notice the size of each room. The gracious entry with skylight and planter leads into the living room and connecting dining room. Soaring, sloped ceilings add to the feeling of spaciousness. The kitchen features a large breakfast room with a sloped ceiling. French doors open onto a deck. Upstairs are three good-sized bedrooms and abundant closet space; the master has His and Hers walk-in closets. The lower level features a family room with fireplace and wet bar. Two sets of French doors lead out to a spacious patio.

LIFESTYLE
HOME PLANS

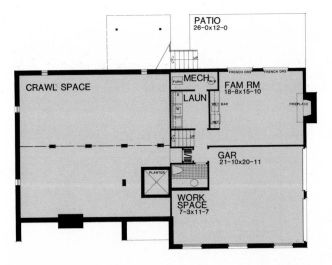

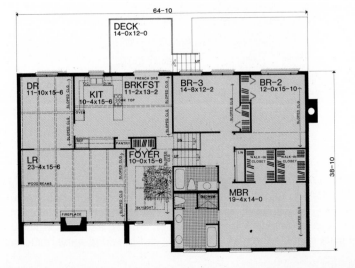

Design V34288

First Floor: 1,598 square feet
Second Floor: 1,335 square feet
Total: 2,933 square feet

D

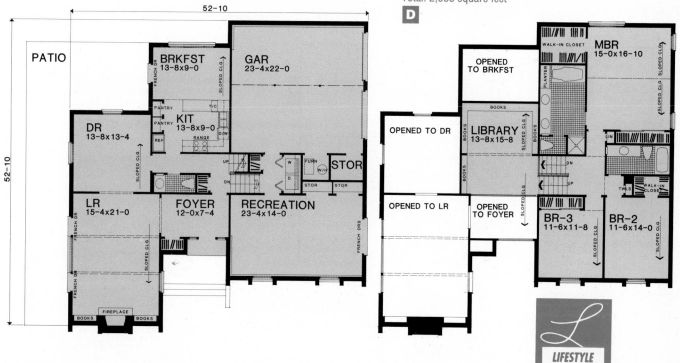

● This handsome brick contemporary boasts four levels of livability. Located off the foyer, the impressive living room features a fireplace flanked by built-in bookshelves. Next door is a formal dining room. The U-shaped kitchen has a pass-through to the breakfast room and lots of pantry space. Downstairs is a large recreation room. The upper level has three bedrooms; notice the sumptuous bath in the master suite. Up a few steps is a large library with wraparound, built-in bookshelves, sloped ceilings, and a balcony overlooking the foyer.

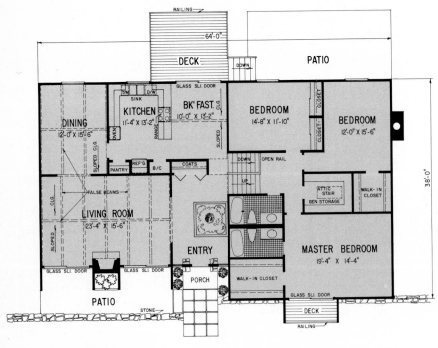

DECK
64'-0"
RAILING

PATIO
DOWN

GLASS SLI. DOOR

KITCHEN
11'-4" X 13'-2"
SINK
D/W
OVEN
RANGE

BK' FAST.
10'-0" X 13'-2"
SLOPED CLG.

BEDROOM
14'-8" X 11'-10"
SLOPED

CLOSET
CLOSET

BEDROOM
12'-0" X 15'-6"

DINING
12'-0" X 15'-6"
SLOPED CLG.

PANTRY
REF'G
B/C
COATS

DOWN
OPEN RAIL
UP

LIVING ROOM
23'-4" X 15'-6"
FALSE BEAMS
CLG
SLOPED

ATTIC STAIR
GEN. STORAGE

WALK-IN CLOSET

38'-0"

ENTRY

MASTER BEDROOM
19'-4" X 14'-4"

GLASS SLI. DOOR
GLASS SLI. DOOR

PORCH

WALK-IN CLOSET

PATIO
STONE

GLASS SLI. DOOR

DECK
RAILING

LIFESTYLE HOME PLANS

Design V34136
Middle Level: 965 square feet
Upper Level: 1,150 square feet
Lower Level: 560 square feet
Total: 2,675 square feet

D

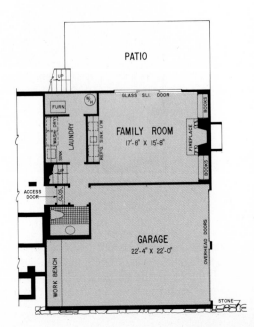

PATIO

UP
FURN.
W.H.
GLASS SLI. DOOR

FAMILY ROOM
17'-8" X 15'-8"
BOOKS
FIREPLACE

WASH.
DRY.
SINK
D/M

LAUNDRY
REFIG SINK D/M
BOOKS

ACCESS DOOR
CLOS.

GARAGE
22'-4" X 22'-0"

WORK BENCH

OVERHEAD DOORS

STONE

● Three distinct living levels conveniently locate the areas of livability in this home. On the first level are a slope-ceilinged living room, dining room, and kitchen with attached breakfast nook. The rear deck on this level has steps to the patio below. The upper level contains three bedrooms with two large baths. At the lower level, along with a two-car garage, is a family room plus a laundry and nearby washroom.

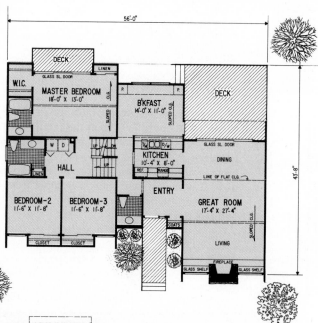

Design V34199

Middle Level: 926 square feet
Upper Level: 874 square feet
Study: 152 square feet
Total: 2,047 square feet

LIFESTYLE HOME PLANS

● Two decks adorn this plan — one reached from the great room and breakfast nook on the entry level, and one from the master bedroom on the upper-level. Other welcome features include a fireplace, an upper-level study, washer/dryer area close to bedrooms, and a large storage area sharing lower-level space with garages for two cars.

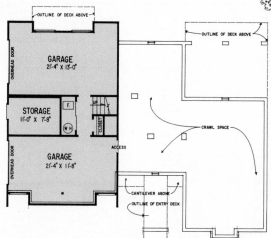

Design V34130

Entry Level: 1,414 square feet
Main Level: 965 square feet
Upper Level: 1,150 square feet
Total: 3,529 square feet

● This unique design separates the master bedroom suite on the entry level from the family bedrooms on the upper level. In between are a living room with fireplace and covered deck, a sloped-ceiling dining room, and kitchen/breakfast room with access to a rear deck. The lower-level patio is reached from both master suite and family room (note the second fireplace and wet bar).

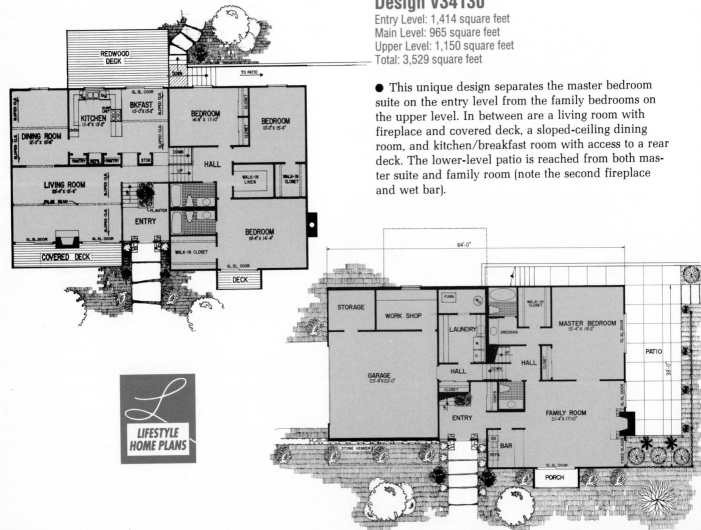

LIFESTYLE HOME PLANS

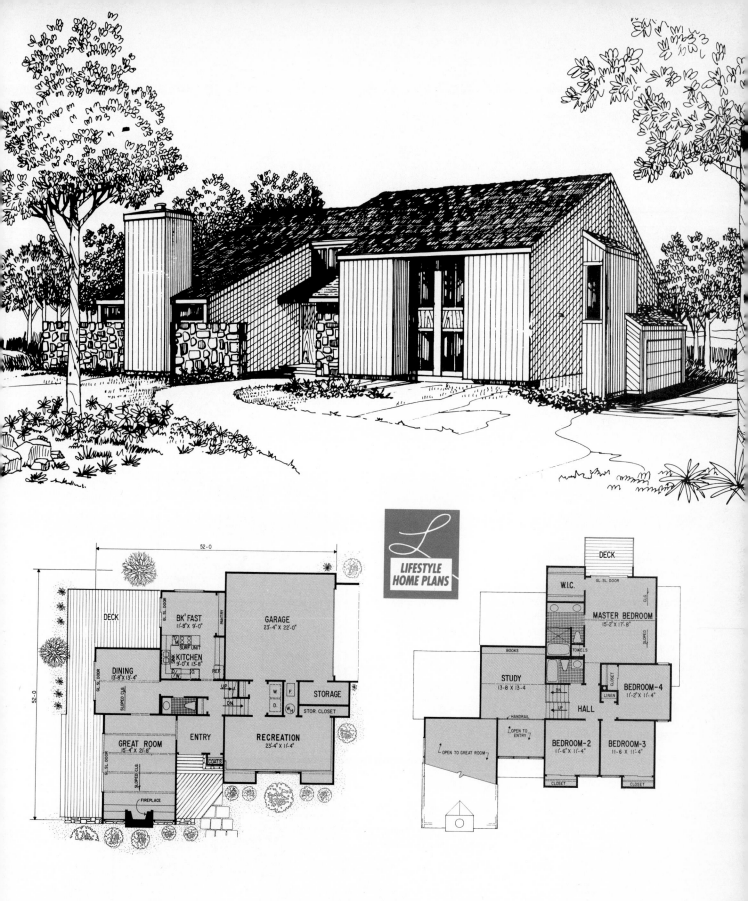

Design V34171

Entry Level: 1,013 square feet
Upper Level: 1,306 square feet
Lower Level: 469 square feet
Total: 2,788 square feet

● The long, wraparound deck in this plan adds a large measure of livability to its entry level living areas. Also consider the fireplace in the great room and the hallway powder room. Upstairs are four bedrooms, two full baths, and an upper study. The master bedroom has sliding glass doors to a private deck.

Design V34209

Entry Level: 800 square feet
Upper Level: 896 square feet
Total: 1,696 square feet

● Though small in size, this home's leveled-living arrangement allows a floor plan that easily accommodates family lifestyles. Besides a sunken living room with corner fireplace, a handy L-shaped kitchen, powder room, and dining room are found on the entry level. Side patios extend the possible eating areas, both formal and informal. An indulgent master suite on the second floor has its own fireplace and sitting room. Just a few steps up are two family bedrooms.

LIFESTYLE
HOME PLANS

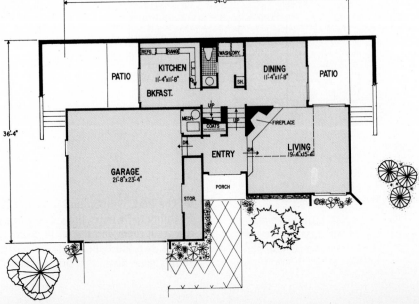

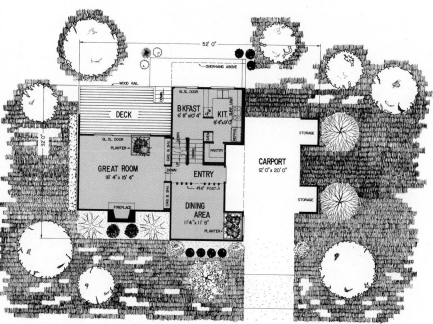

Design V34107

Entry Level: 776 square feet
Middle Level: 592 square feet
Upper Level: 336 square feet
Total: 1,704 square feet

LIFESTYLE
HOME PLANS

● Here's a grand plan for a small family or that can be used as a vacation or second home. A large deck off the great room will be enjoyed in the summer months, while the cozy fireplace warms chillier seasons. Special touches like built-in planters, cabinets, and shelves enhance the rooms on this level. Sleeping areas are found on two levels: family bedrooms on the middle level and a skylit master suite above.

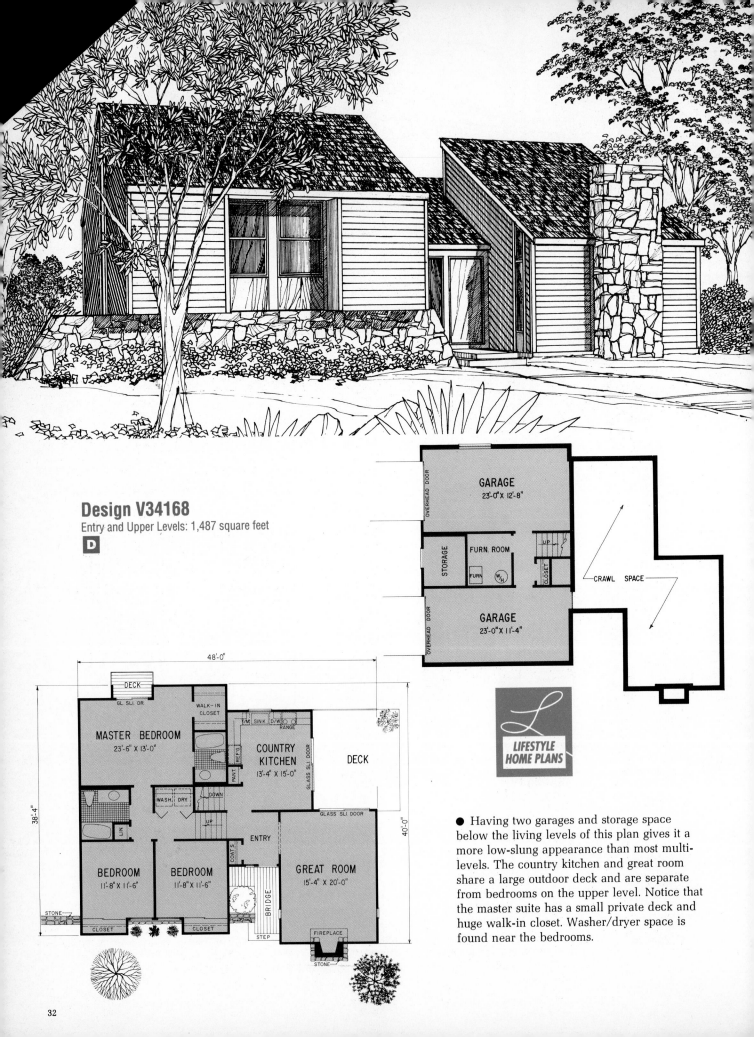

Design V34168

Entry and Upper Levels: 1,487 square feet

D

GARAGE
23'-0" X 12'-8"

OVERHEAD DOOR

STORAGE

FURN. ROOM

FURN

W/H

UP

CLOSET

CRAWL SPACE

OVERHEAD DOOR

GARAGE
23'-0" X 11'-4"

48'-0"

DECK

GL. SLI. DR.

WALK-IN CLOSET

MASTER BEDROOM
23'-6" X 13'-0"

T/M SINK D/W

RANGE

REF'G

PANT.

COUNTRY KITCHEN
13'-4" X 15'-0"

GLASS SLI. DOOR

DECK

38'-4"

WASH. DRY.

DOWN

LIN.

UP

GLASS SLI. DOOR

ENTRY

COATS

40'-0"

BEDROOM
11'-8" X 11'-6"

BEDROOM
11'-8" X 11'-6"

GREAT ROOM
15'-4" X 20'-0"

STONE

CLOSET

CLOSET

BRIDGE

STEP

FIREPLACE

STONE

L

LIFESTYLE HOME PLANS

● Having two garages and storage space below the living levels of this plan gives it a more low-slung appearance than most multi-levels. The country kitchen and great room share a large outdoor deck and are separate from bedrooms on the upper level. Notice that the master suite has a small private deck and huge walk-in closet. Washer/dryer space is found near the bedrooms.

Design V34163

Entry and Upper Levels: 1,394 square feet
Garage Level: 673 square feet
Total: 2,067 square feet

● It will be difficult to decide which room of this house is your favorite. Just off the entry is a galley kitchen and attached breakfast nook with patio. The great room also leads to a patio and has a glowing corner fireplace. Up a few steps are three bedrooms, one a master suite with its own deck. At the garage level is a convenient laundry room.

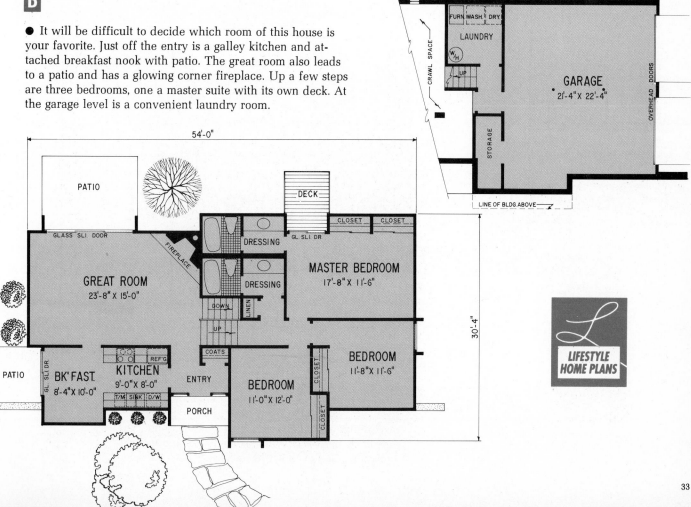

LIFESTYLE HOME PLANS

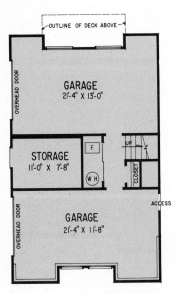

OUTLINE OF DECK ABOVE

GARAGE
21'-4" X 13'-0"

STORAGE
11'-0" X 7'-8"

F.

W H

UP

CLOSET

ACCESS

GARAGE
21'-4" X 11'-8"

OVERHEAD DOOR

OVERHEAD DOOR

LIFESTYLE HOME PLANS

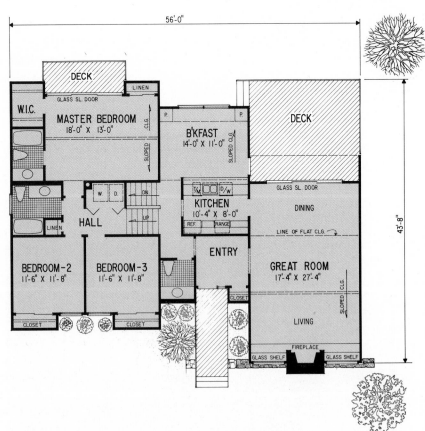

56'-0"

43'-8"

DECK

GLASS SL. DOOR

LINEN

W.I.C.

MASTER BEDROOM
18'-0" X 13'-0"

CLG.

SLOPED

P.

P.

B'KFAST
14'-0" X 11'-0"

SLOPED CLG.

DECK

GLASS SL. DOOR

W. D.

DN.

T/M

D/W

KITCHEN
10'-4" X 8'-0"

REF.

RANGE

DINING

LINEN

HALL

UP

ENTRY

LINE OF FLAT CLG.

BEDROOM-2
11'-6" X 11'-8"

BEDROOM-3
11'-6" X 11'-8"

CLOSET

GREAT ROOM
17'-4" X 27'-4"

SLOPED CLG.

LIVING

CLOSET

CLOSET

FIREPLACE

GLASS SHELF

GLASS SHELF

Design V34198

Entry Level: 926 square feet
Upper Level: 874 square feet
Lower Level: 95 square feet
Total: 1,895 square feet

● The long sloping roof of this contemporary makes possible dramatic ceilings in the great room, breakfast room, and master bedroom. Two decks to the rear magnify indoor/outdoor living. Notice the double garage areas tucked away under the house and the convenient storage room on this level.

Design V34195

Entry and Upper Levels: 1,425 square feet
Lower Level: 721 square feet
Total: 2,146 square feet

D

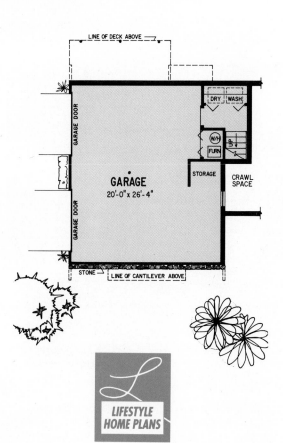

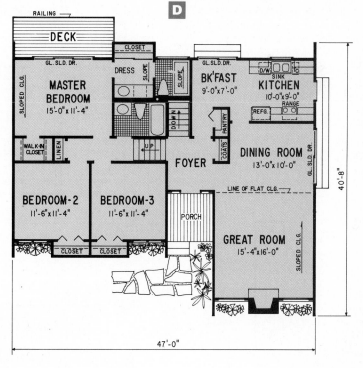

● Two-level floor planning takes a beautiful contemporary turn in this wood-and-stone home. On the entry level is a great room/dining room com-bination located right next to the kitchen and breakfast room. Up a few stairs are sleeping accommodations for everyone; notice the deck off the master bedroom. At the garage level is space for a washer and dryer as well as convenient storage.

● Wood siding and fieldstone create an appealing exterior for this contemporary. Inside is a spacious, well-planned interior. Located off the entry is the impressive great room with both living and dining areas, sloped ceiling, fireplace, and built-in shelves. A nearby galley kitchen is convenient to the formal dining area and breakfast room. The sleeping area occupies the upper level with three sizable bedrooms. The laundry area is strategically placed near the source of dirty linen. Up a few steps is a study balcony. The lower level contains a large family room and spare bedroom.

Design V34207 Entry Level: 926 square feet
Upper Level: 874 square feet; Lower Level: 711 square feet
Study Balcony: 152 square feet; Total: 2,663 square feet

LIFESTYLE HOME PLANS

● Angles and geometric elements influence this contemporary's exterior. The entry leads into the spacious great room with fireplace. Sliding glass doors provide access to the deck. Note the decorative planter set off with a rail. Down a few steps are the dining room and kitchen. A handy garage entrance here makes short work of unloading groceries. The upper level features three good-sized bedrooms and two full baths.

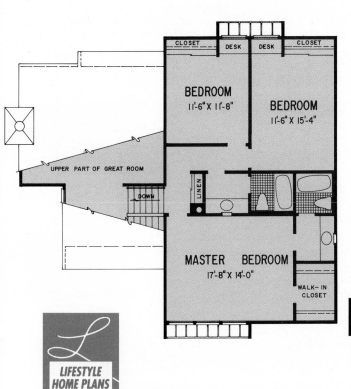

CLOSET — DESK — DESK — CLOSET

BEDROOM
11'-6" X 11'-8"

BEDROOM
11'-6" X 15'-4"

UPPER PART OF GREAT ROOM

DOWN

LINEN

MASTER BEDROOM
17'-8" X 14'-0"

WALK-IN CLOSET

LIFESTYLE HOME PLANS

Design V34152
Upper Level: 906 square feet
Lower Level: 920 square feet
Total: 1,826 square feet

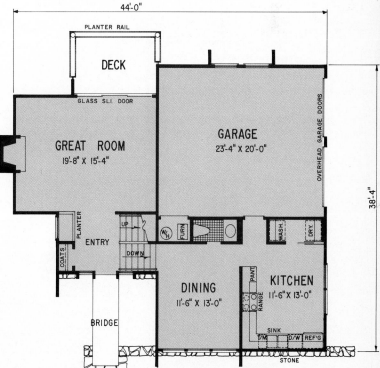

44'-0"

PLANTER RAIL

DECK

GLASS SLI. DOOR

GREAT ROOM
19'-8" X 15'-4"

GARAGE
23'-4" X 20'-0"

OVERHEAD GARAGE DOORS

38'-4"

PLANTER

COATS

ENTRY

UP

DOWN

W.H.

FURN

WASH

DRY

DINING
11'-6" X 13'-0"

PANT

KITCHEN
11'-6" X 13'-0"

RANGE

BRIDGE

SINK

T/M

D/W

REF'G

STONE

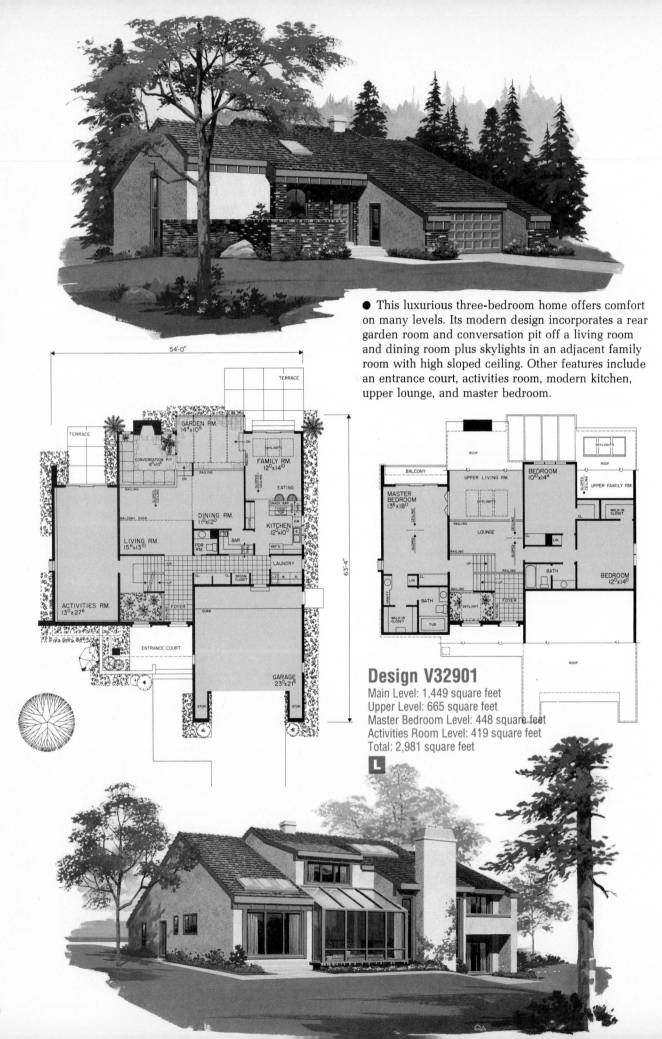

● This luxurious three-bedroom home offers comfort on many levels. Its modern design incorporates a rear garden room and conversation pit off a living room and dining room plus skylights in an adjacent family room with high sloped ceiling. Other features include an entrance court, activities room, modern kitchen, upper lounge, and master bedroom.

Design V32901

Main Level: 1,449 square feet
Upper Level: 665 square feet
Master Bedroom Level: 448 square feet
Activities Room Level: 419 square feet
Total: 2,981 square feet

Design V32932 Main & Family Room Levels: 2,070 square feet
Upper Level: 680 square feet; Master Bedroom Level: 640 square feet
Total: 3,390 square feet

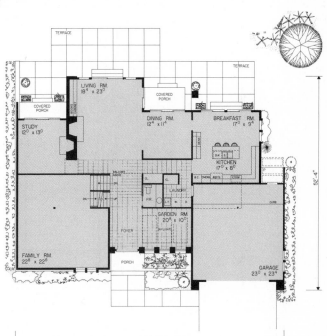

● This attractive split-level comtempo-
rary home includes a garden room just
off the foyer. Note also the master bedroom with whirlpool bath, large living
room, and large family room.

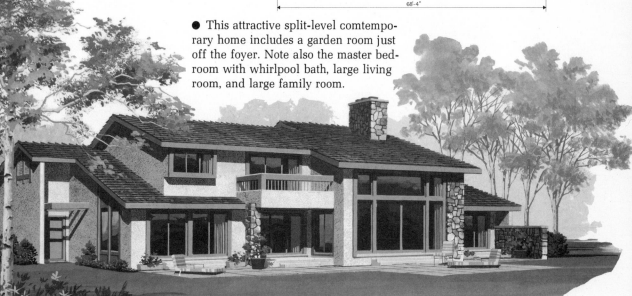

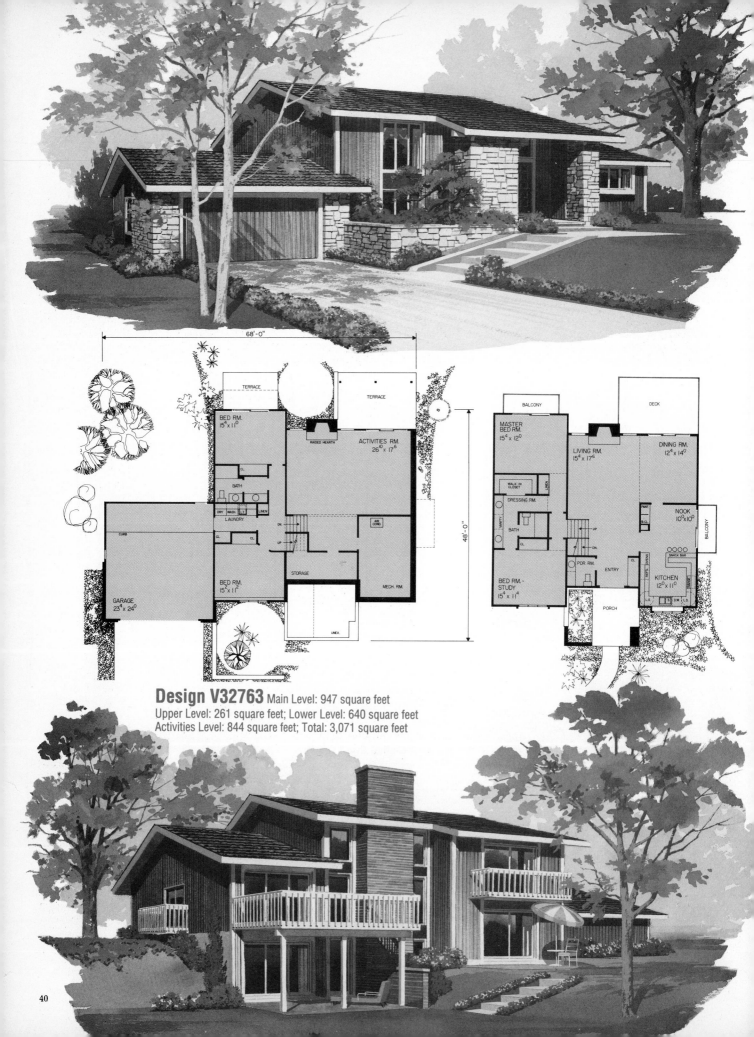

68'-0"

48'-0"

TERRACE

TERRACE

BED RM.
15⁴ x 11⁰

RAISED HEARTH

ACTIVITIES RM.
26¹⁰ x 17⁶

BATH

CL.

DRY. WASH. L.S. LINEN

LAUNDRY

DN.

AIR COND.

CURB

CL. CL.

UP

GARAGE
23⁴ x 24⁰

BED RM.
15⁵ x 11⁰

STORAGE

MECH. RM.

UNEX.

BALCONY

DECK

MASTER
BED RM.
15⁴ x 12⁰

LIVING RM.
15⁴ x 17⁶

DINING RM.
12⁴ x 14⁰

WALK-IN
CLOSET

DRESSING RM.

PANT.

B.CL.

NOOK
10⁰ x 10⁰

VANITY

BATH

CL.

UP

DN.

SNACK BAR

BALCONY

PDR. RM.

ENTRY

CL.

KITCHEN
12⁰ x 11⁰

BED RM.-
STUDY
15⁴ x 11⁴

PORCH

D.W. L.S.

Design V32763 Main Level: 947 square feet
Upper Level: 261 square feet; Lower Level: 640 square feet
Activities Level: 844 square feet; Total: 3,071 square feet

Design V32679 Main Level: 1,179 square feet
Upper Level: 681 square feet; Family Room Level: 643 square feet
Lower Level: 680 square feet; Total: 3,183 square feet

● This spacious modern Contemporary home offers plenty of livability on many levels. Main level includes a breakfast room in addition to a dining room. Adjacent is a sloped-ceiling living room with raised hearth. The upper level features isolated master bedroom suite with adjoining study or sitting room and balcony. Family room level includes a long rectangular family room with adjoining terrace on one end and adjoining bar with washroom at the other end. A spacious basement is included. Two other bedrooms are positioned in the lower level with their own view of the terrace and quiet privacy. Note the rear deck.

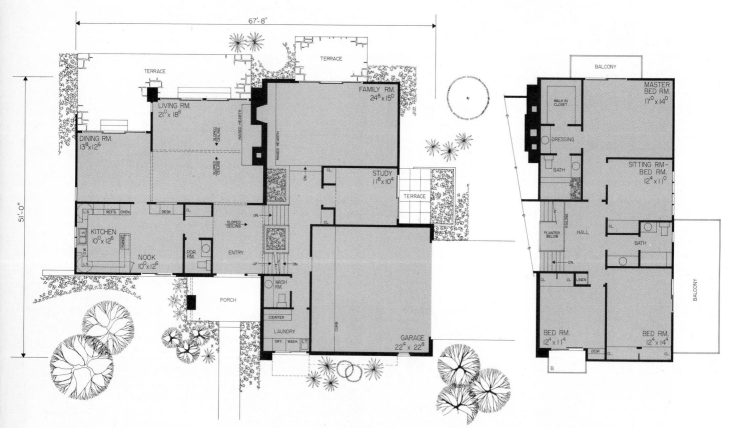

Design V32536 Main Level: 1,077 square feet
Upper Level: 1,319 square feet; Lower Level: 914 square feet; Total: 3,310 square feet

● Here are three levels of outstanding livability all packed in a delightfully contemporary exterior. The low pitched roof has a wide overhang with exposed rafter tails. The stone masses contrast effectively with the vertical siding and the glass areas. The extension of the sloping roof provides the recessed feature of the front entrance with the patterned double doors. The homemaker's favorite highlight will be the layout of the kitchen. No crossroom traffic here. Only a few steps from the formal and informal eating areas, it is the epitome of efficiency. A sloping beamed ceiling, sliding glass doors and a raised hearth fireplace enhance the appeal of the living room. The upper level offers the option of a fourth bedroom or a sitting room functioning with the master bedroom. Note the three balconies. On the lower level, the big family room, quiet study, laundry and extra washroom are present.

Design V32247

Main Level: 979 square feet
Upper Level: 1,049 square feet
Lower Level: 915 square feet
Total: 2,943 square feet

Floor plan labels:

69'-3"
50'-10"

TERRACE DECK TERRACE

MASTER BED RM. 18⁰ x 16⁰
KIT. 15⁶ x 11⁸
DINING RM. 15⁶ x 11⁸
LIVING RM. 15⁶ x 25⁴
SNACK BAR BUFFET
STOR. BELOW
PANTRY RANGE OVEN
DRESS. RM.
BATH
BATH
BED RM. 13⁰ x 15⁰
BED RM. 10⁸ x 15⁰
WOOD BOX
STORAGE BELOW
CABINET VANITY CABINET
DECK

BALCONY ABOVE
STORAGE FAMILY RM. 23⁴ x 19⁴ STORAGE
BEAMED CEILING
STORAGE
AIR COND.
PDR. RM.
UNEXCAVATED UNEXCAVATED
LOWER HALL
L.R.
GARAGE 20⁰ x 21⁶
FOYER
PORCH
BALCONY ABOVE

43

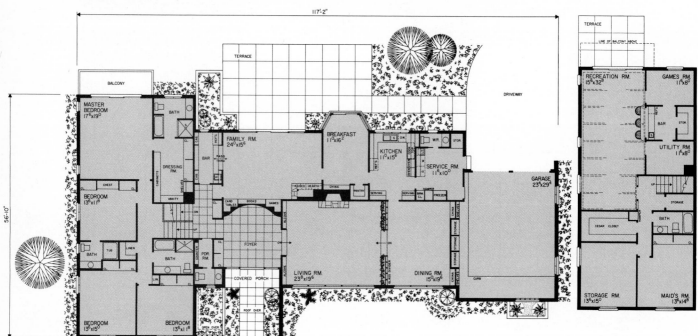

Floor plan labels:

117'-2"

56'-10"

TERRACE

BALCONY

MASTER BEDROOM 17⁶x19⁰

BATH

DRESSING RM.

CHEST

BEDROOM 13⁶x11⁶

BATH

TUB

LINEN

BEDROOM 13⁶x15⁰

BEDROOM 13⁶x11⁸

BATH

PDR. RM.

FOYER

COVERED PORCH

ROOF OVER

OPEN OVER

FAMILY RM. 24⁰x15⁶

BAR

CARD TABLES

BOOKS

GAMES

RAISED HEARTH

CHINA

ALCOVE

LIVING RM. 23⁶x19⁶

BREAKFAST 11⁰x16²

KITCHEN 11⁰x15⁶

SERVING

PANTRY

DINING RM. 15⁰x19⁰

SERVICE RM. 11⁸x10⁰

W.R.

STOR.

SERVING

HAMPER

FREEZER

STORAGE

GARAGE 23⁴x29⁴

CURB

DRIVEWAY

TERRACE

LINE OF BALCONY ABOVE

RECREATION RM. 15⁶x32⁰

GAMES RM. 11⁴x8⁰

BAR

STOR.

UTILITY RM. 11⁴x8⁰

STORAGE

CEDAR CLOSET

BATH

STORAGE RM. 13⁶x15⁰

MAID'S RM. 13⁶x14⁸

Design V32173
Main Level: 2,290 square feet; Upper Level: 1,621 square feet
Lower Level: 1,638 square feet; Total: 5,549 square feet

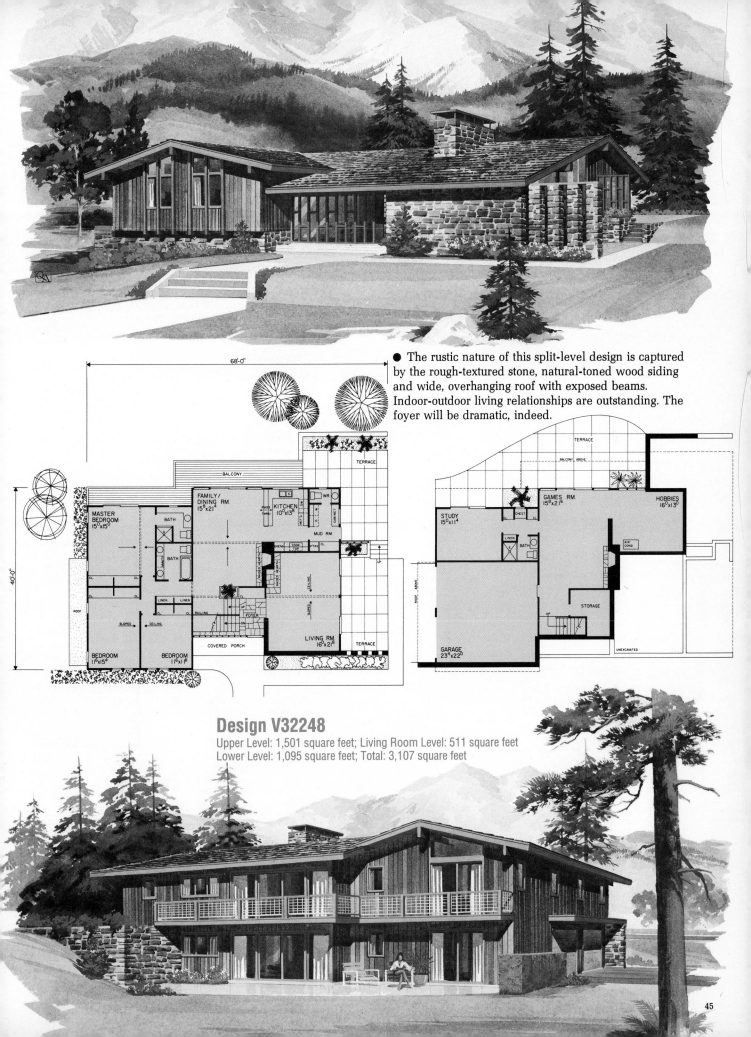

● The rustic nature of this split-level design is captured by the rough-textured stone, natural-toned wood siding and wide, overhanging roof with exposed beams. Indoor-outdoor living relationships are outstanding. The foyer will be dramatic, indeed.

Design V32248

Upper Level: 1,501 square feet; Living Room Level: 511 square feet
Lower Level: 1,095 square feet; Total: 3,107 square feet

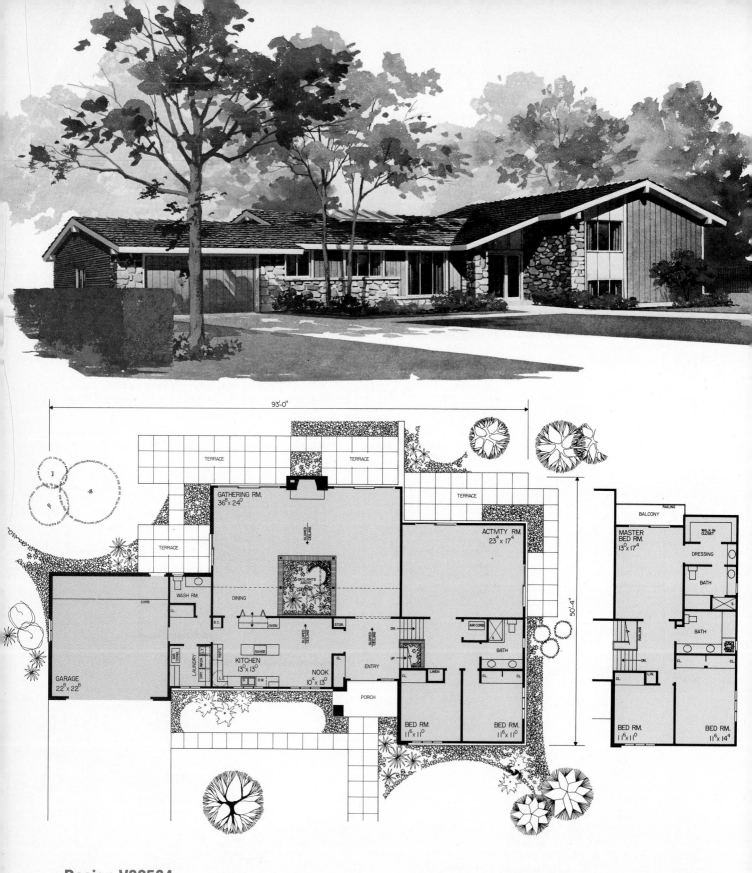

Design V32584 Main Level: 1,604 square feet; Upper Level: 1,018 square feet; Lower Level: 1,026 square feet; Total: 3,648 square feet

● Imagine an indoor garden with a skylight above in the huge gathering room plus a planter beside the lower level stairs. The gathering room also has a sloped ceiling, fireplace and two sets of sliding glass doors leading to the rear terrace and one set to the side terrace. That sure is luxury. But the appeal does not stop there. There are sloped ceilings in the foyer and break-fast nook. The kitchen has an island range, built-in oven and pass-thru to the dining room. Plus a large activities room. A great place for those informal activities. Five bedrooms in all to serve the large family. Including a master suite with a private balcony, dressing room, walk-in closet and bath.

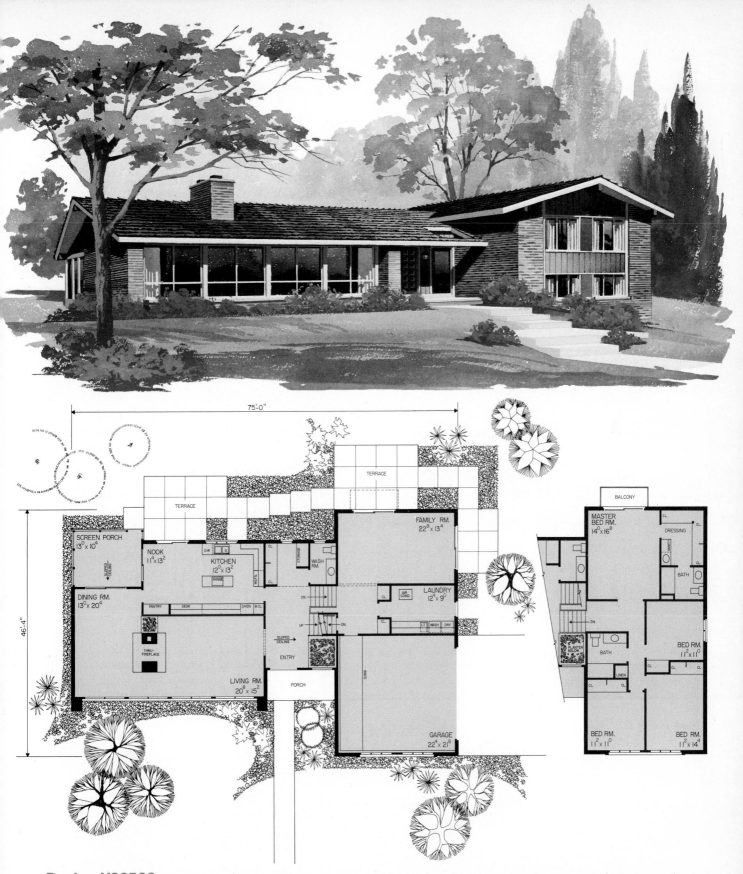

Design V32588 Main Level: 1,354 square feet; Upper Level: 1,112 square feet; Lower Level: 562 square feet; Total: 3,028 square feet

● A thru-fireplace with an accompanying planter for the formal dining room and living room. That's old-fashioned good cheer in a contemporary home. The dining room has an adjacent screened-in porch for outdoor dining in the summertime. There are companions for these two formal areas, an informal breakfast nook and a family room. Each having sliding glass doors to separate rear terraces. Built-in desk, pantry, ample work space and island range are features of the L-shaped kitchen. The large laundry on the lower level houses the heating and cooling equipment. Three family bedrooms, bath and master bedroom suite are on the upper level.

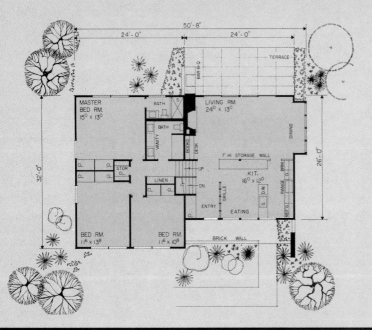

Design V31093

Main Level: 654 square feet Upper Level: 768 square feet
Lower Level: 492 square feet; Total: 1,914 square feet

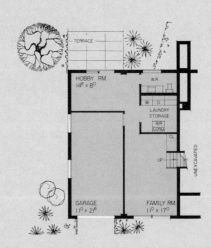

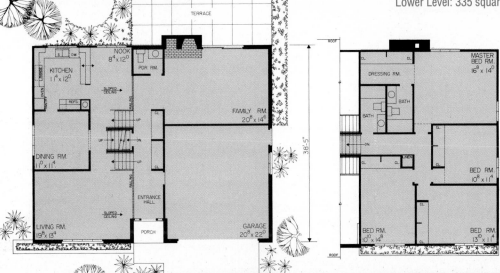

Design V32375
Main Level: 993 square feet; Upper Level: 1,064 square feet
Lower Level: 335 square feet; Total: 2,392 square feet

● For those who like tri-level living, these three contemporary designs have much to offer. Their exteriors are most-distinctive. There are low-pitched, wide-overhanging roofs, effective use of contrasting exterior materials, raised planters and recessed front entrances. The interiors also are quite dramatic with sloped ceilings in Design V32375, right, and Design V32845, below, to enhance the spaciousness. Each of the designs has a fireplace and economically grouped plumbing facilities.

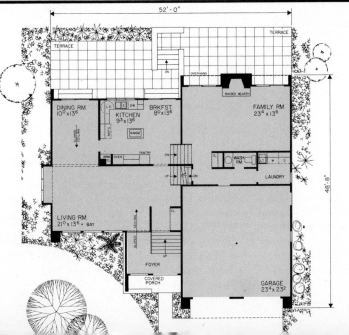

Design V32845
Main Level: 804 square feet Upper Level: 1,089 square feet
Lower Level: 619 square feet; Total: 2,512 square feet

● This multi-level design will be ideal on a sloping site, both in the front and the rear of the house. The contemporary exterior is made up of vertical wood siding. The sloping roofline adds to the exterior appeal and creates a sloped ceiling in the formal living and dining rooms. An attractive bay window highlights the living room as will sliding glass doors in the dining room. The U-shaped kitchen and breakfast room also are located on this main level.

49

Design V32393 Entry Level: 392 square feet; Upper Level: 841 square feet; Lower Level: 848 square feet; Total: 2,081 square feet

● For those with a flair for something refreshingly contemporary both inside and out. This modest sized multi-level has a unique exterior and an equally interesting interior. The low-pitched, wide-overhanging roof protects the inviting double front doors and the large picture window. The raised planter and the side balcony add an extra measure of appeal. Inside, the living patterns will be delightful! The formal living room will look down into the dining room. Like the front entry, the living room has direct access to the lower level. The kitchen is efficient and spacious enough to accommodate an informal breakfast eating area. The laundry room is nearby. The all-purpose family room has beamed ceiling, fireplace and sliding glass doors to rear terrace. The angular, open stairwell to the upper level is dramatic, indeed. Notice how each bedroom has direct access to an outdoor balcony.

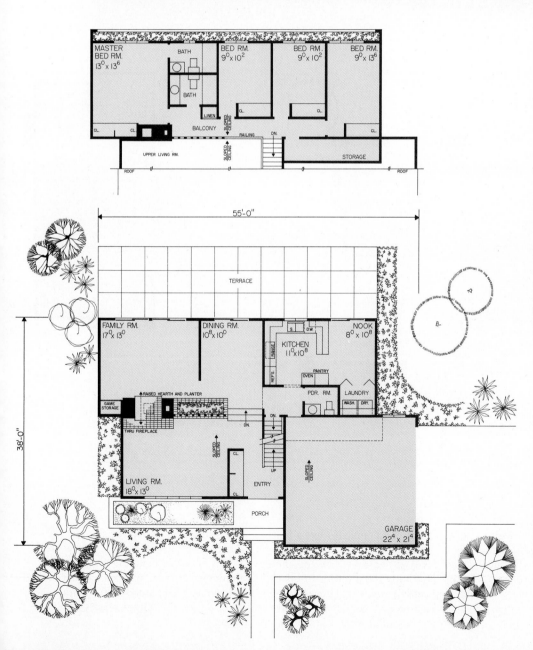

MASTER BED RM. 13⁰ x 13⁶
BATH
BED RM. 9⁰ x 10²
BED RM. 9⁰ x 10²
BED RM. 9⁰ x 13⁶
BATH
LINEN
CL.
CL.
CL.
CL.
BALCONY
SLOPED CEILING
RAILING
DN.
UPPER LIVING RM.
SLOPED CEILING
STORAGE
CL.
ROOF
ROOF

55'-0"
38'-0"

TERRACE

FAMILY RM. 17⁰ x 13⁰
DINING RM. 10⁸ x 10⁰
S.
D.W.
KITCHEN 11⁰ x 10⁸
NOOK 8⁰ x 10⁸
RANGE
REFG.
PANTRY
OVEN
GAME STORAGE
RAISED HEARTH AND PLANTER
PDR. RM.
LAUNDRY
WASH. DRY.
THRU FIREPLACE
DN.
DN.
SLOPED CEILING
CL.
UP
SLOPED CEILING
LIVING RM. 18⁰ x 13⁰
ENTRY
CL.
PORCH
GARAGE 22⁴ x 21⁴

Design V32377

Living Room Level: 388 square feet
Main Level: 782 square feet
Upper Level: 815 square feet
Total: 1,985 square feet

● What an impressive up-to-date multi-level home this is. Its refreshing configuration will command a full measure of attention. Separating the living and slightly lower levels is a thru-fireplace which has a raised hearth in the family room. An adjacent planter with vertical members provides additional interest and beauty. The rear terrace is accessible from nook, family and dining rooms. Notice the powder room, the convenient laundry area and the basement stairs. Four bedrooms serviced by two full baths comprise the upper level which looks down into the living room. A large walk-in storage closet will be ideal for those seasonal items. An attractive outdoor planter extends across the rear just outside the bedroom windows. This will surely be a house that will be fun in which to live.

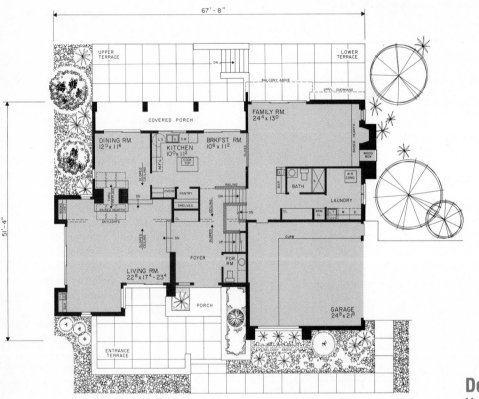

Design V32893

Main Level: 1,297 square feet
Upper Level: 1,256 square feet
Lower Level: 654 square feet
Total: 3,207 square feet

D

● Here is a contemporary split-level with a lot of appeal. To the right of the foyer and up a few steps you will find three bedrooms and a bath. Also, a master bedroom suite with an oversized tub, shower, walk-in closet and sliding glass doors to a balcony. (One of the front bedrooms also has a balcony.) A sunken living room is on the main level. It has a wet bar and shares with the dining room a thru-fireplace, sloped ceiling and a skylight. A spacious kitchen and breakfast room are nearby. They offer easy access to the covered porch - ideal for summer meals. The lower level has a large family room with sliding glass doors to the lower terrace, another wet bar and a fireplace. The laundry, full bath, large closet and garage access are just steps away.

TWO COUPLES/SINGLES RESIDENCE

CONVERTIBLE ONE-FAMILY RESIDENCE

Design V32828 First Floor: 817 square feet - Living Area; Foyer & Laundry: 261 square feet
Second Floor: 852 square feet - Living Area; Foyer & Storage: 214 square feet; Total: 2,144 square feet

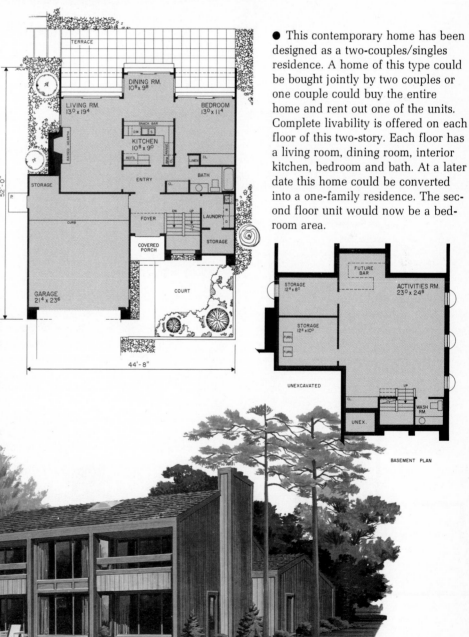

● This contemporary home has been designed as a two-couples/singles residence. A home of this type could be bought jointly by two couples or one couple could buy the entire home and rent out one of the units. Complete livability is offered on each floor of this two-story. Each floor has a living room, dining room, interior kitchen, bedroom and bath. At a later date this home could be converted into a one-family residence. The second floor unit would now be a bedroom area.

Design V32926

First Floor: 1,570 square feet; Second Floor: 598 square feet
Lower Level; 1,080 square feet; Total: 3,248 square feet

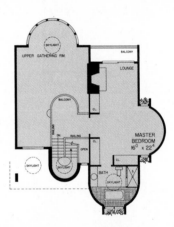

● This striking Contemporary design offers plenty of leisure living on three levels including an activities room with bar, exercise room with sauna, a gathering room, circular glass windows, and skylights. Note the outstanding master bedroom suite with skylight over the bath, adjoining lounge, and adjacent balcony.

Design V32735

Upper Level: 1,545 square feet
Lower Level: 1,633 square feet
Total: 3,178 square feet

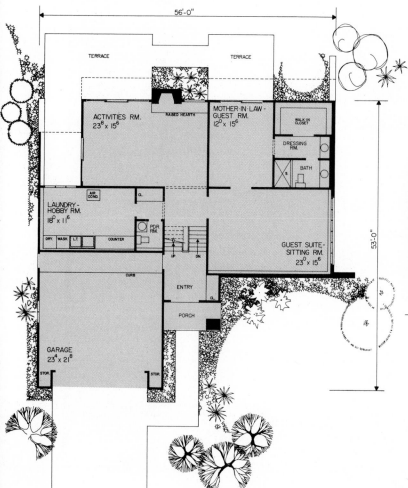

● Whether entering this house through the double front doors, or from the garage, access is gained to the lower level by descending seven stairs. Here, there is a bonus of livability. If desired, this level could be used to accommodate a live-in relative while still providing the family with a fine informal activities room and a separate laundry/hobby room and extra powder room. Up seven risers from the entry is the main living level. It has a large gathering room; a sizable nook which could be called upon to function as a separate dining room; an efficient kitchen with pass-thru to a formal dining area and a two bedroom, two bath and study sleeping zone. Don't miss the balconies and deck.

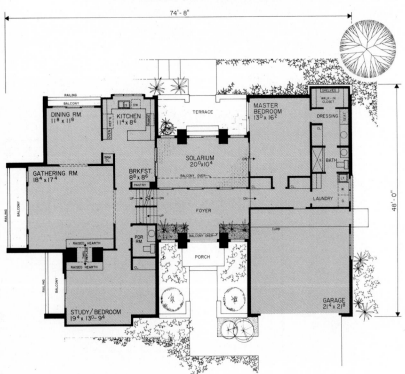

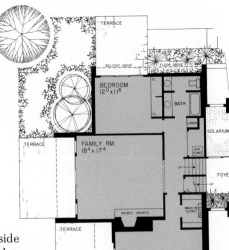

Design V32836 Foyer Level: 998 square feet; Main Level: 1,146 square feet
Lower Level: 1,090 square feet; Studio Level: 241 square feet; Total: 3,475 square feet

● Here is a dramatic, hip-roofed contemporary with exciting living patterns. Inside the double front doors, flanked by planting areas, is the foyer level which includes the solarium, master bedroom and laundry. Up seven steps from the foyer is the main level comprised of a gathering room with a thru-fireplace opening to the study, formal dining and informal breakfast rooms and an efficient, U-shaped kitchen. Across from the gathering room is the short flight of stairs to the upper level studio. Like the breakfast room immediately below, the studio looks down into the solarium. The skylight provides both studio and solarium with an abundance of natural light. Heat is absorbed and stored in the thermal brick floor of this centrally located solarium. The floor will then radiate heat into the living areas to stabilize the temperature when necessary. The lower sleeping level is down a few steps from the foyer. It functions well with its terrace and the children's bedrooms. Don't miss the three main level balconies and the three lower level terraces. They will create wonderful indoor-outdoor living relationships for the entire family to enjoy.

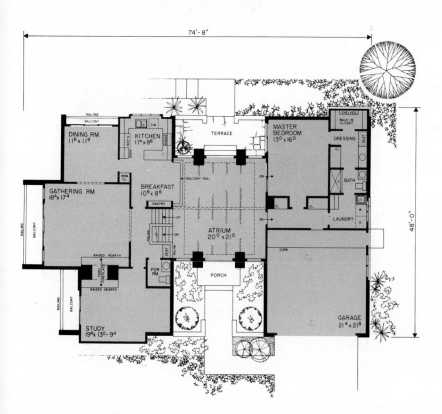

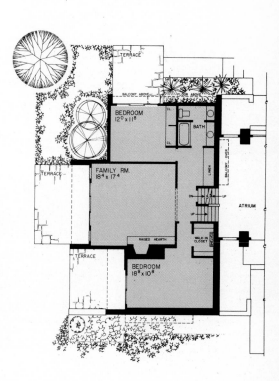

Design V32837 Main Level: 1,165 square feet; Atrium Level: 998 square feet; Lower Level: 1,090 square feet; Total: 3,253 square feet

● This atrium plan is housed in the same dramatic exterior as the solarium plan on the opposite page. The exterior remains exactly the same but the floor plan has been altered to house an atrium. Enclosed in glass, the atrium admits daytime solar warmth, which radiates into the other rooms for direct-gain heating. Seeing that this plan includes a basement underneath the atrium, it lacks the thick, heat-storing thermal floor which is featured in the solarium version. For this reason, the plan calls for a furnace in the basement as the primary heat source. The floor plan of this atrium version is similar to its solarium counterpart except that the studio level has been omitted. As a result it has three living levels instead of four, plus a basement.

The master suite is outstanding. It is complete with dressing room, two large closets, bathroom and access to the laundry. The rear terrace is accessible by way of sliding glass doors. Fireplaces can be enjoyed in three rooms, gathering, study and lower level family room. Continue to study this unique design and its solarium counterpart for their many features.

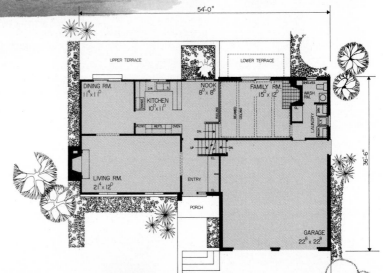

Design V32608

Main Level: 728 square feet; Upper Level: 874 square feet
Lower Level: 310 square feet; Total: 1,912 square feet

L **D**

● Here is tri-level livability with a fourth basement level for bulk storage and, perhaps, a shop area. There are four bedrooms, a handy laundry, two eating areas, formal and informal living areas and two fireplaces. Sliding glass doors in the formal dining room and the family room open to a terrace. The U-shaped kitchen has a built-in range/oven and storage pantry. The breakfast nook overlooks the family room.

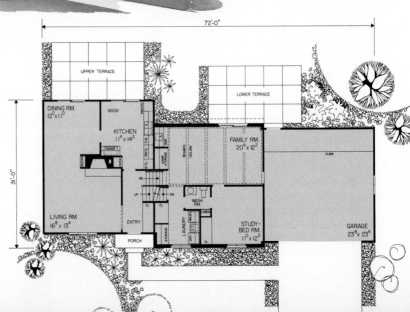

Design V32628

Main Level: 649 square feet; Upper Level: 672 square feet
Lower Level: 624 square feet; Total: 1,945 square feet

D

● Traditional, yet contemporary! With lots of extras, too. Like a wet bar and game storage in the family room. A beamed ceiling, too, and a sliding glass door onto the terrace. In short, a family room designed to make your life easy and enjoyable. There's more. A living room with a traditionally styled fireplace and built-in bookshelves. And a dining room with a sliding glass door that opens to a second terrace. Here's the appropriate setting for those times when you want a touch of elegance.

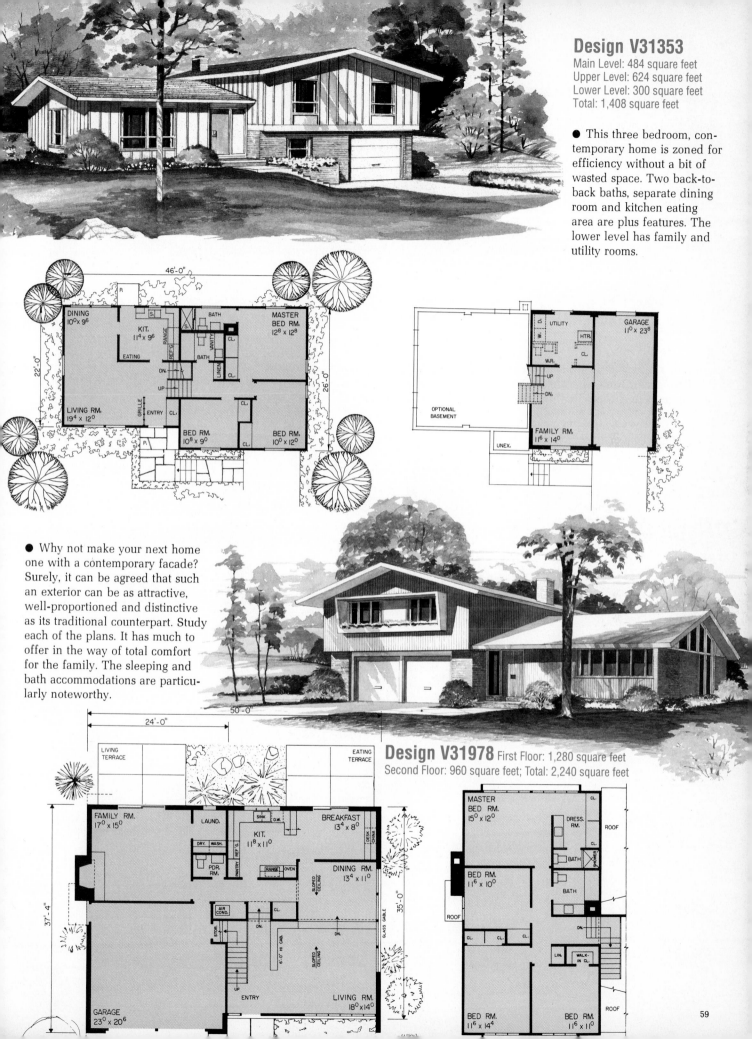

Design V31353

Main Level: 484 square feet
Upper Level: 624 square feet
Lower Level: 300 square feet
Total: 1,408 square feet

● This three bedroom, contemporary home is zoned for efficiency without a bit of wasted space. Two back-to-back baths, separate dining room and kitchen eating area are plus features. The lower level has family and utility rooms.

● Why not make your next home one with a contemporary facade? Surely, it can be agreed that such an exterior can be as attractive, well-proportioned and distinctive as its traditional counterpart. Study each of the plans. It has much to offer in the way of total comfort for the family. The sleeping and bath accommodations are particularly noteworthy.

Design V31978
First Floor: 1,280 square feet
Second Floor: 960 square feet; Total: 2,240 square feet

59

Design V32111 Main Level: 1,036 square feet

Upper Level: 1,339 square feet; Study Level; 306 square feet; Lower Level: 1,419 square feet; Total: 4,100 square feet

● If you have a sloping site, you'd better give this dramatic contemporary a second, or even a third, look. Should your property have a view worth enjoying from the main level living areas, the large expanses of glass would undoubtedly be your most favorite feature. Notice how the glass wall is pushed outward like the bow of a ship.

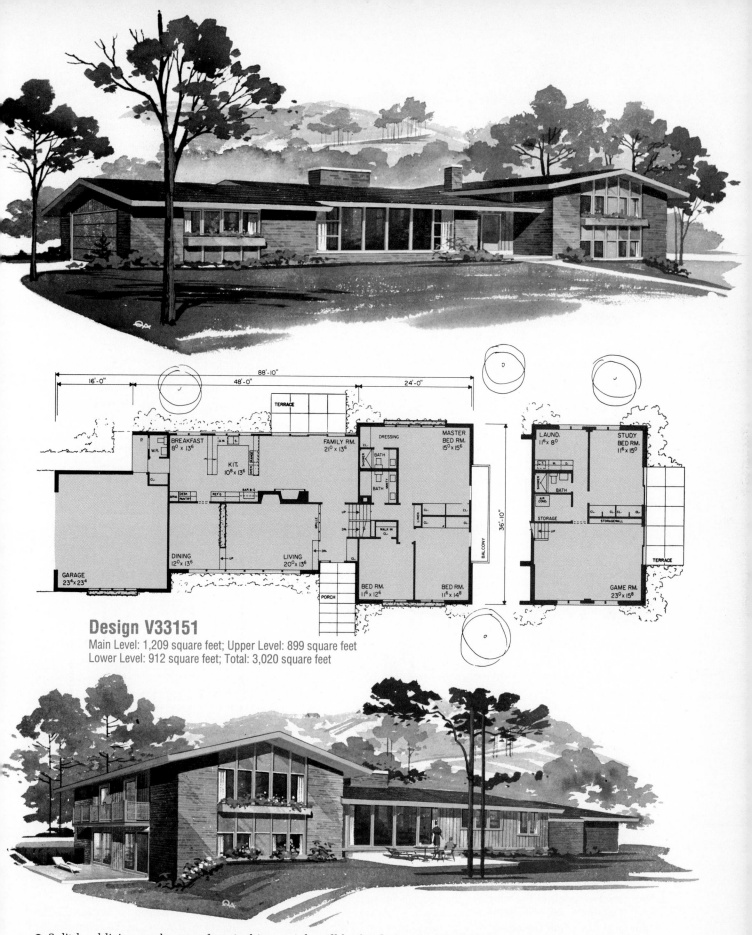

Design V33151

Main Level: 1,209 square feet; Upper Level: 899 square feet
Lower Level: 912 square feet; Total: 3,020 square feet

● Split-level living can be great fun. And it certainly will be for the occupants of this impressive house. First and foremost, you and your family will appreciate the practical zoning. The upper level is the quiet sleeping level. List the features. They are many. The main level is zoned for both formal and informal living. Don't miss the sunken living room or the twin fireplaces. The lower level provides that extra measure of livability for all to enjoy.

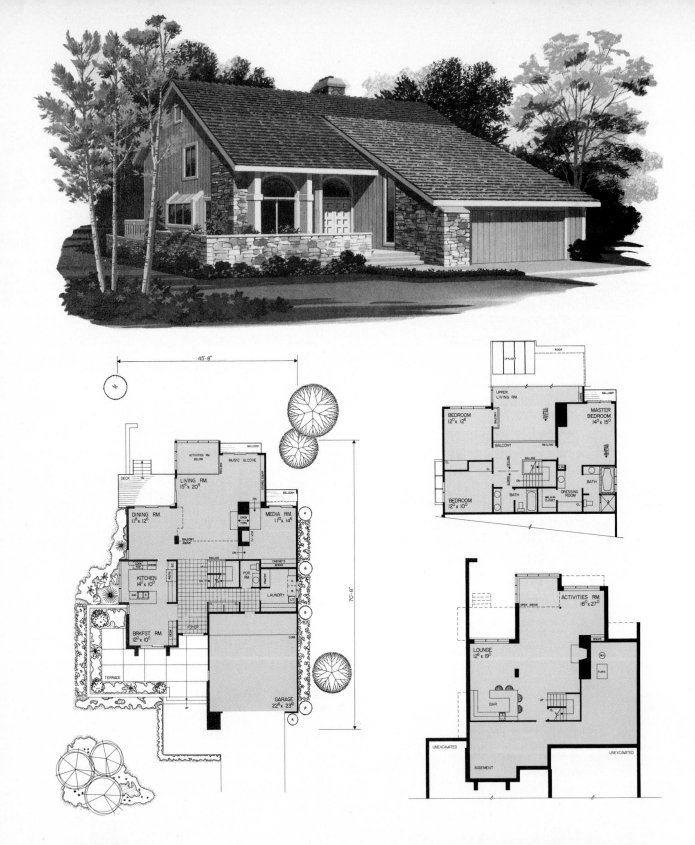

Design V32944 Main Level: 1,545 square feet; Upper Level: 977 square feet; Lower Level: 933 square feet; Total: 3,455 square feet

● This eye-catching contemporary features three stacked levels of livability. And what livability it will truly be! The main level has a fine U-shaped kitchen which is flanked by the informal breakfast room and formal dining room. The living room will be dramatic, indeed. Its sloping ceiling extends through the upper level. It overlooks the lower level activities room and has wonderfully expansive window areas for full enjoyment of surrounding vistas. A two-way fireplace can be viewed from dining, living and media rooms. A sizable deck and two cozy balconies provide for flexible outdoor living. Don't miss the music alcove with its wall for stereo equipment. Upstairs, the balcony overlooks the living room. It serves as the connecting link for the three bedrooms. The lower level offers more cheerful livability with the huge activities room plus lounge area. Note bar, fireplace.

TRADITIONAL SPLIT-LEVELS . . .

have been included in this section that reflect exteriors of a variety of classic styles. Tudor, Spanish, Western, French and Early American versions have been adapted to the split-level type of floor plan. The split-level house may be built on a flat or sloping site. It is a favorite of many because it features a desirable separation of functions. The main level is generally the living level and contains the living, dining and breakfast rooms, plus kitchen. The upper level is exclusively the sleeping level with its baths. The lower level is devoted to laundry and family room. Some split-levels feature a fourth basement level.

Design V32218

Main Level: 889 square feet; Upper Level: 960 square feet
Lower Level: 936 square feet; Total: 2,785 square feet

● Styled in the Tudor tradition, the warmth and charm of the exterior sets the tone for an exceptionally livable interior. Were you to ask each member of your family to choose his/her favorite feature there would be many outstanding highlights to consider.

Design V32841

Main Level: 1,044 square feet; Upper Level: 851 square feet
Lower Level: 753 square feet; Total: 2,648 square feet

D

● This spacious tri-level with traditional stone exterior offers excellent comfort and zoning for the modern family. The rear opens to balconies and a deck that creates a covered patio below. A main floor gathering room is continued above with an upper gathering room. The lower level offers an activities room with raised hearth, in addition to an optional bunk room with bath. A modern kitchen on main level features a handy snack bar, in addition to a dining room. A study on main level could become an optional bedroom. The master bedroom is located on the upper level, along with a rectangular bunk room with its own balcony.

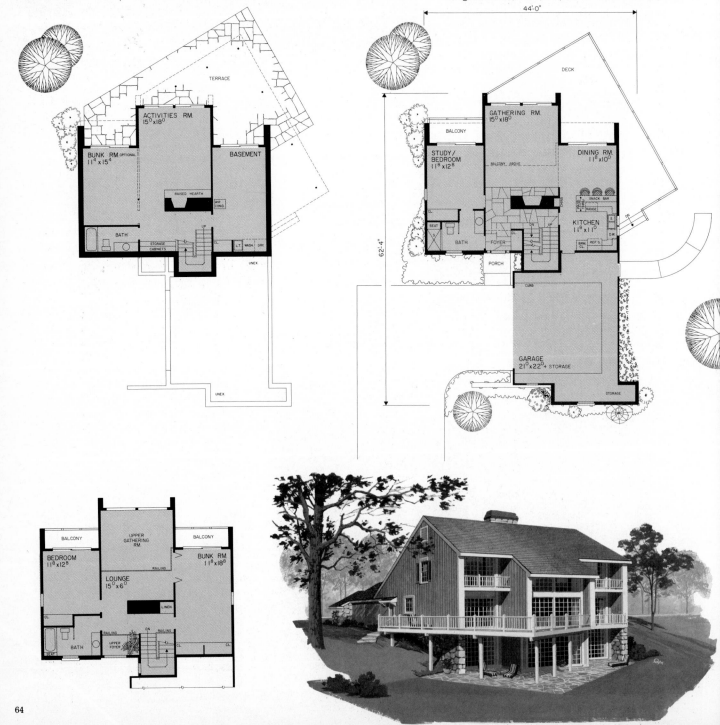

Design V32842

Entrance Level: 156 square feet; Upper Level: 1,038 square feet
Lower Level: 1,022 square feet; Total: 2,216 square feet

● This narrow, 42 foot width, house can be built on a narrow lot to cut down overall costs. Yet its dramatic appeal surely is worth a million. The projecting front garage creates a pleasing curved drive. One enters this house through the covered porch to the entrance level foyer. At this point the stairs lead down to the living area consisting of formal living room, family room, kitchen and dining area then up the stairs to the four bedroom-two bath sleeping area. The indoor-outdoor living relationship at the rear is outstanding.

Design V32758

Main Level: 1,143 square feet
Upper Level: 792 square feet
Lower Level: 770 square feet
Total: 2,705 square feet

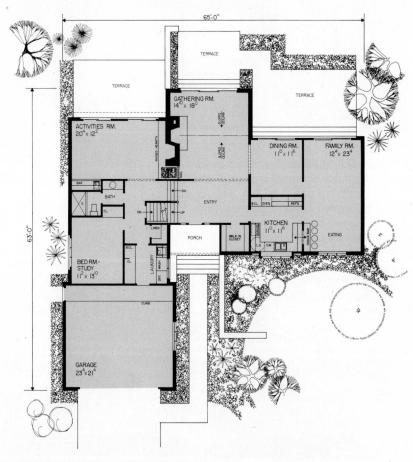

● An outstanding Tudor with three levels of exceptional livability, plus a basement. A careful study of the exterior reveals many delightful architectural details which give this home a character of its own. Notice the appealing recessed front entrance. Observe the overhanging roof with the exposed rafters. Don't miss the window treatment, the use of stucco and simulated beams, the masses of brick and the stylish chimney. Inside, the living potential is unsurpassed. Imagine, there are three living areas - the gathering, family and activities rooms. Having a snack bar, informal eating area and dining room, eating patterns can be flexible. In addition to the three bedroom, two-bath upper level, there is a fourth bedroom with adjacent bath on the lower level.

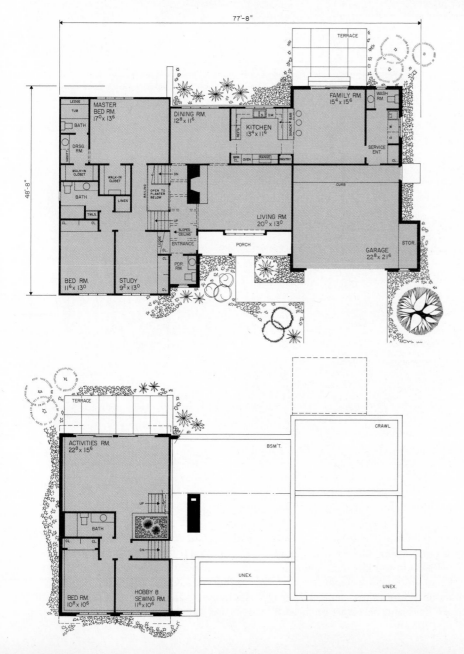

Design V32773

Main Level: 1,157 square feet
Upper Level: 950 square feet
Lower Level: 912 square feet
Total: 3,019 square feet

● Here is an exquisitely styled Tudor tri-level which retains the low-slung characteristics of a one-story house. The contrasting use of material surely makes the exterior eye-catching. Another outstanding feature will be the covered front porch. A delightful way to enter this home. Many fine features also will be found inside this design. Formal living and dining room, U-shaped kitchen with snack bar and family room find themselves located on the main level. Two of the three bedrooms are on the upper level with two baths. Activities room, third bedroom and hobby/ sewing room are on the lower level — a real bonus. Notice the built-in planter on the lower level which is visible from the other two levels. A powder room and a washroom both are on the main level. A study is on the upper level which is a great place for a quiet retreat. The basement will be convenient for storage of any bulk items.

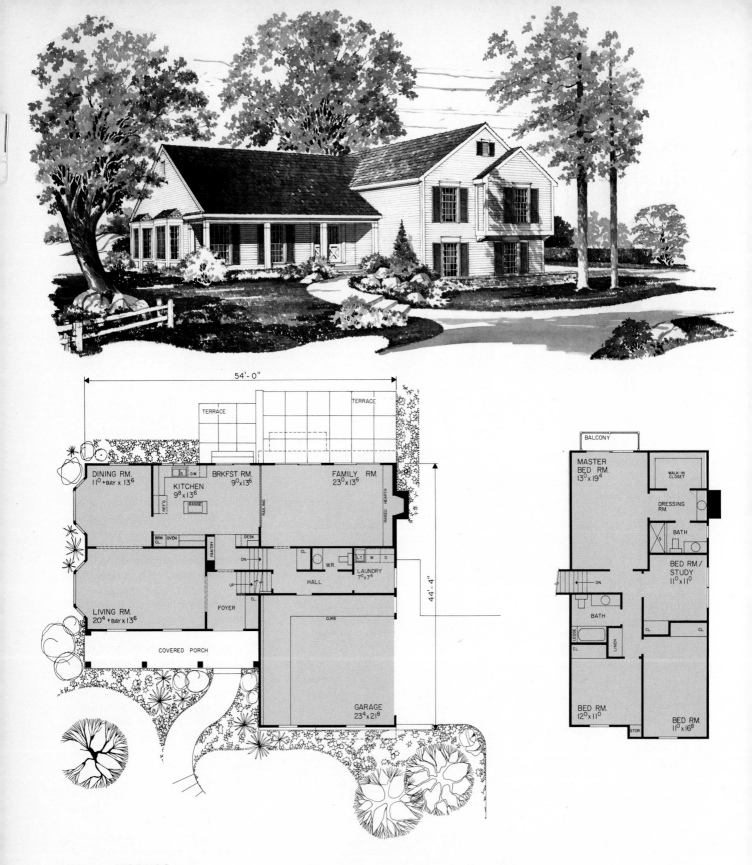

Design V32786 Main Level: 871 square feet; Upper Level: 1,132 square feet; Lower Level: 528 square feet; Total: 2,531 square feet

● A bay window in each the formal living room and dining room. A great interior and exterior design feature to attract attention to this tri-level home. The exterior also is enhanced by a covered front porch to further the Colonial charm. The interior livability is outstanding, too. An abundance of built-ins in the kitchen create an efficient work center. Features include an island range, pantry, broom closet, desk and breakfast room with sliding glass doors to the rear terrace. The lower level houses the informal family room, wash room and laundry. Further access is available to the outdoors by the family room to the terrace and laundry room to the side yard.

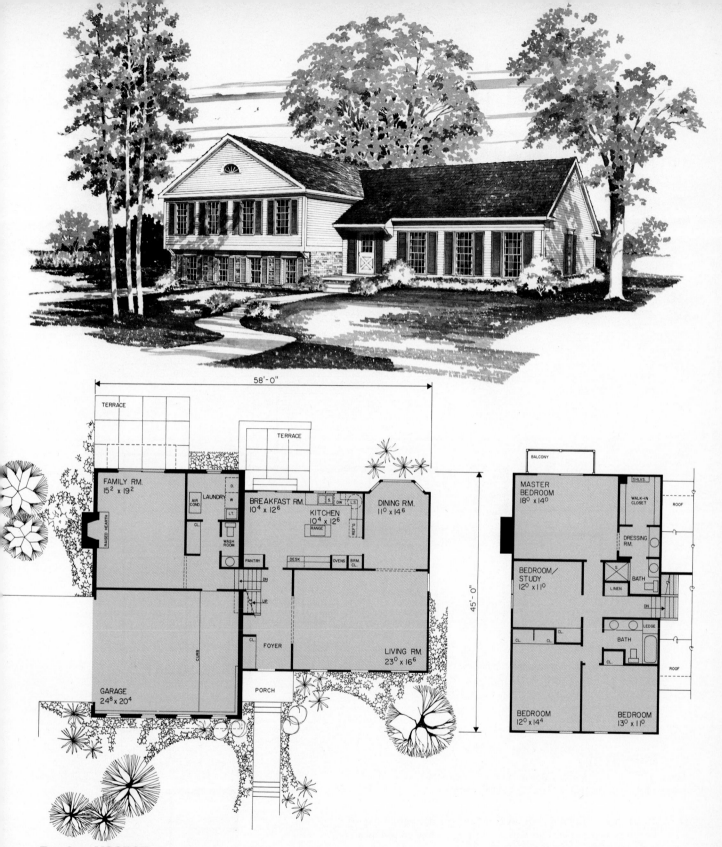

Design V32787 Main Level: 976 square feet; Upper Level: 1,118 square feet; Lower Level: 524 square feet; Total: 2,618 square feet

L D

● Three level living! Main, upper and lower levels to serve you and your family with great ease. Start from the bottom and work your way up. Family room with raised hearth fireplace, laundry and wash room on the lower level. Formal living and dining rooms, kitchen and breakfast room on the main level. Stop and take note at the efficiency of the kitchen with its many outstanding extras. The upper level houses the three bedrooms, study (or fourth bedroom if you prefer) and two baths. This design has really stacked up its livability to serve its occupants to their best advantage. This design has great interior livability and exterior charm.

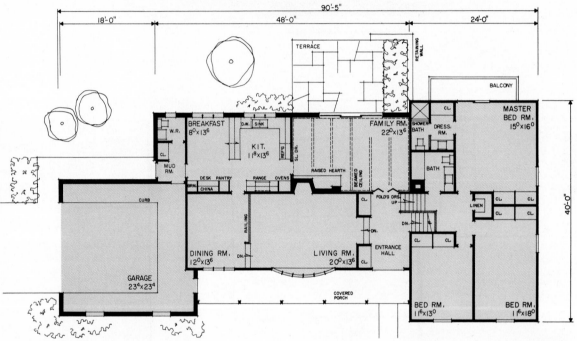

Main floor plan labels:

TERRACE, RETAINING WALL, BALCONY, BREAKFAST 8⁰x13⁶, W.R., D.W., SINK, FAMILY RM. 22⁰x13⁶, SHOWER BATH, DRESS. RM., CL., MASTER BED RM. 15⁰x16⁰, CL., MUD RM., KIT. 11⁸x13⁶, REF'G, SL. DR., RAISED HEARTH, BEAMED CEILING, BATH, DESK, PANTRY, RANGE, OVENS, FOLD'G DRS., UP, LINEN, CL., CL., BRM, CHINA, CL., DN., CL., CURB, RAILING, DN., DINING RM. 12⁰x13⁶, DN., LIVING RM. 20⁰x13⁶, ENTRANCE HALL, CL., GARAGE 23⁴x23⁴, COVERED PORCH, BED RM. 11⁶x13⁰, BED RM. 11⁶x18⁰

Dimensions: 90'-5", 18'-0", 48'-0", 24'-0", 40'-0"

Design V31927

Main Level: 1,272 square feet; Upper Level: 960 square feet
Lower Level: 936 square feet; Total: 3,168 square feet

● Living in this traditional split level home will be a great experience. For here is a design that has everything. It has good looks and an abundance of livability features. The long, low appearance is accentuated by the large covered porch which shelters the bowed window and the inviting double front doors. Whatever your preference for exterior materials they will show well on this finely proportioned home. They start with four bedrooms and three full baths and continue with: beamed ceiling family room, sunken living room, formal dining room, informal breakfast room, extra wash room, outstanding kitchen and two attractive fireplaces.

Lower floor plan labels:

TERRACE, LAUNDRY-SEWING, LAUNDRY TRAY, WASH, DRY, STUDY-BED RM. 11⁰x15⁰, BATH, AIR COND., CL., DESK, BOOKS, CL., SHELVES, UP, REF'G, SINK, SNACK BAR, UNEX., GAME RM. 22⁶x14⁰

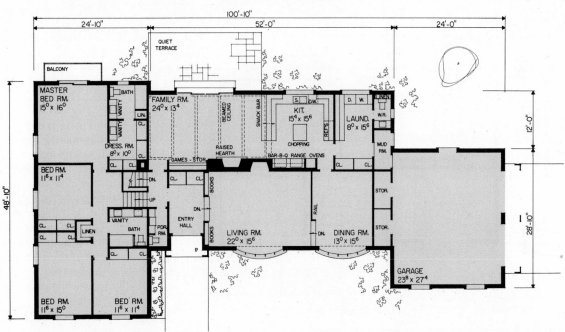

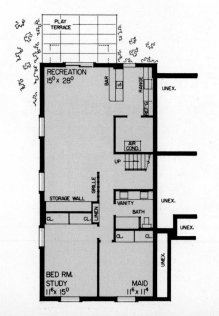

Design V31270

Main Level: 1,648 square feet; Upper Level: 1,200 square feet
Lower Level: 1,200 square feet; Total: 4,048 square feet

● A French Provincial adaptation with an enormous amount of livability on three levels. Whether called upon to function as a four or six bedroom home, there will be plenty of space in which to move around. Whatever the activities of the family–formal or informal–this floor plan contains the facilities to cater to them. For instance, there is the family room of the main level and the recreation room of the lower level to more than adequately serve informal pursuits. Then there is the sunken living room. The main level laundry will save many steps. There are two fireplaces and exceptional storage facilities. Four bedrooms highlight upper level.

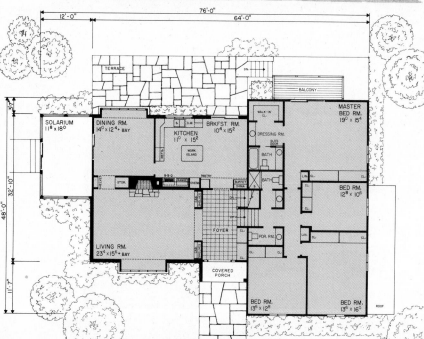

Design V32254

Main Level: 1,220 square feet
Upper Level: 1,344 square feet
Lower Level: 659 square feet
Total: 3,223 square feet

● Tudor charm is deftly exemplified by this outstanding four level design. The window treatment, the heavy timber work and the chimney pots help set the character of this home. Contributing an extra measure of appeal is the detailing of the delightful porch. The garden view of this home is equally appealing. The upper level balcony looks down onto the two terraces. The covered front entry leads to the spacious formal entrance hall with its slate floor. . .

Design V32243

Main Level: 1,274 square feet; Upper Level: 960 square feet
Lower Level: 936 square feet; Total: 3,170 square feet

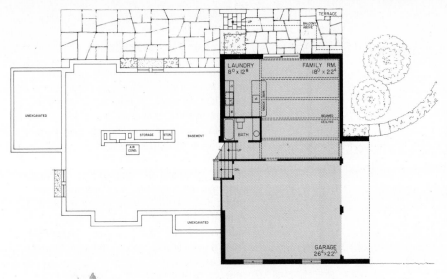

. . . Straight ahead is the kitchen and nook. The open planning of this area results in a fine feeling of spaciousness. Both living and dining rooms are wonderfully large. Each room highlights a big bay window. Notice the built-in units. Upstairs there are four bedrooms, two full baths and a powder room. Count the closets. The lower level is reserved for the all-purpose room, the separate laundry and a third full bath. The garage is adjacent. A fourth level is a basement with an abundance of space for storage and hobbies.

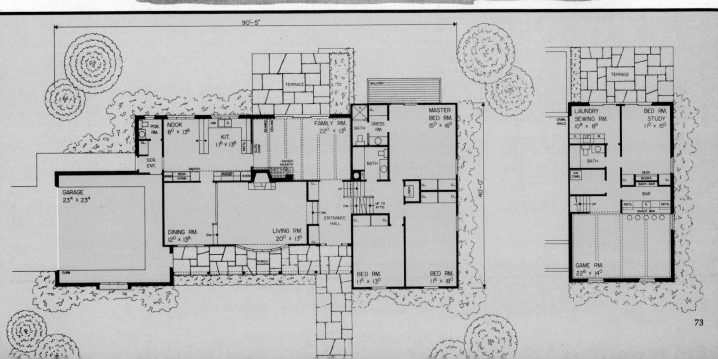

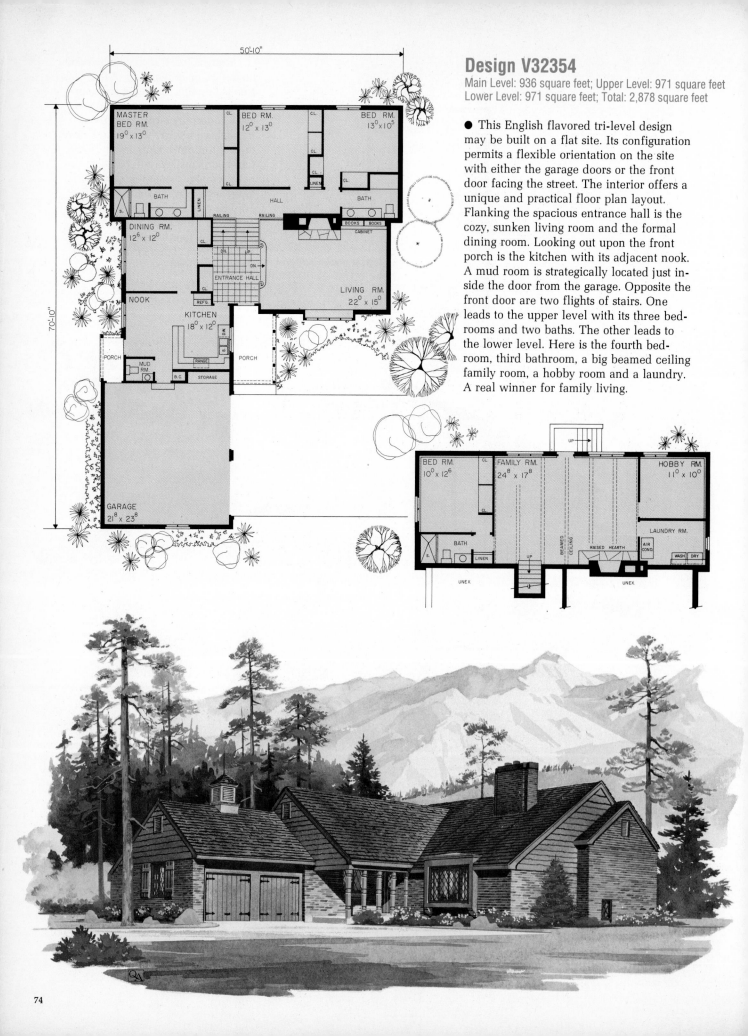

Design V32354

Main Level: 936 square feet; Upper Level: 971 square feet
Lower Level: 971 square feet; Total: 2,878 square feet

● This English flavored tri-level design may be built on a flat site. Its configuration permits a flexible orientation on the site with either the garage doors or the front door facing the street. The interior offers a unique and practical floor plan layout. Flanking the spacious entrance hall is the cozy, sunken living room and the formal dining room. Looking out upon the front porch is the kitchen with its adjacent nook. A mud room is strategically located just inside the door from the garage. Opposite the front door are two flights of stairs. One leads to the upper level with its three bedrooms and two baths. The other leads to the lower level. Here is the fourth bedroom, third bathroom, a big beamed ceiling family room, a hobby room and a laundry. A real winner for family living.

Floor plan labels:

50'-10"
70'-10"

MASTER BED RM. 19⁰ x 13⁰
BED RM. 12⁰ x 13⁰
BED RM. 13⁰ x 10⁵
BATH
LINEN
HALL
RAILING
RAILING
BOOKS BOOKS
CABINET
DINING RM. 12⁶ x 12⁰
CL.
DN. UP
DN.
ENTRANCE HALL
CL.
LIVING RM. 22⁰ x 15⁰
NOOK
REF'G.
KITCHEN 18⁰ x 12⁰
RANGE
DW
PORCH
PORCH
MUD RM.
B.C. STORAGE
GARAGE 21⁸ x 23⁸

BED RM. 10⁰ x 12⁶
FAMILY RM. 24⁸ x 17⁸
HOBBY RM. 11⁰ x 10⁰
UP
BATH
LINEN
BEAMED CEILING
RAISED HEARTH
LAUNDRY RM.
AIR COND.
UP
WASH DRY
UNEX.
UNEX.

Design V32624

Main Level: 904 square feet; Upper Level: 1,120 square feet
Lower Level: 404 square feet; Total: 2,428 square feet

L D

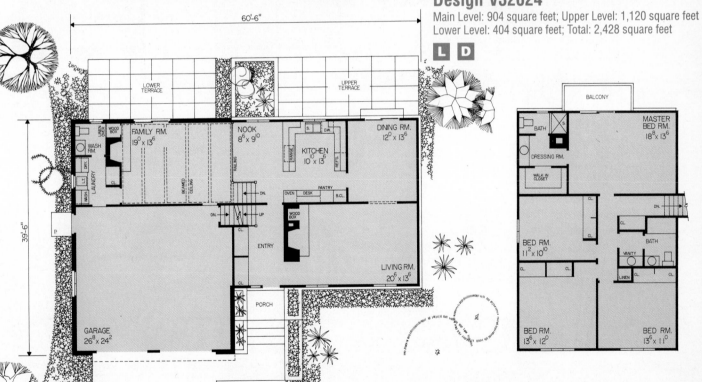

● This is tri-level living at its best. The exterior is that of the most popular Tudor styling. A facade which will hold its own for many a year to come. Livability will be achieved to its maximum on the four (including basement) levels. The occupants of the master bedroom can enjoy the outdoors on their private balcony. Additional outdoor enjoyment can be gained on the two terraces. That family room is more than 19' x 13' and includes a beamed ceiling and fireplace with wood box. Its formal companion, the living room, is similar in size and also will have the added warmth of a fireplace.

Design V32143 Main Level: 832 square feet; Upper Level: 864 square feet; Lower Level: 864 square feet; Total: 2,560 square feet

● Here the Spanish Southwest comes to life in the form of an enchanting multi-level home. There is much to rave about. The architectural detailing is delightful, indeed. The entrance courtyard, the twin balconies and the roof treatment are particular- ly noteworthy. Functioning at the rear of the house are the covered patio and the balcony with its lower patio. Well zoned, the upper level has three bedrooms and two baths; the main level has its formal living and dining rooms to the rear and kitchen area looking onto the courtyard; the lower level features the family room, study and laundry. Be sure to notice the extra wash room and the third full bath. There are two fireplaces each with a raised hearth. A dramatic house wherever built!

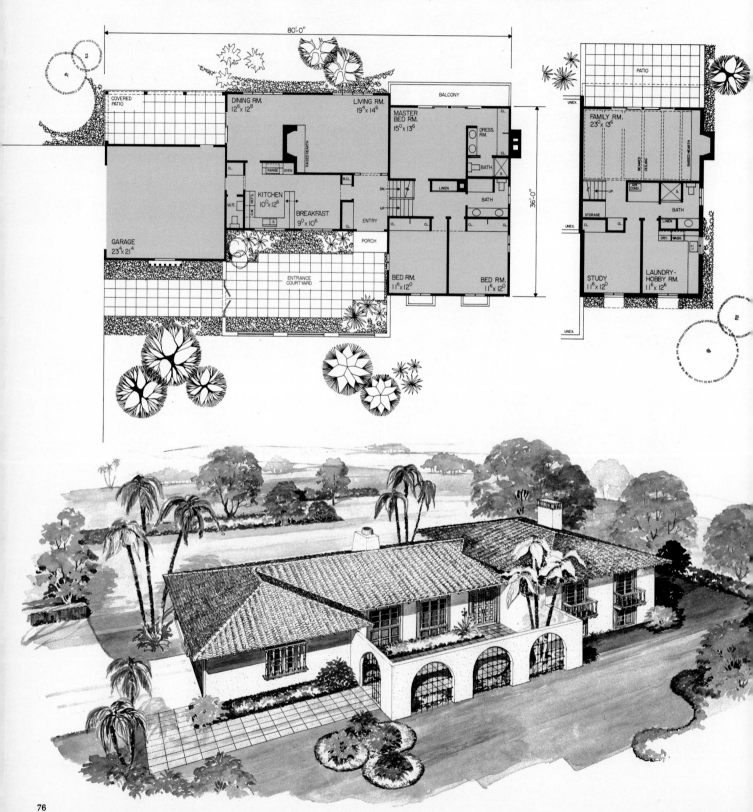

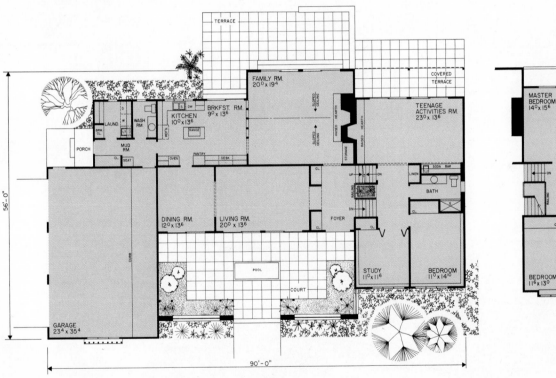

Design V32850

Main Level: 1,530 square feet; Upper Level: 984 square feet; Lower Level: 951 square feet; Total: 3,465 square feet

L D

● Entering through the entry court of this Spanish design is very impressive. Partially shielded from the street, this court features planting areas and a small pool. Enter into the foyer and this split-level interior will begin to unfold. Down six steps from the foyer is the lower level housing a bedroom and full bath, study and teenage activities room. Adults, along with teenagers, will enjoy the activities room which has a raised hearth fireplace, soda bar and sliding glass doors leading to a covered terrace. Six steps up from the foyer is the upper level bedroom area. The main level has the majority of the living areas. Formal living and dining rooms, informal family room, kitchen with accompanying breakfast room and mud room consisting of laundry and wash room. This home even has a three-car garage. Livability will be achieved with the greatest amount of comfort in this home.

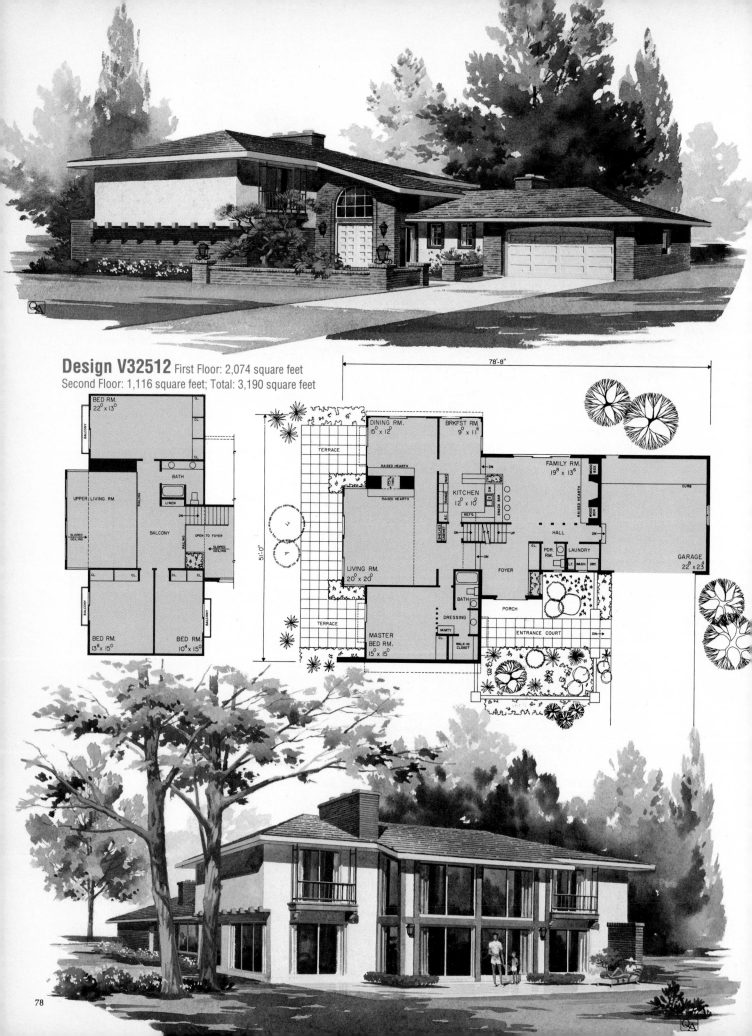

Design V32512 First Floor: 2,074 square feet
Second Floor: 1,116 square feet; Total: 3,190 square feet

Second Floor Plan:
- BED RM. 22⁰ x 13⁰
- CL.
- BALCONY
- UPPER LIVING RM.
- BATH
- LINEN
- SLOPED CEILING
- BALCONY
- DN.
- RAILING
- OPEN TO FOYER
- SLOPED CEILING
- CL.
- BED RM. 13⁸ x 15⁰
- BED RM. 10⁴ x 15⁰
- BALCONY

First Floor Plan:
- 78'-8"
- 51'-0"
- TERRACE
- DINING RM. 15⁰ x 12⁰
- BRKFST RM. 9⁰ x 11⁶
- RAISED HEARTH
- RAISED HEARTH
- FAMILY RM. 19⁸ x 13⁶
- WOOD BOX
- RAISED HEARTH
- CURB
- WOOD BOX
- KITCHEN 12⁰ x 10⁰
- RANGE
- REFG.
- SNACK BAR
- B.C.
- SHELVES CABINET
- UP
- DN.
- HALL
- DN.
- LIVING RM. 20⁰ x 20⁰
- EL.
- PDR. RM.
- LAUNDRY
- LT. WASH. DRY.
- GARAGE 22⁸ x 23⁴
- FOYER
- BATH
- DRESSING
- VANITY
- PORCH
- MASTER BED RM. 15⁰ x 15⁰
- WALK-IN CLOSET
- CL.
- ENTRANCE COURT
- DN.
- TERRACE

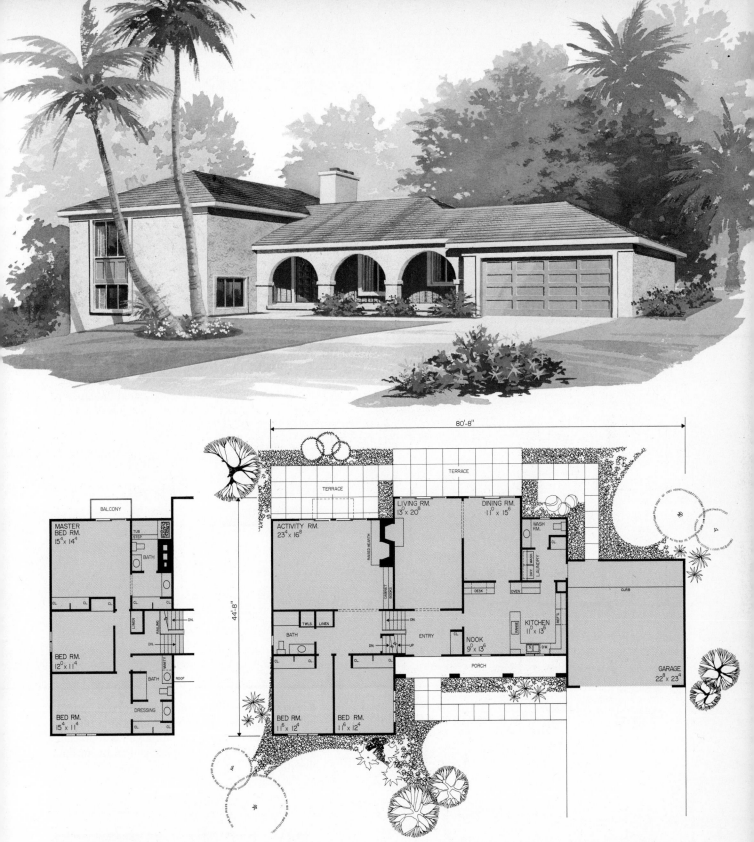

Design V32574 Main Level: 984 square feet; Upper Level: 968 square feet; Lower Level: 976 square feet; Total: 2,928 square feet

● Spanish flair! This home has four bedrooms plus a master suite with a private balcony, dressing room, a luxury bath with a step-up tub and four closets. Also featuring extravagant living space. The activity room is more than 23' by 16' and offers a raised hearth fireplace and a built-in bookcase. Double sliding glass doors open onto the terrace. The main level houses the formal living room with another fireplace and a formal dining room. Both with sliding glass doors that open onto a second terrace. Plus an exceptional kitchen! U-shaped for convenience, it features a built-in desk as well as an oven and range. A separate breakfast nook gaurantees to make every meal something special. Steps away, a first floor laundry to keep all your work in one area.

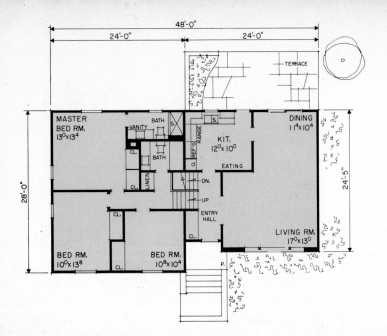

● Here are three charming split-levels designed for the modest budget. They will not require a large, expensive piece of property. Nevertheless, each is long on livability and offers all the features necessary to guarantee years of convenient living.

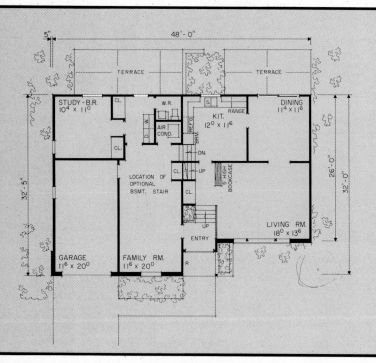

● Charming? It certainly is. And with good reason, too. This delightfully proportioned split level is highlighted by fine window treatment, interesting roof lines, an attractive use of materials and an inviting front entrance with double doors.

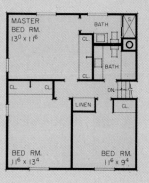

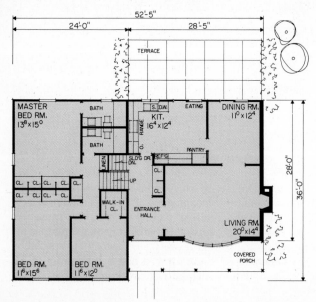

● Four level livability. And what livability it will be! This home will be most economical to build. As the house begins to take form you'll appreciate even more all the livable space you and your family will enjoy. List features that appeal to you.

Design V31358 Main Level: 576 square feet; Upper Level: 672 square feet; Lower Level: 328 square feet; Total: 1,576 square feet

Design V31770 Main Level: 636 square feet; Upper Level: 672 square feet; Lower Level: 528 square feet; Total: 1,836 square feet

Design V31882 Main Level: 800 square feet; Upper Level: 864 square feet; Lower Level: 344 square feet; Total: 2,008 square feet

● Projecting over the lower level in Garrison Colonial style is the upper level containing three bedrooms a compartmented bath with twin lavatories and two handy linen closets. The main level consists of an L-shaped kitchen with convenient eating space, a formal dining room with sliding glass doors to the terrace and a sizable living room. On the lower level there is access to the outdoors, a spacious family room and a laundry-wash room area.

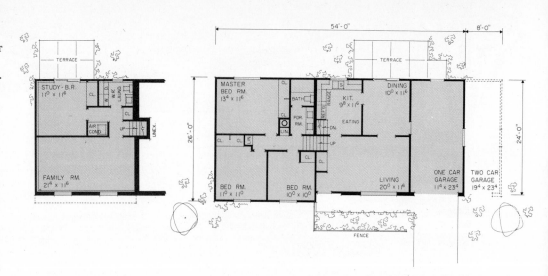

● Here are four levels just waiting for the opportunity to serve the living requirements of the active family. The traditional appeal of the exterior will be difficult to beat. Observe the window treatment, the double front doors, the covered front porch and the wrought iron work.

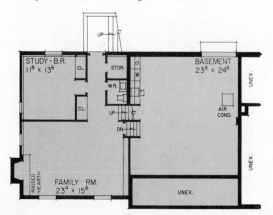

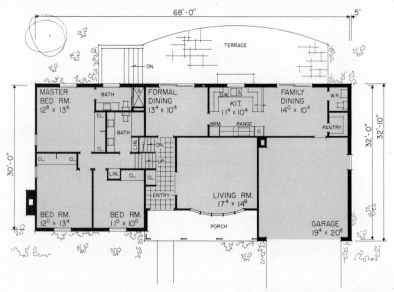

Design V31308 Main Level: 496 square feet; Upper Level: 572 square feet; Lower Level: 537 square feet; Total: 1,605 square feet

Design V31981

Main Level: 784 square feet; Upper Level: 912 square feet; Lower Level: 336 square feet; Total: 2,032 square feet

L **D**

● Here are three multi-level designs which are ideal for those who wish to build on a relatively narrow site. These split-levels have delightful exteriors and each offers exceptional family livability. Formal and informal areas are in each along with efficiently planned work centers. Outdoor areas are easily accessible from various rooms in these plans. Note that two of the upper level plans even have balconies.

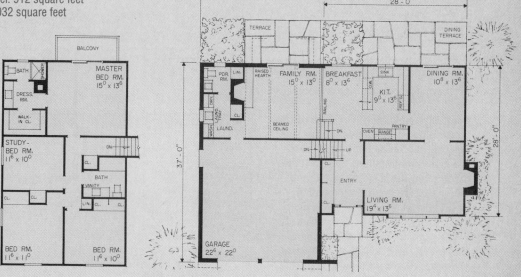

Design V31768 Main Level: 844 square feet; Upper Level: 740 square feet; Lower Level: 740 square feet; Total: 2,324 square feet

Design V32171

Main Level: 795 square feet; Upper Level: 912 square feet
Lower Level: 335 square feet; Total: 2,042 square feet

 L D

● This English Tudor, split-level adaptation has much to recommend it. Perhaps, its most significant feature is that it can be built economically on a relatively small site. The width of the house is just over 52 feet. But its size does not inhibit its livability. There are many fine qualities. Observe the living room fireplace in addition to the one in the family room with a wood box. The breakfast room overlooks the lower level family room. It also has a pass-thru to the kitchen. Don't miss the balcony off the master bedroom. Also worthy of note, a short flight of stairs leads to the huge attic storage area.

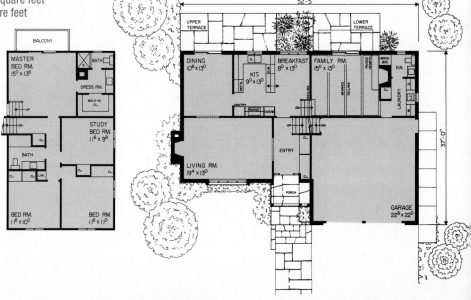

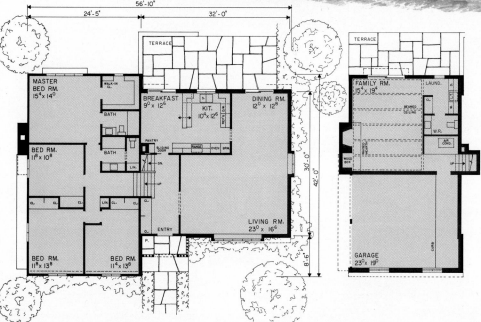

Design V32137
Main Level: 987 square feet
Upper Level: 1,043 square feet
Lower Level: 463 square feet
Total: 2,493 square feet

● Tudor design adapts to split-level living. The result is a unique charm for all to remember. As for the livability, the happy occupants of this tri-level home will experience wonderful living patterns. A covered porch protects the front entry. The center hall routes traffic coveniently to the spacious formal living and dining area; the informal breakfast room and kitchen zone; the upper level bedrooms and the lower level all-purpose family room. List the numerous features that contribute to fine living.

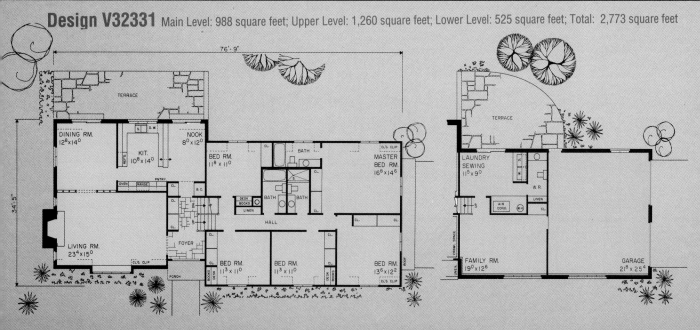

Design V32331 Main Level: 988 square feet; Upper Level: 1,260 square feet; Lower Level: 525 square feet; Total: 2,773 square feet

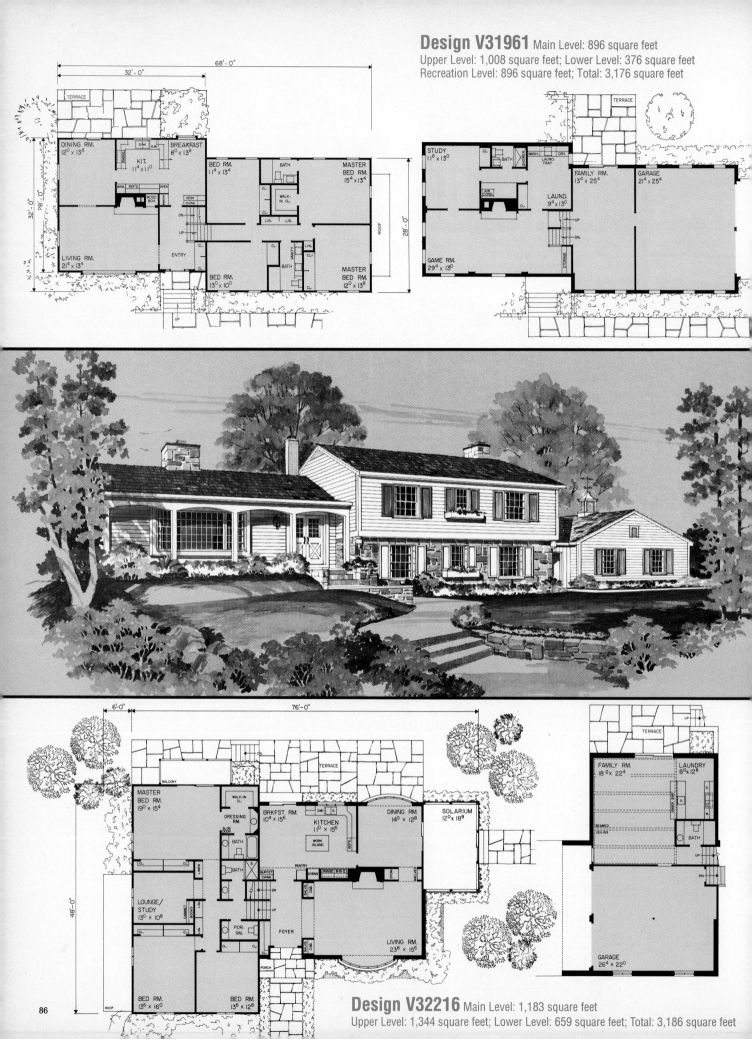

Design V31961 Main Level: 896 square feet
Upper Level: 1,008 square feet; Lower Level: 376 square feet
Recreation Level: 896 square feet; Total: 3,176 square feet

Design V31961 — Floor plans

68'-0"
32'-0"
32'-0"
28'-0"
28'-0"

TERRACE
DINING RM. 12⁰ x 13⁸
KIT. 11⁴ x 11⁰
BREAKFAST 8⁰ x 13⁸
BED RM. 11⁴ x 13⁴
BATH
MASTER BED RM. 15⁴ x 13⁴
WALK-IN CL.
WOOD BOX
OVEN
DESK CHINA
LIVING RM. 21⁴ x 13⁴
ENTRY
BED RM. 13⁰ x 10⁰
BATH
VANITY
MASTER BED RM. 12⁰ x 13⁸
ROOF
UP

STUDY 11⁸ x 13⁰
BATH
SHOWER
WASH. LAUND. TRAY DRY.
TERRACE
FAMILY RM. 13⁴ x 25⁴
GARAGE 21⁴ x 25⁴
AIR COND.
LAUND. 9⁴ x 13⁰
GAME RM. 29⁴ x 13⁰
STORAGE
UP
DN.

Design V32216 — Floor plans

6'-0"
76'-0"
48'-0"

TERRACE
BALCONY
MASTER BED RM. 19⁰ x 15⁴
WALK-IN CL.
DRESSING RM.
BATH
BRKFST. RM. 10⁴ x 15⁶
KITCHEN 11⁰ x 15⁶
WORK ISLAND
DINING RM. 14⁰ x 12⁸
SOLARIUM 12⁰ x 18⁸
LOUNGE/ STUDY 13⁰ x 10⁸
BATH
LINEN
BUFFET CHINA
PANTRY
OVENS
RANGE
FOYER
PDR. RM.
LIVING RM. 23⁸ x 15⁶
PORCH
BED RM. 13⁶ x 16⁰
BED RM. 13⁶ x 12⁸
ROOF

TERRACE
UP
FAMILY RM. 18⁰ x 22⁴
LAUNDRY 8⁰ x 12⁸
BEAMED CEILING
BATH
GARAGE 26⁴ x 22⁰

86

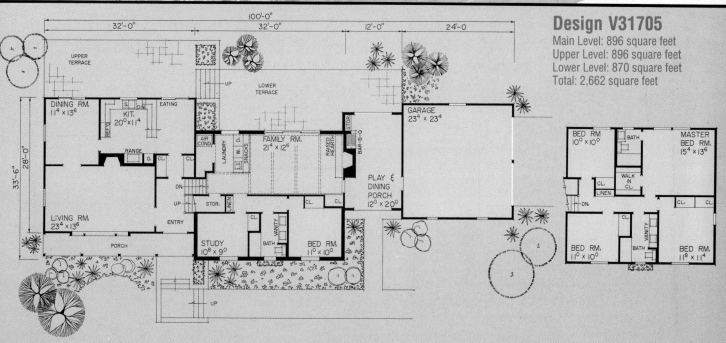

Design V31705

Main Level: 896 square feet
Upper Level: 896 square feet
Lower Level: 870 square feet
Total: 2,662 square feet

Main Level / Lower Level floor plan labels:

UPPER TERRACE

LOWER TERRACE

DINING RM. 11⁴ x 13⁶

KIT. 20⁰ x 11⁴

EATING

S. D.W.

REF'G.

RANGE

O. CL.

AIR COND.

LAUNDRY W. D.

SNACKS

FAMILY RM. 21⁴ x 12⁶

RAISED HEARTH

STOR.

BAR-B-Q

GARAGE 23⁴ x 23⁴

LIVING RM. 23⁴ x 13⁶

DN.

UP

STOR.

LINEN

ENTRY

PORCH

STUDY 10⁸ x 9⁰

VANITY

BATH

CL.

CL.

CL.

BED RM. 11⁰ x 10⁰

PLAY & DINING PORCH 12⁰ x 20⁰

UP

Dimensions: 100'-0", 32'-0", 32'-0", 12'-0", 24'-0", 33'-6", 28'-0"

Upper Level floor plan labels:

BED RM. 10⁰ x 10⁰

BATH

MASTER BED RM. 15⁴ x 13⁶

WALK IN CL.

CL.

LINEN

CL.

CL.

DN.

VANITY

BATH

BED RM. 11⁰ x 10⁰

BED RM. 11⁸ x 11⁴

Design V31977 Main Level: 896 square feet; Upper Level: 884 square feet; Lower Level: 896 square feet; Total: 2,676 square feet

● This split-level is impressive. It has a two-story center portion, flanked by a projecting living wing on one side and a garage on the other side, yet it still maintains that ground-hugging quality. There is an orderly flow of traffic. You will go up to the sleeping zone; down to the hobby/recreation level; straight ahead to the kitchen and breakfast room; left to the living room.

Design V32125 Main Level: 728 square feet; Upper Level: 672 square feet; Lower Level: 656 square feet; Total: 2,056 square feet

● A long list of features are available to recommend this four level, traditional home. First of all, it is a real beauty. The windows, shutters, doorway, horizontal siding and stone all go together with great proportion to project an image of design excellence. Inside, the livability is outstanding. There are three bedrooms, plus a study (make it the fourth bedroom if you wish); two full baths and a washroom; a fine kitchen with eating space; formal living and dining areas and an all-purpose family room.

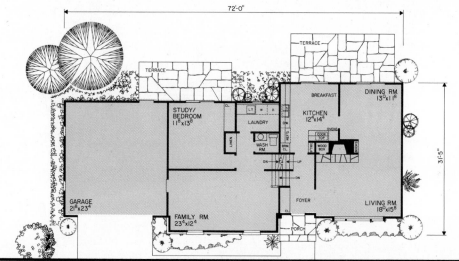

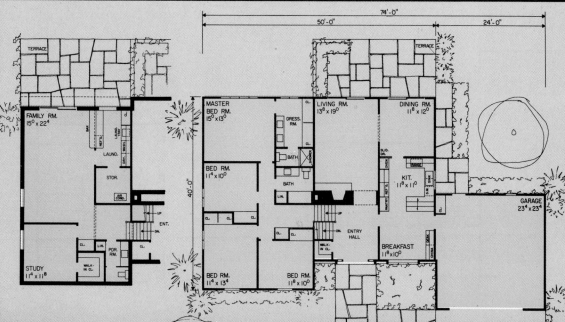

Design V31985

Main Level: 884 square feet
Upper Level: 960 square feet
Lower Level: 888 square feet
Total: 2,732 square feet

● Here is a split-level that expresses all that is warm and inviting in the traditional vein. Delightfully proportioned, the projecting wings add that desired look of distinction. The double front doors open into a spacious entry hall. Straight ahead is the living room with the dining room but a step away. The kitchen is strategically located with a pass-thru to the breakfast room.

● Here are three optional elevations that function with the same basic floor plan. No need to decide now which is your favorite since the blueprints for this design include details for each optional exterior.

If yours is a restricted building budget, your construction dollar could hardly return greater dividends in the way of exterior appeal and interior livability. Also, you won't need a big, expensive site on which to build.

In addition to the four bedrooms and 2½ baths, there are two living areas, two places for dining, a fireplace and a basement. Notice the fine accessibility of the rear outdoor terrace.

Design V32366
First Floor: 1,078 square feet
Second Floor: 880 square feet
Total: 1,958 square feet

D

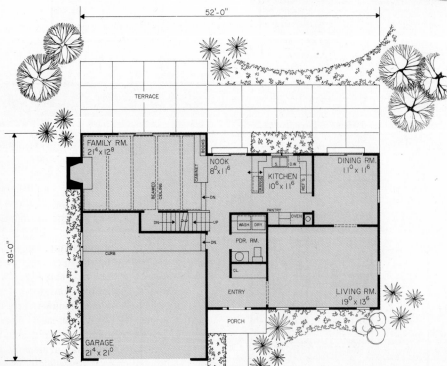

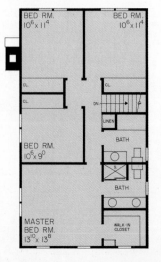

Design V31230

Main Level: 728 square feet
Recreation Level: 728 square feet
Upper Level: 792 square feet
Study Level: 316 square feet
Total: 2,564 square feet

● Here is a side-to-side split-level. It has a bow window that enlivens the front of the house. Note that the basement area has a workshop and recreation room. The bedroom area provides the master bedroom with its own private bath.

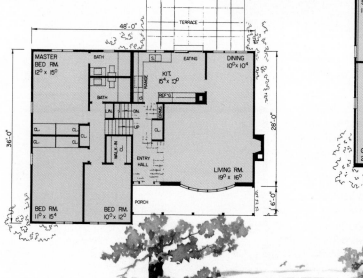

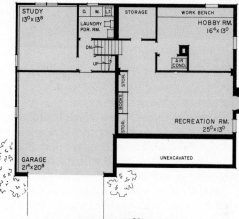

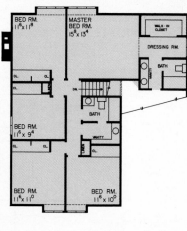

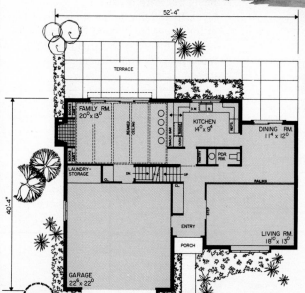

Design V32373

First Floor: 1,160 square feet
Second Floor: 1,222 square feet
Total: 2,382 square feet

● It would be difficult to find more livability wrapped in such an attractive facade. This charming, Tudor adaptation will return big dividends per construction dollar. It is compact and efficient. And, of course, it will not require a big, expensive piece of property. The two-car garage is an integral part of the structure for convenience and economic advantages.

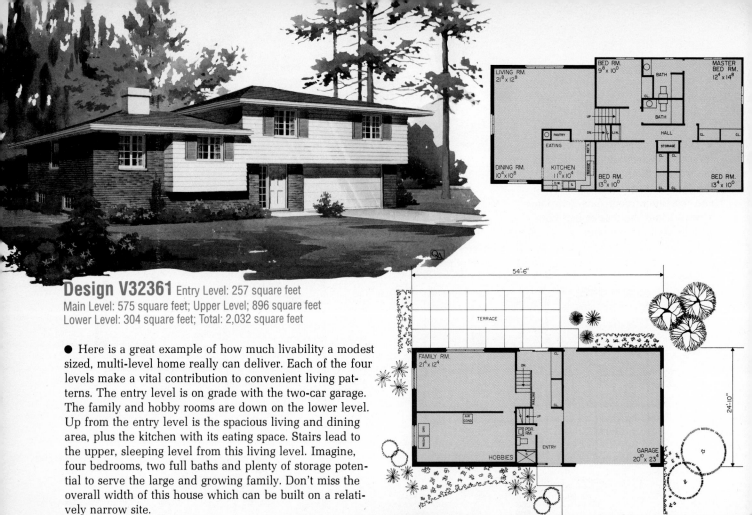

Design V32361 Entry Level: 257 square feet

Main Level: 575 square feet; Upper Level; 896 square feet
Lower Level: 304 square feet; Total: 2,032 square feet

● Here is a great example of how much livability a modest sized, multi-level home really can deliver. Each of the four levels make a vital contribution to convenient living patterns. The entry level is on grade with the two-car garage. The family and hobby rooms are down on the lower level. Up from the entry level is the spacious living and dining area, plus the kitchen with its eating space. Stairs lead to the upper, sleeping level from this living level. Imagine, four bedrooms, two full baths and plenty of storage potential to serve the large and growing family. Don't miss the overall width of this house which can be built on a relatively narrow site.

Design V31324 Main Level: 682 square feet

Upper Level: 672 square feet; Lower Level: 656 square feet; Total: 2,010 square feet

● Wonderfully proportioned, this tri-level has delightful symmetry. Designed to satisfy the requirements of the medium-sized building budget, the exterior houses an extremely practical floor plan. Although the upper level, sleeping area features three bedrooms and two full baths, this home could function admirably as a four bedroom. The fourth bedroom is acquired by utilizing the extra bedroom on the lower level. In addition to the study/bedroom of the lower level, there is the separate laundry, the extra washroom and the multi-purpose family room.

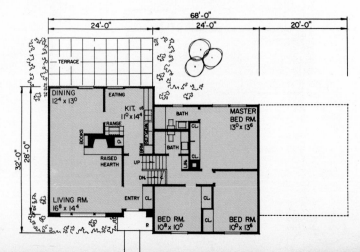

92

● This compact tri-level will build economically. Its charming, traditional facade will never fail to elicit enthusiastic comment. Designed to assure the most economical use of lumber, this house is a perfect rectangle. When built on a site which slopes to the rear, the lower level can become exposed. This permits the family room to function with the outdoor terrace. The extra bedroom becomes completely livable. This house then features four bedrooms and two full baths.

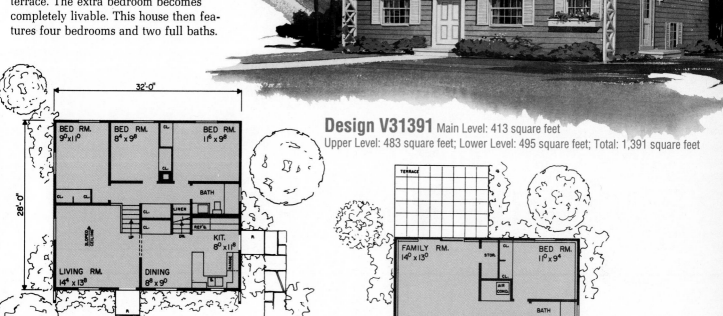

Design V31391 Main Level: 413 square feet
Upper Level: 483 square feet; Lower Level: 495 square feet; Total: 1,391 square feet

Design V31292 Main Level: 640 square feet
Upper Level: 672 square feet; Lower Level: 646 square feet; Total: 1,958 square feet

● A traditionally styled tri-level design that is perfect for you and your family. Upon entering this home, you will find a raised living room. Just a few steps away, there is a nice-sized kitchen-eating area. It will make feeding the family a breeze. An adjacent dining room is for formal dining. To your left of the entryway, a conveniently situated office/study is available. It is ideal for a home business. Another convenience is the first floor laundry and washroom. Note the spacious family room with fireplace and sliding glass doors leading to the terrace. Two bedrooms, a full bath and a master bedroom will be found on the upper level.

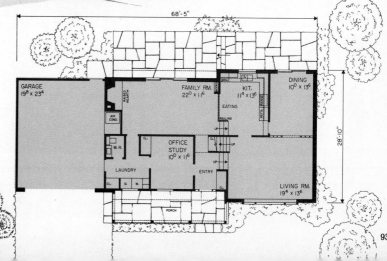

93

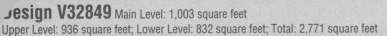

Design V32849 Main Level: 1,003 square feet
Upper Level: 936 square feet; Lower Level: 832 square feet; Total: 2,771 square feet

● Enter into the front foyer of this traditional design and you will be impressed by the dramatic sloped ceiling. Sunken two steps, the formal living room is to the right. This room is highlighted by a fireplace with adjacent wood box, sloped ceiling and a multi-paned bay window. Formal and informal dining, kitchen, laundry and washroom also share the main level with the living room and foyer. The lower level houses the family room, bedroom/study, full bath and mechanical room; the upper level, three bedrooms and two more full baths. Notice the excellent indoor-outdoor living relationships. There is a side terrace accessible from each of the dining areas plus a rear terrace. The front projecting garage reduces the size of the lot required for this home.

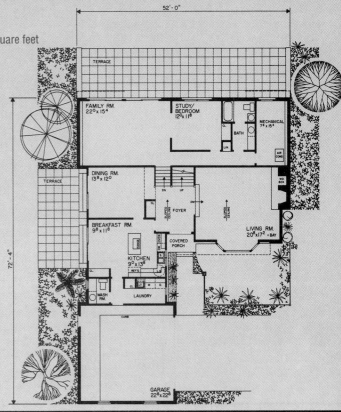

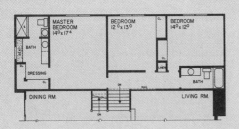

Design V31930 Main Level: 947 square feet; Upper Level: 768 square feet; Lower Level: 740 square feet; Total: 2,455 square feet

● The warmth of this inspiring Colonial adaptation is not restricted to the exterior. Its charm is readily apparent upon stepping through the double front doors. The sunken living room and family room will be in great demand.

Design V31348 Main Level: 750 square feet; Upper Level: 672 square feet; Lower Level: 664 square feet; Total: 2,086 square feet

74'-10"

TERRACE

TERRACE

NOOK
8⁰ x 12⁰

DINING RM.
10⁸ x 12⁰

FAMILY RM.
23⁰ x 12⁶

KIT.
9⁴ x 12⁰

PANTRY

34'-10"

WOOD BOX

RAISED HEARTH

UP

DN

DN

AIR COND.

PDR. RM.

ENTRY HALL

LIVING RM.
19⁰ x 13⁰

STUDY-B.R.
10⁴ x 13⁶

LAUND.

PORCH

GARAGE
21⁸ x 23⁴

BED RM.
10⁴ x 13⁶

BED RM.
10⁴ x 10⁰

LIN

BATH

MASTER BED RM.
12⁸ x 13⁶

DRESS. RM.

● The massive center section with its pediment gable and flanking wings highlights the exterior of this design. U-shaped, the kitchen is flanked by the separate dining room and the breakfast eating area.

● A relatively small split-level that
will surely return loads of livability for
the building dollar. Certainly your
building budget will purchase a well
designed home. One that will be hard
to beat for exterior appeal.

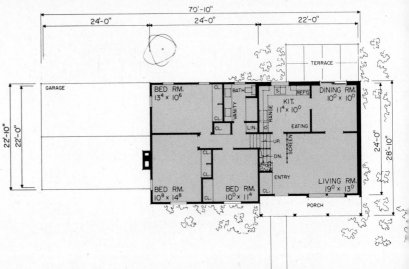

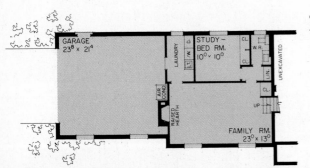

● Impressive, indeed, wherever located.
Gabled roofs, muntined windows with
shutters, a covered front porch, paneled
double doors and a cupola over the garage give a Colonial touch to the exterior
of this smartly planned split-level.

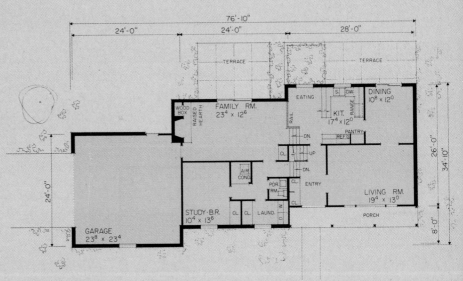

● You'll have fun living in this home. There will be
four bedrooms, three baths, large formal living and
dining rooms, an efficient kitchen with breakfast nook,
a covered porch and much more to serve your family.

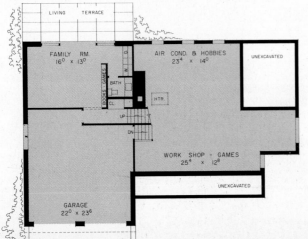

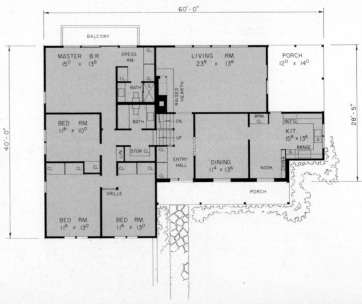

Design V31717 Main Level: 556 square feet; Upper Level: 624 square feet; Lower Level: 596 square feet; Total: 1,776 square feet

Design V31347 Main Level: 750 square feet; Upper Level: 672 square feet; Lower Level: 664 square feet; Total: 2,086 square feet

Design V33148 Main Level: 808 square feet; Upper Level: 960 square feet; Lower Level: 374 square feet; Total: 2,142 square feet

Design V31935 Main Level: 904 square feet; Upper Level: 864 square feet; Lower Level: 840 square feet; Total: 2,608 square feet

● If there was ever a design that looked a part of the ground it was built on, this particular multi-level looks just that. This design will adapt equally well to a flat or sloping site. There would be no question about the family's ability to adapt to what the interior has to offer. Everything is present to satisfy the family's desire to "live a little". Features include: a covered porch, balcony, two fire-places, extra study, family room with a beamed ceiling, complete laundry and a basement level for added recreational and storage space. Blueprints include non-basement details.

OPTIONAL NON-BASEMENT

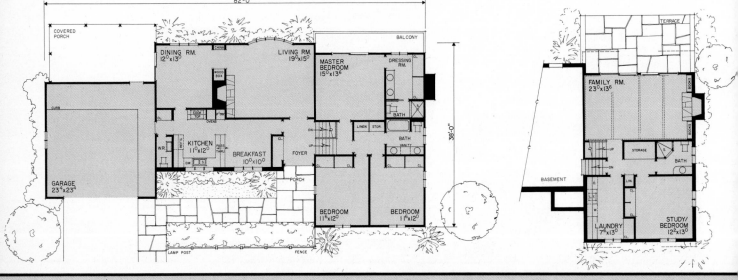

Design V32291
Main Level: 942 square feet; Upper Level: 1,101 square feet
Lower Level: 534 square feet; Total: 2,577 square feet

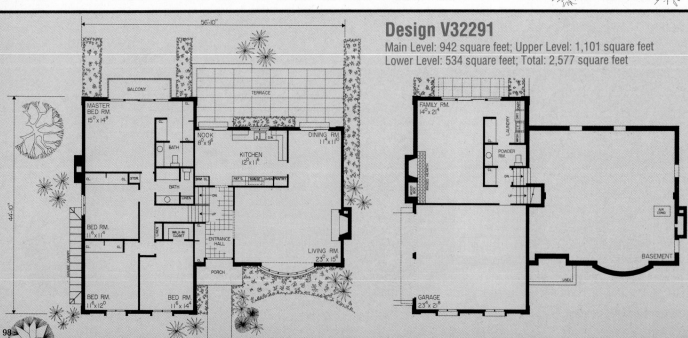

Design V31265 Main Level: 1,298 square feet; Upper Level: 964 square feet; Lower Level: 964 square feet; Total: 3,226 square feet

● Impressive, may be just the word to describe this appealingly formal, traditional tri-level. Changes in level add interest to its plan and make this already spacious house seem even larger. A glamorous living room, two steps below entry level, features a handsome fireplace and a broad, bay window. Raised two additional steps to emphasize the sunken area, the formal dining room is partitioned from the living room by a built-in planter. Up a few stairs from the entry hall, the sleeping level houses three bedrooms and two baths. The lower level has areas which will lend themselves to flexible living patterns.

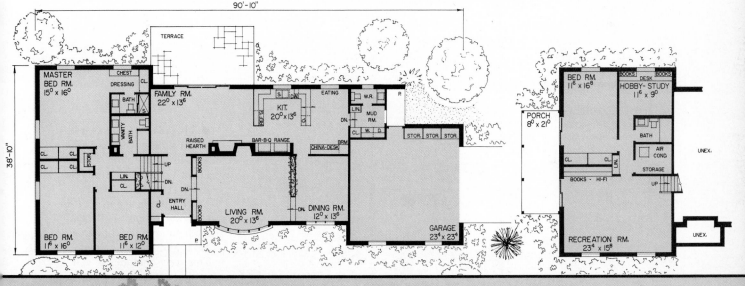

Design V31267

Upper Level: 1,114 square feet
Lower Level: 1,194 square feet
Total: 2,308 square feet

● This plan combines traditional styling with modern split-level planning. The lower level features a large living room with raised-hearth fireplace and built-in shelving. A short hallway leads to both the dining room and family kitchen. This room includes a well-equipped work area with peninsula range and snack bar plus space for an informal eating or sitting area. Sliding glass doors in all three rooms lead out to a covered porch. The four-bedroom upper level includes a master with a dressing room.

SPLIT-FOYER DESIGNS . . . *usually incorporate two levels of livability*

accessed from stairways leading in two directions off the main entry foyer. The lower level of these designs is often at least partly below ground. Many of the beautiful designs presented here feature lower-level sleeping zones or recreation areas, covered patios and upper level decks, and working areas for the handyman or craftsman.

Design V34019

First Floor: 676 square feet
Second Floor: 969 square feet
Total: 1,645 square feet

L

LIFESTYLE
HOME PLANS

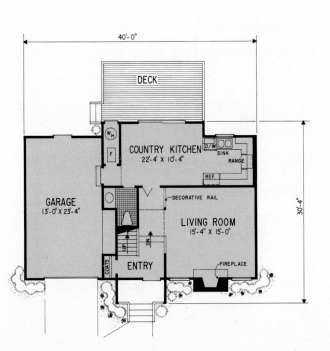

● Those looking for an economical, easy-to-build home, look no further. The rectangular shape of this design will help hold down construction costs. The first level features a spacious living room with fireplace and a large country kitchen. The kitchen work area is contained to one side, leaving room for both eating and sitting areas. A wood deck is just a few steps away. An open stair leads up to the second level which contains three good-sized bedrooms; the master boasts a huge walk-in closet, a bath with double vanity, and an optional fireplace. The washer and dryer are conveniently near the source of dirty laundry.

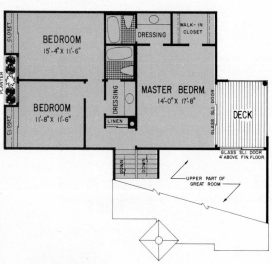

Design V34146

Upper Level: 900 square feet
Lower Level: 837 square feet
Total: 1,737 square feet

LIFESTYLE
HOME PLANS

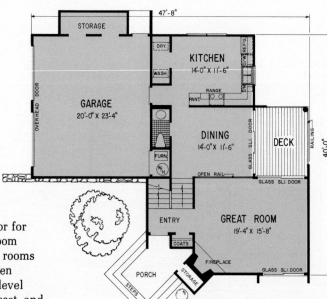

● Contrasting siding and stone make for an interesting exterior for this attractive split-foyer. Just off the entry, a spacious great room boasts a corner fireplace and overlooks the dining room. Both rooms enjoy access to a deck. Also on this level is an L-shaped kitchen which includes space for an informal eating area. The upper level features three bedrooms; the master includes bath, walk-in closet, and private deck.

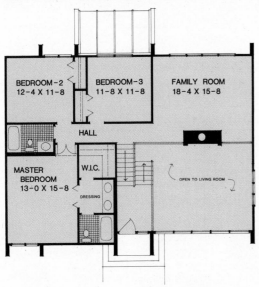

BEDROOM-2
12-4 X 11-8

BEDROOM-3
11-8 X 11-8

FAMILY ROOM
18-4 X 15-8

HALL

MASTER
BEDROOM
13-0 X 15-8

W.I.C.

DRESSING

OPEN TO LIVING ROOM

- Steeply pitched rooflines create a dramatic facade to match this impressive floor plan. The lower level features enormous living and dining rooms, separated by a large fireplace. Also on this level, a spacious kitchen includes an island with cooktop and prep counter and a cheery breakfast room. Sliding glass doors provide access to a large patio. The upper level contains the three-bedroom, two-bath sleeping area. In addition, there's a balcony family room which overlooks the two-story living room.

Design V34295

Upper Level: 1,108 square feet
Lower Level: 1,191 square feet
Total: 2,299 square feet

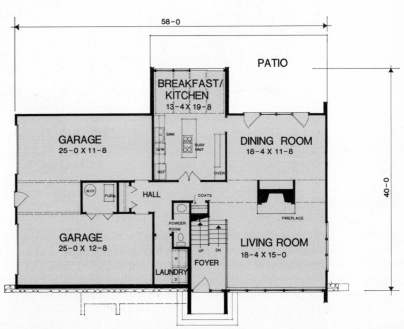

58-0

PATIO

BREAKFAST/
KITCHEN
13-4 X 19-8

GARAGE
25-0 X 11-8

SINK

SURF
UNIT

DINING ROOM
18-4 X 11-8

D/W

REF

OVEN

40-0

W/H

FURN

HALL

COATS

FIREPLACE

GARAGE
25-0 X 12-8

POWDER
ROOM

LIVING ROOM
18-4 X 15-0

UP   DN

LAUNDRY

FOYER

LIFESTYLE
HOME PLANS

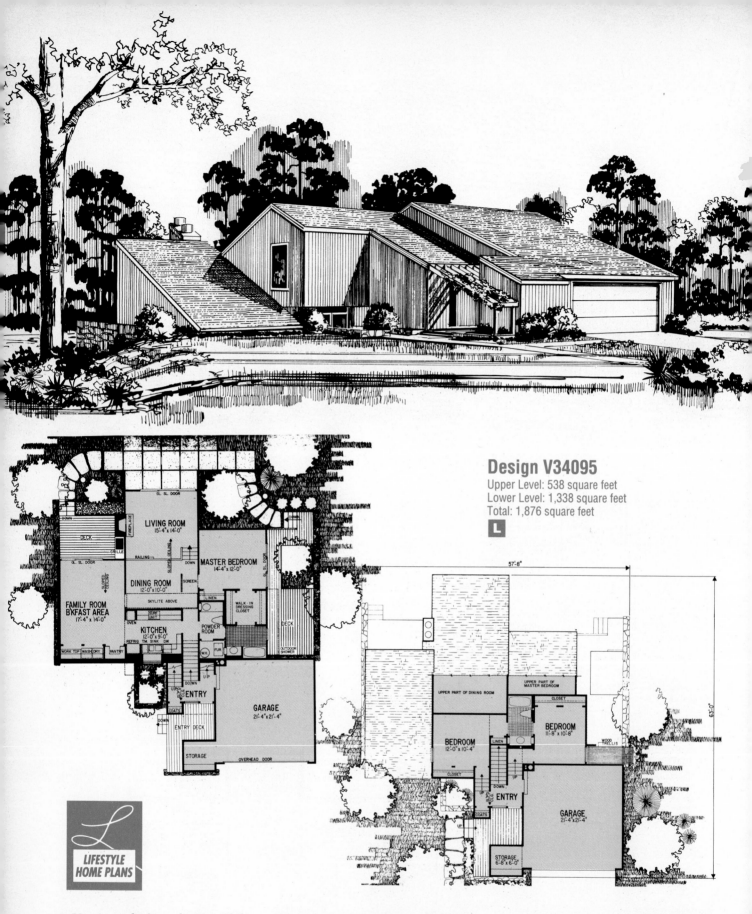

Design V34095

Upper Level: 538 square feet
Lower Level: 1,338 square feet
Total: 1,876 square feet

● Here's a split-foyer design with lots of visual appeal. Steeply pitched rooflines and sloped ceilings create a dramatic appearance both inside and out. From the entry, stairs lead down to a galley kitchen with lots of counter space for food preparation. Next door is a large family room and breakfast area with adjacent deck and barbecue. Beyond the kitchen is a formal dining room which overlooks the sunken living room with fireplace. The master suite is also on this level and features a large private deck. The upper level contains two bedrooms with separate staircases.

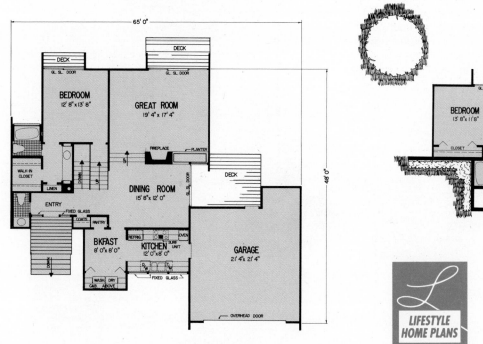

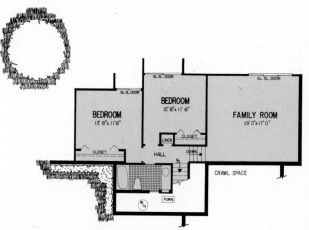

Design V34104
Upper Level: 1,269 square feet
Lower Level: 873 square feet
Total: 2,142 square feet

LIFESTYLE HOME PLANS

L

● This spacious contemporary features living areas on both levels. The entry leads into the formal dining room and beyond to the raised great room with fireplace. A deck off the dining room provides a perfect spot for outdoor meals. The galley kitchen and breakfast room are just steps away. Upstairs from the entry is the master bedroom with its own private deck. The lower level features two bedrooms and a sunken family room. Sliding glass doors in all three rooms lead outside.

● This striking contemporary was designed with indoor/outdoor living in mind. Each living space has access to a deck. Stairs lead up from the entry foyer to a large dining room with a deck and adjacent kitchen with a U-shaped work area and a breakfast room. Upstairs is an enormous living room with a wet bar and two decks — perfect for entertaining. There's also a sunken conversation pit warmed by a fireplace for smaller groups. Another set of stairs leads to the three-bedroom sleeping area. Notice the deck off each bedroom.

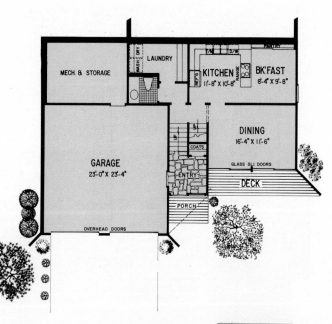

MECH. & STORAGE

LAUNDRY

WASH DRY

PANTRY

KITCHEN
11'-8" X 10'-8"

BK'FAST
8'-4" X 9'-8"

REF'G

RANGE

D/W

GARAGE
23'-0" X 23'-4"

COATS

ENTRY

DINING
16'-4" X 11'-6"

GLASS SLI. DOORS

DECK

PORCH

OVERHEAD DOORS

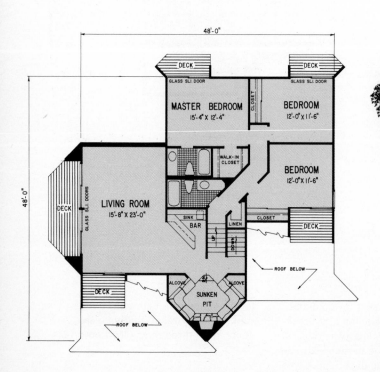

48'-0"

48'-0"

DECK

DECK

GLASS SLI. DOOR

GLASS SLI. DOOR

MASTER BEDROOM
15'-4" X 12'-4"

BEDROOM
12'-0" X 11'-6"

CLOSET

WALK-IN CLOSET

DECK

GLASS SLI. DOORS

LIVING ROOM
15'-8" X 23'-0"

BEDROOM
12'-0" X 11'-6"

SINK

BAR

LINEN

CLOSET

DECK

ROOF BELOW

DECK

ALCOVE

ALCOVE

SUNKEN PIT

ROOF BELOW

Design V34121
Upper Level: 1,591 square feet
Lower Level: 602 square feet
Total: 2,193 square feet

LIFESTYLE
HOME PLANS

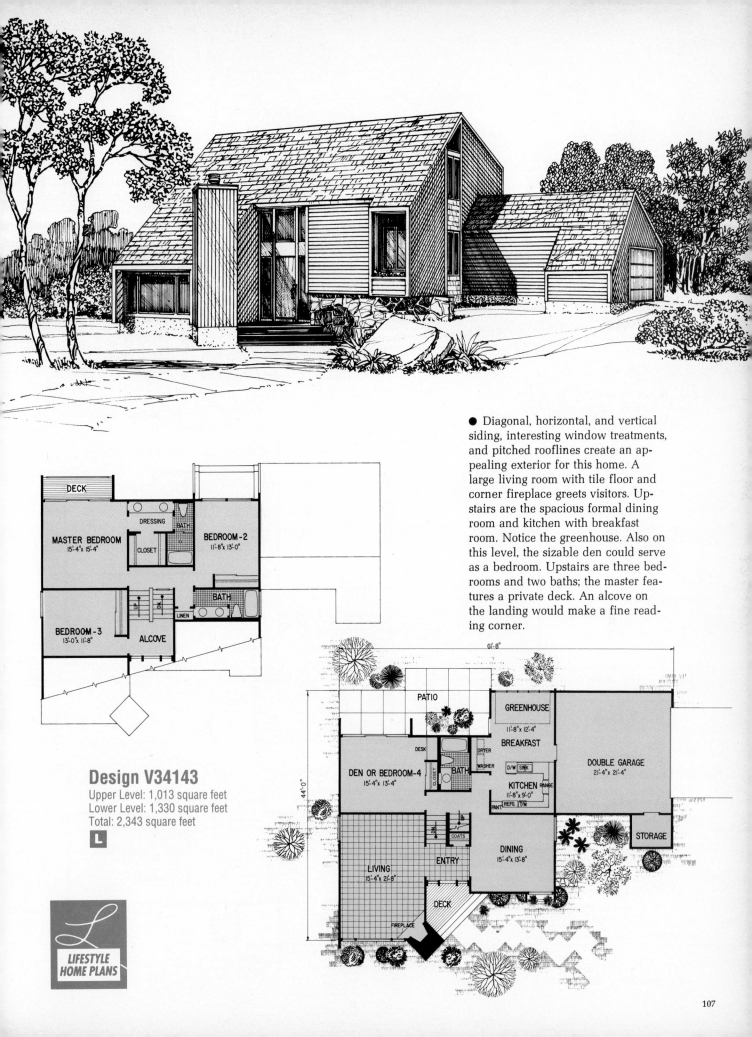

● Diagonal, horizontal, and vertical siding, interesting window treatments, and pitched rooflines create an appealing exterior for this home. A large living room with tile floor and corner fireplace greets visitors. Upstairs are the spacious formal dining room and kitchen with breakfast room. Notice the greenhouse. Also on this level, the sizable den could serve as a bedroom. Upstairs are three bedrooms and two baths; the master features a private deck. An alcove on the landing would make a fine reading corner.

Upper Level Floor Plan:

- DECK
- MASTER BEDROOM 15'-4" x 15'-4"
- DRESSING
- BATH
- CLOSET
- BEDROOM-2 11'-8" x 13'-0"
- BATH
- LINEN
- BEDROOM-3 13'-0" x 11'-8"
- ALCOVE

Design V34143

Upper Level: 1,013 square feet
Lower Level: 1,330 square feet
Total: 2,343 square feet

L

Lower Level Floor Plan:

- 61'-8"
- PATIO
- GREENHOUSE 11'-8" x 12'-4"
- BREAKFAST
- DOUBLE GARAGE 21'-4" x 21'-4"
- DESK
- DRYER
- WASHER
- BATH
- CLOSET
- DEN OR BEDROOM-4 15'-4" x 13'-4"
- D/W SINK
- KITCHEN 11'-8" x 9'-0" RANGE
- REFG. T/M
- PANT.
- 44'-0"
- STORAGE
- DN
- COATS
- DINING 15'-4" x 13'-8"
- LIVING 15'-4" x 21'-8"
- ENTRY
- DECK
- FIREPLACE

LIFESTYLE HOME PLANS

76'-0"

42'-0"

GARAGE
23'-8" x 23'-4"

MASTER BEDROOM
17'-4" x 13'-6"

BEDROOM-2
12'-0" x 11'-10"

BEDROOM-3
11'-0" x 13'-6"

POWDER

CLOSET

CLOSET

RAIL

DOWN

CLOSET

DRESSING

LINEN

COATS

UP

DOWN

SLOPE CLG.

LIVING ROOM
21'-0" x 13'-6"

CABS BOOKS

CABS BOOKS

PANTRY OVEN

GRILL

KITCHEN
9'-0" x 17'-8"

FOYER

REFG.

D/W

SINK

DINING
12'-4" x 15'-8"

PORCH

OVERHEAD DOOR

SURF. UNIT

Design V34240

Entry Level: 1,781 square feet
Lower Level: 931 square feet
Total: 2,712 square feet

D

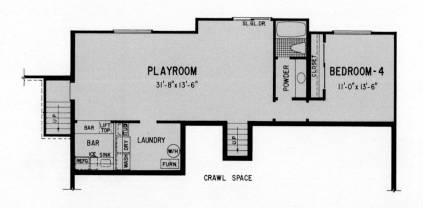

PLAYROOM
31'-8" x 13'-6"

SL. GL. DR.

POWDER

CLOSET

BEDROOM-4
11'-0" x 13'-6"

UP

BAR

LIFT TOP

TUB

BAR

ICE

SINK

REFG.

WASH

DRY

LAUNDRY

W/H

FURN.

UP

CRAWL SPACE

● This design has the appearance of a cozy cottage yet boasts tremendous living space inside. Off the foyer is a spacious living room with a fireplace flanked by built-in shelves and cabinets, a sloped ceiling, and bay window. Also on this level, the well-equipped kitchen includes a pantry, barbecue, lots of counter space, and a pass-through to the dining room which has its own fireplace. The sleeping area is contained on the upper level with three nice-sized bedrooms and two baths. A fourth bedroom is found on the lower level along with a mammoth playroom and tavern. Also notice the laundry room.

● You can't help but feel spoiled by this design. Behind the handsome facade lies a spacious, amenity-filled plan. Downstairs from the entry is the large living room with sloped ceiling and fireplace. Nearby is the U-shaped kitchen with a pass-through to the din-

ing room — a convenient step-saver. Also on this level, the master suite boasts a fireplace and a sliding glass door onto the deck. The living and dining rooms also feature deck access. Upstairs are two bedrooms and shared bath. A balcony sitting area overlooks

the living room. The enormous lower-level playroom includes a fireplace, a large bar, and sliding glass doors to the patio. Also notice the storage room with built-in workbench.

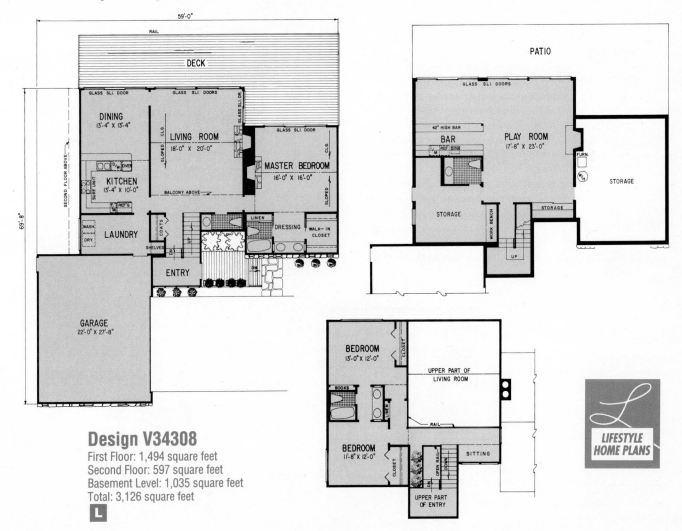

Design V34308
First Floor: 1,494 square feet
Second Floor: 597 square feet
Basement Level: 1,035 square feet
Total: 3,126 square feet

LIFESTYLE HOME PLANS

Design V34248

First Floor: 1,157 square feet
Second Floor: 841 square feet
Total: 1,998 square feet

● This appealing contemporary packs lots of livability into a moderate amount of space. Downstairs from the entry is the enormous great room. This multi-purpose room features a living area with a sloped ceiling and fireplace and dining area with a sliding glass door to the patio. Conveniently adjacent is the kitchen with L-shaped work area. A small window greenhouse provides a cheerful backdrop for the breakfast nook. Also on this level, the master bedroom includes a walk-in closet, bathroom with double vanities, and patio access. Two more bedrooms and a shared bath are located upstairs as well as a large study balcony overlooking the great room.

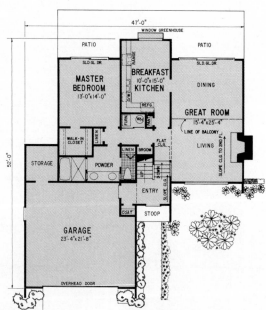

LIFESTYLE
HOME PLANS

Design V34247

First Floor: 1,096 square feet
Second Floor: 1,157 square feet
Total: 2,253 square feet

● This design features a first-floor plan near-ly identical to V34248. A raised-hearth fire-place placed at one end of the great room creates a living-area focus. The difference between the two plans lies upstairs. This de-sign boasts four nice-sized bedrooms and two full baths. This additional space makes this plan ideal for larger families.

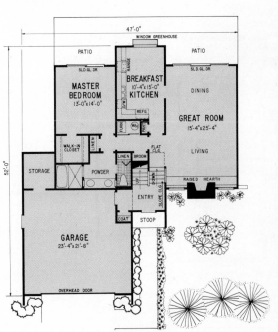

LIFESTYLE HOME PLANS

Design V34179

Upper Level: 1,064 square feet
Lower Level: 1,215 square feet
Total: 2,279 square feet

L

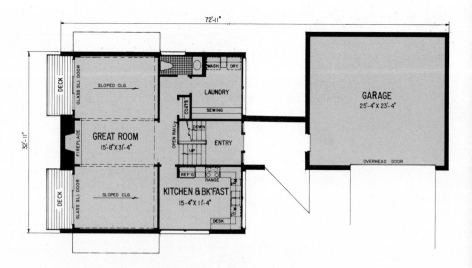

LIFESTYLE HOME PLANS

● This handsome contemporary sports an attractive brick facade. Inside, an amenity-filled plan will make you feel at home. The upper level features an enormous great room with a large fire-place, soaring sloped ceilings, and two decks. This multi-purpose room provides space for entertaining, dining, and relaxing. A large kitchen and breakfast area are a few steps away. Down the open stair are three, good-sized bedrooms and two full baths. Two bedrooms feature private decks.

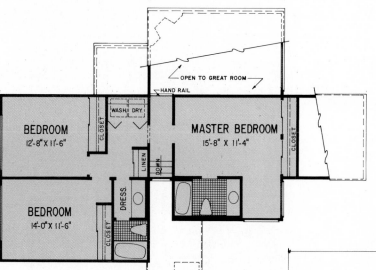

Design V34159

First Floor: 802 square feet
Second Floor: 894 square feet
Total: 1,696 square feet

L

LIFESTYLE
HOME PLANS

BEDROOM
12'-8" X 11'-6"

BEDROOM
14'-0" X 11'-6"

OPEN TO GREAT ROOM

HAND RAIL

WASH. DRY.

CLOSET

LINEN

DOWN

DRESS.

CLOSET

MASTER BEDROOM
15'-8" X 11'-4"

CLOSET

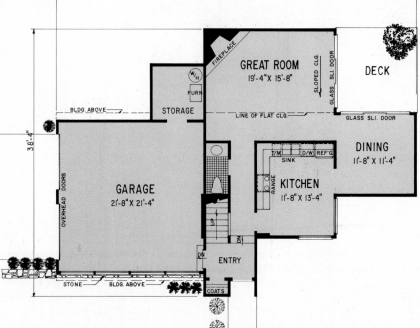

54'-0"

38'-4"

FIREPLACE

GREAT ROOM
19'-4" X 15'-8"

SLOPED CLG.

GLASS SLI. DOOR

DECK

BLDG. ABOVE

STORAGE

W.H.

FURN.

LINE OF FLAT CLG.

GLASS SLI. DOOR

GARAGE
21'-8" X 21'-4"

OVERHEAD DOORS

T/M

SINK

D/W

REF'G.

RANGE

KITCHEN
11'-8" X 13'-4"

DINING
11'-8" X 11'-4"

UP

DN

DN

ENTRY

STONE

BLDG. ABOVE

COATS

● Careful planning and attractive design turn this modest-sized plan into a place to call home. Immediately off the entry is an efficient kitchen with L-shaped work area. Extra space by the windows could easily accommodate a breakfast area. A few steps away is a dining room for formal occasions. For entertaining or just plain relaxing, look to the spacious great room with sloped ceiling and warming corner fireplace. Doors in this room and the dining room provide access to a deck. Three nice-sized bedrooms are found upstairs. Notice the windowed alcove in the master — a perfect spot for a cozy sitting area.

DECK

GLASS SLI. DOOR

WALK-IN CLOSET

MASTER BEDROOM
17'-8" X 14'-0"

DRESSING

HAND RAIL

DOWN DOWN

LINEN DRESSING

LANDING

ATTIC ACCESS

BEDROOM
11'-6" X 11'-8"

BEDROOM
11'-6" X 15'-4"

CLOSET DESK DESK CLOSET

TRELLIS

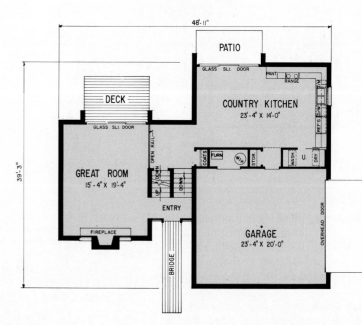

48'-11"

PATIO

GLASS SLI. DOOR

PANT. RANGE

DECK

GLASS SLI. DOOR

COUNTRY KITCHEN
23'-4" X 14'-0"

REF'G DOWN

39'-3"

OPEN RAIL'G

COATS FURN W/H STOR WASH- U. DRY

GREAT ROOM
15'-4" X 19'-4"

UP DOWN DOWN

ENTRY

FIREPLACE

GARAGE
23'-4" X 20'-0"

OVERHEAD DOOR

BRIDGE

Design V34182

Entry and Lower Level: 933 square feet
Upper Level: 972 square feet
Total: 1,905 square feet

D

● Here's a compact, hard-working plan with lots of livability. A spacious great room with fireplace provides a large multi-purpose living area. Sliding glass doors lead out to an inviting deck. Down a few steps is an enormous country kitchen. There's room for the large L-shaped work area and a sizable dining area — even a sitting area, if you wish. Also notice the adjacent patio. The three-bedroom upstairs includes two with built-in desks and a master with a walk-in closet and private deck.

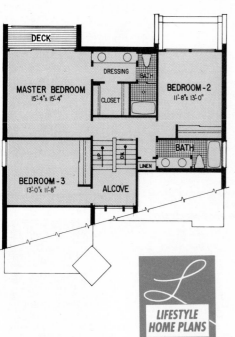

 LIFESTYLE HOME PLANS

Design V34181

Entry and Lower Level: 1,412 square feet
Upper Level: 1,041 square feet
Total: 2,453 square feet

L

● This attractive brick facade houses a spacious, comfortable floor plan. The entry opens onto a large living room with corner fireplace and tiled floor. Up a flight of stairs is a den which could also function as a bedroom. Also on this level is a large kitchen and formal dining room. The kitchen features an efficient work space and breakfast area with greenhouse. Upstairs is another bedroom. Extra space on the landing could accommodate a sitting area. The remaining two bedrooms are up another flight. The master features a large walk-in closet and a private deck.

Design V34289

Upper Level: 1,989 square feet
Lower Level: 1,085 square feet
Total: 3,074 square feet

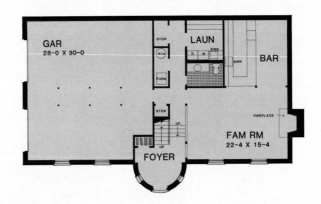

GAR
28-0 X 30-0

STOR

LAUN

BAR

W/H

SINK

D   W

SINK

FURN

STOR

UP

UP

FOYER

FIREPLACE

FAM RM
22-4 X 15-4

LIFESTYLE HOME PLANS

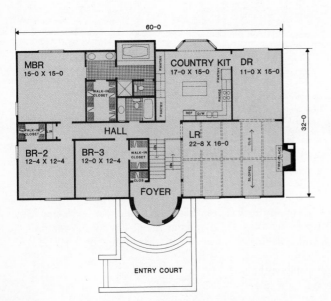

60-0

MBR
15-0 X 15-0

PANTRY

COUNTRY KIT
17-0 X 15-0

DR
11-0 X 15-0

WALK-IN CLOSET

PANTRY

32-0

WALK-IN CLOSET

LIN

REF   D/W

RANGE

HALL

LR
22-8 X 16-0

BR-2
12-4 X 12-4

BR-3
12-0 X 12-4

WALK-IN CLOSET

CLG

DN

CLG

SLOPED

FIREPLACE

FOYER

ENTRY COURT

● This design combines traditional styling features such as half timbers, a circular tower, and multi-paned windows, with modern split-foyer planning. Upstairs from the foyer are the main living areas. There's a spacious beamed-ceiling living room with fireplace and adjoining dining room. Conveniently nearby is the large country kitchen with bay window and island work center. Also notice the extensive pantry space. Three bedrooms round out this level; the master features a sumptuous bath with twin vanities, stall shower, and large platform tub. The lower level includes an enormous family room with fireplace and bar.

DECK
24-0 X 20-0

MASTER BEDROOM
16-0 X 16-0

W I C

DRESSING

BEDROOM - 3
11-0 X12-0

LIVING ROOM
18-4 X 18-0

FIREPLACE

SHOWER

LINEN

DINING
13-0 X 15-0

TRAY CLG.

TRAY CLG.

PANTRY

LINEN

FOYER

REF.

D/W

BEDROOM - 2
14-8 X 13-0

KITCHEN

SINK

SURF. UNIT

OVEN

BREAKFAST

UP

DN

ENTRY

48-0

56-0

PATIO

GAME ROOM
23-4 X 15-8

STORAGE

PLAY ROOM
24-8 X 18-0

GARAGE
21-8 X 22-8

W/H

FURN.

MECH.

SINK

UP

WASHER

DRYER

Design V34389
Upper Level: 2,060 square feet
Lower Level: 1,045 square feet
Total: 3,105 square feet

● Old world charm greets visitors to this lovely home. Notice the stucco-and-quoin facade, hipped roof, and wrought-iron railings. The living room with tray ceiling and fireplace is the centerpiece of the plan. The adjoining dining room also boasts a tray ceiling and is convenient to the large kitchen with island cooktop. Separated from the other bedrooms, the master suite is to the rear and features a walk-in closet, oversized bath with bay window, and access to the rear deck. The lower level contains a game room and play room, both adjacent to a covered patio.

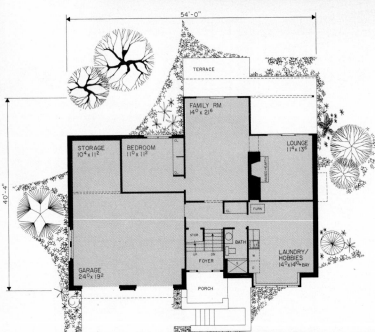

54'-0"

40'-4"

TERRACE

FAMILY RM.
14⁰ x 21⁶

STORAGE
10⁴ x 11²

BEDROOM
11⁰ x 11²

LOUNGE
11⁴ x 13⁶

RAISED HEARTH

CL

CL

FURN

STGR

UP DN

FOYER

BATH

LT

W D

LAUNDRY/
HOBBIES
14⁰ x 14⁰ + BAY

GARAGE
24⁰ x 19²

PORCH

Design V32843

Upper Level: 1,861 square feet
Lower Level: 1,181 square feet
Total: 3,042 square feet

L

DECK

LIVING RM.
14⁰ x 21⁶

BEDROOM
11⁰ x 13⁶

BEDROOM/
STUDY
11⁰ x 13⁶

DINING
12⁰ x 13⁶

OPT. DOOR

OPEN
THRU

CL

LIN

CAB'T

OVEN

REFS.

BATH

CL

KITCHEN
15⁴ x 8⁰

RANGE

SNACK BAR

S DW

BATH

S

UP DN

CL

FOYER

PANTRY

BREAKFAST
15⁴ x 9⁶

DECK

LINEN

DRESSING RM.

MASTER
BEDROOM
14⁰ x 16⁰

PORCH

● Bi-level living will be enjoyed to its fullest in this Spanish styled design. There is a lot of room for the various family activities. Informal living will take place on the lower level in the family room and lounge. The formal living and dining rooms, sharing a thru-fire-place, are located on the upper level.

Design V32844 Upper Level: 1,882 square feet
Lower Level: 1,168 square feet; Total: 3,050 square feet

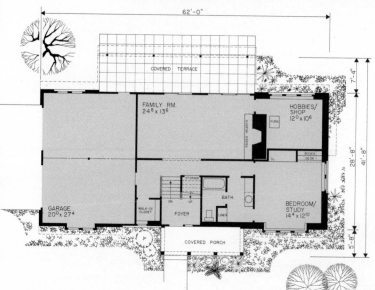

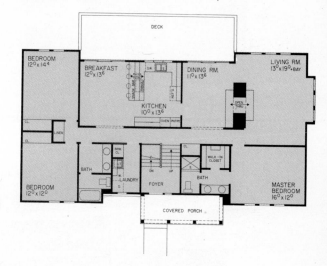

● Bi-level living will be enjoyed to the fullest in this Tudor design. The split-foyer type design will be very efficient for the active family. Three bedrooms are on the upper level, a fourth on the lower level.

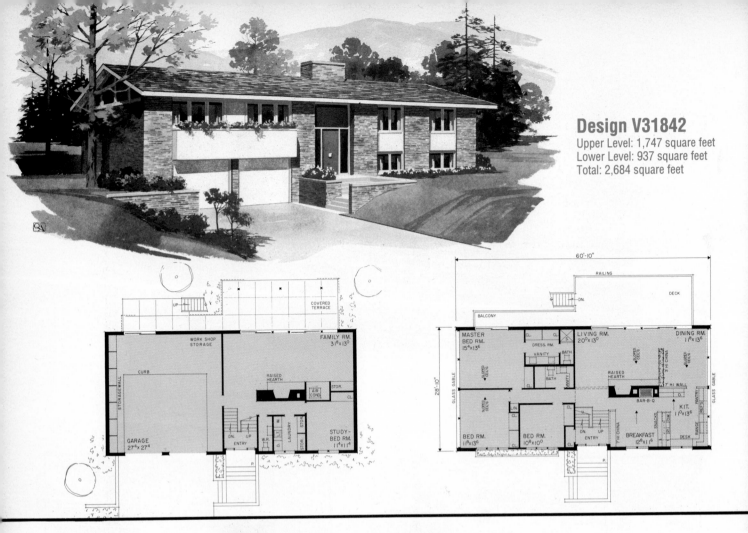

Design V31842

Upper Level: 1,747 square feet
Lower Level: 937 square feet
Total: 2,684 square feet

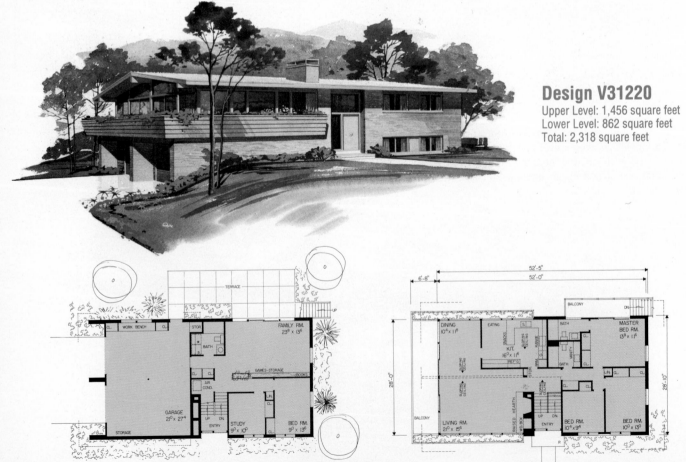

Design V31220

Upper Level: 1,456 square feet
Lower Level: 862 square feet
Total: 2,318 square feet

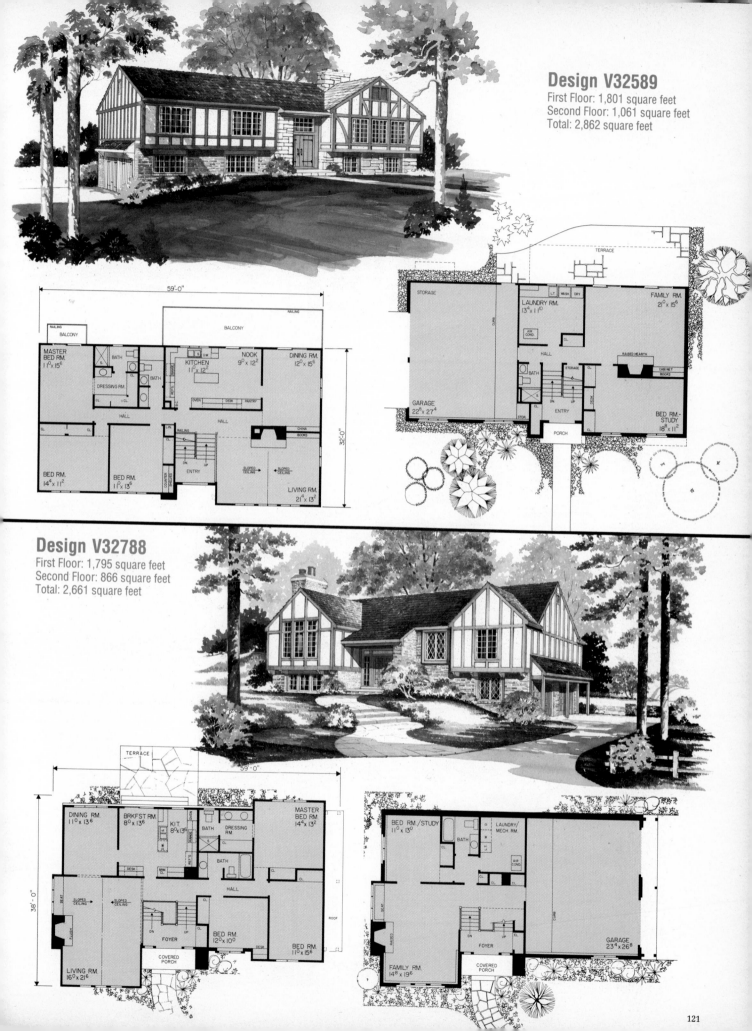

Design V32589

First Floor: 1,801 square feet
Second Floor: 1,061 square feet
Total: 2,862 square feet

Design V32788

First Floor: 1,795 square feet
Second Floor: 866 square feet
Total: 2,661 square feet

Design V31850 Upper Level: 1,456 square feet
Lower Level: 728 square feet; Total: 2,184 square feet

● This attractive, traditional bi-level house surely will prove to be an outstanding investment. While it is a perfect rectangle - which leads to economical construction - it has a full measure of eye-appeal. Setting the character of the exterior is the effective window treatment, plus the unique design of the recessed front entrance.

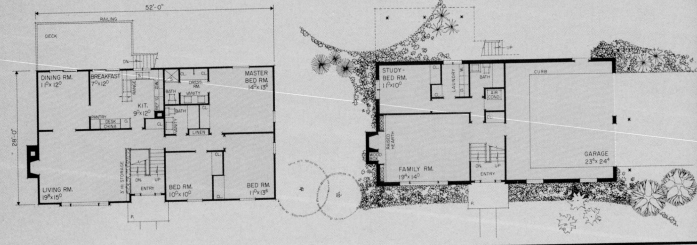

Design V31386 Upper Level: 880 square feet
Lower Level: 596 square feet; Total: 1,476 square feet

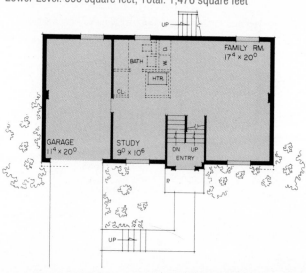

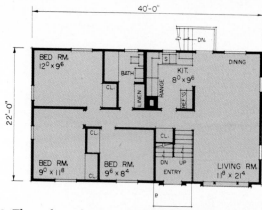

● These three designs feature traditional exterior styling with a split-foyer, bi-level living interior. Owners of a bi-level design achieve a great amount of livability from an economical plan without sacrificing any of the fine qualities of a much larger and more expensive plan.

Design V31210 Upper Level: 1,248 square feet
Lower Level: 676 square feet; Total: 1,924 square feet

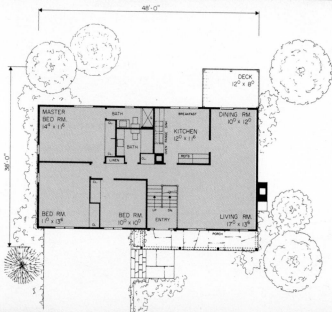

Design V33198

Upper Level: 1,040 square feet
Lower Level: 986 square feet; Total: 2,026 square feet

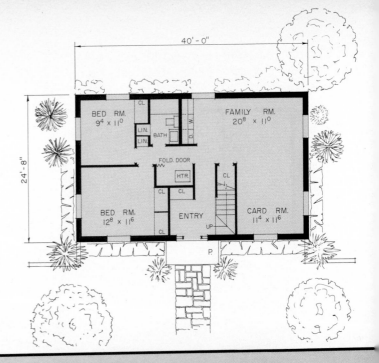

Design V32334

Upper Level: 1,694 square feet
Lower Level: 1,020 square feet; Total: 2,714 square feet

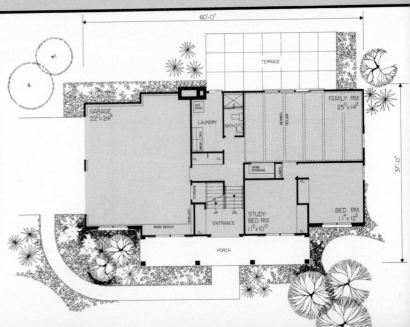

Design V31341 Upper Level: 1,248 square feet; Lower Level: 676 square feet; Total: 1,924 square feet

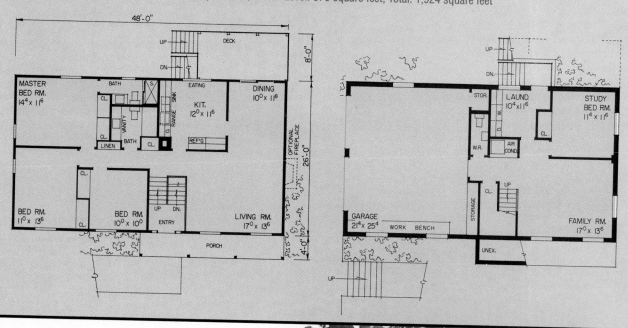

Upper Level floor plan:
- 48'-0" overall width
- MASTER BED RM. 14⁴ x 11⁶
- BATH
- CL.
- VANITY
- LINEN
- BATH
- EATING
- KIT. 12⁰ x 11⁶
- REF'G
- RANGE / SINK
- UP / DN.
- DECK
- DINING 10⁰ x 11⁸
- OPTIONAL FIREPLACE
- 8'-0"
- 26'-0"
- 4'-0"
- BED RM. 11⁰ x 13⁶
- CL.
- BED RM. 10⁰ x 10⁰
- ENTRY
- UP / DN.
- LIVING RM. 17⁰ x 13⁶
- PORCH

Lower Level floor plan:
- UP / DN.
- STOR.
- LAUND. 10⁴ x 11⁶
- D. W.
- W. R.
- AIR COND.
- STUDY BED RM. 11⁴ x 11⁶
- CL.
- GARAGE 21⁴ x 25⁴
- WORK BENCH
- STORAGE
- CL.
- UP
- UNEX.
- FAMILY RM. 17⁰ x 13⁶

Choose Traditional or Contemporary Styling

● The bi-level, or split foyer design has become increasingly popular. Here are six alternate elevations – three Traditional and three Contemporary – which may be built with either of two basic floor plans. One plan contains 960 square feet on each level and is 24 feet in depth; the other contains 1,040 square feet on each level and is 26 feet in depth. Plans for traditional and contemporary series include each of the three optional elevations.

Design V31377 Traditional Exteriors
24-Foot-Depth Plan

Design V31375 Traditional Exteriors
26-Foot-Depth Plan

Upper Level: 960 square feet; Lower Level: 960 square feet; Total: 1,920 square feet

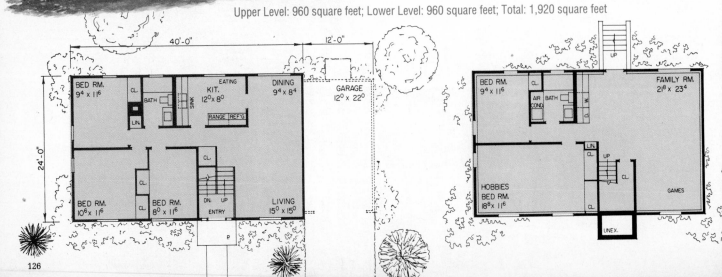

Optional Exteriors
And Floor Plans

● The popularity of the bi-level design can be traced to the tremendous amount of the livable space that such a design provides per construction dollar. While the lower level is partially below grade, it enjoys plenty of natural light and, hence, provides a bright, cheerful atmosphere for total livability. While these two basic floor plans are essentially the same, it is important to note that the larger of the two features a private bath for the master bedroom. Study the plans.

Design V31376 Contemporary Exteriors
24-Foot-Depth Plan

Design V31378 Contemporary Exteriors
26-Foot-Depth Plan

Upper Level: 1,040 square feet; Lower Level: 1,040 square feet; Total: 2,080 square feet

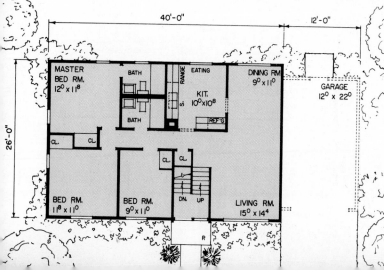

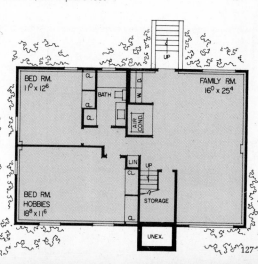

Design V32514
Upper Level: 1,713 square feet
Lower Level: 916 square feet; Total: 2,629 square feet

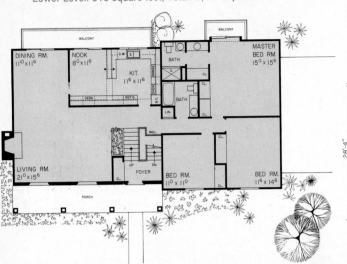

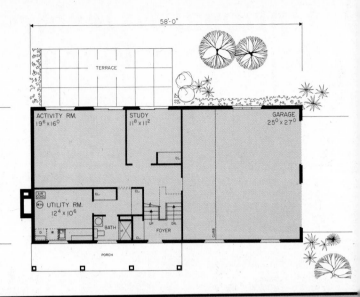

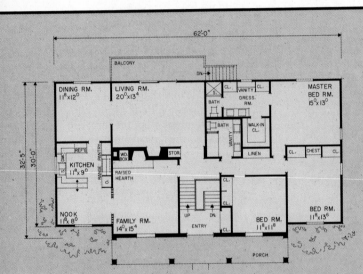

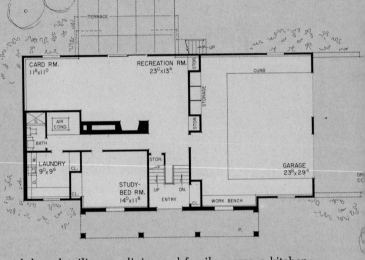

● Here is a unique bi-level. Not only in its delightful exterior appeal, but in its practical planning. The covered porch with its impressive columns, the contrasting use of materials and the traditional window and door detailing are all features which will provoke comment from passers-by. The upper level is a complete living unit of three bedrooms, two baths, separate living, dining and family rooms, a kitchen with an eating area, two fireplaces and an outdoor balcony. The lower level represents extra living space which is bright and cheerful.

Design V32547
Upper Level: 1,946 square feet
Lower Level: 1,340 square feet; Total: 3,286 square feet

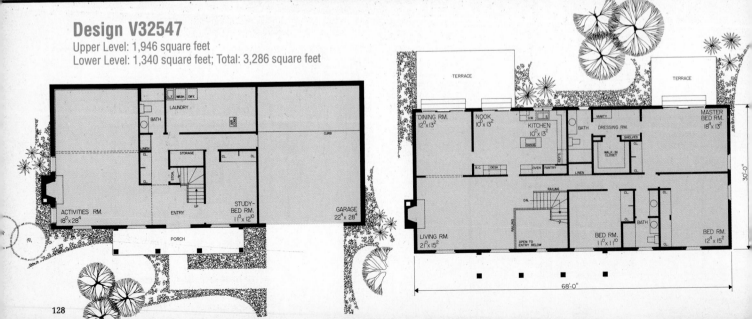

Design V31822 Upper Level: 1,836 square feet; Lower Level: 1,150 square feet; Total: 2,986 square feet

ACTIVITES RM.
21⁶ x 26⁸

SUMMER KIT.
10⁴ x 11²

LAUNDRY
9⁰ x 9⁰

GUEST BED RM.
12⁰ x 13²

BATH

GAMES
10⁰ x 8⁴

ENTRY

GARAGE
23⁰ x 23⁶

PORCH

TERRACE

66'-0"

39'-4"

DINING RM.
12⁰ x 13⁶

NOOK
9⁸ x 13⁶

KITCHEN
10⁴ x 13⁶

STUDY
11⁰ x 13⁶

BED RM.
11⁰ x 17⁸

BATH

GATHERING RM.
19⁸ x 15⁶

LOUNGE
10⁰ x 9⁰

BATH

DRESSING RM.

ENTRY

MASTER BED RM.
21⁰ x 13⁰

PORCH

BALCONY

DECK

Design V32715

Upper Level: 2,299 square feet
Lower Level: 1,524 square feet; Total: 3,823 square feet

● A lounge with built-in seating and a thru-fireplace to the gathering room highlights this upper level. A delightful attraction to view upon entrance of this home. A formal dining room, study and U-shaped kitchen with breakfast nook are present, too. That is a lot of room. There's more! A huge activities room has a fireplace, snack bar and adjacent summer kitchen. This is the perfect set-up for teenage parties or family cook-outs on the terrace. The entire family certainly will enjoy the convenience of this area. All this, plus three bedrooms (optional four without the study), including a luxury master suite with its own outdoor balcony. The upper level, outdoor deck provides partial cover for the lower level terrace. This home offers outdoor living potential on both levels.

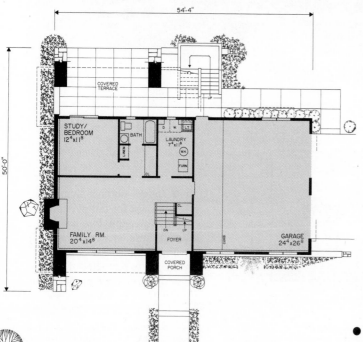

Design V32669

First Floor: 826 square feet
Second Floor: 1,535 square feet
Total: 2,361 square feet

● This comfortable, efficient four-bedroom home offers good traffic flow and personal access to balconies from three upstairs bedrooms. There's a breakfast room adjacent to the kitchen upstairs, plus a dining room and living room also upstairs. An upper-level deck is also accessible from a rear entry. A bedroom/study downstairs opens into a covered terrace. Note the fireplace and first-floor family room, too!

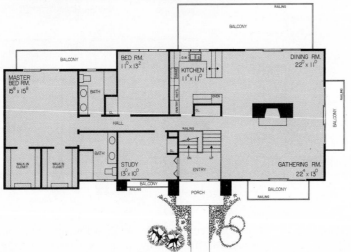

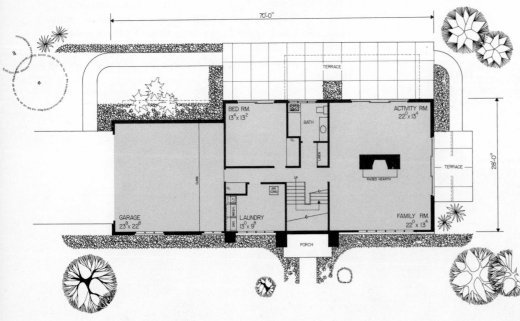

Design V32580

Upper Level: 1,852 square feet
Lower Level: 1,297 square feet
Total: 3,149 square feet

● Indoor-outdoor living hardly-could ask for more! And here's why. Imagine, five balconies and three terraces! These unique balconies add great beauty to the exterior while adding pleasure to those who utilize them from the interior. And there's more. This home has enough space for all to appreciate. Take note of the size of the gathering room, family room and activity room. There's also a large dining room. Four bedrooms too, for the large or growing family. Or three plus a study. Two fireplaces, one to service each of the two levels in this bi-level design. The rear terrace is accessible thru sliding glass doors from the lower level bedroom and activity room. The side terrace functions with the activity/family room area. The master suite has two walk-in closets and a private bath.

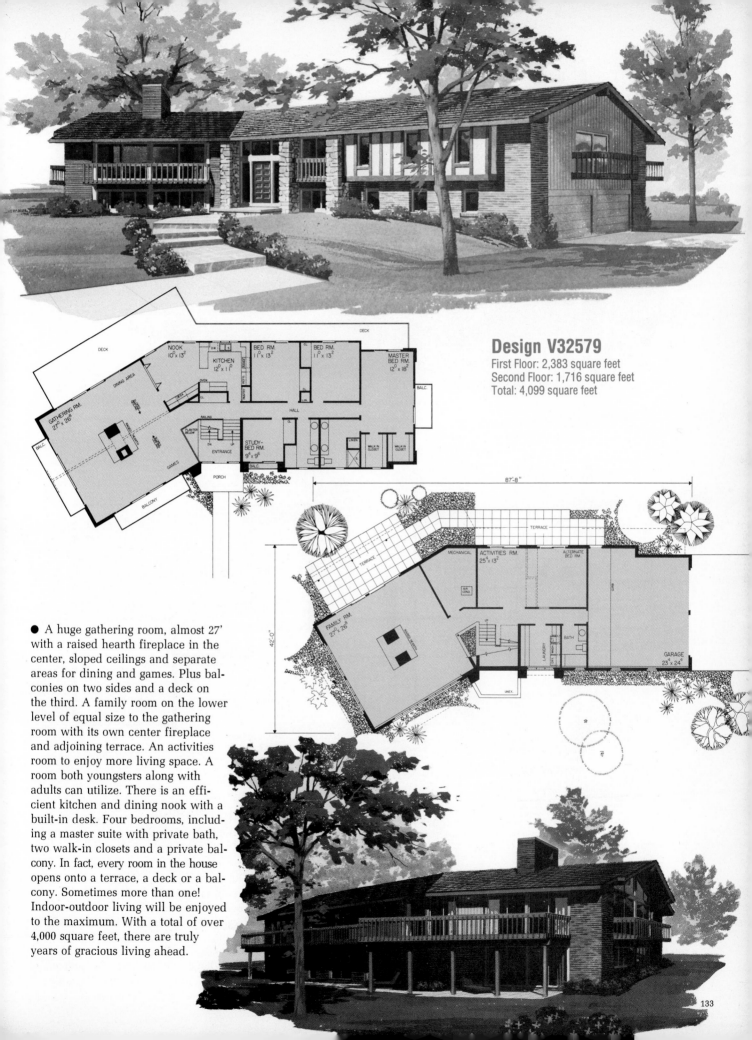

Design V32579

First Floor: 2,383 square feet
Second Floor: 1,716 square feet
Total: 4,099 square feet

● A huge gathering room, almost 27' with a raised hearth fireplace in the center, sloped ceilings and separate areas for dining and games. Plus balconies on two sides and a deck on the third. A family room on the lower level of equal size to the gathering room with its own center fireplace and adjoining terrace. An activities room to enjoy more living space. A room both youngsters along with adults can utilize. There is an efficient kitchen and dining nook with a built-in desk. Four bedrooms, including a master suite with private bath, two walk-in closets and a private balcony. In fact, every room in the house opens onto a terrace, a deck or a balcony. Sometimes more than one! Indoor-outdoor living will be enjoyed to the maximum. With a total of over 4,000 square feet, there are truly years of gracious living ahead.

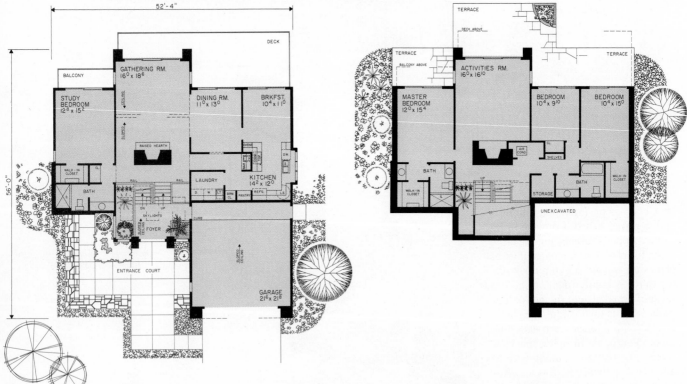

Design V32894
Upper Level: 1,490 square feet
Lower Level: 1,357 square feet; Total: 2,847 square feet

● Contemporary, bi-level living will be enjoyed by all members of the family. Upon entering the foyer, complimented by skylights, stairs will lead you to the upper and lower levels. Up a few steps, you will find yourself in the large gathering room. The fire- place, sloped ceiling and the size of this room will make this a favorite spot. To the left is a study/bedroom with a full bath and walk-in closet. Notice the efficient kitchen and break- fast room with nearby wet bar. The lower level houses two bedrooms and a bath to one side; and a master bed- room suite to the other. Centered is a large activity room with raised-hearth fireplace. It will be enjoyed by all. Note - all of the rear rooms on both levels have easy access to the outdoors for excellent indoor-outdoor livability.

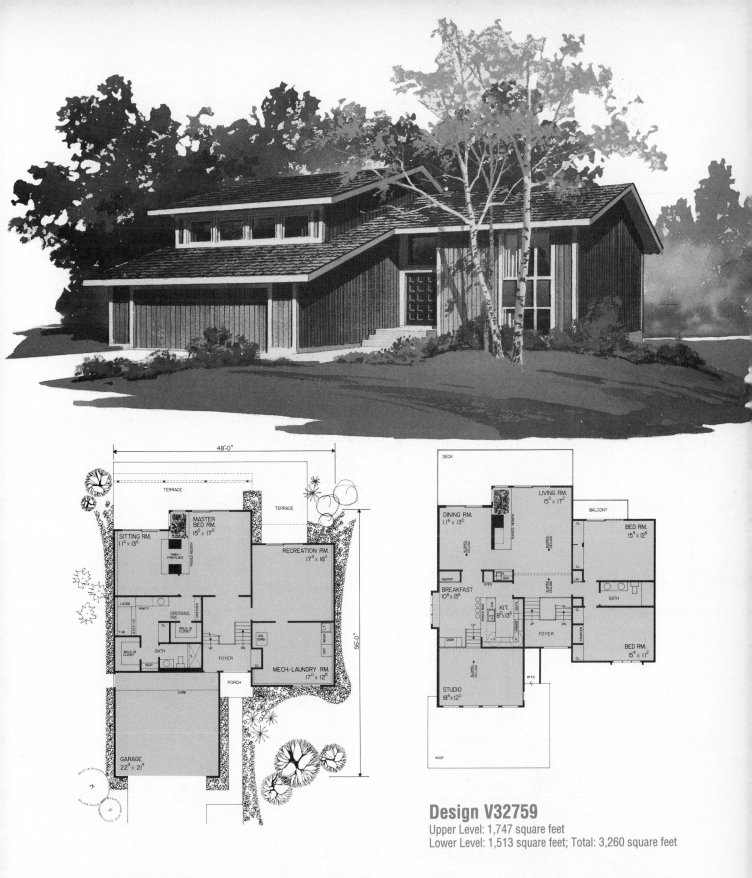

Design V32759

Upper Level: 1,747 square feet
Lower Level: 1,513 square feet; Total: 3,260 square feet

● A contemporary bi-level with a large bonus room on a third level over the garage. This studio will serve as a great room to be creative in or just to sit back in. The design also provides great indoor/outdoor living relationships with terraces and decks. The for-mal living/dining area has a sloped ceiling and built-in wet bar. The dramatic beauty of a raised hearth fireplace and built-in planter will be enjoyed by those in the living room. Both have sliding glass doors to the rear deck. The breakfast area will serve as a pleasant eating room with ample space for a table plus the built-in snack bar. The lower level houses the recreation room, laundry and an outstanding master suite. This master suite includes a thru-fireplace, sitting room, tub and shower and more.

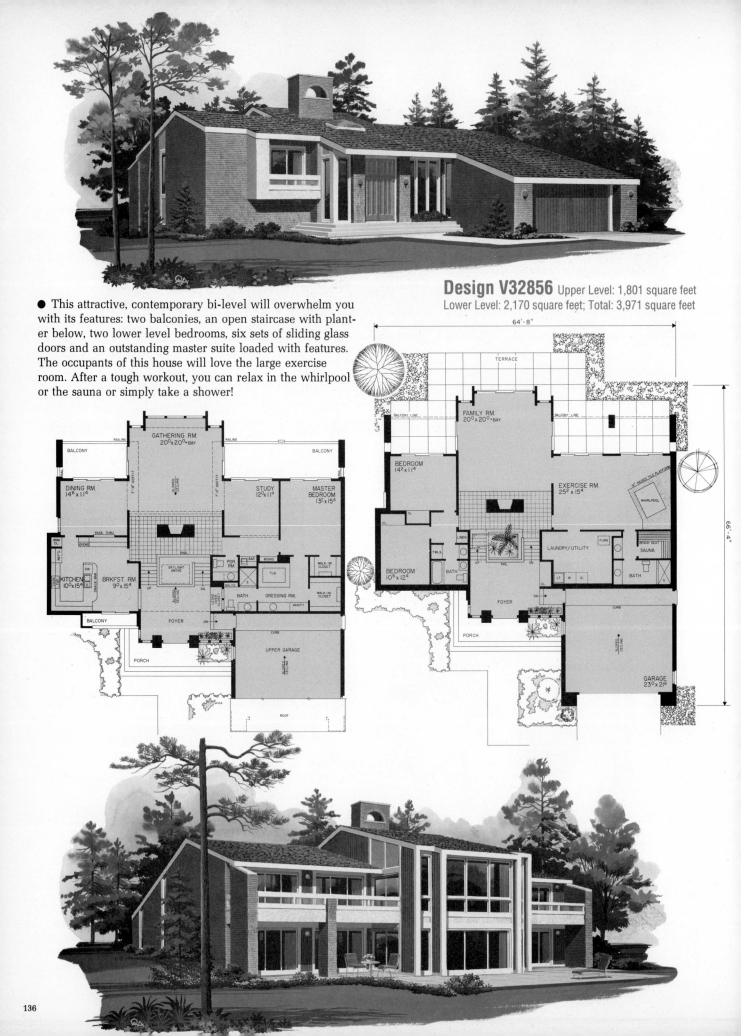

This attractive, contemporary bi-level will overwhelm you with its features: two balconies, an open staircase with planter below, two lower level bedrooms, six sets of sliding glass doors and an outstanding master suite loaded with features. The occupants of this house will love the large exercise room. After a tough workout, you can relax in the whirlpool or the sauna or simply take a shower!

Design V32856 Upper Level: 1,801 square feet
Lower Level: 2,170 square feet; Total: 3,971 square feet

Design V32868

Upper Level: 1,203 square feet
Lower Level: 1,317 square feet; Total: 2,520 square feet

Common Living Areas – Sleeping Privacy

● Two couples sharing the expense of a house has got to be ideal and, of course, economical. The occupants of this house could do just that. The lower level, housing the kitchen, dining room, family and living rooms and the laundry facilities, is the common area to be shared by both couples. Centrally located, the kitchen and dining room act as a space divider to the living and family rooms so both couples can enjoy privacy.

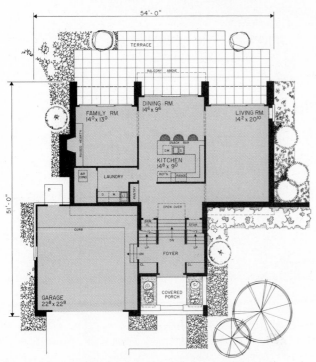

Separate stairways lead to the upper level from the skylit foyer. Each private area has two bedrooms, a dressing room and a full bath. Individual entrances can be locked for additional privacy. Sliding glass doors are in each of the rear rooms on both levels so the outdoors can be enjoyed to its fullest.

Design V32827 Upper Level: 1,618 square feet
Lower Level: 1,458 square feet; Total: 3,076 square feet

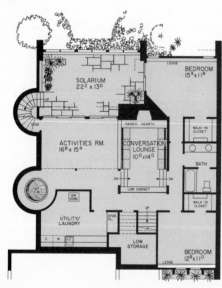

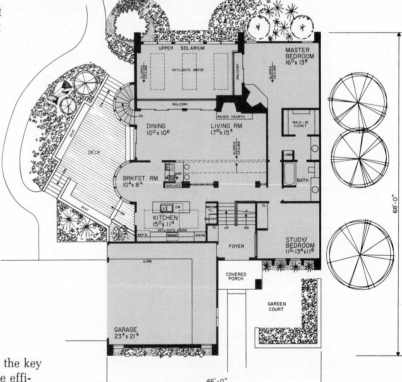

● The two-story solarium with skylights above is the key to energy savings to this bi-level design. Study the efficiency of this floor plan. The conversation lounge on the lower level is a unique focal point.

HILLSIDE HOMES . . .

take advantage of the contours of the site on which they stand. A hillside house can be a one- or two-story or a split-level. Its lower level may be open to the rear, front or sides of the house, with patios and terraces enhancing indoor/outdoor living relationships. Many houses with basements designed for a flat site can be adapted to hillside living by merely exposing the basement and installing windows or doors.

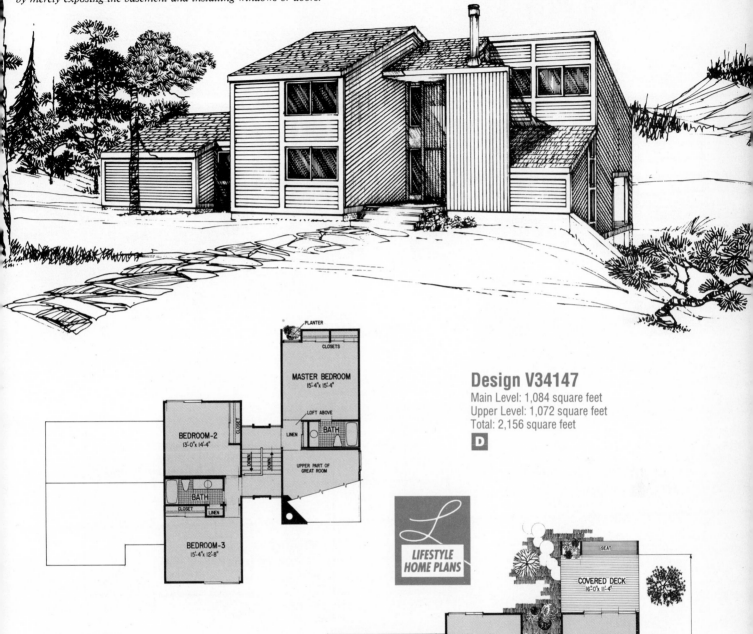

Design V34147

Main Level: 1,084 square feet
Upper Level: 1,072 square feet
Total: 2,156 square feet

D

L LIFESTYLE HOME PLANS

● This hillside haven offers four levels of living. The great room will be a favorite gathering spot: in winter for its corner fireplace; in summer for its cool covered deck. The large U-shaped kitchen complements a formal dining room and is near a washroom and laundry area. Separate sleeping quarters are found on two upper levels — two family bedrooms and a private master suite.

Design V34203

Main Level: 1,470 square feet
Basement Level: 455 square feet
Total: 1,925 square feet

70'-0"

DECK

DECK

28'-0"

STORAGE

D.
W.

LAUNDRY

SL. GL. DOOR

DINING

SINK

KITCHEN
RANGE

W.

SL. GL. DOOR

MASTER BEDROOM
13'-0" X 13'-4"

OPEN TO
DINING

SNACK BAR

REF.

SLOPED CLG.

GARAGE
21'-8" X 21'-0"

FIXED GLASS ABOVE

FURNACE & W/H
LOCATION W/OUT BASEM'T.

W.I.C.

DOWN

CLOSET

CLOSET

SLOPED CLG.

GREAT ROOM
15'-4" X 27'-4"

HALL

BEDROOM - 3
13'-8" X 10'-4"

BEDROOM - 2
13'-0" X 11'-4"

W.I.C.

ENTRY

LIFESTYLE
HOME PLANS

DECK ABOVE

DECK ABOVE

PATIO

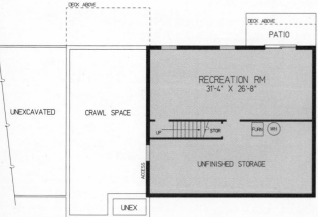

UNEXCAVATED

CRAWL SPACE

RECREATION RM
31'-4" X 26'-8"

UP

STOR.

FURN.

WH

UNFINISHED STORAGE

ACCESS

UNEX

● Though most of the living in this house takes place on one level, if built on a hillside lot, the plan could have a lower-level recreation room with outdoor access. Decks off the dining room and master bedroom would serve as covers for the lower level patios. Living and sleeping zones inside are well placed and harbor plenty of storage and closet space.

Design V34196

Main Level: 1,709 square feet
Basement Level: 1,182 square feet
Total: 2,891 square feet

D

● This low-to-the-ground home shelters several surprises. The first is a cheerful garden court at the entrance. Exposed rafters here allow just the right combination of sun and shade. Inside are more delights, like the three decks off the living room, breakfast room, and master bedroom. And note that the living room is sunken a step down from the main house. The real secret, however, to this home's hillside nature is its optional basement, which, if developed, allows walk-out potential on a lower level.

Design V34127

First Floor: 2,015 square feet
Second Floor: 746 square feet
Basement Level: 1,952 square feet
Total: 4,713 square feet

● The unusual configuration of this home's floor plan provides a totally private master bedroom suite, separated from first-floor access by a windowed bridge. On the main level are three bedrooms, two baths, a family room with deck and fireplace, a formal dining room, and a kitchen with attached nook. The basement level can be developed into a recreation room or guest bedroom with outdoor patio access.

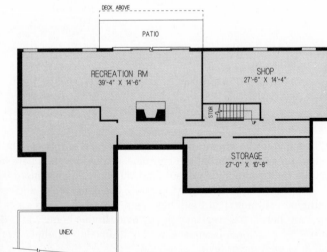

LIFESTYLE HOME PLANS

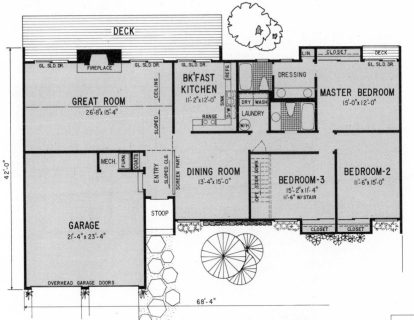

Design V34193

Main Level: 1,712 square feet
Basement Level: 1,653 square feet
Total: 3,365 square feet

● Though seemingly small in size, this home provides a good measure of family living potential. In addition to three bedrooms and two baths, a huge great room, a convenient L-shaped kitchen with breakfast room, and a large central dining area are found on the main level. Lower-level living areas can be developed, making this a great hillside design.

LIFESTYLE
HOME PLANS

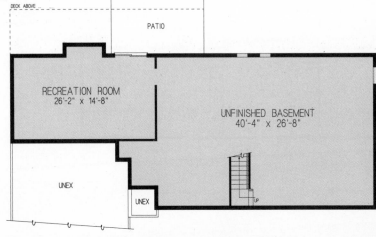

Design V34309

Main Level: 2,430 square feet
Basement Level: 959 square feet
Total: 3,389 square feet

● This rustic, rambling ranch has many of the amenities today's homeowner looks for: four bedrooms, 2½ baths, a great room with deck and fireplace, efficient U-shaped kitchen, and lots of storage. As a hillside plan, the design provides additional living space on its lower level.

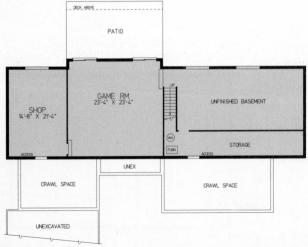

L
LIFESTYLE
HOME PLANS

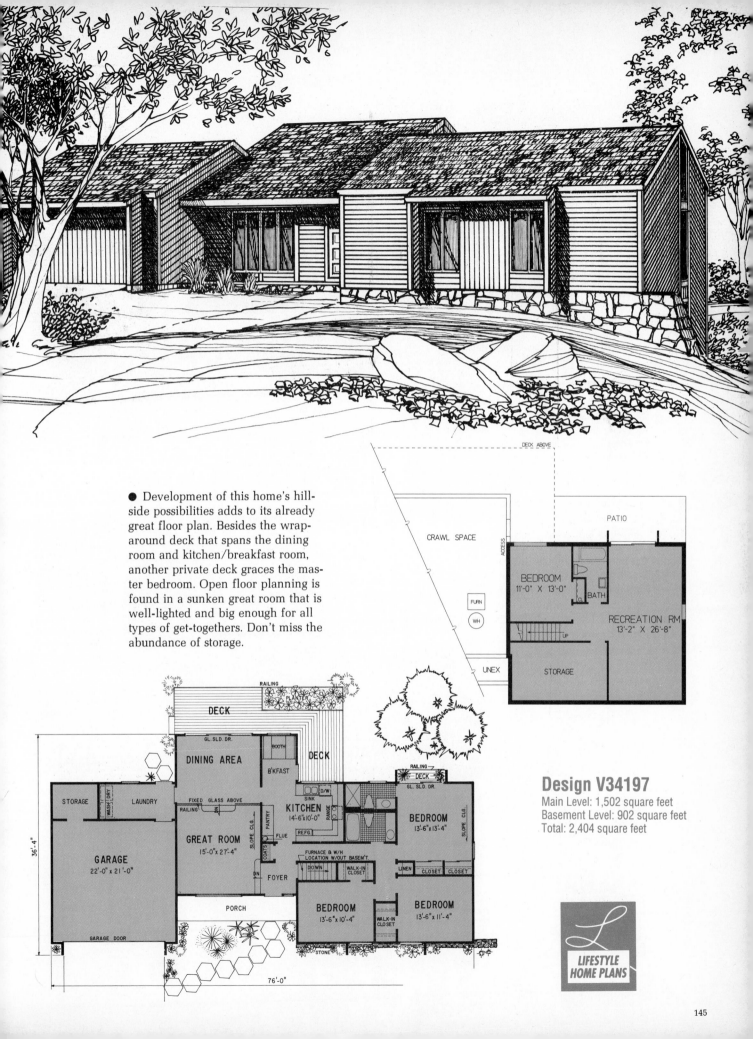

● Development of this home's hillside possibilities adds to its already great floor plan. Besides the wraparound deck that spans the dining room and kitchen/breakfast room, another private deck graces the master bedroom. Open floor planning is found in a sunken great room that is well-lighted and big enough for all types of get-togethers. Don't miss the abundance of storage.

DECK ABOVE

CRAWL SPACE

ACCESS

PATIO

BEDROOM
11'-0" X 13'-0"

BATH

FURN

WH

RECREATION RM
13'-2" X 26'-8"

UP

UNEX

STORAGE

RAILING

PLANTER

DECK

GL. SLD. DR.

DINING AREA

BOOTH

DECK

B'KFAST

RAILING

DECK

GL. SLD. DR.

STORAGE

WASH / DRY

LAUNDRY

FIXED GLASS ABOVE

RAILING

SINK

D/W

KITCHEN
14'-6" x 10'-0"

RANGE

BEDROOM
13'-6" x 13'-4"

SLOPE CLG.

PANTRY

REFG.

GARAGE
22'-0" x 21'-0"

GREAT ROOM
15'-0" x 27'-4"

FLUE

COATS

FURNACE & W/H
LOCATION W/OUT BASEM'T.

LINEN

CLOSET

CLOSET

DOWN

WALK-IN CLOSET

DN

FOYER

PORCH

BEDROOM
13'-6" x 10'-4"

WALK-IN CLOSET

BEDROOM
13'-6" x 11'-4"

GARAGE DOOR

STONE

36'-4"

76'-0"

Design V34197

Main Level: 1,502 square feet
Basement Level: 902 square feet
Total: 2,404 square feet

L

LIFESTYLE
HOME PLANS

Design V34326

Main Level: 2,492 square feet
Basement Level: 956 square feet
Total: 3,448 square feet

D

● Formal and informal living areas in this home double its value and appeal. The potential of expanding the livability in an exposed hillside basement furthers its attractiveness. Notice the interesting angles and levels that are achieved with the sunken living room and sloped-ceiling great room. Two of the family bedrooms share a full bath with dressing room; the master bedroom shares its bath with a fourth bedroom.

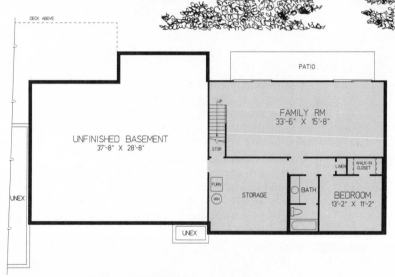

LIFESTYLE HOME PLANS

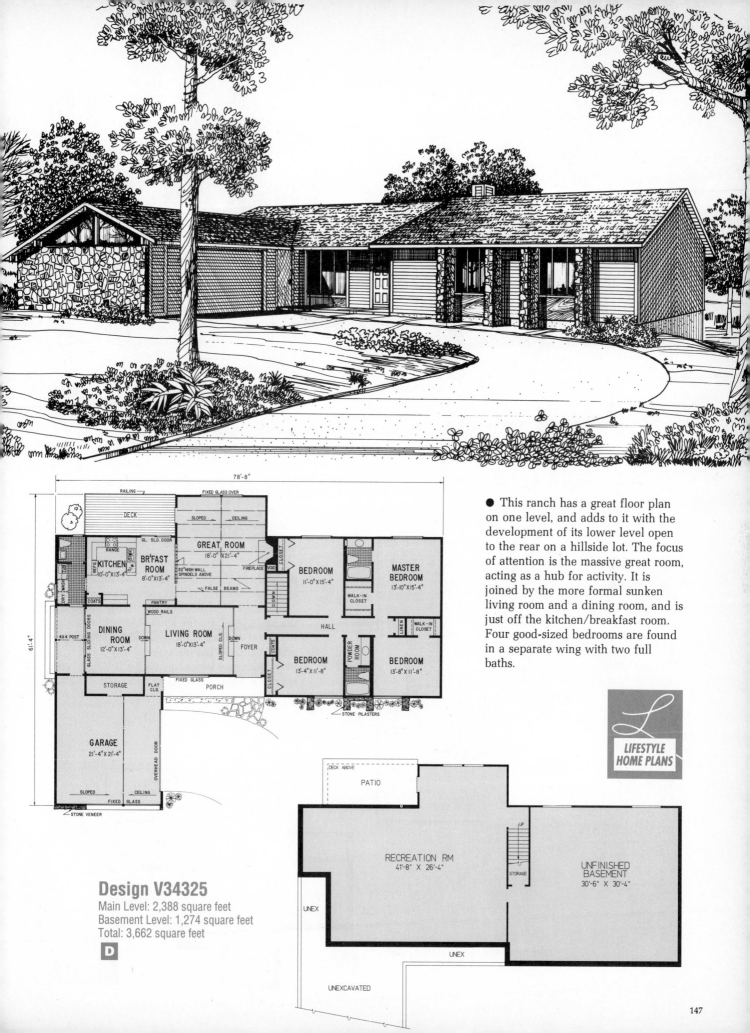

This ranch has a great floor plan on one level, and adds to it with the development of its lower level open to the rear on a hillside lot. The focus of attention is the massive great room, acting as a hub for activity. It is joined by the more formal sunken living room and a dining room, and is just off the kitchen/breakfast room. Four good-sized bedrooms are found in a separate wing with two full baths.

Design V34325

Main Level: 2,388 square feet
Basement Level: 1,274 square feet
Total: 3,662 square feet

D

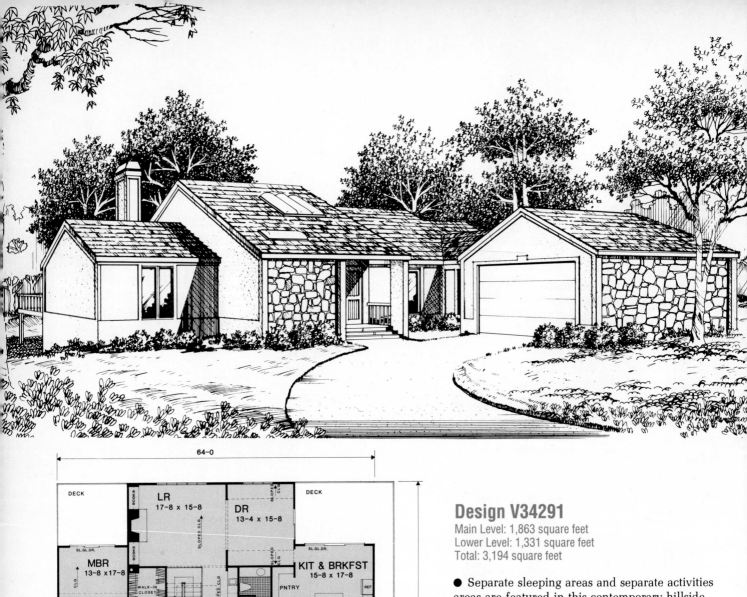

DECK	
LR 17-8 x 15-8	DR 13-4 x 15-8 DECK
MBR 13-8 x 17-8	KIT & BRKFST 15-8 x 17-8

WALK-IN CLOSET

DN

SKYLIGHT ABOVE

PNTRY

REF D/W

FOYER

PORCH

DN

SHOWER

ENTRY COURT

DN

STORAGE

BRMS W D

LAUNDRY

GAR 21-4 x 21-4

64-0

66-8

Design V34291

Main Level: 1,863 square feet
Lower Level: 1,331 square feet
Total: 3,194 square feet

● Separate sleeping areas and separate activities areas are featured in this contemporary hillside. Along with formal living and dining rooms on the main level are the kitchen/breakfast room, two-level outdoor deck, and master suite with grand bath. On the lower level is a children's play room, two bedrooms with a full bath, and space for a fourth bedroom and another bath.

PLAY RM. 19-8 x 15-8

BR-3 13-4 x 13-0

UNFINISHED FUTURE BR-4

MECH

BR-2 15-0 x 16-8

LIN

UP

STOR

FUTURE BATH

WALK-IN CLOSET

L
LIFESTYLE
HOME PLANS

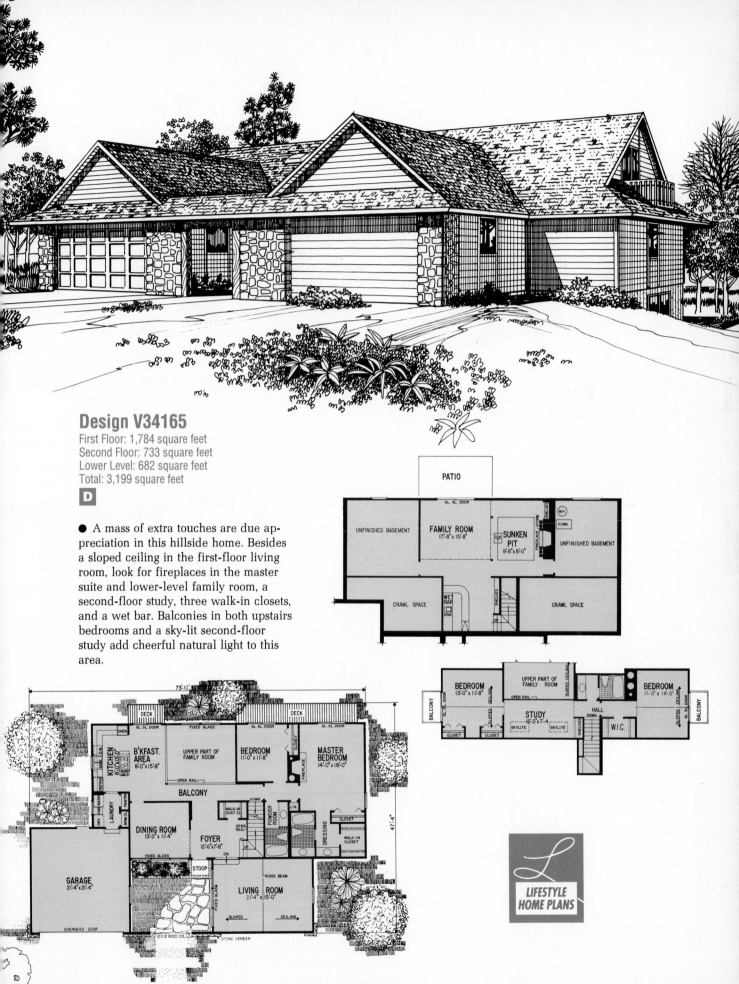

Design V34165

First Floor: 1,784 square feet
Second Floor: 733 square feet
Lower Level: 682 square feet
Total: 3,199 square feet

D

● A mass of extra touches are due appreciation in this hillside home. Besides a sloped ceiling in the first-floor living room, look for fireplaces in the master suite and lower-level family room, a second-floor study, three walk-in closets, and a wet bar. Balconies in both upstairs bedrooms and a sky-lit second-floor study add cheerful natural light to this area.

LIFESTYLE HOME PLANS

Design V34191

Main Level: 1,881 square feet
Lower Level: 1,538 square feet
Total: 3,419 square feet

 D

● Only a few differences in floor planning distinguish the interiors of the homes on these two pages, though the exterior looks are quite different. Design V34191 has a garage which opens to the front with a small storage room at its side. Notice also that this design has a separate utility room whereas V34090 uses the same space for storage. The lower level for both plans features a large playroom with fireplace, a full bath, and a bedroom with two walk-in closets.

LIFESTYLE
HOME PLANS

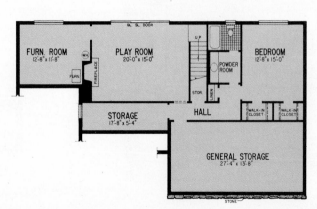

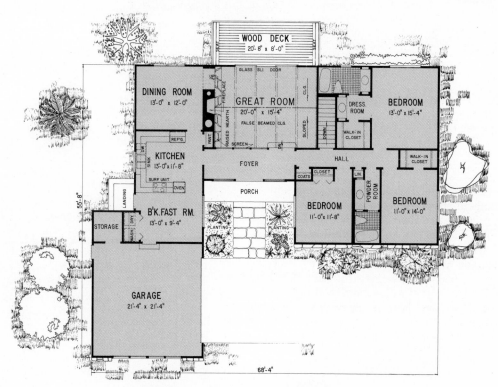

Design V34090

Main Level: 1,858 square feet
Lower Level: 1,538 square feet
Total: 3,396 square feet

● A wonderful combination of wood and stone accents the exterior of this clean-lined home while a gracious floor plan meets the needs of a busy family. Besides a great room with attached deck on the main level, there is a children's play room and plenty of storage area on the lower level. Three bedrooms on the main level are complemented by a fourth below. Note the convenient placement of baths and the many extras such as a raised-hearth fireplace and large walk-in closets.

Design V34215

Main Level: 2,134 square feet
Lower Level: 1,054 square feet
Total: 3,188 square feet

L

● A great bi-level design, this home opens with a naturally lit entry leading to a sunken living area with fireplace and deck. To the left is a formal dining room, kitchen and breakfast area, and powder room with washer/dryer space. To the right is the master suite with a huge bath and private deck, and two family bedrooms sharing a full bath. Bonus area is on the lower level with a fourth bedroom, another full bath, and large family room with wet bar and fireplace.

DECK

DECK

DINING
16'-4" X 12'-0"

LIVING
20'-0" X 15'-4"

MASTER BEDROOM
15'-0" X 15'-4"

PANTRY

W.I.C.

KITCHEN
15'-4" X 10'-0"

RANGE   REFG

HALL

CLOSET

CLOSET

COATS

ENTRY

CLOSET

LIN

BREAKFAST AREA
16'-8" X 10'-8"

WASH DRY

BEDROOM-3
11'-0" X 11'-8"

BEDROOM-2
11'-0" X 11'-8"

DOUBLE GARAGE
21'-8" X 21'-4"

61'-8"

66'-0"

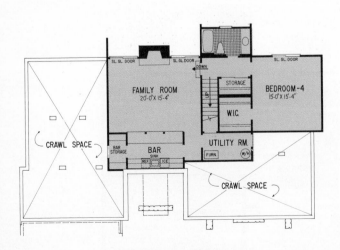

FAMILY ROOM
20'-0" X 15'-4"

SL. GL. DOOR   SL. GL. DOOR   SL. GL. DOOR

DOWN

STORAGE

BEDROOM-4
15'-0" X 15'-4"

W.I.C.

CRAWL SPACE

BAR STORAGE

BAR
SINK

UTILITY RM.

REF. ICE

FURN

W/H

CRAWL SPACE

LIFESTYLE HOME PLANS

Design V34190

Main Level: 2,157 square feet
Lower Level: 1,008 square feet
Total: 3,165 square feet

L

LIFESTYLE
HOME PLANS

● The spaciousness of this design might never be guessed for it conceals part of its great living space in a lower level. Open planning on the main level gives way to formal living and dining rooms, a more casual great room, galley kitchen, laundry with powder room, and three bedrooms with two full baths. Notice the deep wood deck to the rear.

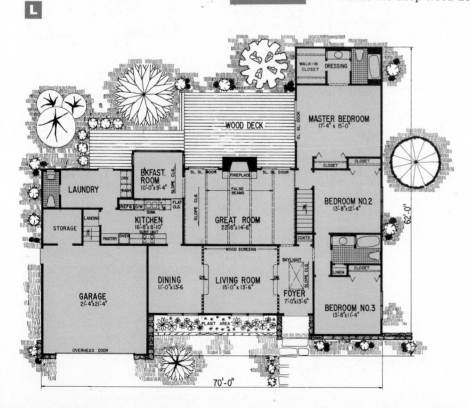

LIFESTYLE HOME PLANS

● Three dramatic levels of livability mean room for everyone in the family to engage in active and quiet pursuits. There are six bedrooms — the master sits alone on the upper level — and three full baths. Also notice the five separate decks, in addition to the lower-level patio. And storage abounds with space in the double garage and three walk-in closets.

Design V34092

Main Level: 1,660 square feet; Upper Level: 606 square feet
Lower Level: 1,092 square feet; Total: 3,358 square feet

L

Design V34091

Main Level: 1,914 square feet
Lower Level: 1,040 square feet
Total: 2,954 square feet

● A sunken, sloped-ceiling great room lies at the heart of this contemporary design. To the left are the dining room with built-in buffet, and a U-shaped kitchen with pass-through to the breakfast room. Sleeping arrangements are nicely accommodated in a separate wing — two family bedrooms and a master suite. A fourth bedroom is on the lower level next to the large family room and service bar.

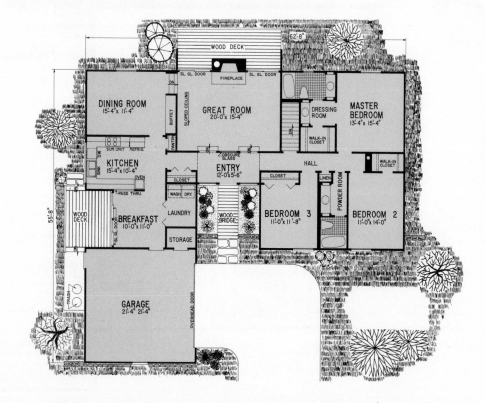

LIFESTYLE HOME PLANS

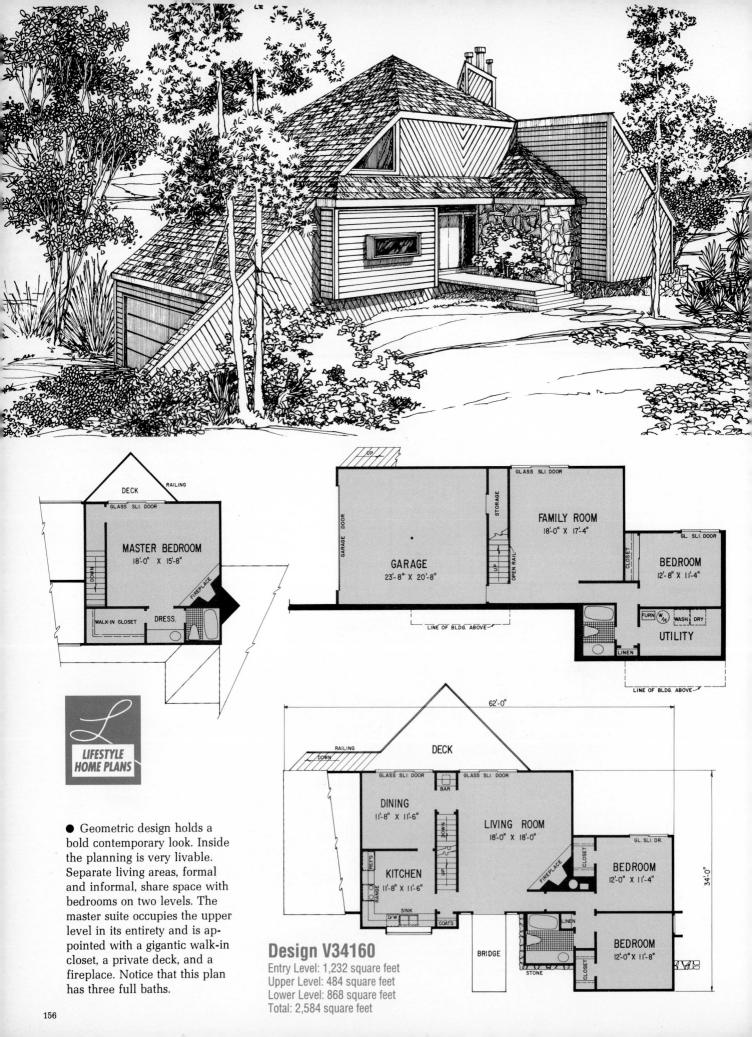

DECK · RAILING
GLASS SLI. DOOR

MASTER BEDROOM
18'-0" X 15'-8"

DOWN
FIREPLACE
WALK-IN CLOSET · DRESS.

UP
GARAGE DOOR
STORAGE
GLASS SLI. DOOR

FAMILY ROOM
18'-0" X 17'-4"

GARAGE
23'-8" X 20'-8"

UP
OPEN RAIL

CLOSET

GL. SLI. DOOR
BEDROOM
12'-8" X 11'-4"

LINE OF BLDG. ABOVE

FURN W/H WASH DRY
UTILITY
LINEN

LINE OF BLDG. ABOVE

62'-0"

RAILING
DOWN
DECK

GLASS SLI. DOOR   GLASS SLI. DOOR
BAR

DINING
11'-8" X 11'-6"

DOWN
UP

LIVING ROOM
18'-0" X 18'-0"

REF'G
RANGE
KITCHEN
11'-8" X 11'-6"

SINK
D/W
COATS

FIREPLACE
CLOSET

GL. SLI. DR.
BEDROOM
12'-0" X 11'-4"

34'-0"

LINEN

BRIDGE

STONE
CLOSET
BEDROOM
12'-0" X 11'-8"

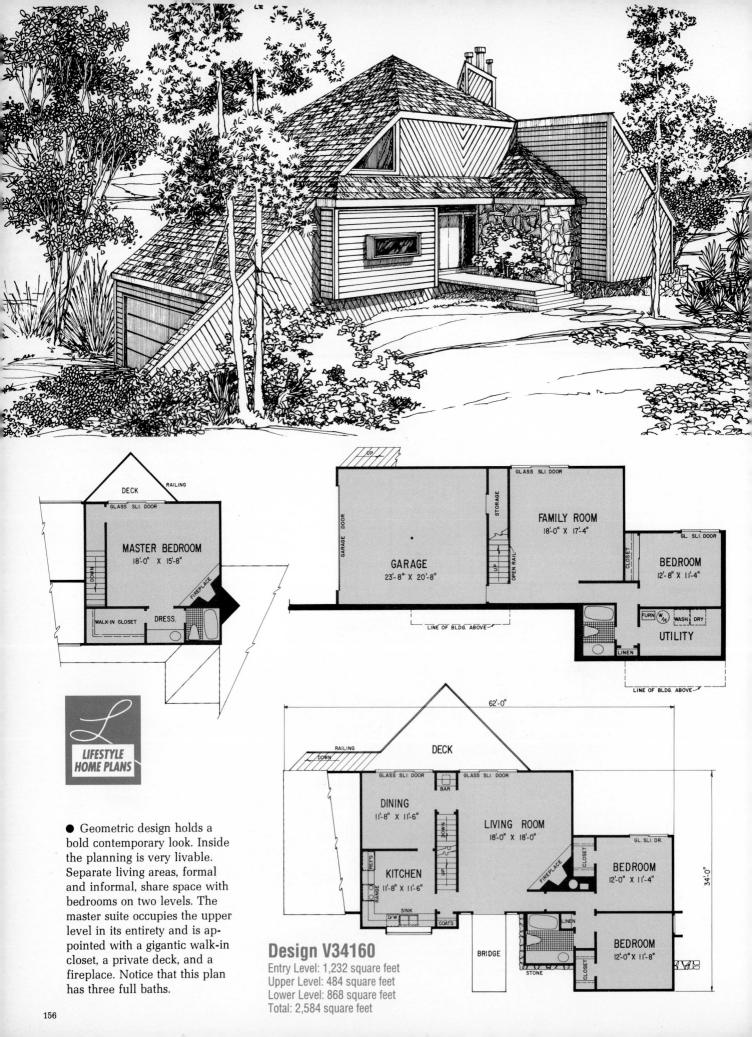
LIFESTYLE
HOME PLANS

● Geometric design holds a
bold contemporary look. Inside
the planning is very livable.
Separate living areas, formal
and informal, share space with
bedrooms on two levels. The
master suite occupies the upper
level in its entirety and is appointed with a gigantic walk-in
closet, a private deck, and a
fireplace. Notice that this plan
has three full baths.

Design V34160

Entry Level: 1,232 square feet
Upper Level: 484 square feet
Lower Level: 868 square feet
Total: 2,584 square feet

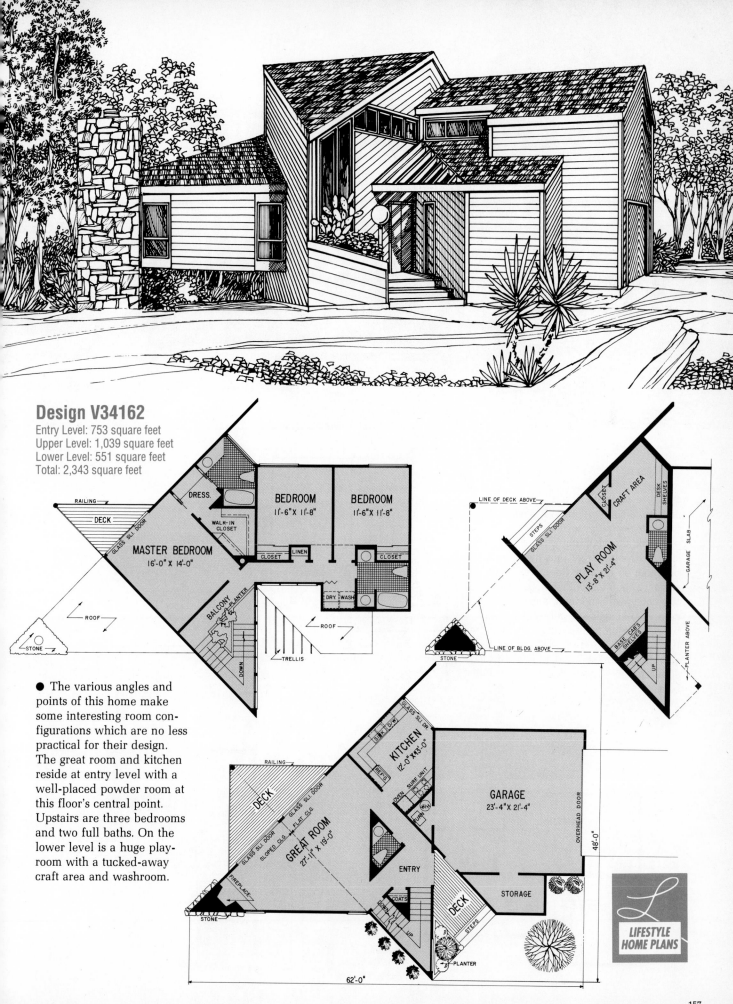

Design V34162

Entry Level: 753 square feet
Upper Level: 1,039 square feet
Lower Level: 551 square feet
Total: 2,343 square feet

RAILING

DECK

GLASS SLI. DOOR

DRESS.

MASTER BEDROOM
16'-0" X 14'-0"

WALK-IN CLOSET

BEDROOM
11'-6" X 11'-8"

BEDROOM
11'-6" X 11'-8"

CLOSET

LINEN

CLOSET

ROOF

STONE

ROOF

BALCONY

PLANTER

DRY

WASH

DOWN

TRELLIS

LINE OF DECK ABOVE

STEPS

GLASS SLI DOOR

CLOSET

CRAFT AREA

DESK

SHELVES

PLAY ROOM
13'-8" X 21'-4"

GARAGE SLAB

BASE CAB'S SHELVES

UP

PLANTER ABOVE

STONE

LINE OF BLDG. ABOVE

● The various angles and points of this home make some interesting room configurations which are no less practical for their design. The great room and kitchen reside at entry level with a well-placed powder room at this floor's central point. Upstairs are three bedrooms and two full baths. On the lower level is a huge playroom with a tucked-away craft area and washroom.

RAILING

DECK

GLASS SLI. DOOR

SLOPED CLG.

FLAT CLG.

GLASS SLI DOOR

GREAT ROOM
27'-11" X 19'-0"

FIREPLACE

STONE

SINK

D/W

REFG

OVEN

SURF. UNIT

FURN.

KITCHEN
12'-0" X 13'-0"

GARAGE
23'-4" X 21'-4"

OVERHEAD DOOR

ENTRY

COATS

DOWN

UP

DECK

STEPS

PLANTER

STORAGE

48'-0"

62'-0"

𝓛
LIFESTYLE
HOME PLANS

157

There's a lot to love in this wood-and-stone contemporary. From three wood decks to the second-floor balcony overlook, the planning is just right. The split-bedroom design puts the master bedroom on the first floor. It is luxuriously appointed with a sloped ceiling, fireplace, walk-in closet, and deck access. A U-shaped kitchen serves both breakfast room and dining room. On the basement level is a large playroom, a washroom, and shop area that could be converted to a fourth bedroom with full bath.

Design V34331

First Floor: 1,580 square feet
Second Floor: 730 square feet
Basement Level: 1,323 square feet
Total: 3,633 square feet

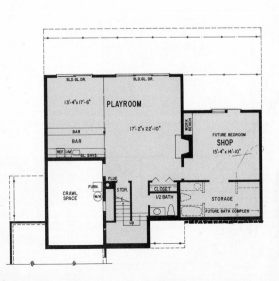

LIFESTYLE
HOME PLANS

LIFESTYLE
HOME PLANS

BEDROOM-2
11'-0"x14'-4"

OPEN TO LIVING

OPEN RAIL

BALCONY

BEDROOM-3
13'-4"x14'-0"

FIXED GLASS

CLOSET

Design V34241

First Floor: 1,580 square feet
Second Floor: 702 square feet
Basement Level: 967 square feet
Total: 3,249 square feet

L

● Similar to Design V34331, this home introduces some differences that may make it better suited to some lifestyles or building situations. Note, for instance, that the garage is placed at the basement level, alongside the playroom. An outside storage area is created just off the garage. The first floor has remained essentially the same, but there are subtle changes in the second-floor layout.

WOOD RAIL

WOOD DECK

WOOD DECK

DINING
13'-4"x12'-4"

LIVING
17'-4"x23'-0"

SLD. GL. DR.

SLD. GL. DR.

SLD. GL. DR.

MASTER BEDROOM
15'-8"x15'-0"

REFG.

KITCHEN
12'-10"x10'-0"

SLOPE CLG TO 2ND FL.

LINE OF BALCONY

SLOPE

CEILING

D/W

WOOD DECK

BREAKFAST
13'-4"x11'-0"

SLD.GL.DR.

POWDER RM.

BATH

DRESSING

WALK-IN CLOSET

DRY.

WASH

PANTRY

FOYER

ENTRY DECK

STONE VENEER

38'-0"

50'-0"

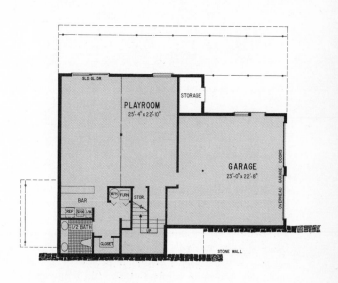

SLD. GL. DR.

PLAYROOM
25'-4"x22'-10"

STORAGE

GARAGE
23'-0"x22'-8"

OVERHEAD GARAGE DOORS

BAR

W/H

FURN.

STOR.

REF.

SINK

1/2 BATH

CLOSET

UP

STONE WALL

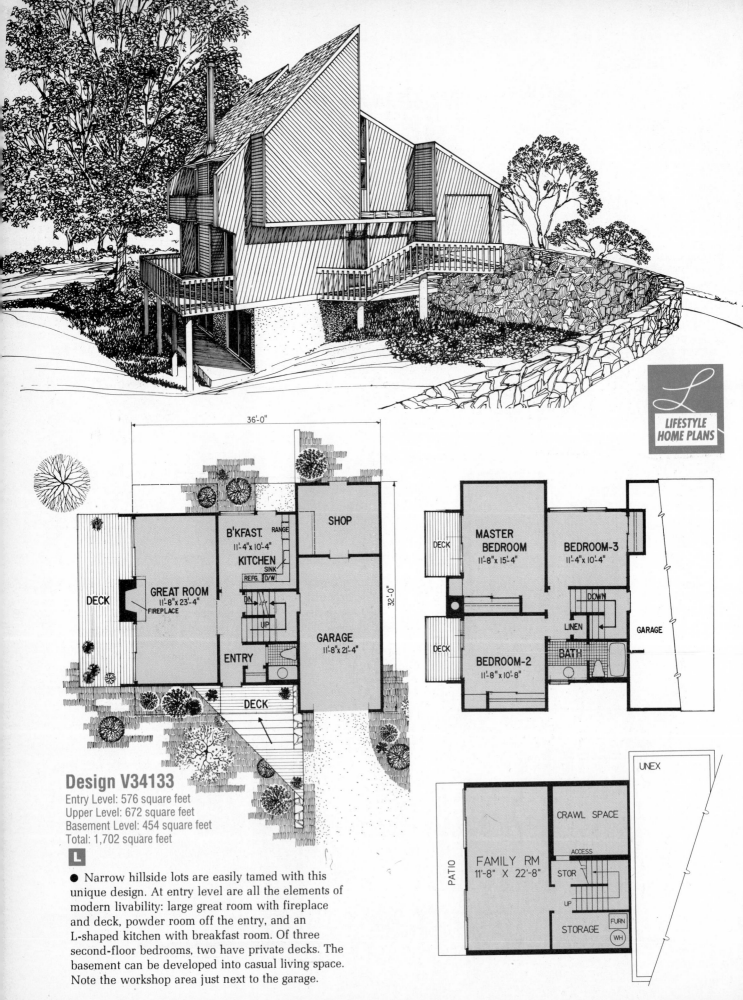

LIFESTYLE HOME PLANS

36'-0"

32'-0"

DECK

GREAT ROOM
11'-8" x 23'-4"
FIREPLACE

B'KFAST.
11'-4" x 10'-4"

KITCHEN
SINK
REFG. D/W
RANGE

SHOP

DN UP

ENTRY

DECK

GARAGE
11'-8" x 21'-4"

DECK

MASTER
BEDROOM
11'-8" x 15'-4"

BEDROOM-3
11'-4" x 10'-4"

DECK

DOWN

LINEN

BEDROOM-2
11'-8" x 10'-8"

BATH

GARAGE

UNEX

PATIO

FAMILY RM
11'-8" X 22'-8"

CRAWL SPACE

ACCESS

STOR

UP

STORAGE

FURN

WH

Design V34133

Entry Level: 576 square feet
Upper Level: 672 square feet
Basement Level: 454 square feet
Total: 1,702 square feet

L

● Narrow hillside lots are easily tamed with this unique design. At entry level are all the elements of modern livability: large great room with fireplace and deck, powder room off the entry, and an L-shaped kitchen with breakfast room. Of three second-floor bedrooms, two have private decks. The basement can be developed into casual living space. Note the workshop area just next to the garage.

Design V34249

First Level: 1,138 square feet
Second Level: 693 square feet
Lower Level: 610 square feet
Total: 2,441 square feet

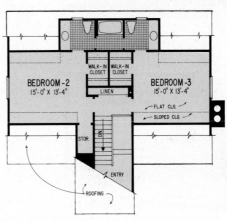

● This wonderfully compact plan incorporates a split-bedroom configuration with separate formal and informal living areas. Be sure to appreciate the full-width wood deck, complemented by a window greenhouse in the breakfast room. Each of the three bedrooms has a walk-in closet; the master suite has deck access through sliding glass doors.

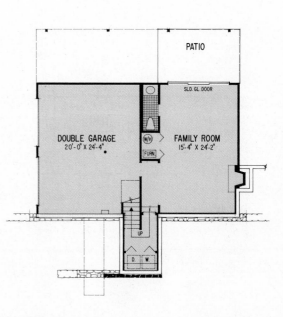

PATIO

FAMILY ROOM
27'-0"x13'-2"

GL. SLD. DR.

SHOP & STOR.
22'-8"x13'-2"

W/H · HVAC

FUTURE

UP

BEDROOM-3
11'-8"x 13'-6"

CLOSET

BEDROOM-2
13'-0"x 11'-10"

MASTER BEDROOM
15'-4"x 15'-4"

DECK

CLOSET   CLOSET

LINEN

BEDROOM-4
11'-8"x 11'-2"

BRIDGE

DOWN

CLOSET

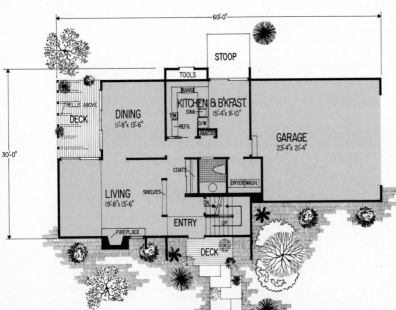

60'-0"

30'-0"

STOOP

TOOLS

RANGE

KITCHEN & B'KFAST.
15'-4"x 9'-10"

SINK

D/W

REFG.

PANTRY

TRELLIS ABOVE

DECK

DINING
11'-8"x 13'-6"

T/W

GARAGE
23'-4"x 21'-4"

COATS

SHELVES

DN

DRYER WASH.

LIVING
19'-8"x 13'-6"

FIREPLACE

ENTRY

UP

DECK

L
LIFESTYLE
HOME PLANS

Design V34149

Entry Level: 910 square feet
Upper Level: 1,104 square feet
Lower Level: 392 square feet
Total: 2,406 square feet

● The exciting exterior lines of this arresting plan contain three levels of contemporary living. At entry level are gathering and working areas with a wood deck to complement the living and dining rooms. Four bedrooms are found on the upper level. The master bedroom has a large closet and private deck. On the lower level is room for casual living and a shop and storage area. There is potential space for a full bath as well.

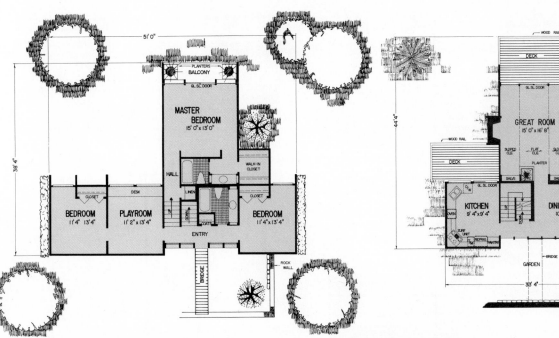

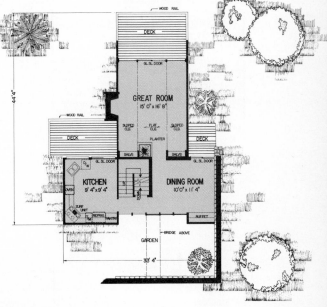

Design V34106

Upper Level: 1,019 square feet
Lower Level: 735 square feet
Total: 1,754 square feet

● A wooden footbridge over a sheltered garden highlights the exterior of this striking contemporary. Inside, split-level planning separates living and sleeping areas. The lower level includes a formal dining room, a spacious great room, and three decks. The upper level features the master bedroom, two other bedrooms, and a playroom. Notice the private balcony off the master bedroom.

BEDROOM-4
13'-0"x11'-8"

BEDROOM-2
15'-0"x11'-8"

DRESS. DRESS.

CLOSET CLOSET

ATTIC STAIR

WASH DRY

LIN. LIN.

CLOSET

BEDROOM-5
13'-0"x11'-0"

BEDROOM-3
15'-0"x11'-0"

CLOSET

DOWN

UPPER ENTRY

SECOND FLOOR

DECK

WINDOW GREENHOUSE

PANTRY

BREAKFAST
9'-0"x8'-0"

SLD. GL. DR.

SLD. GL. DR.

STORAGE STORAGE

MASTER BEDROOM
13'-0"x14'-0"

KITCHEN
10'-8"x10'-0"

REFRIG. W. SINK RANGE

DINING

GARAGE
21'-8"x21'-4"

GREAT ROOM
15'-0"x25'-4"

LIVING

WALK-IN CLOSET

LINEN

TOWEL

DOWN

UP DN

GARAGE DOOR

POWDER

SHOWER

COATS

ENTRY

PORCH

STONE WALL

42'-0"

62'-0"

LIFESTYLE HOME PLANS

Design V34250

Main Level: 1,188 square feet
Upper Level: 1,084 square feet
Lower Level: 777 square feet
Total: 3,049 square feet

D

1/2 BATH

SLD. GL. DR.

RECREATION ROOM
23'-6"x17'-4"

CRAWL SPACE

ICE MAKER

SINK

BAR

STORAGE

BAR

CLOSET

GLASS SHELVES

W.H.

FURN.

CLOSET

UP

UP

● This spacious contemporary will be great for large families. A sizable great room accommodates living and dining areas. Also on this level are the kitchen with breakfast room and the master suite. An enormous recreation room with a wet bar provides additional living space. The upper level contains four bedrooms and two baths.

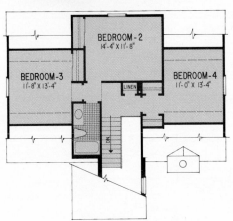

Design V34254

Main Level: 1,160 square feet
Upper Level: 715 square feet
Lower Level: 614 square feet
Total: 2,489 square feet

● Unique siding and masonry work make this hillside home a showplace. Inside there's plenty of living space in the lower-level family room and main-level great room. The kitchen with breakfast area is conveniently adjacent to the great room. The split sleeping area thoughtfully places the master bedroom on the main level and the remaining three bedrooms on the upper level for utmost peace and quiet.

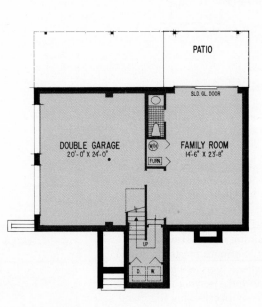

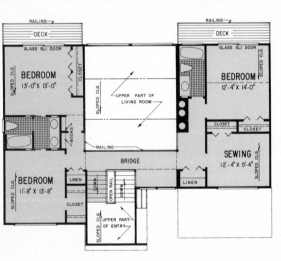

LIFESTYLE HOME PLANS

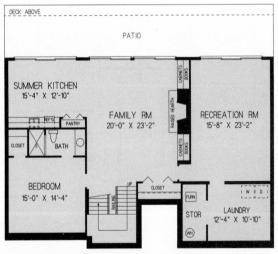

Floor plan labels (upper level):

RAILING — DECK — GLASS SLI. DOOR

BEDROOM 13'-0" X 13'-0" — SLOPED CLG. — CLOSET

UPPER PART OF LIVING ROOM

SLOPED CLG.

BEDROOM 12'-4" X 14'-0" — SLOPED CLG. — GLASS SLI. DOOR — DECK — RAILING

BOOKS — RAILING — CLOSET — CLOSET

BRIDGE

BEDROOM 11'-8" X 13'-8" — SLOPED CLG. — LINEN — LINEN — SEWING 12'-4" X 9'-4" — SLOPED CLG.

DOWN — OPEN RAIL — DOWN — CLOSET

UPPER PART OF ENTRY — SLOPED CLG.

Floor plan labels (lower level):

DECK ABOVE — PATIO

SUMMER KITCHEN 15'-4" X 12'-10" — CABINETS — BOOKS

FAMILY RM. 20'-0" X 23'-2" — RAISED HEARTH — RECREATION RM. 15'-8" X 23'-2"

CLOSET — REF'G. — PANTRY — BATH — CABINETS — BOOKS

BEDROOM 15'-0" X 14'-4" — UP — RAILING — CLOSET — FURN. — STOR. — W D — LAUNDRY 12'-4" X 10'-10" — WH

Design V34141

Main Level: 1,809 square feet
Upper Level: 1,293 square feet
Lower Level: 1,828 square feet
Total: 4,930 square feet

● A spacious two-story living room is the centerpiece of this plan with its large fireplace and access to the rear deck. Next door is the kitchen and breakfast room and adjacent formal dining room. Also on this level, an enormous master bedroom with fireplace. Upstairs are three bedrooms and a sewing room linked by a balcony overlooking the living room.

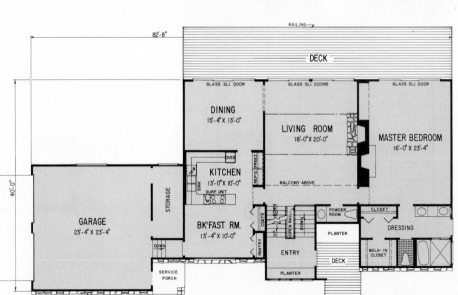

Floor plan labels (main level):

82'-8" — RAILING — DECK

GLASS SLI. DOOR — GLASS SLI. DOORS — GLASS SLI. DOOR

DINING 15'-4" X 13'-0" — LIVING ROOM 18'-0" X 20'-0" — MASTER BEDROOM 16'-0" X 23'-4"

OVEN — KITCHEN 13'-0" X 10'-0" — SINK — SURF. UNIT — REFG. — FREEZ. — BALCONY ABOVE

40'-0" — GARAGE 23'-4" X 23'-4" — STORAGE

BK'FAST RM. 13'-4" X 10'-0" — PANTRY — COATS — UP — OPEN RAIL — DOWN — POWDER ROOM — CLOSET — DRESSING

DOWN — ENTRY — PLANTER — DECK — PLANTER — WALK-IN CLOSET

SERVICE PORCH

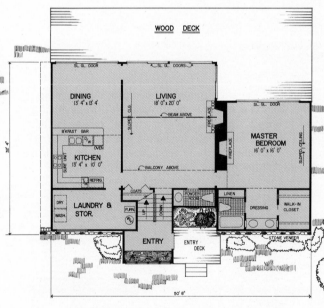

WOOD DECK

DINING
13' 4" x 13' 4"

LIVING
18' 0" x 20' 0"

B'KFAST BAR

KITCHEN
13' 4" x 10' 0"

MASTER
BEDROOM
16' 0" x 16' 0"

SLOPED CEILING

BEAM ABOVE

BALCONY ABOVE

SL. GL. DOOR

SL. GL. DOORS

LAUNDRY &
STOR.

DRY
WASH.

FURN.

COATS

UP
DOWN

POWDER
ROOM

LINEN

DRESSING

WALK-IN
CLOSET

ENTRY

ENTRY
DECK

STONE VENEER

50' 8"

32' 4"

Design V34115

Main Level: 1,494 square feet
Upper Level: 597 square feet
Total: 2,091 square feet

LIFESTYLE
HOME PLANS

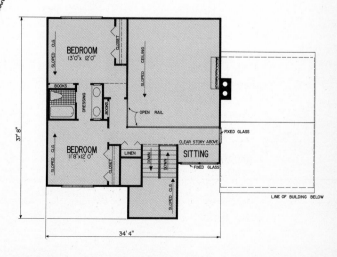

BEDROOM
13' 0" x 12' 0"

BEDROOM
11' 8" x 12' 0"

SITTING

SLOPED CEILING

SLOPED CLG.

SLOPED CLG.

SLOPED CLG.

CLOSET

CLOSET

BOOKS

DRESSING

LINEN

BOOKS

DOWN
DOWN

OPEN RAIL

CLEAR STORY ABOVE

FIXED GLASS

FIXED GLASS

LINE OF BUILDING BELOW

37' 8"

34' 4"

● Here is a home that's moderately sized without sacrificing livability. Just off the entry is a large, two-story living room. There's also a dining room with a breakfast bar/pass-through to the kitchen. To the rear is an enormous deck for sunning and relaxing. A split-sleeping area features two upper-level bedrooms and a main-level master bedroom. Notice the fireplace and sloped ceilings.

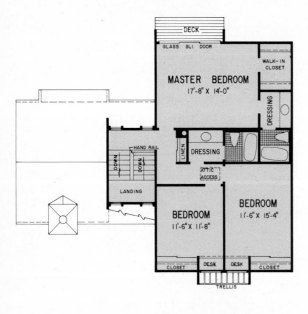

Design V34139

Main Level: 862 square feet
Upper Level: 920 square feet
Total: 1,782 square feet

D

● This home benefits from open, comfortable planning. Off the entry is a spacious great room with fireplace and access to a deck. Down a few steps is the country kitchen. There's enough room here for both a dining area and sitting area. Upstairs are three good-sized bedrooms and two baths. Notice the private deck off the master bedroom.

LIFESTYLE HOME PLANS

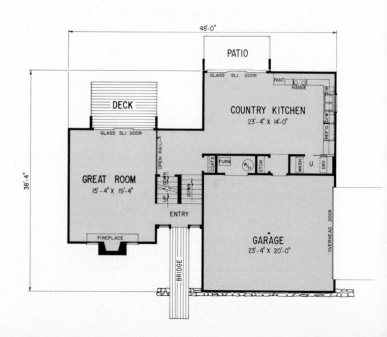

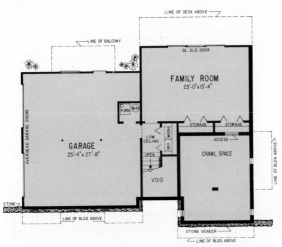

FAMILY ROOM
23'-0"x15'-4"

GARAGE
25'-4" x 27'-8"

CRAWL SPACE

VOID

● This home lives like a one-story but has the bonus space of a lower-level family room. This arrangement will help keep noise and activity contained. The main level features the primary living and working areas: raised great room with fireplace, formal dining room and kitchen with breakfast room. Up a few steps is the three-bedroom sleeping area.

Design V34189
Main Level: 1,779 square feet
Lower Level: 471 square feet
Total: 2,250 square feet

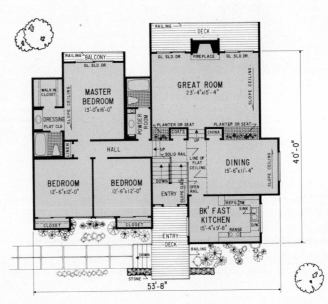

DECK

MASTER BEDROOM
13'-0"x16'-0"

GREAT ROOM
23'-4"x15'-4"

FIREPLACE

BEDROOM
12'-6"x12'-0"

BEDROOM
12'-6"x12'-0"

HALL

ENTRY

DINING
15'-6"x11'-4"

BK'FAST KITCHEN
15'-4"x9'-8"

ENTRY DECK

40'-0"

53'-8"

LIFESTYLE
HOME PLANS

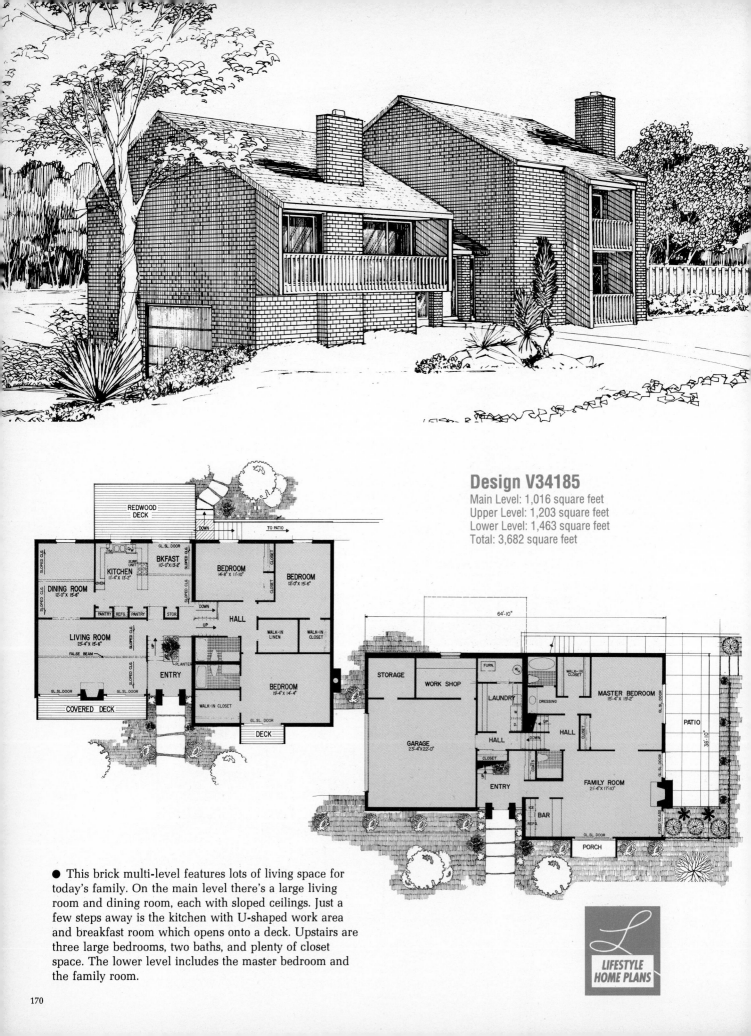

Design V34185

Main Level: 1,016 square feet
Upper Level: 1,203 square feet
Lower Level: 1,463 square feet
Total: 3,682 square feet

REDWOOD DECK

DOWN

TO PATIO

GL. SL. DOOR

BKFAST
10'-0" X 13'-2"

KITCHEN
11'-4" X 13'-2"

OVEN

SURF. UNIT

SLOPED CLG.

BEDROOM
14'-8" X 11'-10"

CLOSET

BEDROOM
12'-0" X 15'-6"

CLOSET

DINING ROOM
12'-0" X 15'-6"

SLOPED CLG.

PANTRY REFS. PANTRY STOR.

DOWN

UP

HALL

WALK-IN LINEN

WALK-IN CLOSET

LIVING ROOM
23'-4" X 15'-6"

SLOPED CLG.

FALSE BEAM

ENTRY

PLANTER

UP

BEDROOM
15'-4" X 14'-4"

GL. SL. DOOR

GL. SL. DOOR

COVERED DECK

WALK-IN CLOSET

GL. SL. DOOR

DECK

64'-10"

STORAGE

WORK SHOP

FURN.

W.H.

WALK-IN CLOSET

LAUNDRY

DRESSING

W

D

UP

MASTER BEDROOM
15'-4" X 19'-2"

GL. SL. DOOR

GARAGE
23'-4" X 22'-0"

HALL

DOWN

HALL

CLOSET

PATIO

36'-10"

CLOSET

ENTRY

COATS

FAMILY ROOM
21'-4" X 17'-10"

ICE

BAR

REF.

GL. SL. DOOR

PORCH

● This brick multi-level features lots of living space for
today's family. On the main level there's a large living
room and dining room, each with sloped ceilings. Just a
few steps away is the kitchen with U-shaped work area
and breakfast room which opens onto a deck. Upstairs are
three large bedrooms, two baths, and plenty of closet
space. The lower level includes the master bedroom and
the family room.

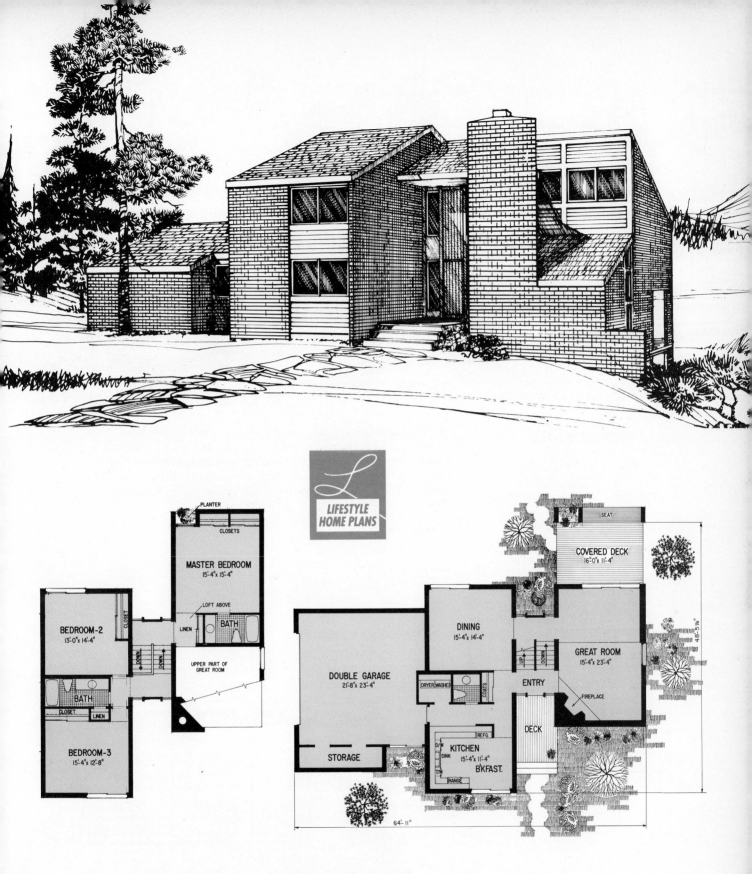

PLANTER

CLOSETS

MASTER BEDROOM
15'-4" x 15'-4"

LOFT ABOVE

LINEN   BATH

UPPER PART OF
GREAT ROOM

CLOSET

BEDROOM-2
13'-0" x 14'-4"

DOWN   DOWN

BATH

CLOSET   LINEN

BEDROOM-3
15'-4" x 12'-8"

L
LIFESTYLE
HOME PLANS

SEAT

COVERED DECK
16'-0" x 11'-4"

48'-5½"

DINING
15'-4" x 14'-4"

GREAT ROOM
15'-4" x 23'-4"

DOUBLE GARAGE
21'-8" x 23'-4"

UP   DOWN

DRYER WASHER   COATS

ENTRY

FIREPLACE

REFG.

DECK

D/W
SINK   KITCHEN
15'-4" x 11'-4"
B'KFAST.

RANGE

STORAGE

64'-11"

Design V34180

Main Level: 1,138 square feet
Upper Level: 1,130 square feet
Total: 2,268 square feet

● The highlight of this plan is the spaciousness of its rooms —
each one is larger than average. The main level features a great
room with corner fireplace and adjacent covered deck. There's
also a formal dining room and kitchen with breakfast area. One
level up is the master bedroom and bath. Two more bedrooms
and a shared bath are upstairs for utmost peace and quiet.

Design V34102

Main Level: 1,237 square feet
Upper Level: 982 square feet
Total: 2,219 square feet

● Varying rooflines create an attractive exterior for this home. Inside, the well-planned interior includes a two-story living room, formal dining room and kitchen with breakfast area. Also found on this level, the master bedroom opens onto the rear terrace. Three more bedrooms are upstairs as well as a balcony family room overlooking the living room.

LIFESTYLE HOME PLANS

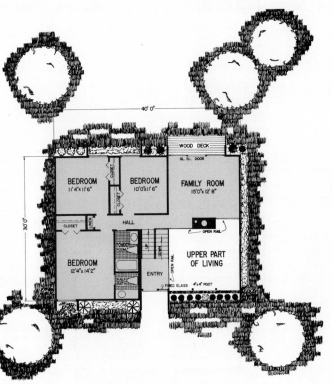

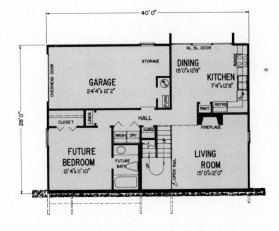

Design V34099

Upper Level: 947 square feet
Main Level: 486 square feet
Future Bedroom: 256 square feet
Total: 1,689 square feet

● The rectangular shape of this contemporary makes it economical to build, without skimping on living space. The main level features a living room with fireplace and a kitchen with dining area. Also on this level is space for a bedroom and bath that may be finished later. Three more bedrooms and a family room are found on the upper level.

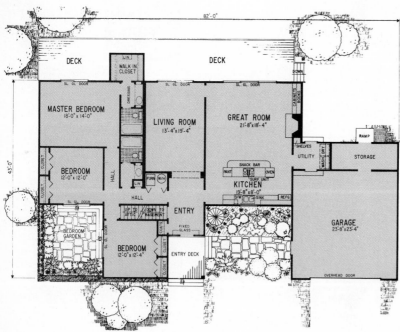

Design V34192

Main Level: 1,990 square feet
Lower Level: 1,185 square feet
Total: 3,175 square feet

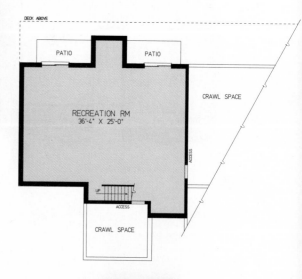

● This ground-hugging contemporary boasts a surprisingly spacious interior. The plan has room for every occasion with both a living room and great room. Separated from the great room by a snack bar pass-through is the large galley kitchen. A three-bedroom sleeping area complete with private patio garden rounds out the plan.

LIFESTYLE
HOME PLANS

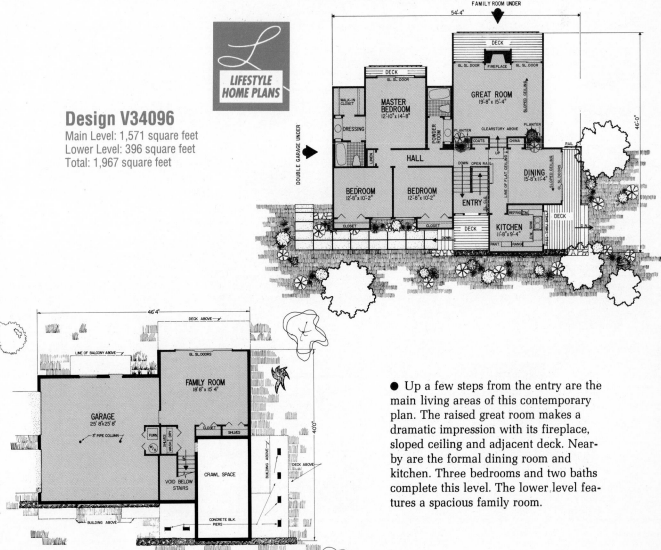

Design V34096

Main Level: 1,571 square feet
Lower Level: 396 square feet
Total: 1,967 square feet

LIFESTYLE HOME PLANS

● Up a few steps from the entry are the main living areas of this contemporary plan. The raised great room makes a dramatic impression with its fireplace, sloped ceiling and adjacent deck. Nearby are the formal dining room and kitchen. Three bedrooms and two baths complete this level. The lower level features a spacious family room.

Design V34188

Main Level: 1,293 square feet
Upper Level: 1,094 square feet
Total: 2,387 square feet

L **D**

● A handsome wood and glass exterior makes this home a showplace. A well-planned interior places the living room, dining room, kitchen with breakfast area and the master bedroom on the main level. The upper level houses three bedrooms, 1½ baths and a family room overlooking the living room. Also notice the access to terraces from the main level.

L LIFESTYLE HOME PLANS

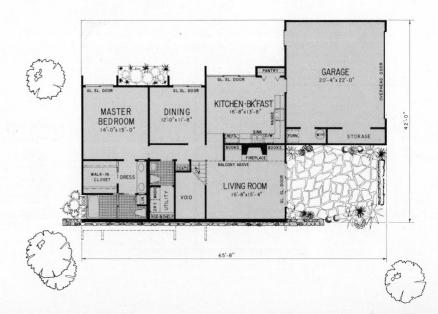

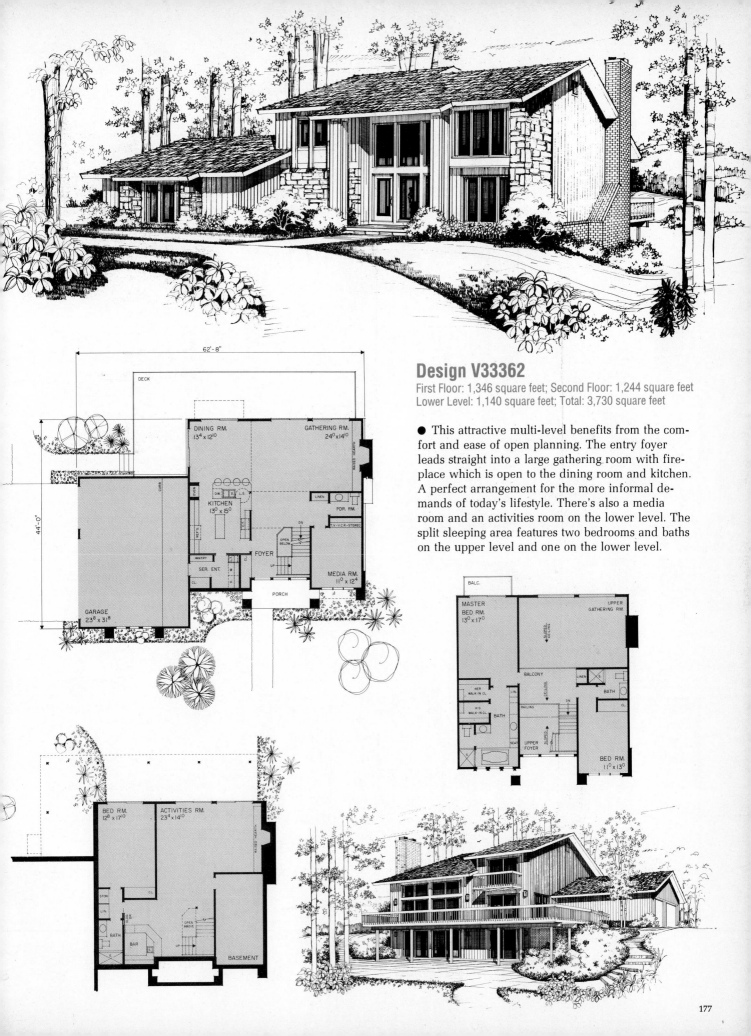

Design V33362

First Floor: 1,346 square feet; Second Floor: 1,244 square feet
Lower Level: 1,140 square feet; Total: 3,730 square feet

● This attractive multi-level benefits from the comfort and ease of open planning. The entry foyer leads straight into a large gathering room with fireplace which is open to the dining room and kitchen. A perfect arrangement for the more informal demands of today's lifestyle. There's also a media room and an activities room on the lower level. The split sleeping area features two bedrooms and baths on the upper level and one on the lower level.

Design V33361
Main Level: 3,548 square feet
Lower Level: 1,036 square feet
Total: 4,584 square feet

● Here's a dandy hillside home that can easily accommodate the largest of families and is perfect for both formal and informal entertaining. Straight back from the entry foyer is a grand gathering room/dining room combination. It is complemented by the breakfast room and a front-facing media room. The sleeping wing contains three bedrooms and two full baths. On the lower level is an activities room with summer kitchen and a fourth bedroom that makes the perfect guest room.

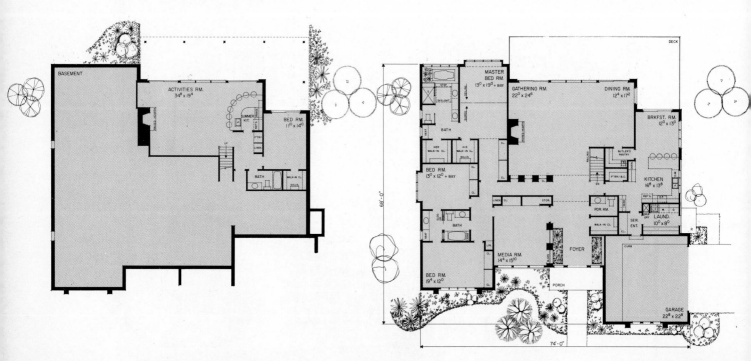

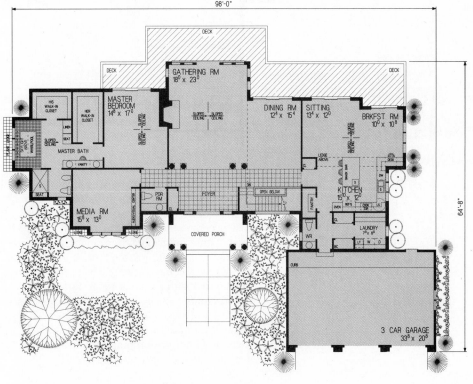

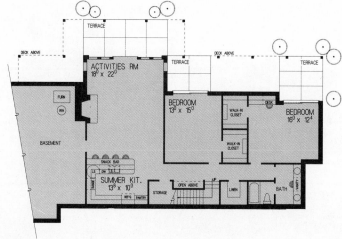

Design V33311

First Floor: 2,662 square feet
Second Floor: 1,548 square feet
Total: 4,210 square feet

● Here's a hillside haven for family living with plenty of room to entertain in style. Enter the main level from a dramatic columned portico that leads to a large entry hall. The gathering room is straight back and adjoins a formal dining area. A true gourmet kitchen with plenty of room for casual eating and conversation is nearby. The abundantly appointed master suite on this level is complemented by a luxurious bath. Note the media room to the front of the house. On the lower level are two more bedrooms, a full bath, a large activity area with fireplace and a convenient summer kitchen.

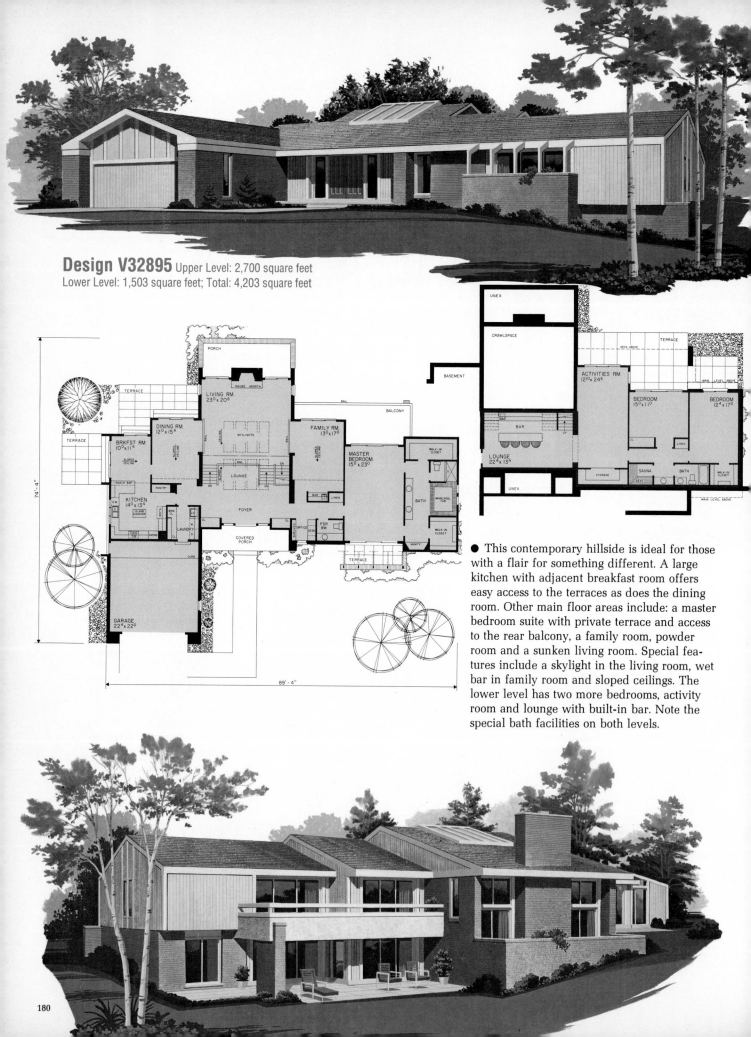

Design V32895 Upper Level: 2,700 square feet
Lower Level: 1,503 square feet; Total: 4,203 square feet

● This contemporary hillside is ideal for those with a flair for something different. A large kitchen with adjacent breakfast room offers easy access to the terraces as does the dining room. Other main floor areas include: a master bedroom suite with private terrace and access to the rear balcony, a family room, powder room and a sunken living room. Special features include a skylight in the living room, wet bar in family room and sloped ceilings. The lower level has two more bedrooms, activity room and lounge with built-in bar. Note the special bath facilities on both levels.

Design V32896

Upper Level: 1,856 square feet; **Lower Level:** 1,454 square feet; **Total:** 3,310 square feet

● This design is very inviting with its contemporary appeal. A large kitchen with an adjacent snack bar makes light meals a breeze. The adjoining breakfast room offers a scenic view through sliding glass doors. Notice the sloped ceiling in the dining and gathering rooms. A fireplace in the gathering room adds a cozy air. An interesting feature is the master bedroom's easy access to the study. Also, take note of the sliding doors in the master bedroom which lead to a private balcony. On the lower level, a large activities room will be a frequently used spot by family members. The fireplace and wet bar add a nice touch for entertaining friends. Also, notice the sliding glass doors which lead to the terrace. Take note of the two or optional three bedrooms - the choice is yours.

Design V32552 Main Level: 1,437 square feet; Upper Level: 1,158 square feet; Lower Level: 1,056 square feet; Total: 3,651 square feet

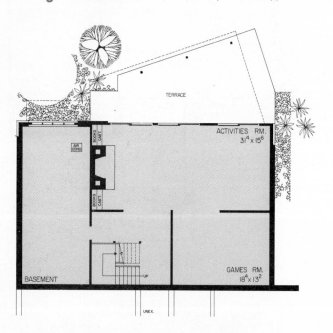

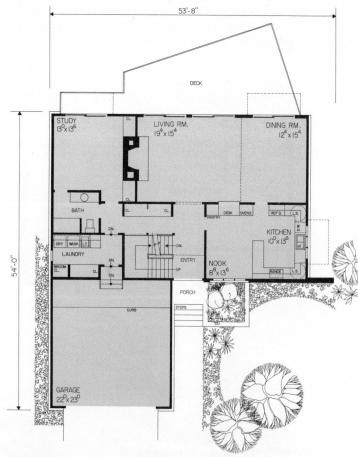

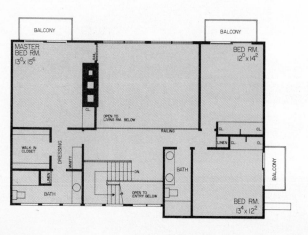

● Whatever you call this design - a hillside home or a two-story with an exposed basement - it will deliver an abundance of family livability. Study the three levels carefully. Notice how the upper level hall and master bedroom look down into the living room. Observe the study with access to a full bath.

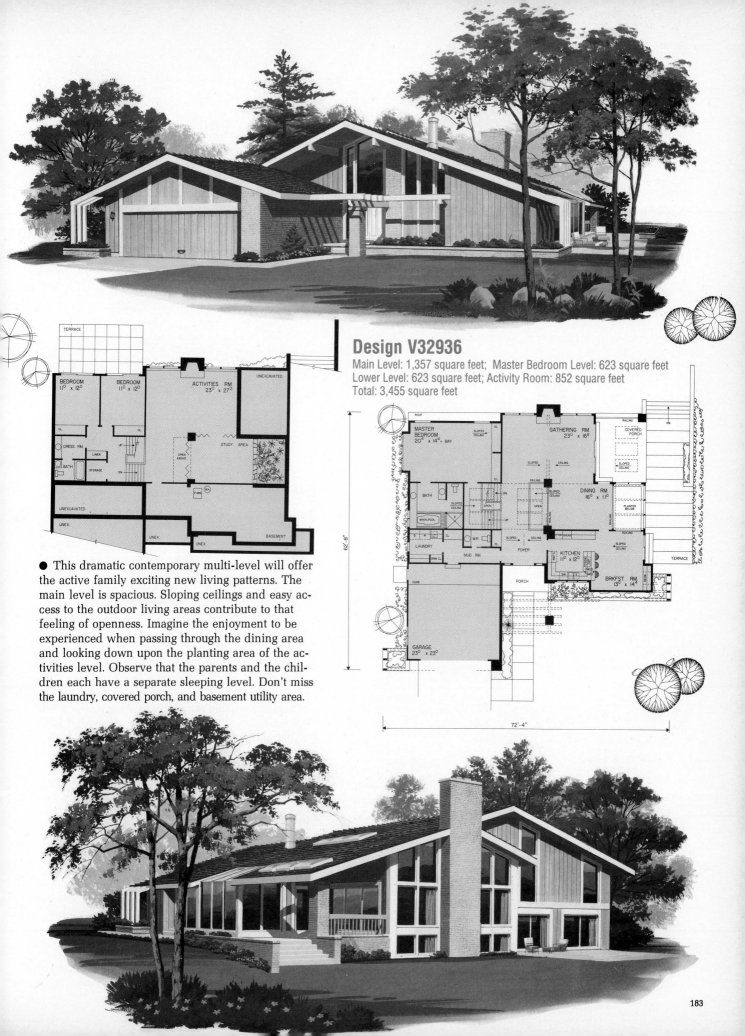

Design V32936

Main Level: 1,357 square feet; **Master Bedroom Level:** 623 square feet
Lower Level: 623 square feet; **Activity Room:** 852 square feet
Total: 3,455 square feet

● This dramatic contemporary multi-level will offer the active family exciting new living patterns. The main level is spacious. Sloping ceilings and easy access to the outdoor living areas contribute to that feeling of openness. Imagine the enjoyment to be experienced when passing through the dining area and looking down upon the planting area of the activities level. Observe that the parents and the children each have a separate sleeping level. Don't miss the laundry, covered porch, and basement utility area.

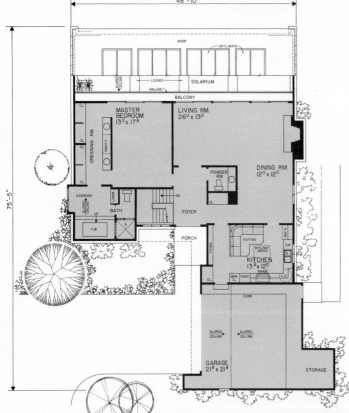

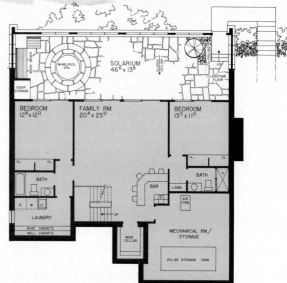

Design V32835 Upper Level: 1,626 square feet
Lower Level: 2,038 square feet; Total: 3,664 square feet

● Passive solar techniques with the help of an active solar component - they can work together or the active solar component can act as a back-up system - heat and cool this striking contemporary design. The lower level solarium is the primary passive element. It admits sunlight during the day for direct-gain heating. The warmth, which was absorbed into the thermal floor, is then radiated into the structure at night. The earth berms on the three sides of the lower level help keep out the winter cold and summer heat. The active system uses collector panels to gather the sun's heat. The heat is transferred via a water pipe system to the lower level storage tank where it is circulated throughout the house by a heat exchanger. Note that where active solar collectors are a design OPTION, which they are in all of our active/passive designs, they must be contracted locally. The collector area must be tailored to the climate and sun angles that characterize your building location.

Design V32937 Main Level: 1,096 square feet
Lower Level: 1,104 square feet; Upper Level: 1,115 square feet; Total: 3,315 square feet

L

● This contemporary multi-level home features an extended rear balcony that covers a rear patio, plus a master bedroom suite, complete with whirlpool and raised-hearth pass-thru. Two other bedrooms and a second bath are on the upper level.

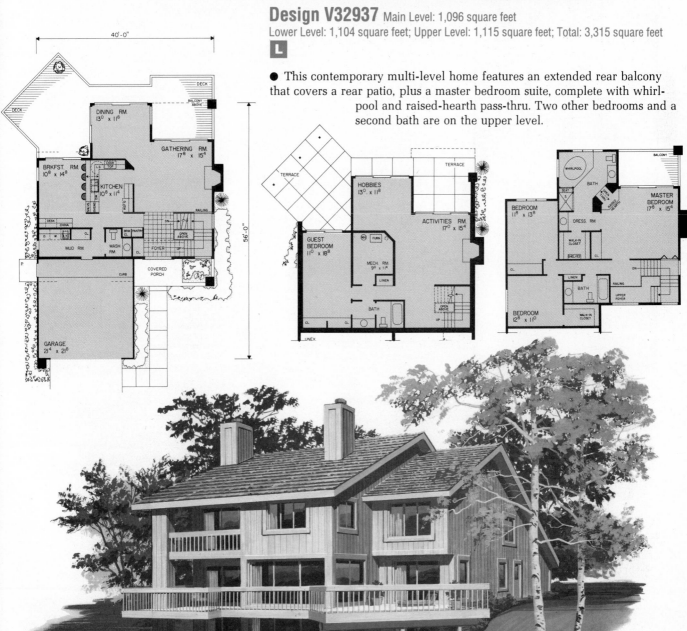

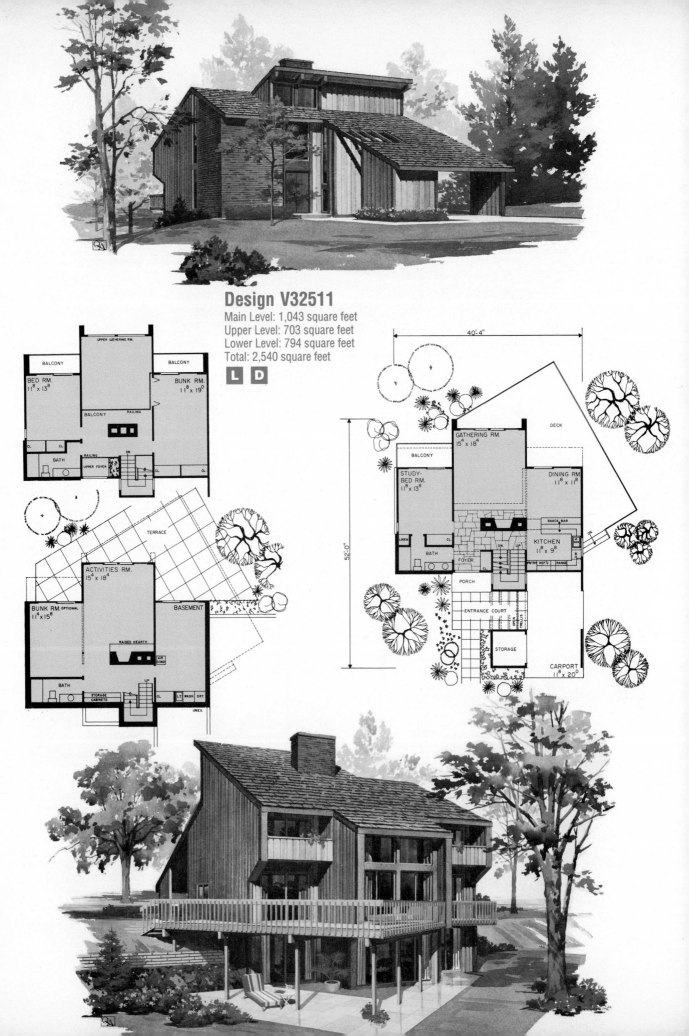

Design V32511

Main Level: 1,043 square feet
Upper Level: 703 square feet
Lower Level: 794 square feet
Total: 2,540 square feet

L **D**

Design V32716 Main Level: 1,013 square feet
Upper Level: 885 square feet; Lower Level: 1,074 square feet; Total: 2,972 square feet

L

● A genuine master suite! It overlooks the gathering room through shut-
tered windows and includes a private balcony. A 9' x 9' sitting/dressing
room and a full bath. There's more, a two-story gathering room with a
raised hearth fireplace, sloped ceiling and sliding glass doors onto the
main balcony. Plus, a family room and a study both having a fireplace.
A kitchen with lots of built-ins and a separate dining nook.

Design V32848 Main Level: 2,028 square feet; Lower Level: 1,122 square feet; Total: 3,150 square feet

● This contemporary design is characterized by the contrast in diagonal and vertical wood siding. The private front court adjacent to the covered porch is a nice area for evening relaxation and creates an impressive entry. Once inside the house, the livability begins to unfold. Three bedrooms are arranged to one side of the entry with two baths sharing back-to-back plumbing. The master bedroom has a balcony. A view of the front court will be enjoyed from the kitchen and breakfast room. Along with the breakfast room, both the formal dining room and the screened porch will have easy access to the kitchen. A formal living room will be enjoyed on many occasions. It is detailed by a sloped ceiling and the warmth of a fireplace. A fourth bedroom is on the lower level. This level is opened to the outdoors by three sets of sliding glass doors. A second fireplace, this one with a raised hearth, is in the family room. A full bath and two work rooms also are located on the lower level.

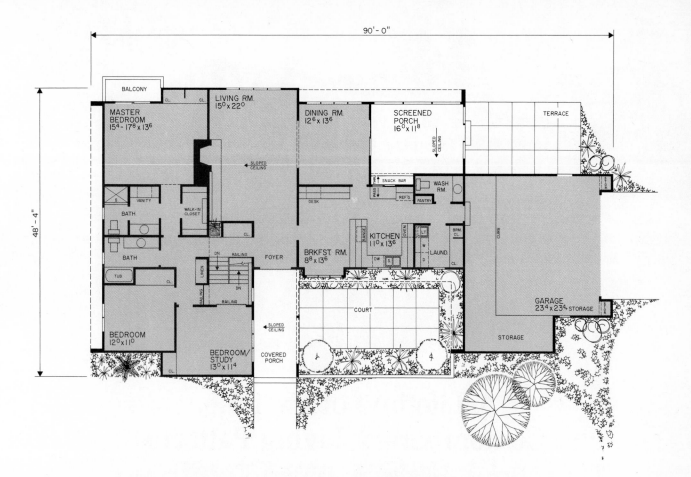

90'- 0"

48'- 4"

BALCONY

MASTER BEDROOM
15⁴- 17⁸ x 13⁶

LIVING RM.
15⁰ x 22⁰

DINING RM.
12⁶ x 13⁶

SCREENED PORCH
16⁰ x 11⁸

TERRACE

SLOPED CEILING

CL.   CL.

SLOPED CEILING

SNACK BAR

WASH RM.

PASS THRU

REF'G   PANTRY

BATH

VANITY

WALK-IN CLOSET

DESK

KITCHEN
11⁰ x 13⁶

RANGE   OVEN   LT

BRM. CL.

BATH

CL.

FOYER

BRKFST. RM.
8⁸ x 13⁶

DW   S.   W   LAUND.   D

CURB

GARAGE
23⁴ x 23⁴   STORAGE

TUB

CL.

DN   RAILING

LINEN

DN

RAILING   RAILING

STORAGE

BEDROOM
12⁰ x 11⁰

SLOPED CEILING

COURT

STORAGE

BEDROOM/ STUDY
13⁰ x 11⁴

CL.

COVERED PORCH

Contemporary Hillside Living

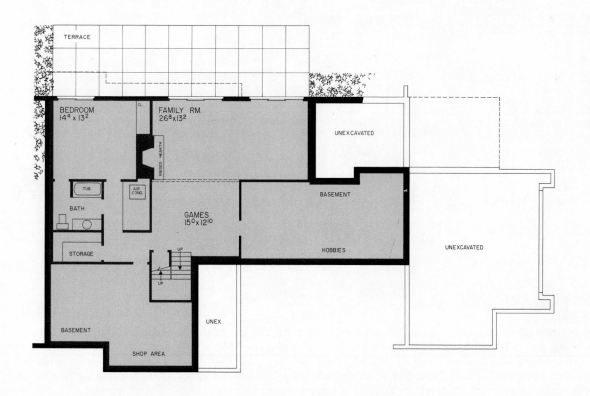

TERRACE

BEDROOM
14⁴ x 13²

CL.

FAMILY RM.
26⁸ x 13²

UNEXCAVATED

TUB

RAISED HEARTH

AIR COND.

BATH

BASEMENT

STORAGE

GAMES
15⁰ x 12¹⁰

UP

UP

HOBBIES

UNEXCAVATED

BASEMENT

UNEX.

SHOP AREA

A Lifetime of Exciting, Contemporary Living Patterns

● Here is a home for those with a bold, contemporary living bent. The exciting exteriors give notice of an admirable flair for something delightfully different. The varying roof planes and textured blank wall masses are distinctive. Two sets of panelled front doors permit access to either level. The inclined ramp to the upper main level is dramatic, indeed. The rear exterior highlights a veritable battery of projecting balconies. This affords direct access to outdoor living for each of the major rooms in the house. Certainly an invaluable feature should your view be particularly noteworthy. Notice two covered outdoor balconies plus a covered terrace. Indoor-outdoor living at its greatest.

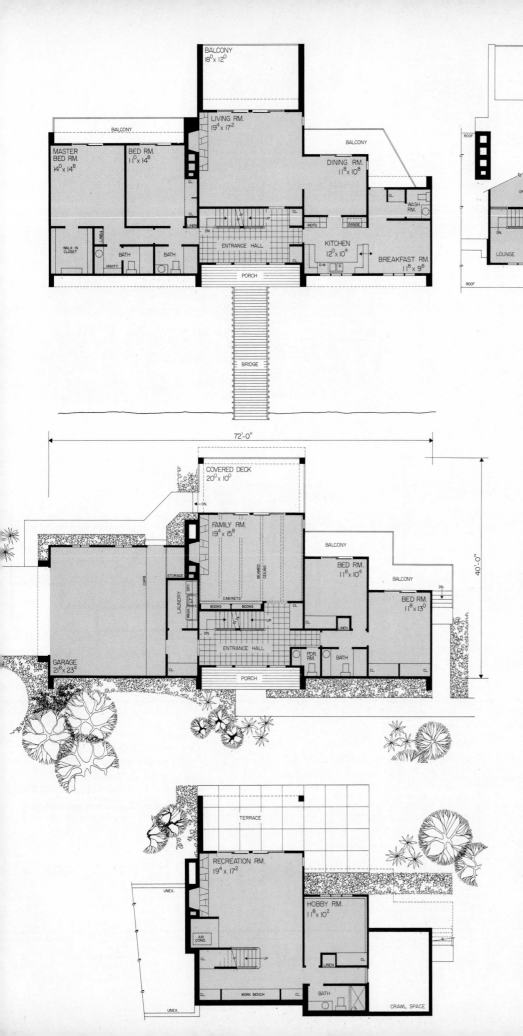

BALCONY
18⁰ x 12⁰

BALCONY

LIVING RM.
19⁴ x 17²

MASTER
BED RM.
14⁰ x 14⁸

BED RM.
11⁰ x 14⁸

BALCONY

DINING RM.
11⁸ x 10⁸

CL.

WASH
RM.

LINEN

CL.

REF'S

RANGE

KITCHEN
12⁰ x 10⁴

WALK IN
CLOSET

LINEN

BATH

BATH

ENTRANCE HALL

DN.   UP

CL.

D.W.

BREAKFAST RM.
11⁸ x 9⁶

VANITY

PORCH

STUDIO
11⁸ x 12⁸

ROOF

ROOF

ROOF

OPEN TO LIVING RM. BELOW

RAILING

DN.

CL.

LOUNGE

CL.

ROOF

ROOF

BRIDGE

72'-0"

COVERED DECK
20⁰ x 10⁰

DN.

FAMILY RM.
19⁴ x 15⁸

BALCONY

BED RM.
11⁸ x 10⁴

BALCONY

BED RM.
11⁸ x 13⁰

STORAGE

BEAMED CEILING

DN.

CL.

40'-0"

CURB

LAUNDRY

WASH DRY

CABINETS

BOOKS   BOOKS

CL.

LINEN

GARAGE
21⁸ x 23⁴

ENTRANCE HALL

DN.   UP

CL.

PDR.
RM.

BATH

CL.

PORCH

TERRACE

RECREATION RM.
19⁴ x 17²

UNEX.

HOBBY RM.
11⁸ x 10²

AIR.
COND.

UP

CL.   CL.   WORK BENCH   CL.   BATH   LINEN   CL.

UNEX.

CRAWL SPACE

Design V32392

Main Level: 1,691 square feet
Lower Entry Level: 1,127 square feet
Upper Level: 396 square feet
Lower Level: 844 square feet
Total: 4,050 square feet

● Try to imagine the manner in which you and your family will function in this four-level hillside design. Surely it will be an adventure in family living that will be hard to surpass. For instance, can you picture a family member painting or sewing in the upper level studio, while another is building models or developing pictures in the lower level hobby room? Or, can you visualize a group in quiet conversation in the living room, another lounging in the family room, while a third plays table tennis or pool in the recreation room? Be sure not to overlook the fireplace in each of these living areas. As for sleeping and bath facilities, your family will have plenty, four bedrooms and four baths, plus a powder room and a wash room. They also will enjoy the eating facilities with a breakfast room, a dining room and an outdoor balcony nearby. Then, too, there is the lounge of the upper level.

Design V32934
Main Level: 2,472 square feet; Lower Level: 2,145 square feet
Total: 4,617 square feet

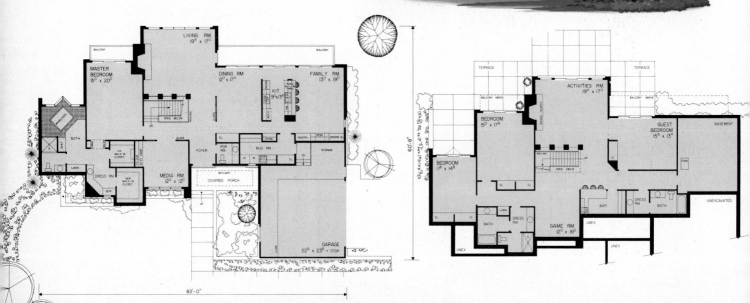

Design V32770
Main Level: 1,182 square feet
Upper Level: 998 square feet
Total: 2,180 square feet

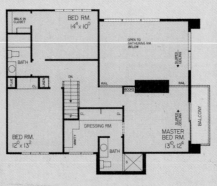

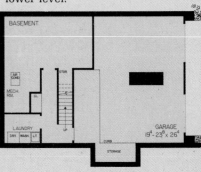

● If you are looking for a home with loads of livability, then consider these two-story contemporary homes which have an exposed lower level.

Design V32548
Main Level: 1,109 square feet; Upper Level: 739 square feet;
Lower Level: 869 square feet; Total: 2,717 square feet

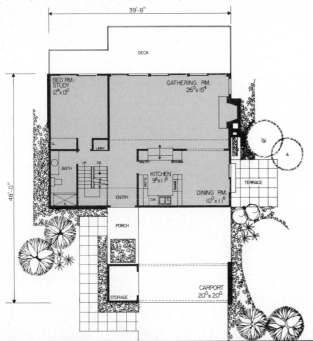

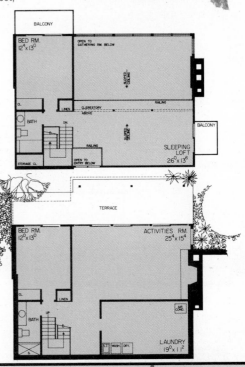

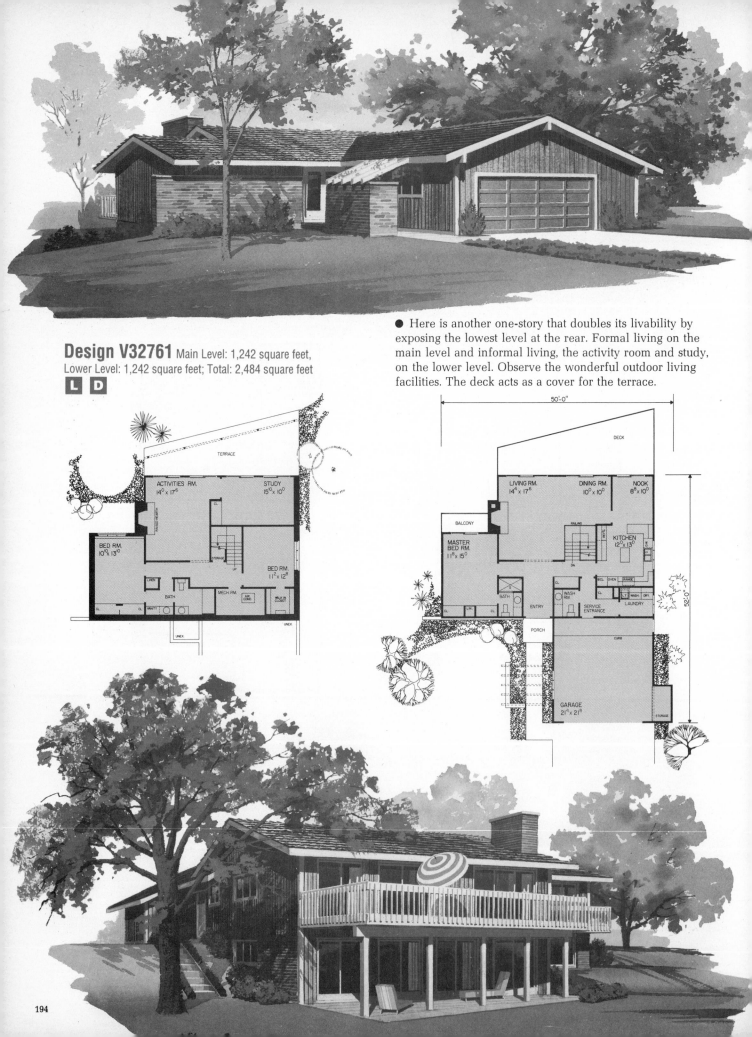

Design V32761 Main Level: 1,242 square feet,
Lower Level: 1,242 square feet; Total: 2,484 square feet

L **D**

● Here is another one-story that doubles its livability by exposing the lowest level at the rear. Formal living on the main level and informal living, the activity room and study, on the lower level. Observe the wonderful outdoor living facilities. The deck acts as a cover for the terrace.

TERRACE

ACTIVITIES RM.
14⁰ x 17⁶

STUDY
15⁰ x 10⁰

BED RM.
10⁰ x 13⁰

BED RM.
11² x 12⁸

STORAGE
UP

BATH

LINEN

VANITY

MECH. RM.

AIR COND.

WALK IN CLOSET

UNEX.

UNEX.

50'-0"

DECK

LIVING RM.
14⁴ x 17⁶

DINING RM.
10⁰ x 10⁰

NOOK
8⁸ x 10⁰

BALCONY

RAILING

KITCHEN
12⁰ x 13⁰

MASTER BED RM.
11⁸ x 15⁰

DN

BATH

ENTRY

CL.

OVEN RANGE

WASH RM.

SERVICE ENTRANCE

WASH. DRY.

LAUNDRY

52'-0"

PORCH

CURB

GARAGE
21⁴ x 21⁶

STORAGE

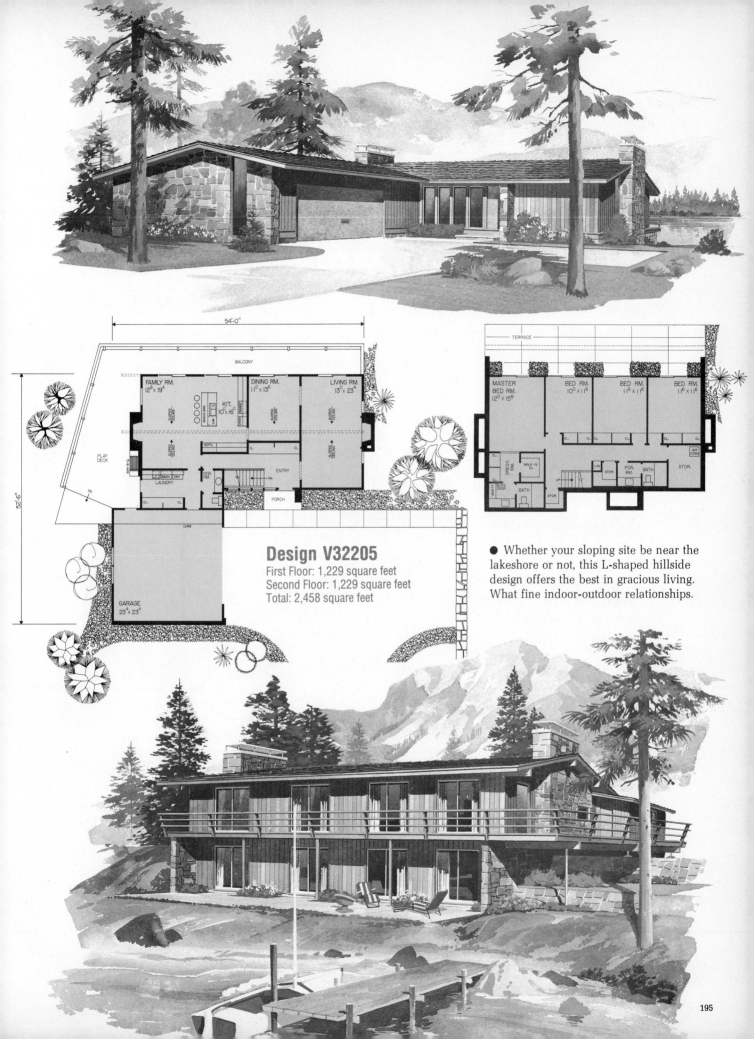

Design V32205

First Floor: 1,229 square feet
Second Floor: 1,229 square feet
Total: 2,458 square feet

● Whether your sloping site be near the lakeshore or not, this L-shaped hillside design offers the best in gracious living. What fine indoor-outdoor relationships.

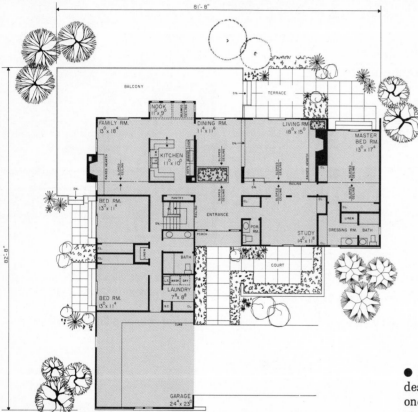

Design V32502
Main Level: 2,606 square feet
Lower Level: 1,243 square feet; Total: 3,849 square feet

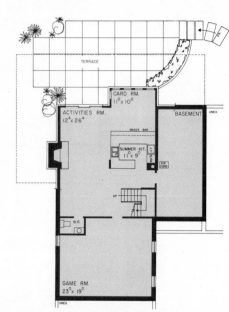

● A home with two faces. From the street this design gives all the appearances of being a one-story, L-shaped home. One can only guess at the character of the rear elevation as dictated by the sloping terrain. A study of the interior of this design reveals a tremendous convenient living potential.

Design V32504
Main Level: 1,918 square feet
Lower Level: 1,910 square feet; Total: 3,828 square feet

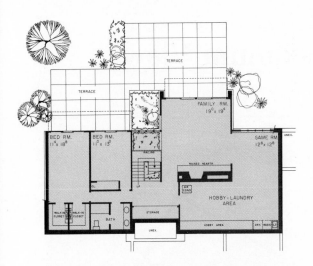

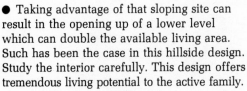

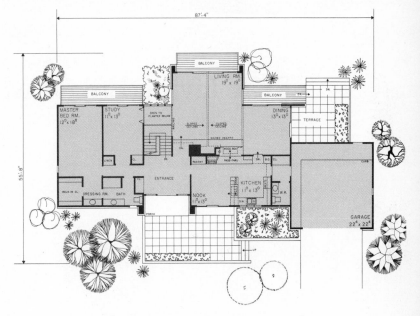

● Taking advantage of that sloping site can result in the opening up of a lower level which can double the available living area. Such has been the case in this hillside design. Study the interior carefully. This design offers tremendous living potential to the active family.

Rear Living Enjoys Maximum View

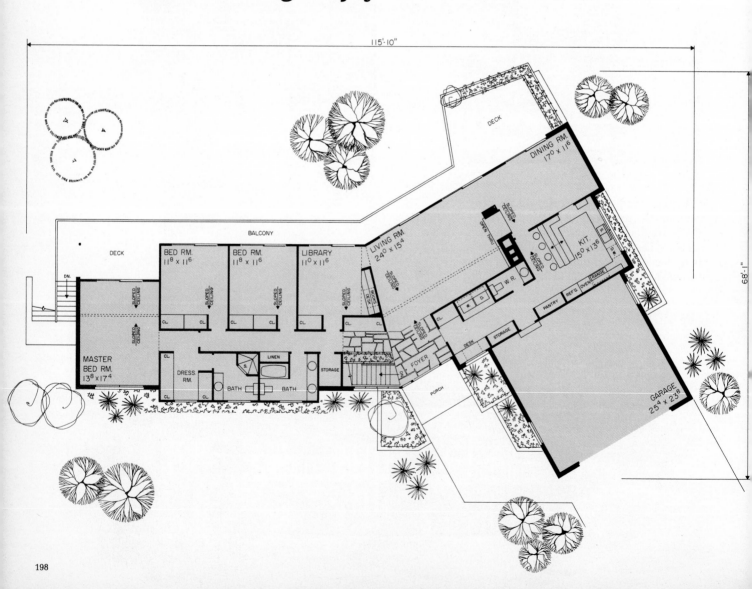

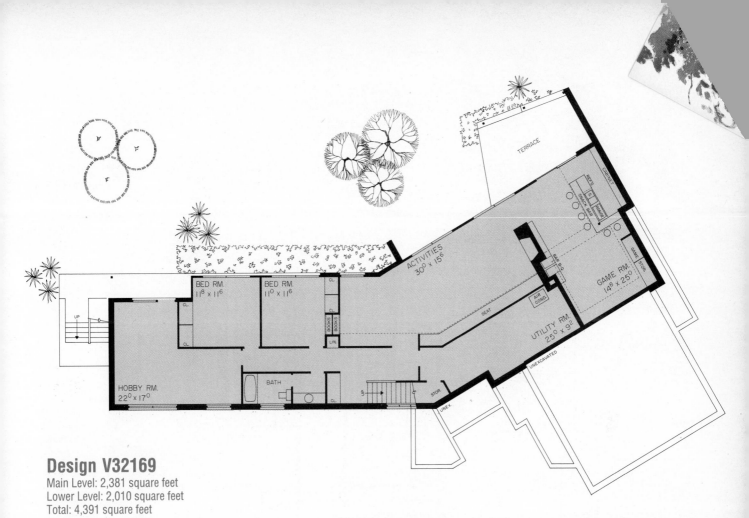

Design V32169

Main Level: 2,381 square feet
Lower Level: 2,010 square feet
Total: 4,391 square feet

● Behold, the view! If, when looking toward the rear of your site, nature's scene is breathtaking or in any way inspiring, you may wish to maximize your enjoyment by orienting your living areas to the rear of your plan. In addition to greater enjoyment of the landscape, such floor planning will provide extra privacy from the street. The angular configuration can enhance the enjoyment of a particular scene, plus it adds appeal to the exterior of the design. A study of both levels reveals that the major living areas look out upon the rear yard. Further, the upper level rooms have direct access to the decks and balcony. The kitchen with its large window over the sink is not without its view. With five bedrooms, plus a library, a game, activities and hobby room, the active family will have an abundance of space to enjoy individualized pursuits. Can't you envision your family living in this house?

This hillside home gives all the appearances of being a one-story ranch home; and what a delightful one at that! Should the contours of your property slope to the rear, this plan permits the exposing of the lower level. This results in the activities room and bedroom/study gaining direct access to outdoor living. Certainly a most desirable aspect for active, outdoor family living. The large and growing family will be admirably served with five bedrooms and three baths. An extra washroom and separate laundry add to the convenient living potential.

Design V32549

Main Level: 2,260 square feet
Lower Level: 1,406 square feet; Total: 3,666 square feet

Design V32213

Main Level: 1,671 square feet
Lower Level: 1,033 square feet; Total: 2,704 square feet

● Whether you locate this contemporary bi-level home on a sloping or flat site, it will certainly command its share of attention and provide the family with wonderful living patterns. The front entry is a separate level with stairs leading directly to the lower and the upper levels.

The most captivating feature of this home may very well be the spacious living and dining areas. An exposed beam is the apex of sloped ceilings. The projecting, glass-gabled end allows for a full measure of natural light. Two pairs of sliding glass doors open onto the balcony. The living balcony wraps around both front and rear to provide appealing planting areas. The kitchen is an efficient one in which to work, while the breakfast nook is but a step away. The sleeping zone has three bedrooms plus two full baths. Don't overlook the fireplace with its wood box.

Elegance And Grandeur On Two Levels

● The above illustrations of the front and rear views of this hillside contemporary design are impressive. And indeed rightly so! For the varied design features are so numerous and they are so delightfully incorporated under the wide overhanging roofs that the result is almost breathtaking at first glance. Consider the basic L-shape of the house and garage. Note how it lends itself to a large drive court. Observe the simplicity of the masses of brick and vertical character of the glass areas. Notice the inviting recessed double front doors. Around to the rear, the architectural interest is indeed extremely exciting. The glass areas are as dramatic as is the wood deck. The covered porch and the two covered terraces complete the facilities for gracious outdoor living fun.

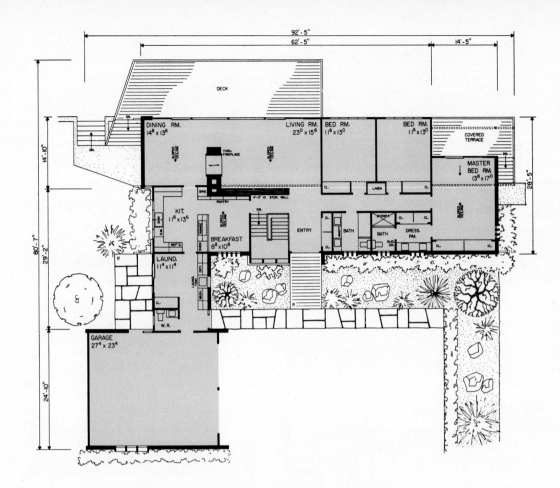

Design V31963 Main Level: 2,248 square feet; Lower Level: 1,948 square feet; Total: 4,196 square feet

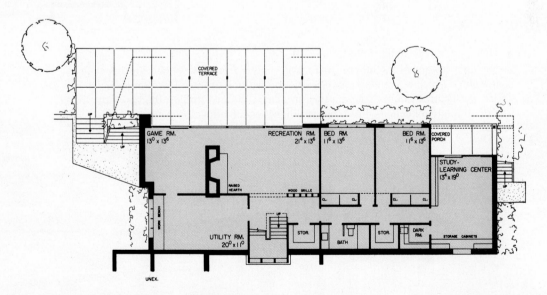

● Over four thousand square feet are available for use by the young, active family. And use them, they certainly will! There are five bedrooms to sleep a large active crew. The living areas are varied and numerous. In addition to the conventional formal living and dining rooms, there is a study/learning center. This is where all the mechanical paraphenalia like the tape recorder, film and slide projectors, phonograph, radio and television will be kept. A great way to keep all the equipment together. Note adjacent dark room. Then there is the recreation room with raised hearth fireplace. The game room will house the pool table, while the utility room will cater to the hobbyists. There are three full baths, plus an extra wash room and laundry adjacent to the kitchen.

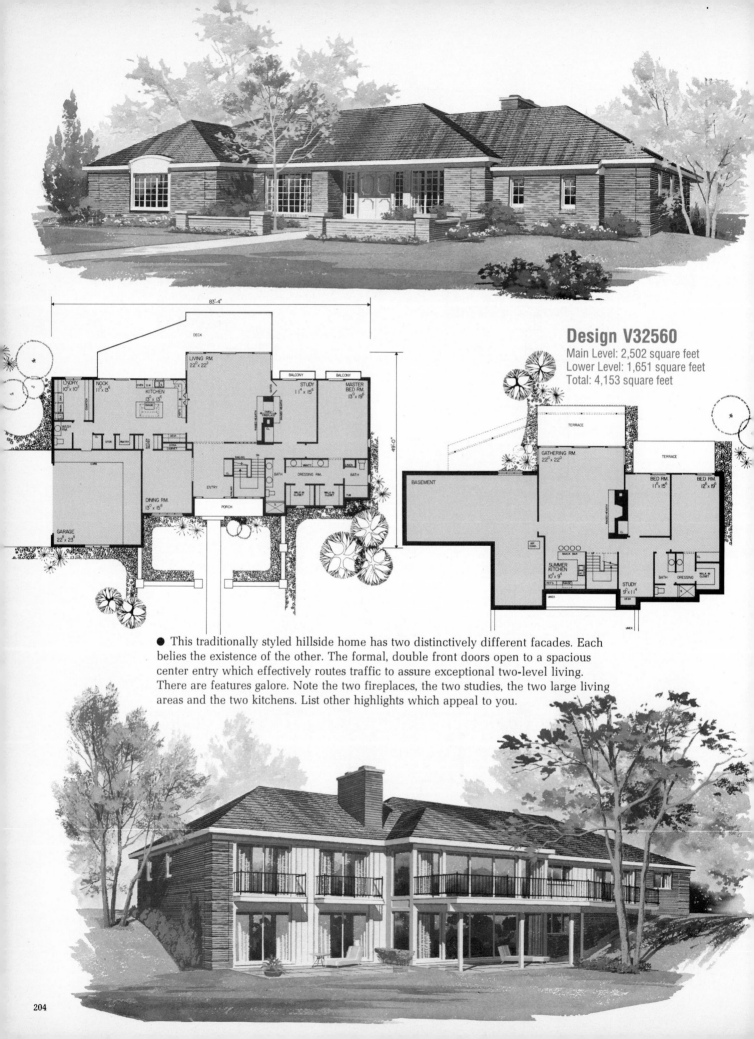

Design V32560

Main Level: 2,502 square feet
Lower Level: 1,651 square feet
Total: 4,153 square feet

● This traditionally styled hillside home has two distinctively different facades. Each belies the existence of the other. The formal, double front doors open to a spacious center entry which effectively routes traffic to assure exceptional two-level living. There are features galore. Note the two fireplaces, the two studies, the two large living areas and the two kitchens. List other highlights which appeal to you.

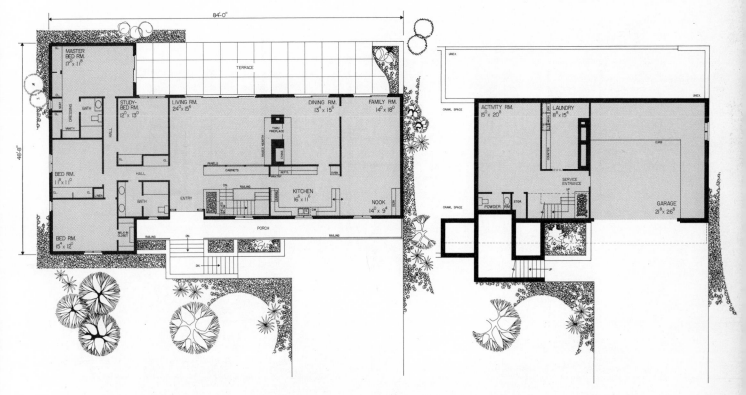

Design V32576 Main Level: 2,805 square feet; Lower Level: 785 square feet; Total: 3,590 square feet

● This delightfully styled hip-roofed house features all the living facilities on one level with an additional lower level housing an activity room, powder room, laundry and garage. The result is a very captivating design. Formal living patterns will prevail in this house.

The living room and dining room will have a delightful view of the rear yard, possess a dramatic thru-fireplace and has natural light through the openness that the sliding glass doors provide, along with access to the terrace. Two full baths serve the three bedrooms

and the cozy study/bedroom. Food preparation could hardly have better facilities than those offered by this well-planned front, U-shaped kitchen. The pass-thru from the kitchen to the nook make the quick, informal meal an enjoyable one.

● This is an exquisitely styled Tudor tri-level designed to serve its happy occupants for many years. The contrasting use of material surely makes the exterior eye-catching.

Design V32847
Main Level: 1,874 square feet; Lower Level: 1,131 square feet; Total: 3,005 square feet

L D

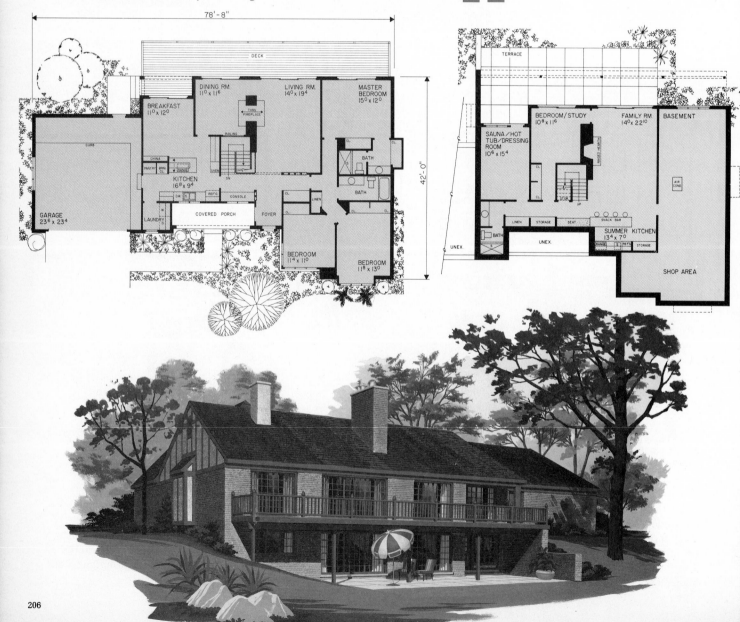

Design V32846
Main Level: 2,341 square feet; Lower Level: 1,380 square feet; Total: 3,721 square feet

● The street view of this Spanish design shows a beautifully designed one-story home, but now take a look at the rear elevation. This home has been designed to be built into a hill so the lower level can be opened to the sun. By so doing, the total livability is almost doubled. A unique feature of the lower level is the summer kitchen.

Design V31974 Main Level: 1,680 square feet; Lower Level: 1,344 square feet; Total: 3,024 square feet

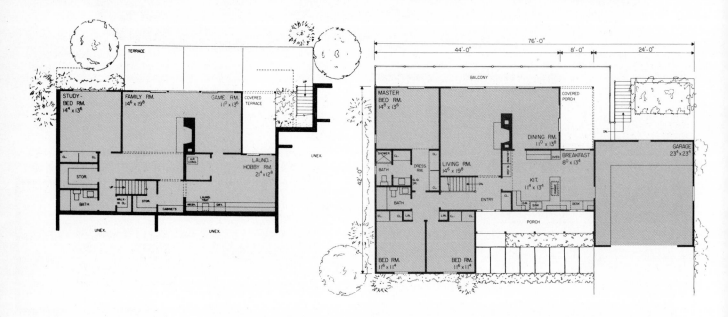

● You would never guess from looking at the front of this traditional design that it possessed such a strikingly different rear. From the front, you would guess that all of its livability is on one floor. Yet, just imagine the tremendous amount of livability that is added to the plan as a result of exposing the lower level - 1,344 square feet of it. Living in this hillside house will mean fun. Obviously, the most popular spot will be the balcony. Then again, maybe it could be the terrace adjacent to the family room. Both the terrace and the balcony have a covered area to provide protection against unfavorable weather. The interior of the plan also will serve the family with ease.

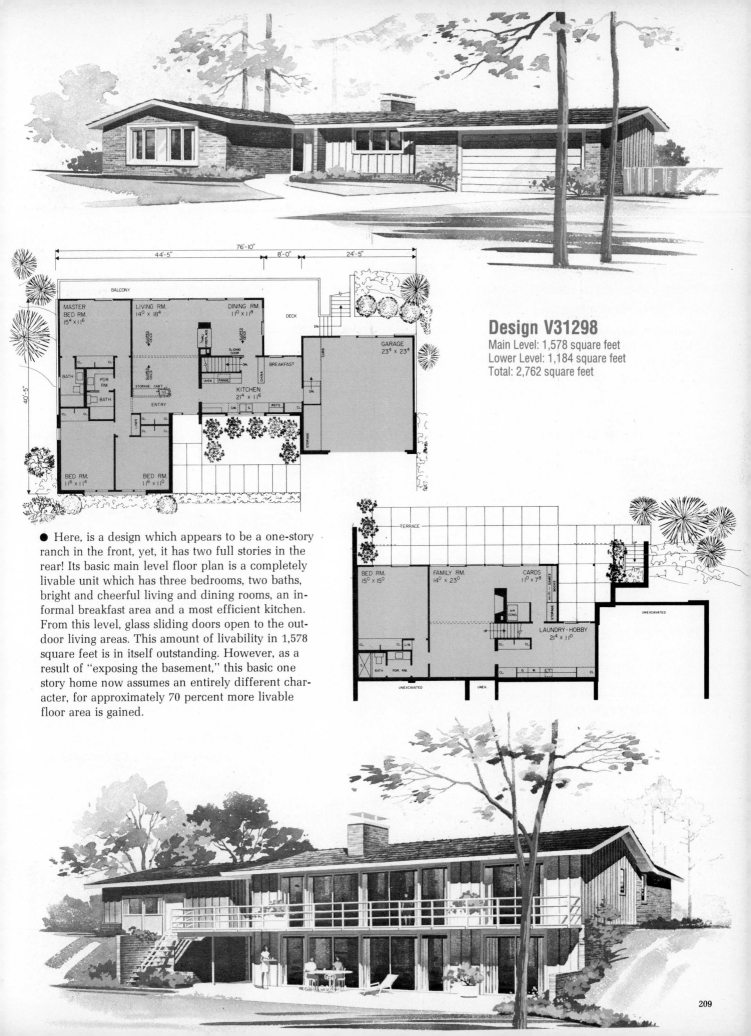

Design V31298

Main Level: 1,578 square feet
Lower Level: 1,184 square feet
Total: 2,762 square feet

● Here, is a design which appears to be a one-story ranch in the front, yet, it has two full stories in the rear! Its basic main level floor plan is a completely livable unit which has three bedrooms, two baths, bright and cheerful living and dining rooms, an informal breakfast area and a most efficient kitchen. From this level, glass sliding doors open to the outdoor living areas. This amount of livability in 1,578 square feet is in itself outstanding. However, as a result of "exposing the basement," this basic one story home now assumes an entirely different character, for approximately 70 percent more livable floor area is gained.

209

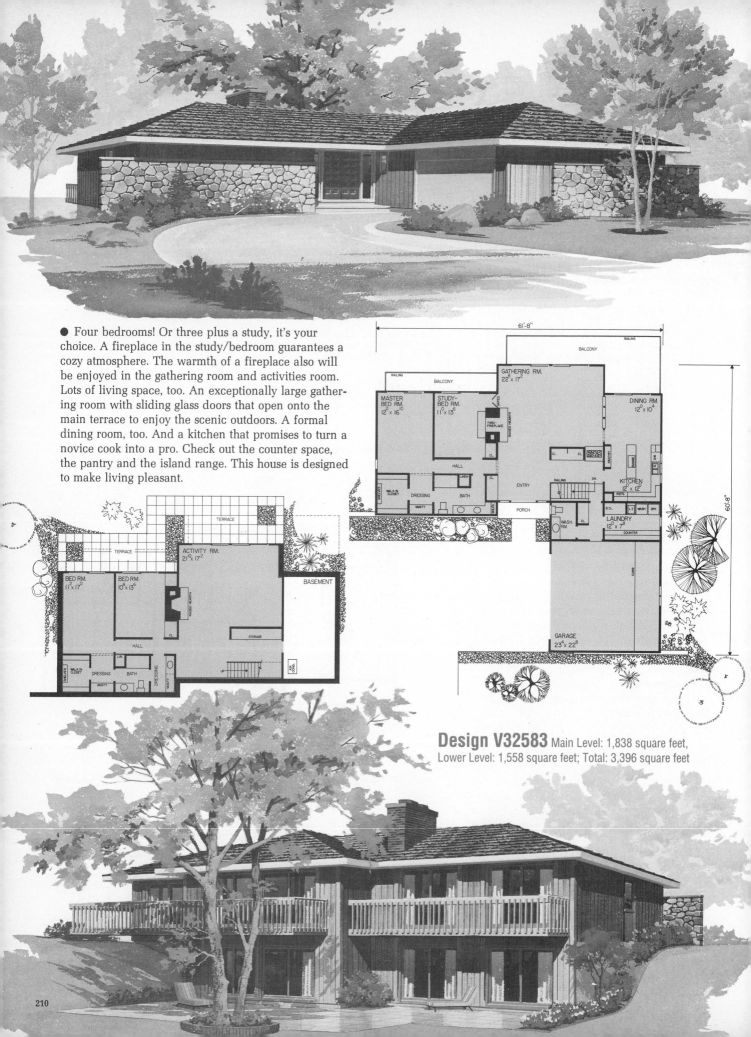

● Four bedrooms! Or three plus a study, it's your choice. A fireplace in the study/bedroom guarantees a cozy atmosphere. The warmth of a fireplace also will be enjoyed in the gathering room and activities room. Lots of living space, too. An exceptionally large gathering room with sliding glass doors that open onto the main terrace to enjoy the scenic outdoors. A formal dining room, too. And a kitchen that promises to turn a novice cook into a pro. Check out the counter space, the pantry and the island range. This house is designed to make living pleasant.

Design V32583 Main Level: 1,838 square feet, Lower Level: 1,558 square feet; Total: 3,396 square feet

Design V32769 Main Level: 1,898 square feet,
Lower Level: 1,134 square feet; Total: 3,032 square feet

● This traditional hillside design has fine architectural styling. It possesses all of the qualities that a great design should have to serve its occupants fully.

Design V31976

Upper Level: 1,616 square feet
Lower Level: 1,472 square feet
Total: 3,088 square feet

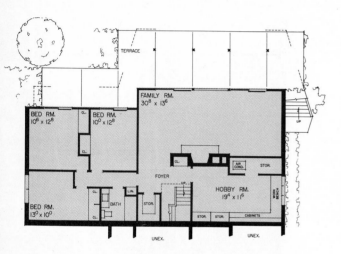

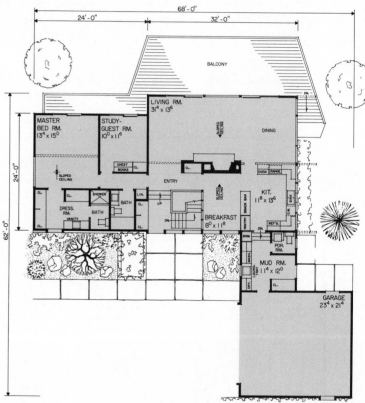

● Here's a hillside design just patterned for the large, active family. Whatever the pursuits and interests of the various members, you'd have to guess there would be more than enough space to service one and all with plenty of room to spare. If the children were teenagers, just imagine the fun they would have with their bedrooms, their family room and their hobby room on the lower level. The parents would be equally thrilled with their more formal facilities on the upper level.

Design V31739 Main Level: 1,281 square feet; Sleeping Level: 857 square feet; Lower Level: 687 square feet; Total: 2,825 square feet

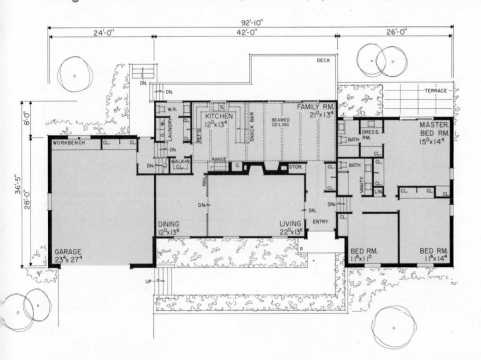

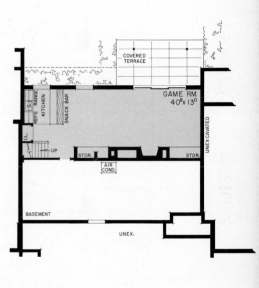

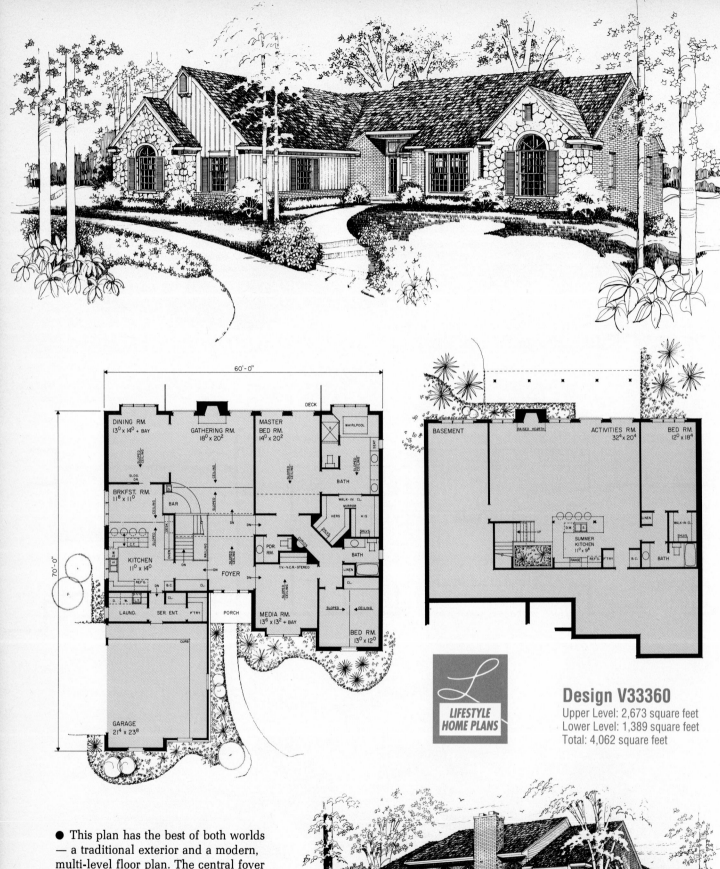

60'-0"

70'-0"

DINING RM. 13⁰ x 14⁰ + BAY

GATHERING RM. 18⁰ x 20²

MASTER BED RM. 14⁰ x 20²

DECK

WHIRLPOOL

BATH

BRKFST. RM. 11⁸ x 11⁰

BAR

WALK-IN CL.

MIRROR

HERS   HIS   SHLVS

KITCHEN 11⁰ x 14⁰

OVEN

DN

BATH

PDR. RM.

DN

FOYER

DN

T.V.-V.C.R.-STEREO

LINEN

CL.

LAUND.   SER. ENT.   P'TRY   PORCH

MEDIA RM. 13⁶ x 13² + BAY

BED RM. 13⁰ x 12⁰

CURB

GARAGE 21⁴ x 23⁸

BASEMENT   RAISED HEARTH   ACTIVITIES RM. 32⁴ x 20⁴   BED RM. 12⁰ x 18⁴

LINEN   WALK-IN CL.

SUMMER KITCHEN 11⁰ x 9⁸

RANGE   REF'G.   P'TRY

B.C.   BATH   SHLVS

L
LIFESTYLE HOME PLANS

Design V33360

Upper Level: 2,673 square feet
Lower Level: 1,389 square feet
Total: 4,062 square feet

● This plan has the best of both worlds — a traditional exterior and a modern, multi-level floor plan. The central foyer routes traffic effectively to all areas: the kitchen, gathering room, sleeping area, media room and the stairs leading to the lower level. Highlights include a master suite with luxurious bath and lower-level activities room with fireplace and kitchen. Also note the bedroom on this level.

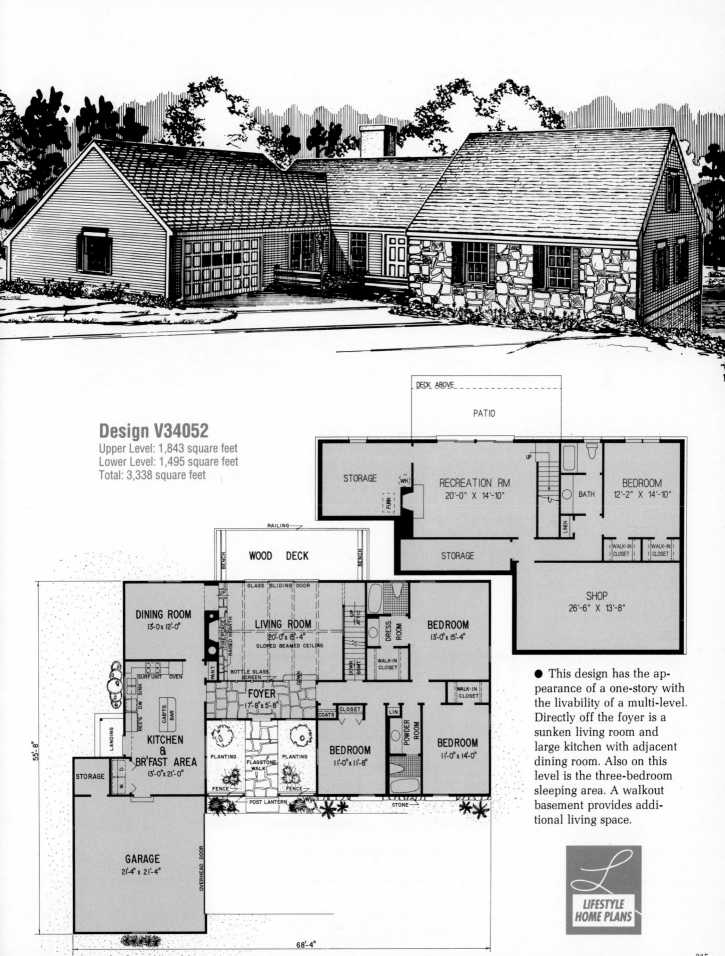

Design V34052

Upper Level: 1,843 square feet
Lower Level: 1,495 square feet
Total: 3,338 square feet

DECK ABOVE

PATIO

STORAGE

RECREATION RM
20'-0" X 14'-10"

WH

FURN

UP

BATH

LINEN

BEDROOM
12'-2" X 14'-10"

STORAGE

WALK-IN CLOSET

WALK-IN CLOSET

SHOP
26'-6" X 13'-8"

RAILING

WOOD DECK

BENCH

BENCH

GLASS SLIDING DOOR

UP

LIVING ROOM
20'-0" X 15'-4"
SLOPED BEAMED CEILING

DINING ROOM
13'-0 x 12'-0"

FIRE PLACE
RAISED HEARTH

PANT.

UP ATTIC

DRESS. ROOM

BEDROOM
13'-0" x 15'-4"

SURF UNIT   OVEN

REFG. DW SINK

CAB'TS   BAR

BOTTLE GLASS
SCREEN

DOWN
BSMT.

DOWN

WALK-IN CLOSET

FOYER
17'-8" x 5'-8"

LANDING

KITCHEN &
BR'FAST AREA
13'-0"x 21'-0"

W. D.

COATS   CLOSET

LIN

POWDER
ROOM

WALK-IN CLOSET

STORAGE

PLANTING

FLAGSTONE
WALK

PLANTING

BEDROOM
11'-0" x 11'-8"

BEDROOM
11'-0" x 14'-0"

FENCE

FENCE

POST LANTERN

STONE

55'-8"

GARAGE
21'-4" x 21'-4"

OVERHEAD DOOR

68'-4"

● This design has the appearance of a one-story with the livability of a multi-level. Directly off the foyer is a sunken living room and large kitchen with adjacent dining room. Also on this level is the three-bedroom sleeping area. A walkout basement provides additional living space.

LIFESTYLE
HOME PLANS

215

● This design is available with floor plans in three different sizes.
Each plan features a sunken great room with fireplace, dining room
and kitchen with island cooktop and breakfast area. Three bedrooms
and two baths make up the sleeping area. A walk-out basement adds
to the living space.

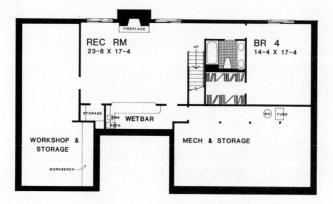

Optional Lower Level: 1,130 square feet

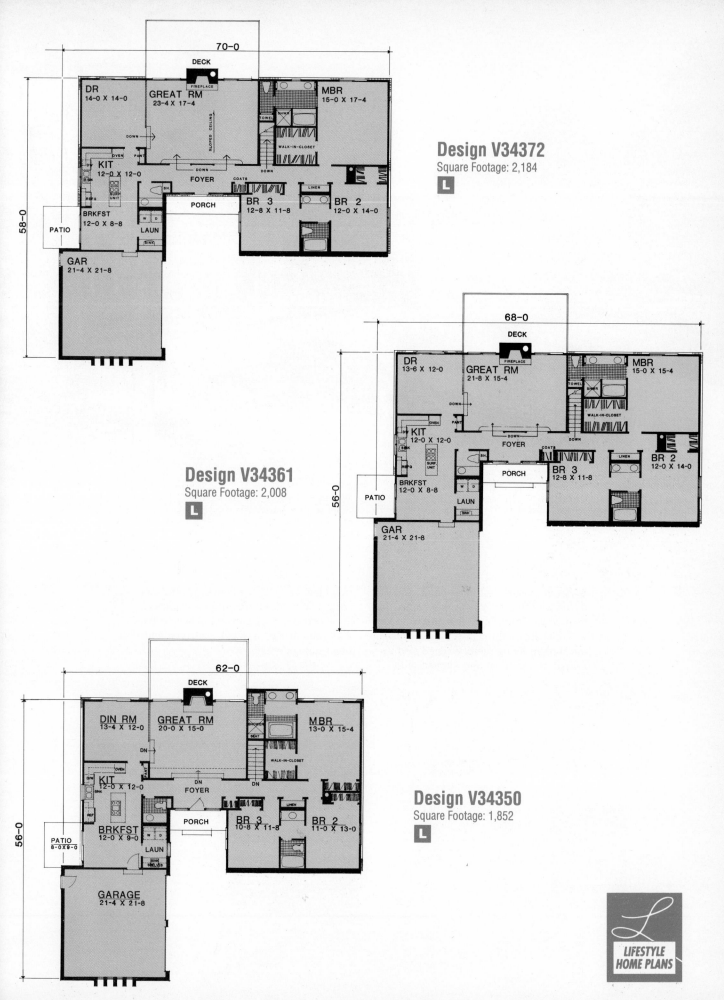

Design V34372
Square Footage: 2,184
L

Design V34361
Square Footage: 2,008
L

Design V34350
Square Footage: 1,852
L

LIFESTYLE HOME PLANS

Design V34543
Main Level: 2,321 square feet
Lower Level: 717 square feet
Total: 3,038 square feet

● An interesting entrance porch and trellis welcome visitors to this home. Immediately off the foyer is a cozy den which shares a through-fireplace with the sunken living room. There's also a formal dining room and kitchen with breakfast area. Three bedrooms and two baths complete this level. Downstairs is an enormous recreation room with a bar and patio access, a fourth bedroom and huge storage areas.

LIFESTYLE HOME PLANS

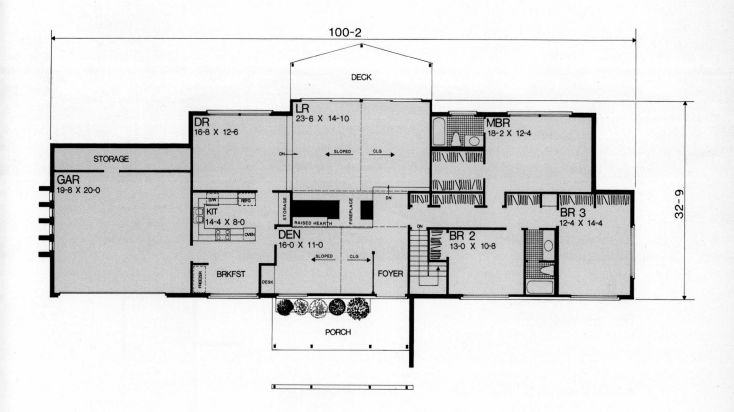

100-2

DECK

32-9

LR
23-6 X 14-10

DR
16-8 X 12-6

MBR
18-2 X 12-4

STORAGE

GAR
19-8 X 20-0

DN

SLOPED

CLG

DN

BR 3
12-4 X 14-4

STORAGE

D/W

REFG

KIT
14-4 X 8-0

RAISED HEARTH

FIREPLACE

DN

OVEN

DEN
16-0 X 11-0

BR 2
13-0 X 10-8

FREEZER

BRKFST

DESK

SLOPED

CLG

FOYER

PORCH

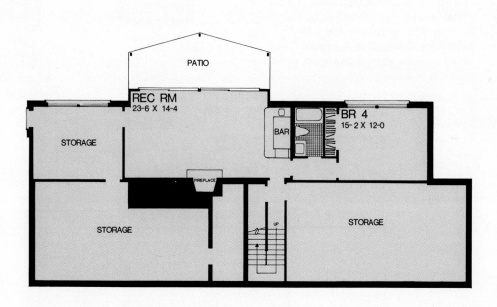

PATIO

REC RM
23-6 X 14-4

BR 4
15-2 X 12-0

BAR

STORAGE

FIREPLACE

STORAGE

UP

STORAGE

Design V34535

Main Level: 3,755 square feet
Lower Level: 583 square feet
Total: 4,338 square feet

● What stands out in this plan is its spaciousness. A large living room with fireplace leads into the sun-splashed garden room. A dining room off the kitchen provides a spot for formal meals. Occupying its own wing, the sleeping area features three bedrooms and a study. Note the lavish bath in the master suite. (Don't miss the extra living space of the walk-out basement.)

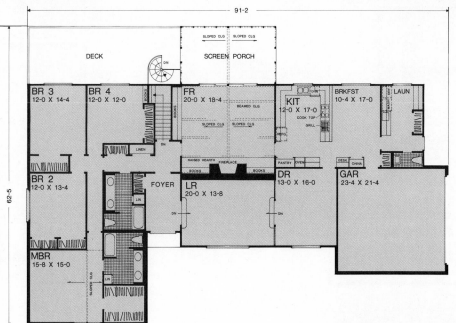

DECK

SCREEN PORCH

SLOPED CLG   SLOPED CLG

91-2

62-5

BR 3
12-0 X 14-4

BR 4
12-0 X 12-0

FR
20-0 X 18-4

BEAMED CLG

KIT
12-0 X 17-0

COOK TOP

BRKFST
10-4 X 17-0

LAUN

BOOKS

LINEN

SLOPED CLG   SLOPED CLG

GRILL

REFG

DN

RAISED HEARTH   FIREPLACE

BOOKS   BOOKS

PANTRY   OVEN

DESK   CHINA

BR 2
12-0 X 13-4

FOYER

LR
20-0 X 13-8

DR
13-0 X 16-0

GAR
23-4 X 21-4

LIN

DN

DN

MBR
15-8 X 15-0

SLOPED CLG

LIN

Design V34538

Main Level: 3,032 square feet
Lower Level: 1,802 square feet
Total: 4,834 square feet

L
LIFESTYLE
HOME PLANS

REC RM
26-4 X 17-8

UP

BONUS RM
16-2 X 14-8

ASH PIT

BR 5
15-4 X 14-8

LINEN

CEDAR CLOSET

STORAGE

SHOWER

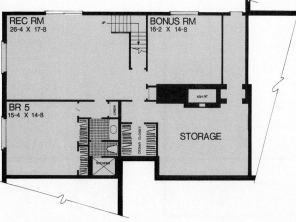

● This plan is ideal for larger families.
The main level features a sunken living
room and family room, dining room and
kitchen with breakfast area, and four
bedrooms. A fifth bedroom is found on
the lower level as well as a large recreation room and bonus room. Don't miss
the screened porch and deck with spiral
staircase for added livability.

Design V34551

Main Level: 5,632 square feet
Lower Level: 525 square feet
Total: 6,157 square feet

D

MBR
15-0 X 23-6

HER DRESSING

HIS DRESSING

SHOWER

BR-2
17-4 X 12-2

BR-3
18-0 X 12-2

BR-4
16-4 X 12-2

STORAGE BAR

LINEN

FAM RM
28-2 X 22-2

BEAMED CLG

PLANTER

LR
14-8 X 22-0

BEAMED CLG

ENTRY

SKYLIGHTS

COVERED PORCH

SLIDING GL DOOR   SLIDING GL DOOR

SLIDING GL DOOR

OVEN

FIREPLACE

OVEN

DR
14-8 X 19-6

BEAMED CLG

BRK'FST AREA

KIT
19-0 X 22-2

SNACK BAR

SINK

LUMINOUS CLG

REF'G FREEZ

PANTRY

LAUN
13-0 X 11-8

DRIP DRY

STORAGE

GARAGE
23-0 X 33-8

BR-5
13-0 X 15-2

BR-6
14-0 X 15-2

72-8

127-10

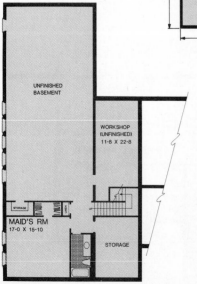

UNFINISHED
BASEMENT

WORKSHOP
(UNFINISHED)
11-8 X 22-8

STORAGE

MAID'S RM
17-0 X 15-10

STORAGE

● The front garden court with its wrought-iron gate helps create a distinctive exterior for this home. An equally distinguished interior features formal dining and living rooms flanking the entry, a large family room to the rear and a spacious kitchen with snack bar and breakfast area. Seven bedrooms and five baths will accommodate even the largest of families. Don't miss the rear covered porch.

L
LIFESTYLE
HOME PLANS

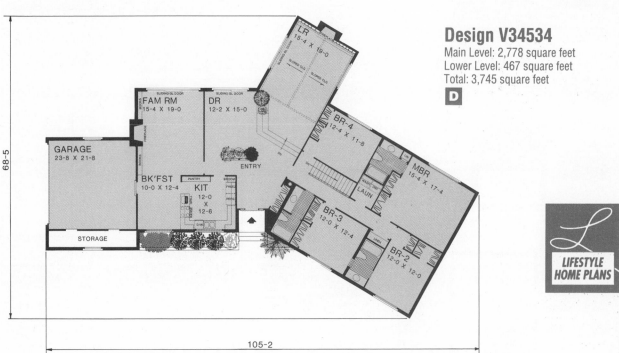

Design V34534
Main Level: 2,778 square feet
Lower Level: 467 square feet
Total: 3,745 square feet

D

LR
15-4 X 19-0

FAM RM
15-4 X 19-0

DR
12-2 X 15-0

BR-4
12-4 X 11-8

GARAGE
23-8 X 21-8

MBR
15-4 X 17-4

BK'FST
10-0 X 12-4

KIT
12-0 X 12-6

PANTRY

LAUN

BR-3
12-0 X 12-4

ENTRY

STORAGE

BR-2
12-0 X 12-0

68-5

105-2

LIFESTYLE
HOME PLANS

OFFICE
14-5 X 11-4

PLAYROOM
17-0 X 30-8

STORAGE

UTILITY
STORAGE

● The angles of this plan create a unique interior for this home. The entry leads to both the dining room and the living room, set at an angle. A family room with fireplace and a well-planned kitchen are nearby. The four-bedroom sleeping area is angled away from the living areas. From here stairs lead down to a walk-out basement containing a playroom, an office and storage.

Design V34084

Main Level: 2,133 square feet
Lower Level: 1,050 square feet
Total: 3,183 square feet

LIFESTYLE
HOME PLANS

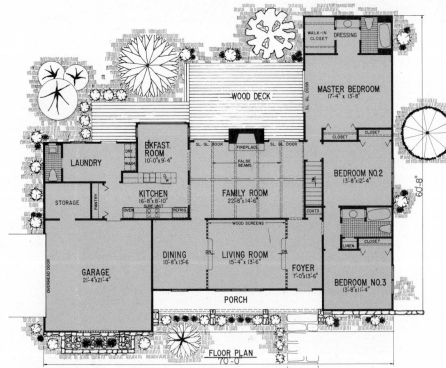

FLOOR PLAN
70'-0"

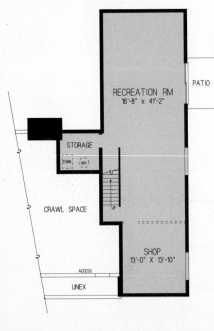

● This wood and stone contemporary features a well-planned interior for small- to medium-sized families. The formal living room and dining room are near the entry foyer — a nice arrangement for entertaining. A large family room takes care of informal occasions. Also on this level: the kitchen, laundry, and three-bedroom sleeping wing. A walk-out basement offers additional living space.

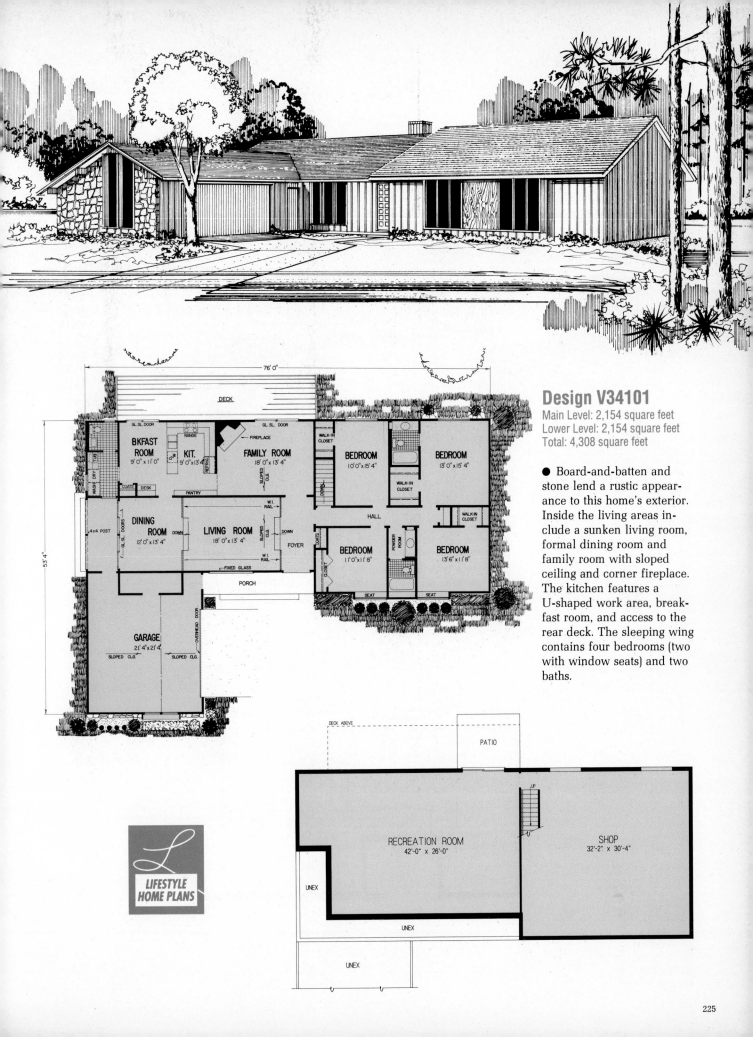

Design V34101
Main Level: 2,154 square feet
Lower Level: 2,154 square feet
Total: 4,308 square feet

● Board-and-batten and stone lend a rustic appearance to this home's exterior. Inside the living areas include a sunken living room, formal dining room and family room with sloped ceiling and corner fireplace. The kitchen features a U-shaped work area, breakfast room, and access to the rear deck. The sleeping wing contains four bedrooms (two with window seats) and two baths.

Floor plan labels (main level):

- DECK
- 76' 0"
- 53' 4"
- BKFAST ROOM 9' 0" x 11' 0"
- KIT. 9' 0" x 13' 4"
- FAMILY ROOM 18' 0" x 13' 4"
- GL. SL. DOOR
- FIREPLACE
- WALK-IN CLOSET
- BEDROOM 10' 0" x 15' 4"
- BEDROOM 13' 0" x 15' 4"
- WALK-IN CLOSET
- HALL
- WALK-IN CLOSET
- DINING ROOM 12' 0" x 13' 4"
- LIVING ROOM 18' 0" x 13' 4"
- FOYER
- BEDROOM 11' 0" x 11' 6"
- POWDER ROOM
- BEDROOM 13' 6" x 11' 8"
- SLOPED CLG.
- W.I. RAIL
- PANTRY
- DESK
- COATS
- WASH DRY TUB
- 4x4 POST
- FIXED GLASS
- PORCH
- SEAT
- SEAT
- GARAGE 21' 4" x 21' 4"
- SLOPED CLG.
- OVERHEAD DOOR
- RANGE
- REFRIG

Floor plan labels (lower level):

- DECK ABOVE
- PATIO
- UP
- RECREATION ROOM 42' 0" x 26' 0"
- SHOP 32' 2" x 30' 4"
- UNEX
- UNEX
- UNEX

LIFESTYLE HOME PLANS

225

● This attractive exterior comes with a floor plan in three different sizes to accommodate different size budgets. Each plan features a sunken great room with sloped ceiling and fireplace, dining room, kitchen with island cooktop and breakfast area, and a three-bedroom sleeping area with two baths. An optional walk-out basement adds extra living and storage space.

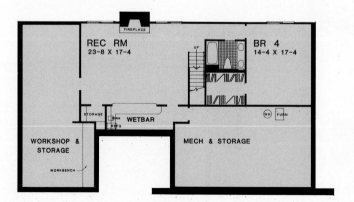

Lower Level: 1,130 square feet

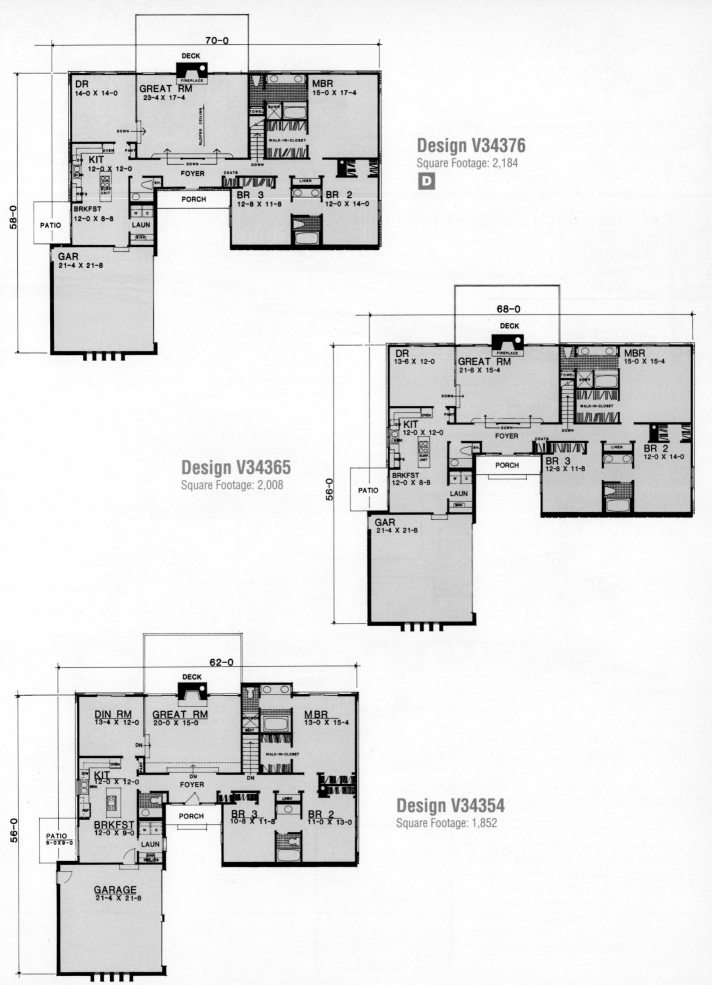

Design V34376
Square Footage: 2,184

D

Design V34365
Square Footage: 2,008

Design V34354
Square Footage: 1,852

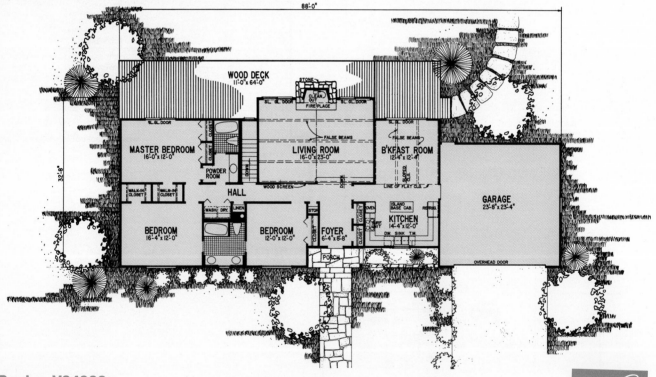

Design V34300

Main Level: 1,824 square feet
Lower Level: 811 square feet
Total: 2,635 square feet

● This cozy ranch house makes a great starter home. Directly off the foyer is the spacious living room with beamed ceiling and enormous stone fireplace. Nearby is the kitchen with island work center and breakfast room. The three-bedroom sleeping area features a master with access to the rear deck. A walk-out basement provides room for future expansion.

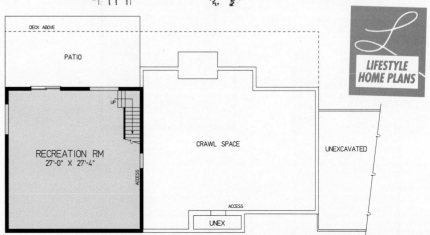

LIFESTYLE HOME PLANS

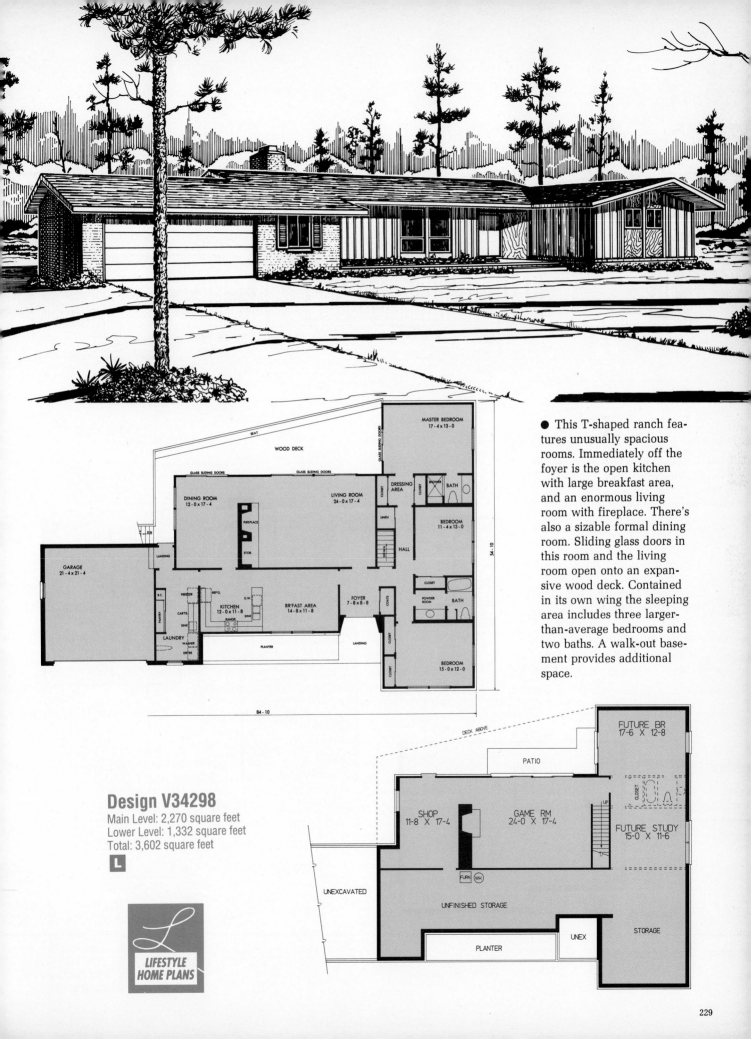

WOOD DECK

SEAT

GLASS SLIDING DOORS — GLASS SLIDING DOORS

DINING ROOM
12 - 0 x 17 - 4

LIVING ROOM
24 - 0 x 17 - 4

MASTER BEDROOM
17 - 4 x 13 - 0

DRESSING AREA

SHOWER BATH

CLOSET

LINEN

FIREPLACE

STOR.

HALL

BEDROOM
11 - 4 x 13 - 0

CLOSET

GARAGE
21 - 4 x 21 - 4

LANDING

B.C.

FREEZER REF'G.

D.W.

PANTRY

CARTS.

KITCHEN
12 - 0 x 11 - 8

SINK

RANGE

SINK

BR'FAST AREA
14 - 8 x 11 - 8

FOYER
7 - 8 x 8 - 8

COATS

CLOSET

POWDER ROOM

BATH

LAUNDRY

WASHER

DRYER

PLANTER

LANDING

CLOSET

BEDROOM
15 - 0 x 12 - 0

54 - 10

84 - 10

● This T-shaped ranch features unusually spacious rooms. Immediately off the foyer is the open kitchen with large breakfast area, and an enormous living room with fireplace. There's also a sizable formal dining room. Sliding glass doors in this room and the living room open onto an expansive wood deck. Contained in its own wing the sleeping area includes three larger-than-average bedrooms and two baths. A walk-out basement provides additional space.

DECK ABOVE

FUTURE BR
17 - 6 X 12 - 8

PATIO

CLOSET

SHOP
11 - 8 X 17 - 4

GAME RM
24 - 0 X 17 - 4

UP

FUTURE STUDY
15 - 0 X 11 - 6

FURN WH

UNEXCAVATED

UNFINISHED STORAGE

PLANTER

UNEX

STORAGE

Design V34298
Main Level: 2,270 square feet
Lower Level: 1,332 square feet
Total: 3,602 square feet

L

L
**LIFESTYLE
HOME PLANS**

● Here's another great starter home with lots of potential. The foyer leads straight back to a spacious living room with fireplace and sliding glass door opening onto the rear deck, and left to the kitchen and dining area. A patio off the kitchen is a great spot for outdoor dining. Down a short hall are three bedrooms and two baths. As the family grows, the walk-out basement can be developed for more living space.

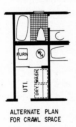

ALTERNATE PLAN
FOR CRAWL SPACE

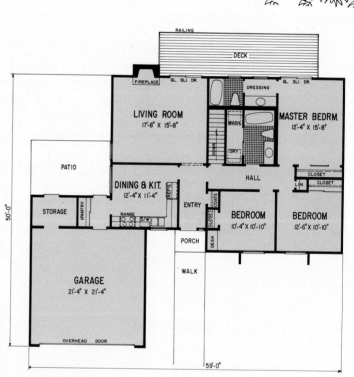

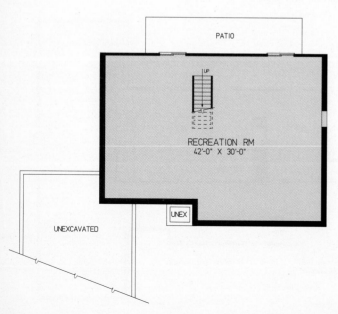

PATIO

RECREATION RM
42'-0" X 30'-0"

UNEX

UNEXCAVATED

Design V34174

Main Level: 1,374 square feet
Lower Level: 1,332 square feet
Total: 2,706 square feet

LIFESTYLE
HOME PLANS

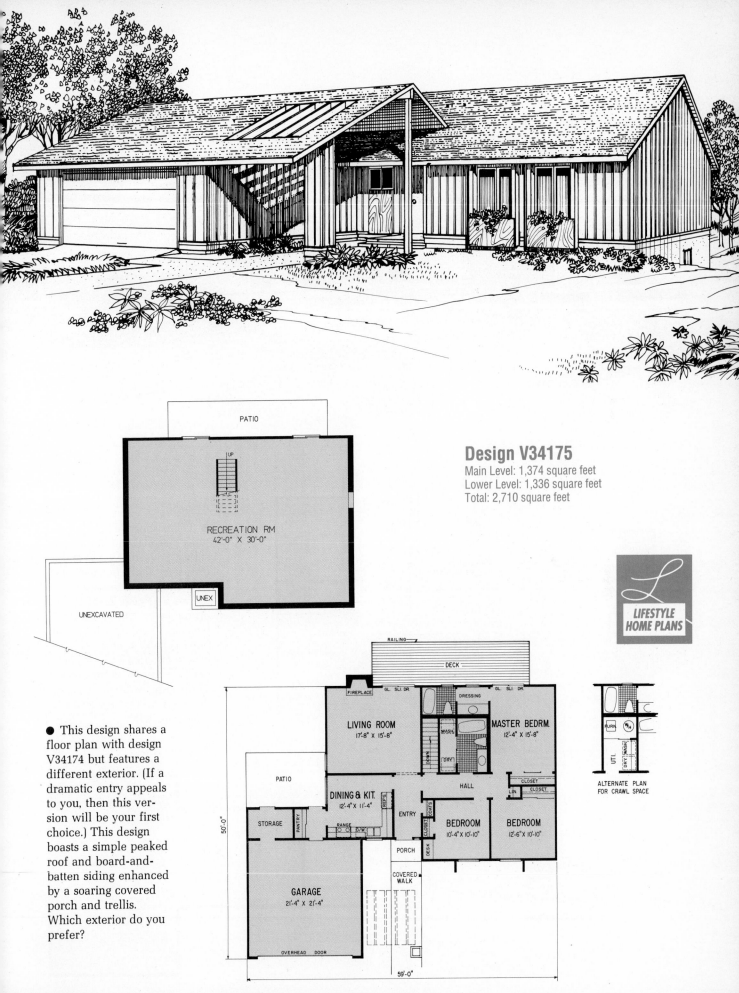

PATIO

UP

RECREATION RM
42'-0" X 30'-0"

UNEX

UNEXCAVATED

Design V34175

Main Level: 1,374 square feet
Lower Level: 1,336 square feet
Total: 2,710 square feet

LIFESTYLE HOME PLANS

● This design shares a floor plan with design V34174 but features a different exterior. (If a dramatic entry appeals to you, then this version will be your first choice.) This design boasts a simple peaked roof and board-and-batten siding enhanced by a soaring covered porch and trellis. Which exterior do you prefer?

RAILING

DECK

FIREPLACE

GL. SLI. DR.

DRESSING

GL. SLI. DR.

LIVING ROOM
17'-8" X 15'-8"

WASH.

DRY

MASTER BEDRM.
12'-4" X 15'-8"

DOWN

HALL

CLOSET

LIN.

CLOSET

ALTERNATE PLAN
FOR CRAWL SPACE

UTI.

FURN.

W.H.

DRY WASH.

PATIO

DINING & KIT.
12'-4" X 11'-4"

REFR.

RANGE

D/W

ENTRY

COATS

CLOSET

DESK

BEDROOM
10'-4" X 10'-10"

BEDROOM
12'-6" X 10'-10"

STORAGE

PANTRY

PORCH

GARAGE
21'-4" X 21'-4"

COVERED WALK

OVERHEAD DOOR

50'-0"

59'-0"

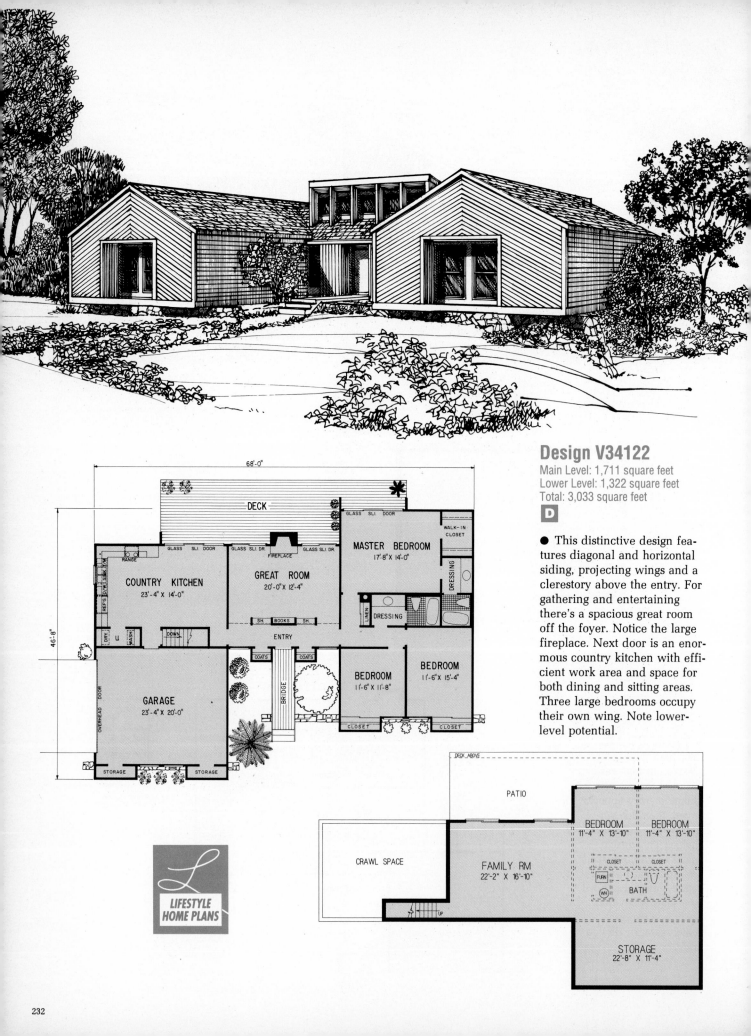

Design V34122

Main Level: 1,711 square feet
Lower Level: 1,322 square feet
Total: 3,033 square feet

D

● This distinctive design features diagonal and horizontal siding, projecting wings and a clerestory above the entry. For gathering and entertaining there's a spacious great room off the foyer. Notice the large fireplace. Next door is an enormous country kitchen with efficient work area and space for both dining and sitting areas. Three large bedrooms occupy their own wing. Note lower-level potential.

68'-0"

46'-8"

DECK

GLASS SLI. DOOR

RANGE

GLASS SLI. DOOR   GLASS SLI. DR.   FIREPLACE   GLASS SLI. DR.

MASTER BEDROOM
17'-8" X 14'-0"

WALK-IN CLOSET

DRESSING

COUNTRY KITCHEN
23'-4" X 14'-0"

GREAT ROOM
20'-0" X 12'-4"

LINEN

DRESSING

PREFG   DW   SINK

DRY   WASH   DOWN

SH   BOOKS   SH

ENTRY

COATS   COATS

BEDROOM
11'-6" X 11'-8"

BEDROOM
11'-6" X 15'-4"

GARAGE
23'-4" X 20'-0"

OVERHEAD DOOR

BRIDGE

CLOSET   CLOSET

STORAGE   STORAGE

DECK ABOVE

PATIO

CRAWL SPACE

FAMILY RM
22'-2" X 16'-10"

BEDROOM
11'-4" X 13'-10"

BEDROOM
11'-4" X 13'-10"

CLOSET   CLOSET

FURN

WH   BATH

UP

STORAGE
22'-8" X 11'-4"

L
LIFESTYLE
HOME PLANS

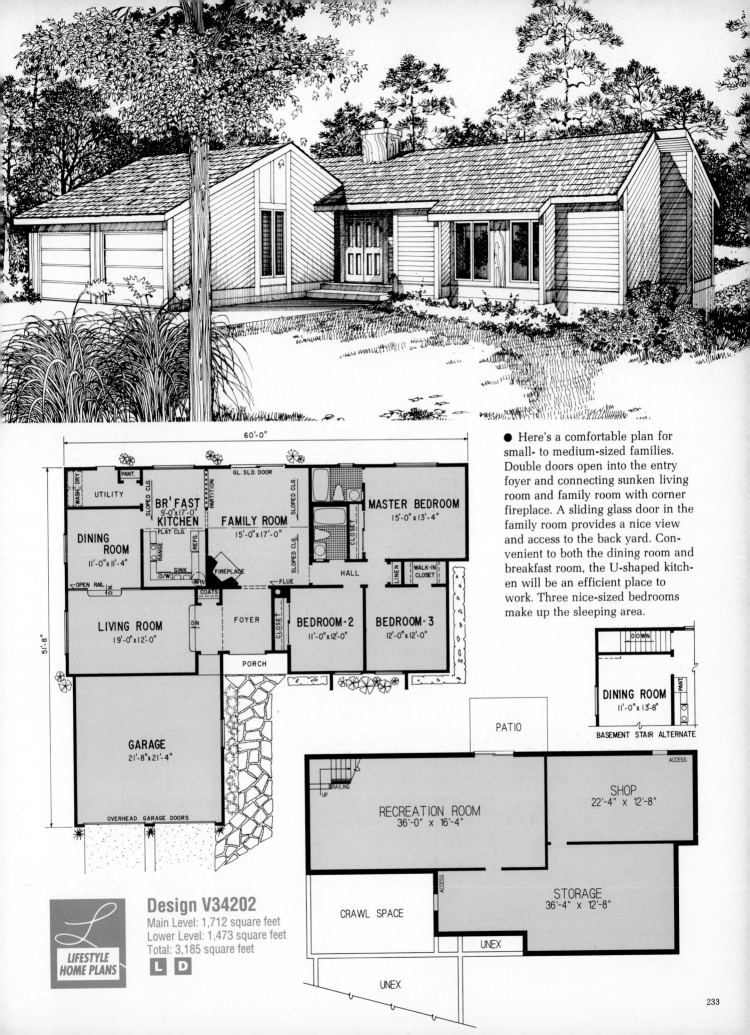

Here's a comfortable plan for small- to medium-sized families. Double doors open into the entry foyer and connecting sunken living room and family room with corner fireplace. A sliding glass door in the family room provides a nice view and access to the back yard. Convenient to both the dining room and breakfast room, the U-shaped kitchen will be an efficient place to work. Three nice-sized bedrooms make up the sleeping area.

60'-0"

UTILITY

WASH DRY

PANT.

SLOPED CLG.

BR' FAST KITCHEN
9'-0" x 17'-0"

DINING ROOM
11'-0" x 11'-4"

RANGE

D/W SINK

REFG.

FLAT CLG.

GL. SLD. DOOR

PARTITION

FAMILY ROOM
15'-0" x 17'-0"

SLOPED CLG.

SLOPED CLG.

MASTER BEDROOM
15'-0" x 13'-4"

CLOSET

FIREPLACE

WH

OPEN RAIL

DN

LIVING ROOM
19'-0" x 12'-0"

COATS

DN

FOYER

FLUE

CLOSET

HALL

LINEN

WALK-IN CLOSET

BEDROOM-2
11'-0" x 12'-0"

BEDROOM-3
12'-0" x 12'-0"

51'-8"

PORCH

GARAGE
21'-8" x 21'-4"

OVERHEAD GARAGE DOORS

DOWN

DINING ROOM
11'-0" x 13'-8"

PANT.

BASEMENT STAIR ALTERNATE

PATIO

RAILING

UP

RECREATION ROOM
36'-0" x 16'-4"

ACCESS

SHOP
22'-4" x 12'-8"

ACCESS

CRAWL SPACE

STORAGE
36'-4" x 12'-8"

UNEX

UNEX

LIFESTYLE HOME PLANS

Design V34202
Main Level: 1,712 square feet
Lower Level: 1,473 square feet
Total: 3,185 square feet

L D

● You can't help but feel spoiled by this home. Beyond the foyer is an enormous great room with conversation pit, fireplace and lots of windows for sweeping views. Also on this level are a dining room, cozy library and kitchen with island and breakfast area. The master bedroom features a large bath and plenty of closet space. The finished basement contains four bedrooms, three baths and a den with fireplace.

Design V34547

Main Level: 3,272 square feet
Lower Level: 2,097 square feet
Total: 5,369 square feet

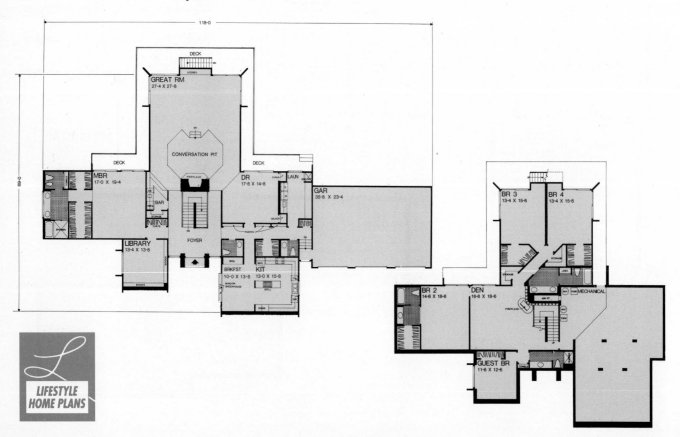

TWO-STORY HOMES WITH WALK-OUT
BASEMENTS . . .

have all the advantages of one-story walk-out basement plans with even more livability on the second floor. This floor may be a full- or half-story and usually holds family bedrooms. Offered here are contemporary and traditional styles in many unique floor-plan arrangements.

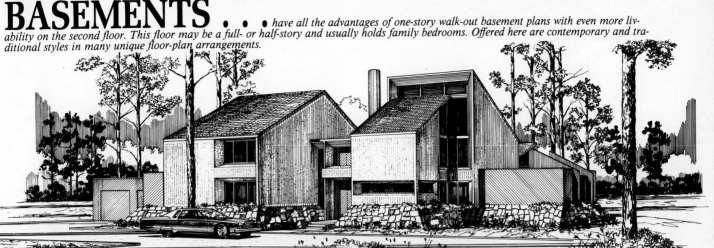

● This home is a showplace both inside and out. A handsome contemporary exterior houses a spacious interior. The first floor features a dramatic living room, formal dining room, kitchen with breakfast area, library with built-in shelves and the master bedroom. Four more bedrooms and two baths are on the second floor. The basement recreation room has a sliding glass door leading outside.

Design V34548

First Floor: 3,064 square feet
Second Floor: 1,450 square feet
Basement: 1,115 square feet
Total: 5,629 square feet

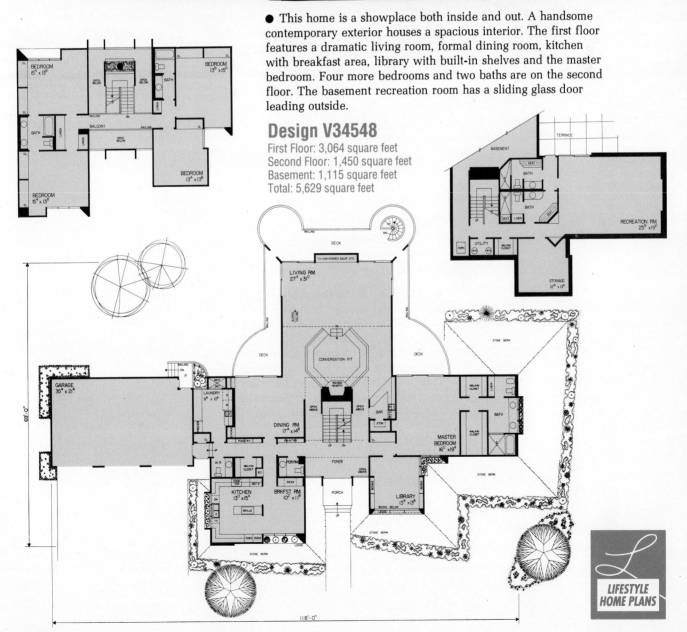

Design V34537

First Floor: 2,208 square feet
Second Floor: 773 square feet
Total: 2,981 square feet

● This design features an especially
well-planned interior. The entry foyer
routes traffic effectively to the living and
dining room and kitchen on the left,
straight back to the guest room, master
bedroom and stairs to the second floor.
This floor contains two more bedrooms,
each with sloped ceilings. A play room
and laundry room are on the lower
level.

LIFESTYLE
HOME PLANS

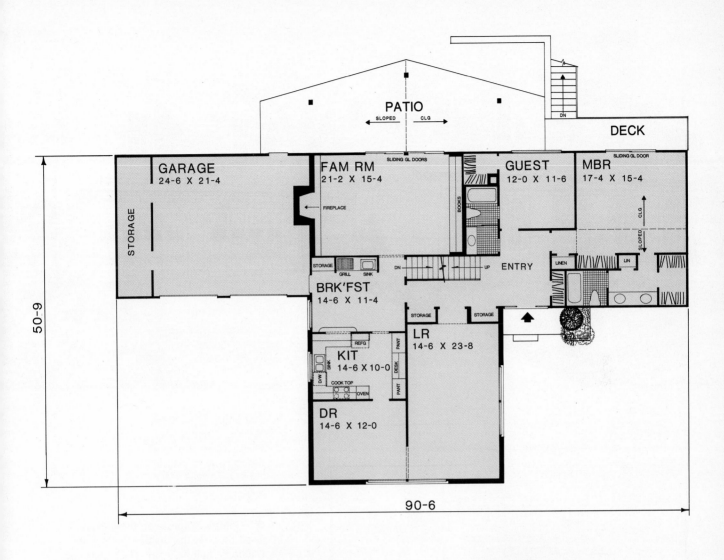

PATIO
SLOPED   CLG

DECK

GARAGE
24-6 X 21-4

STORAGE

FAM RM
21-2 X 15-4

FIREPLACE

SLIDING GL DOORS

BOOKS

GUEST
12-0 X 11-6

MBR
17-4 X 15-4

SLIDING GL DOOR

CLG

SLOPED

STORAGE   GRILL   SINK

DN

UP   ENTRY

LINEN

LIN

BRK'FST
14-6 X 11-4

REFG

STORAGE

STORAGE

50-9

KIT
14-6 X 10-0

SINK

D/W

COOK TOP

OVEN

DESK

PANT

PANT

LR
14-6 X 23-8

DR
14-6 X 12-0

90-6

UP

PATIO

DECK ABOVE

SLIDING GL DOORS

LAUN

WH   FURN

PLAY RM
29-0 X 22-0

WASH   DRY

UP

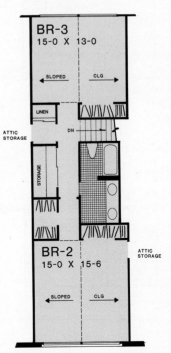

BR-3
15-0 X 13-0

SLOPED   CLG

LINEN

ATTIC
STORAGE

DN

STORAGE

ATTIC
STORAGE

BR-2
15-0 X 15-6

SLOPED   CLG

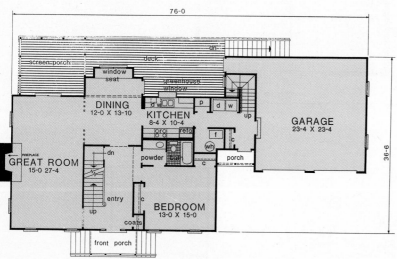

76-0

36-6

screen-porch

deck

dn

window seat

greenhouse window

DINING
12-0 X 13-10

KITCHEN
8-4 X 10-4

d w

p

d w

up

GARAGE
23-4 X 23-4

refg

f

FIREPLACE

GREAT ROOM
15-0 27-4

dn

powder

wh

c

porch

up

entry

c

BEDROOM
13-0 X 15-0

coats

front porch

Design V34397

First Floor: 1,421 square feet
Second Floor: 967 square feet
Basement: 1,380 square feet
Total: 3,768 square feet

L

● A simple colonial on the outside, a great plan on the inside! Distinct attractions include a first-floor bedroom that might make the perfect guest room, a screened porch, a deck, a greenhouse window, great room fireplace, and bonus room on the second floor. The master bedroom has a full bath as does a second bedroom on this floor.

walk-in closet

dress

dress

bath

books

dn

dn

attic access

UNFINISHED BONUS ROOM
11-4 X 23-4

hall

c

MBR
13-4 X 15-0

dn

open to below

lin

BEDROOM
12-0 X 15-0

attic access

c

L
LIFESTYLE HOME PLANS

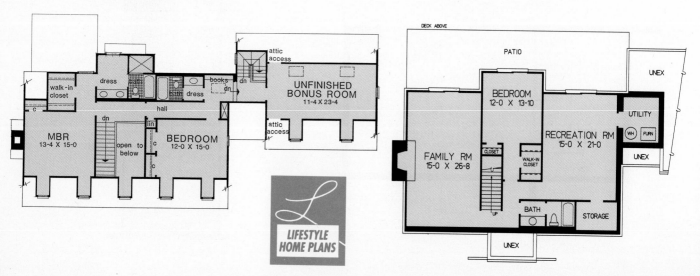

DECK ABOVE

PATIO

UNEX

BEDROOM
12-0 X 13-10

UTILITY

FAMILY RM
15-0 X 26-8

closet

walk-in closet

RECREATION RM
15-0 X 21-0

WH

FURN

UNEX

up

BATH

STORAGE

UNEX

Design V34290

First Floor: 2,104 square feet
Second Floor: 1,147 square feet
Basement Level: 1,911 square feet
Total: 5,162 square feet

● A long, low Colonial facade introduces this classic floor plan, but the foyer and center hall are the true initiation point to all the living areas and sleeping areas throughout the house. Don't overlook the large master suite and its warming fireplace, or the rear screened porch. Upstairs bedrooms are accented with dormer windows and have attic storage access through walk-in closets.

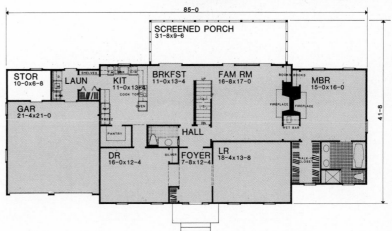

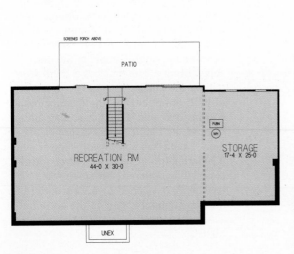

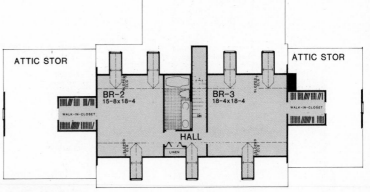

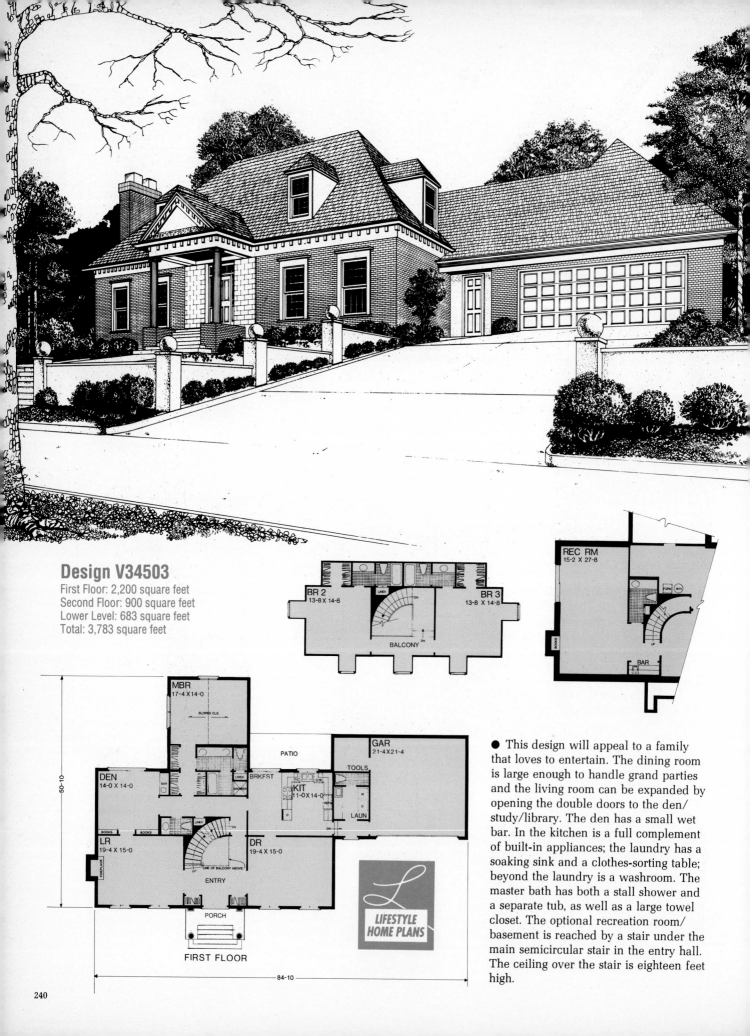

Design V34503

First Floor: 2,200 square feet
Second Floor: 900 square feet
Lower Level: 683 square feet
Total: 3,783 square feet

BR 2
13-8 X 14-8

LINEN

DN

BR 3
13-8 X 14-8

DN

BALCONY

REC RM
15-2 X 27-8

FURN | WH

BOOKS

BAR

MBR
17-4 X 14-0

SLOPED CLG

DEN
14-0 X 14-0

BAR

PATIO

BRKFST

GAR
21-4X21-4

TOOLS

LINEN

SHOWER

KIT
11-0 X 14-0

W | D

LAUN

LR
19-4 X 15-0

BOOKS

BOOKS

LINEN

DN

DR
19-4 X 15-0

FIREPLACE

LINE OF BALCONY ABOVE

UP

ENTRY

PORCH

50-10

84-10

FIRST FLOOR

● This design will appeal to a family that loves to entertain. The dining room is large enough to handle grand parties and the living room can be expanded by opening the double doors to the den/study/library. The den has a small wet bar. In the kitchen is a full complement of built-in appliances; the laundry has a soaking sink and a clothes-sorting table; beyond the laundry is a washroom. The master bath has both a stall shower and a separate tub, as well as a large towel closet. The optional recreation room/basement is reached by a stair under the main semicircular stair in the entry hall. The ceiling over the stair is eighteen feet high.

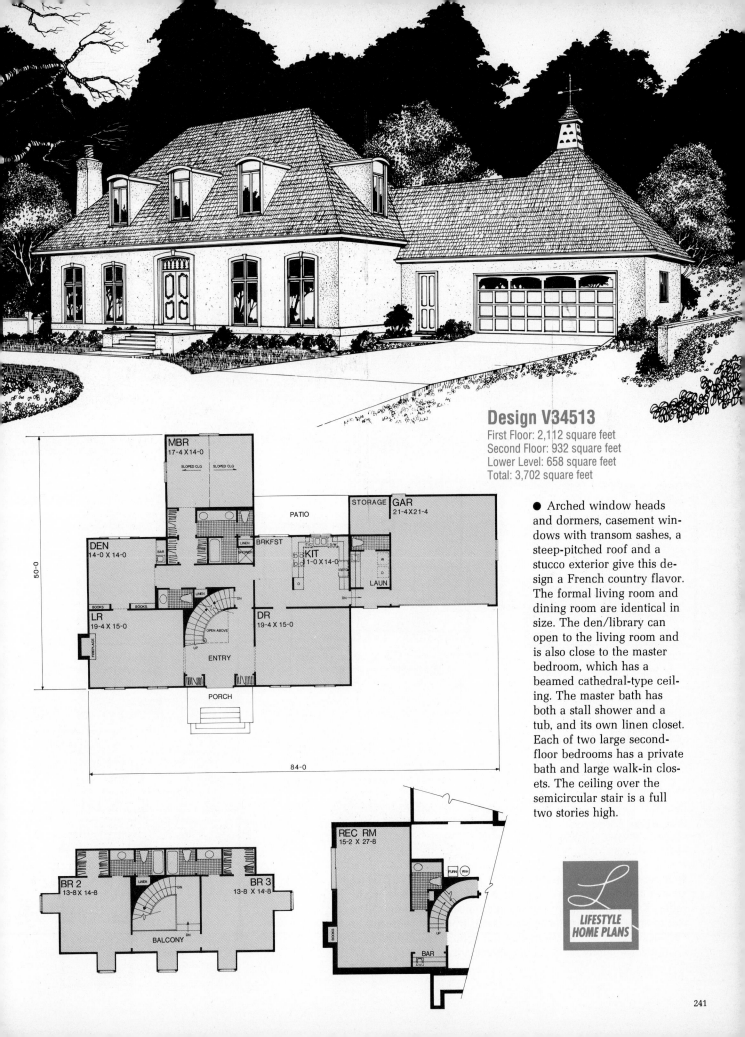

Design V34513

First Floor: 2,112 square feet
Second Floor: 932 square feet
Lower Level: 658 square feet
Total: 3,702 square feet

● Arched window heads and dormers, casement windows with transom sashes, a steep-pitched roof and a stucco exterior give this design a French country flavor. The formal living room and dining room are identical in size. The den/library can open to the living room and is also close to the master bedroom, which has a beamed cathedral-type ceiling. The master bath has both a stall shower and a tub, and its own linen closet. Each of two large second-floor bedrooms has a private bath and large walk-in closets. The ceiling over the semicircular stair is a full two stories high.

LIFESTYLE HOME PLANS

PATIO   PATIO

REC ROOM
13'-4" x 18'-4"

FAMILY ROOM
23'-0" x 14'-8"

SHOP
32'-0" x 10'-4"

ACCESS

UNEX   CRAWL SPACE

UNEX

UP

BEDROOM #2
14'-10" X 15'-0"

LIVING ROOM BELOW

BALCONY   DN

LINEN

WALK-IN
CLOSET   FOYER BELOW

BEDROOM #3
19'-8" X 14'-0"

LINEN   STORAGE

FURN

LIFESTYLE
HOME PLANS

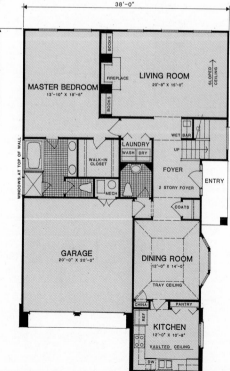

38'-0"

BOOKS

fireplace   LIVING ROOM
20'-6" X 15'-0"

MASTER BEDROOM
13'-10" X 18'-8"   BOOKS

SLOPED CEILING

60'-9"

WINDOWS AT TOP OF WALL

LAUNDRY   WET BAR

WASH DRY   UP

WALK-IN
CLOSET   FOYER

MECH   2 STORY FOYER   ENTRY

COATS

GARAGE
20'-0" X 20'-0"   DINING ROOM
12'-0" X 14'-0"

TRAY CEILING

CHINA   PANTRY

REF

KITCHEN
12'-0" X 10'-8"

VAULTED CEILING

DW

Design V34406

First Floor: 1,497 square feet
Second Floor: 848 square feet
Lower Level: 1,119 square feet
Total: 3,464 square feet

● Tame a narrow lot with this unique side-entry design. The front kitchen and dining room feature high ceilings while the sloped-ceiling living room has a fireplace and built-in bookshelves. The master suite on the first floor is separated from two bedrooms on the second floor, each with its own full bath. A lower-level basement holds a family room and a recreation room.

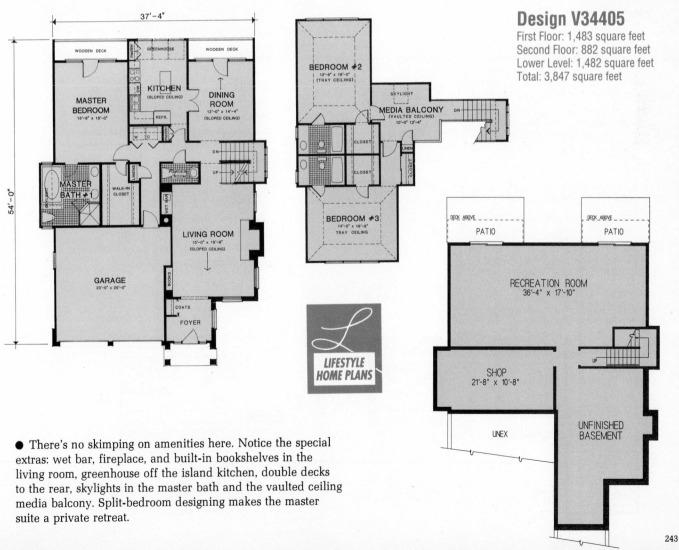

Design V34405

First Floor: 1,483 square feet
Second Floor: 882 square feet
Lower Level: 1,482 square feet
Total: 3,847 square feet

L
LIFESTYLE
HOME PLANS

37'-4"

54'-0"

WOODEN DECK
GREENHOUSE
WOODEN DECK

MASTER
BEDROOM
13'-8" x 18'-0"

KITCHEN
(SLOPED CEILING)

DINING
ROOM
12'-0" x 14'-4"
(SLOPED CEILING)

REFR.

PANTRY

W D

PANTRY

MASTER
BATH #1

WALK-IN
CLOSET

LINENS

POWDER
ROOM

DN

UP

WET BAR

LIVING ROOM
15'-0" x 19'-8"
(SLOPED CEILING)

GARAGE
20'-0" x 20'-0"

BOOKS

COATS

FOYER

BEDROOM #2
13'-8" x 18'-0"
(TRAY CEILING)

SKYLIGHT

MEDIA BALCONY
(VAULTED CEILING)
10'-0" 12'-4"

DN

CLOSET

LINEN

CLOSET

CLOSET

BEDROOM #3
14'-0" x 16'-8"
TRAY CEILING

DECK ABOVE

PATIO

DECK ABOVE

PATIO

RECREATION ROOM
36'-4" x 17'-10"

SHOP
21'-8" x 10'-8"

UP

UNEX

UNFINISHED
BASEMENT

● There's no skimping on amenities here. Notice the special extras: wet bar, fireplace, and built-in bookshelves in the living room, greenhouse off the island kitchen, double decks to the rear, skylights in the master bath and the vaulted ceiling media balcony. Split-bedroom designing makes the master suite a private retreat.

243

Design V34257

First Floor: 1,422 square feet
Second Floor: 949 square feet
Lower Level: 621 square feet
Total: 2,992 square feet

● Here's a great farmhouse design that has bonus livability on the basement level for family activities. On the first floor, look to the great room for casual gatherings which are complemented by a screened porch and a fireplace. More formal entertaining takes place in the front parlor. Across the foyer is a formal dining room. All first-floor rooms are served handily by the central kitchen. All three second-floor bedrooms have more than adequate closet space.

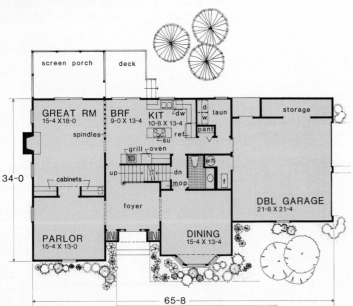

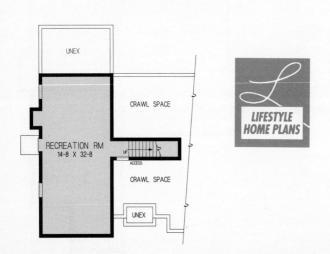

LIFESTYLE HOME PLANS

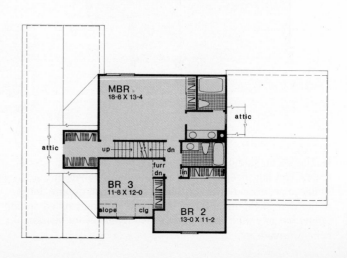

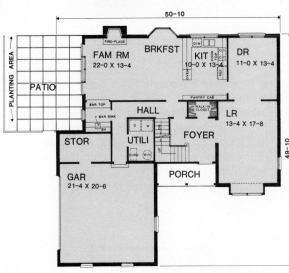

FAM RM
22-0 X 13-4

BRKFST

KIT
10-0 X 13-4

DR
11-0 X 13-4

FIRE-PLACE

PLANTING AREA

PATIO

BAR TOP

BAR SINK

HALL

PANTRY CAB

WALK-IN CLOSET

LR
13-4 X 17-8

STOR

UTILI

FURN

W/H

D W

FOYER

GAR
21-4 X 20-6

PORCH

50-10

49-10

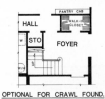

HALL

PANTRY CAB

WALK-IN CLOSET

STO

W

FOYER

H/W

OPTIONAL FOR CRAWL FOUND.

Design V34278

First Floor: 1,269 square feet
Second Floor: 1,203 square feet
Lower Level: 1,232 square feet
Total: 3,704 square feet

D

MBR
12-0 X 17-0

BR-2
11-0 X 13-4

WALK-IN CLOSET

BR-3
15-8 X 11-0

WALK-IN CLOSET

HALL

OPEN

BR-4
12-0 X 13-0

SHOWER SEAT

WALK-IN CLOSET

ROOF BELOW

ROOF BELOW

L
LIFESTYLE HOME PLANS

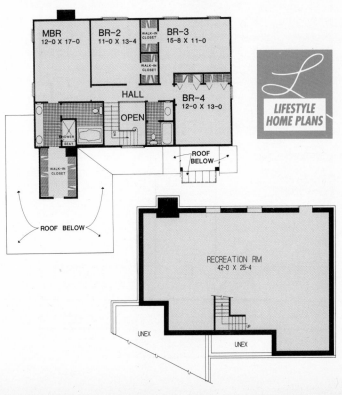

RECREATION RM
42-0 X 25-4

UNEX

UNEX

● Beyond the welcoming front covered porch, this plan offers a lot to those looking for a two-story design, and then some. Besides the primary living areas found in the family room, living room, dining room, and breakfast room, there is lower-level space to really spread out. Notice that there are four bedrooms on the second floor. The master bedroom is a treat with an over-sized walk-in closet and well-appointed bath.

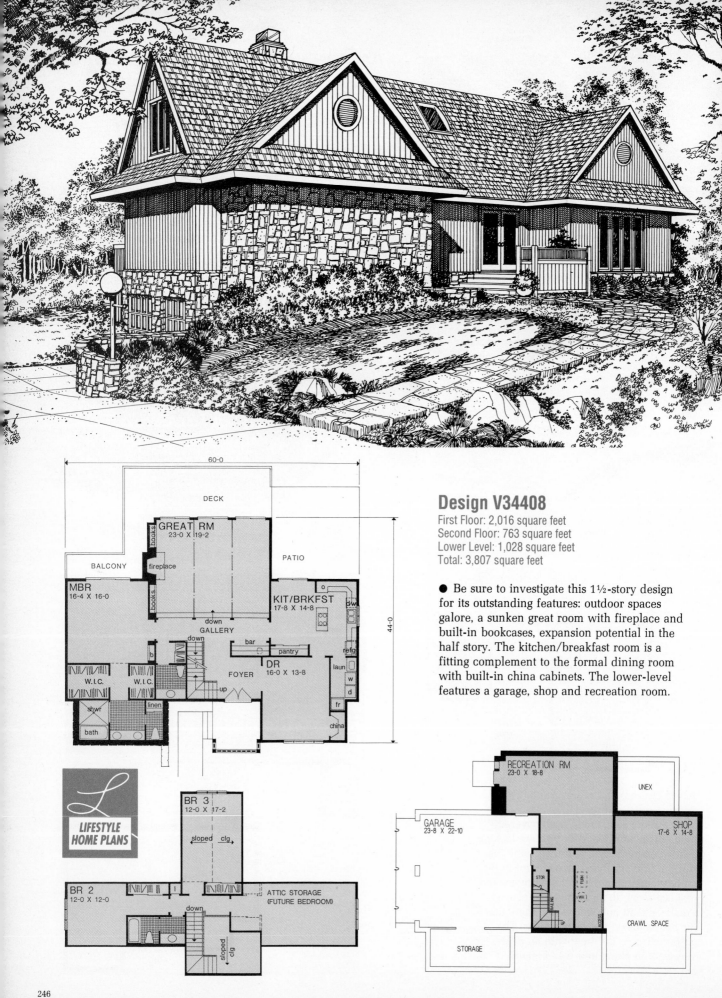

Design V34408

First Floor: 2,016 square feet
Second Floor: 763 square feet
Lower Level: 1,028 square feet
Total: 3,807 square feet

● Be sure to investigate this 1½-story design for its outstanding features: outdoor spaces galore, a sunken great room with fireplace and built-in bookcases, expansion potential in the half story. The kitchen/breakfast room is a fitting complement to the formal dining room with built-in china cabinets. The lower-level features a garage, shop and recreation room.

60-0

DECK

GREAT RM
23-0 X 19-2

books.

BALCONY

fireplace

books.

PATIO

MBR
16-4 X 16-0

KIT/BRKFST
17-8 X 14-8

dw

44-0

down

GALLERY

down

bar

pantry

refg.

b

DR
16-0 X 13-8

laun

FOYER

W.I.C.

W.I.C.

up

china

w

d

fr

shwr

linen

bath

LIFESTYLE HOME PLANS

BR 3
12-0 X 17-2

sloped   clg

RECREATION RM
23-0 X 18-8

UNEX

BR 2
12-0 X 12-0

ATTIC STORAGE
(FUTURE BEDROOM)

GARAGE
23-8 X 22-10

SHOP
17-6 X 14-8

down

STOR

sloped   clg

CRAWL SPACE

STORAGE

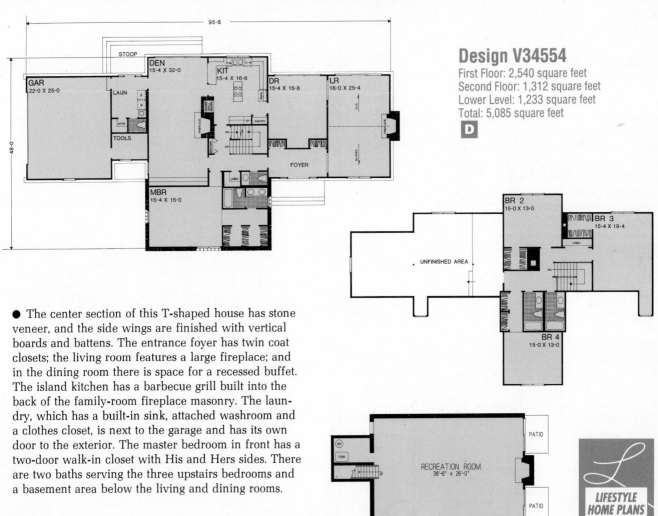

Design V34554

First Floor: 2,540 square feet
Second Floor: 1,312 square feet
Lower Level: 1,233 square feet
Total: 5,085 square feet

D

● The center section of this T-shaped house has stone veneer, and the side wings are finished with vertical boards and battens. The entrance foyer has twin coat closets; the living room features a large fireplace; and in the dining room there is space for a recessed buffet. The island kitchen has a barbecue grill built into the back of the family-room fireplace masonry. The laundry, which has a built-in sink, attached washroom and a clothes closet, is next to the garage and has its own door to the exterior. The master bedroom in front has a two-door walk-in closet with His and Hers sides. There are two baths serving the three upstairs bedrooms and a basement area below the living and dining rooms.

LIFESTYLE HOME PLANS

● Most of the front of this New England farmhouse is veneered with fieldstone; the rest is clapboards with a roof of hand-split cedar shakes. A formal entry with the living room on one side and the dining room on the other leads to the center hall and the stair to the children's rooms on the second floor. Each of these bedrooms has its own bath and walk-in closet. The family room has a large fireplace flanked by built-in bookshelves and a French door leading to a screened porch. The generous master suite has two walk-in closets and a unique compartmented bath.

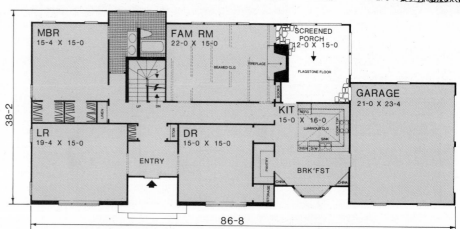

MBR 15-4 X 15-0
FAM RM 22-0 X 15-0
SCREENED PORCH 12-0 X 15-0
BEAMED CLG
FIREPLACE
FLAGSTONE FLOOR
UP DN
LINEN
GARAGE 21-0 X 23-4
LR 19-4 X 15-0
KIT 15-0 X 16-0
REFG
LUMINOUS CLG
COOK TOP
OVEN D/W
SINK
STOR
DR 15-0 X 15-0
ENTRY
PANTRY
BRK'FST
STORAGE
CHINA
CHINA
38-2
86-8

LIFESTYLE HOME PLANS

ATTIC STORAGE
OAK SILL
ATTIC STORAGE
BR-2 13-8 X 15-0
DN
BR-3 16-8 X 15-0
LINEN
STORAGE
ATTIC STORAGE

MAID'S RM 13-4 X 12-8
WASH TUB DRY
FREEZ
UP
REC RM 15-0 X 22-0
STORAGE
FIREPLACE
FURN
WH
UNFINISHED BASEMENT
UNEXCAVATED

Design V34531
First Floor: 1,975 square feet
Second Floor: 856 square feet
Lower Level: 760 square feet
Total: 3,591 square feet

D

Design V34530

First Floor: 3,207 square feet
Second Floor: 1,325 square feet
Lower Level: 1,552 square feet
Total: 6,084 square feet

D

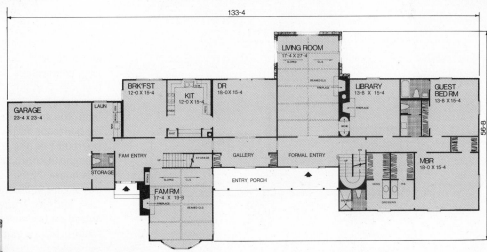

GARAGE 23-4 X 23-4 | LAUN | BRK'FST 12-0 X 15-4 | KIT 12-0 X 15-4 | DR 18-0 X 15-4 | LIVING ROOM 17-4 X 27-4 | LIBRARY 13-8 X 15-4 | GUEST BED RM 13-8 X 15-4

133-4 / 56-8

FAM ENTRY / STORAGE / FAM RM 17-4 X 19-8 / STORAGE / GALLERY / FORMAL ENTRY / ENTRY PORCH / MBR 18-0 X 15-4

GAME RM 16-8 X 34-8

UNFINISHED BASEMENT / BR 4 14-4 X 15-0 / BR 5 13-4 X 15-0

UNEXCAVATED / STORAGE / HALL / STORAGE

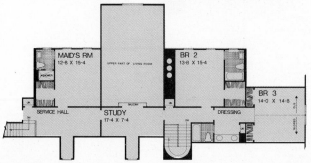

MAID'S RM 12-8 X 15-4 / UPPER PART OF LIVING ROOM / BR 2 13-8 X 15-4

SERVICE HALL / STUDY 17-4 X 7-4 / DRESSING / BR 3 14-0 X 14-8

● This large, country-style home has board-and-batten siding combined with a stone-veneered foundation and a hand-split cedar-shake roof. The living room, which has eighteen-foot beamed ceilings and ten-foot wall windows, will accommodate large groups that can circulate between the living room and library. The first-floor guest room has a private bath and a large closet. In the master bedroom is a convenient dressing room and two deep walk-in closets. Each upstairs bedroom has a private bath and generous closet space. The end bedroom with its large bath has a high sloping ceiling. On the lower level are two more bedrooms, a game room and storage.

LIFESTYLE HOME PLANS

249

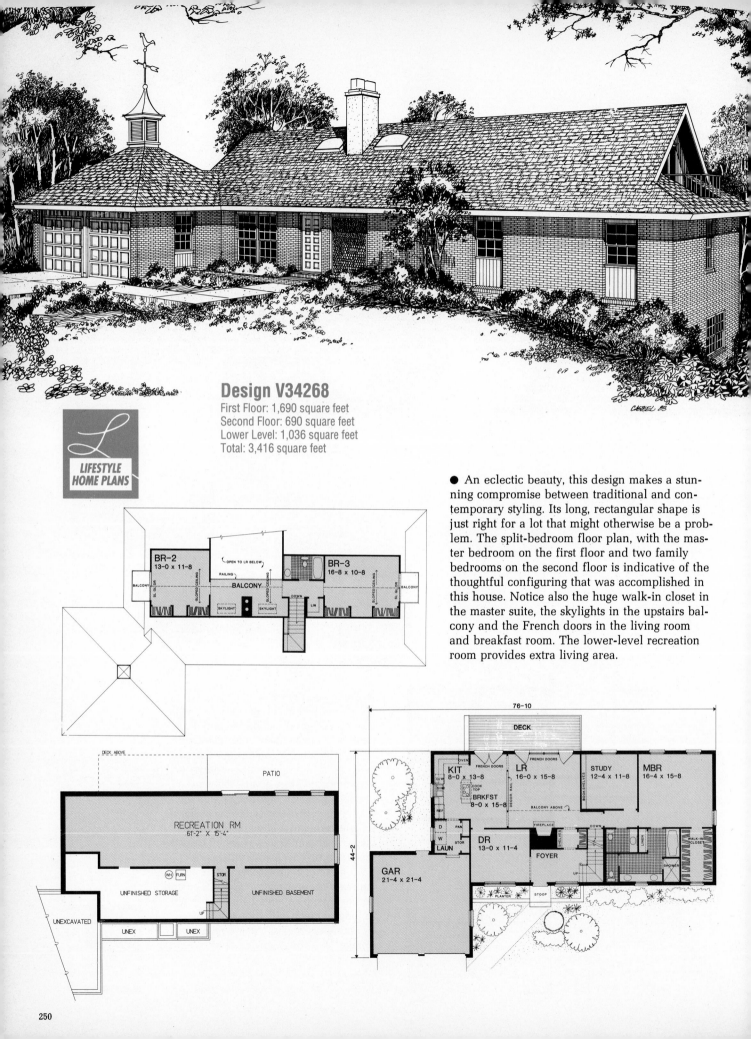

Design V34268

First Floor: 1,690 square feet
Second Floor: 690 square feet
Lower Level: 1,036 square feet
Total: 3,416 square feet

● An eclectic beauty, this design makes a stunning compromise between traditional and contemporary styling. Its long, rectangular shape is just right for a lot that might otherwise be a problem. The split-bedroom floor plan, with the master bedroom on the first floor and two family bedrooms on the second floor is indicative of the thoughtful configuring that was accomplished in this house. Notice also the huge walk-in closet in the master suite, the skylights in the upstairs balcony and the French doors in the living room and breakfast room. The lower-level recreation room provides extra living area.

LIFESTYLE HOME PLANS

Second Floor plan:
BR-2 13-0 x 11-8
OPEN TO LR BELOW
RAILING
BALCONY
BR-3 16-8 x 10-8
BALCONY
SKYLIGHT
DOWN
LIN
SKYLIGHT

Lower Level plan:
DECK ABOVE
PATIO
RECREATION RM 61-2" X 15-4"
WH FURN
STOR
UNFINISHED STORAGE
UNFINISHED BASEMENT
UNEXCAVATED
UNEX
UNEX
UP

First Floor plan:
76-10
DECK
44-2
KIT 8-0 x 13-8
FRENCH DOORS
LR 16-0 x 15-8
FRENCH DOORS
STUDY 12-4 x 11-8
MBR 16-4 x 15-8
BRKFST 8-0 x 15-8
BALCONY ABOVE
BOOK SHELVES
REF
D W
PAN STOR
LAUN
DR 13-0 x 11-4
FIREPLACE
FOYER
DOWN
LINEN
WALK-IN CLOSET
SHOWER
GAR 21-4 x 21-4
UP
PLANTER
STOOP

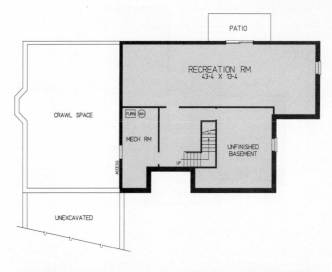

LIFESTYLE HOME PLANS

Design. V34270

First Floor: 2,272 square feet
Second Floor: 582 square feet
Lower Level: 675 square feet
Total: 3,529 square feet

D

● A captivating home — and one that will stand the test of time with its great floor plan. Informal living takes place in the family room and nearby breakfast room attached to the kitchen. The dining room and formal living room are to the rear. Two of the bedrooms (one a fine master suite) are to the right of the entry foyer. Each has its own full bath. Upstairs are two more bedrooms, sharing a full bath between them. Bonus space is found on the lower level.

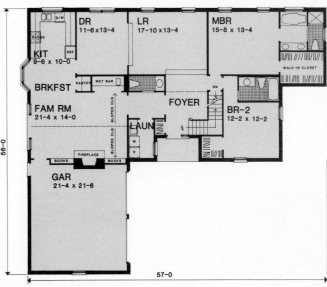

Design V34527

First Floor: 2,258 square feet
Second Floor: 1,169 square feet
Lower Level: 1,552 square feet
Total: 4,979 square feet

● This Georgian exterior encloses a thoroughly modern floor plan. From the front entry, a left turn leads to the library with its front-facing windows. Turn right to enter the formal dining room, just a few steps from the U-shaped kitchen with attached breakfast room. The great room is located to the rear of the home and has a fireplace with flanking built-in bookshelves as its focus. The first-floor master bedroom features its own deck, three closets, and a private bath with double vanity. Upstairs there are three more bedrooms and two full baths. Another bedroom is on the lower level.

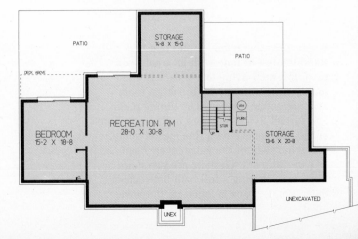

LIFESTYLE
HOME PLANS

Design V34506

First Floor: 2,270 square feet
Second Floor: 865 square feet
Lower Level: 1,345 square feet
Total: 4,480 square feet

L **D**

● This multi-level house with a one-story antebellum Greek Revival exterior was designed for maximum flexibility for family requirements. On the first floor, bedroom two could be made into a sitting room to create a private suite for the master bedroom. Bedroom three could be a library or a home office. The two upstairs bedrooms could be omitted or could be left unfinished for future development. The basement-level bedroom could be used by a college-age student or a servant.

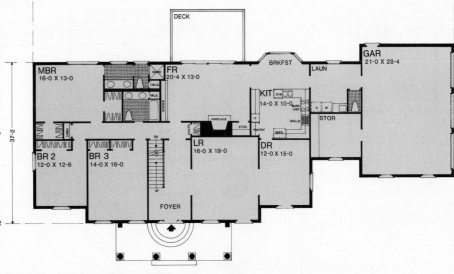

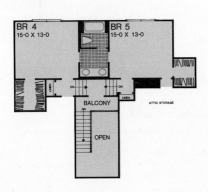

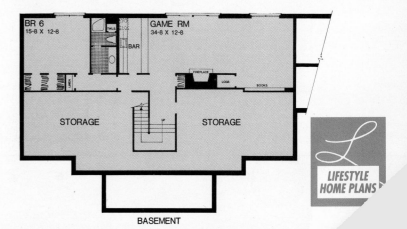

LIFESTYLE HOME PLANS

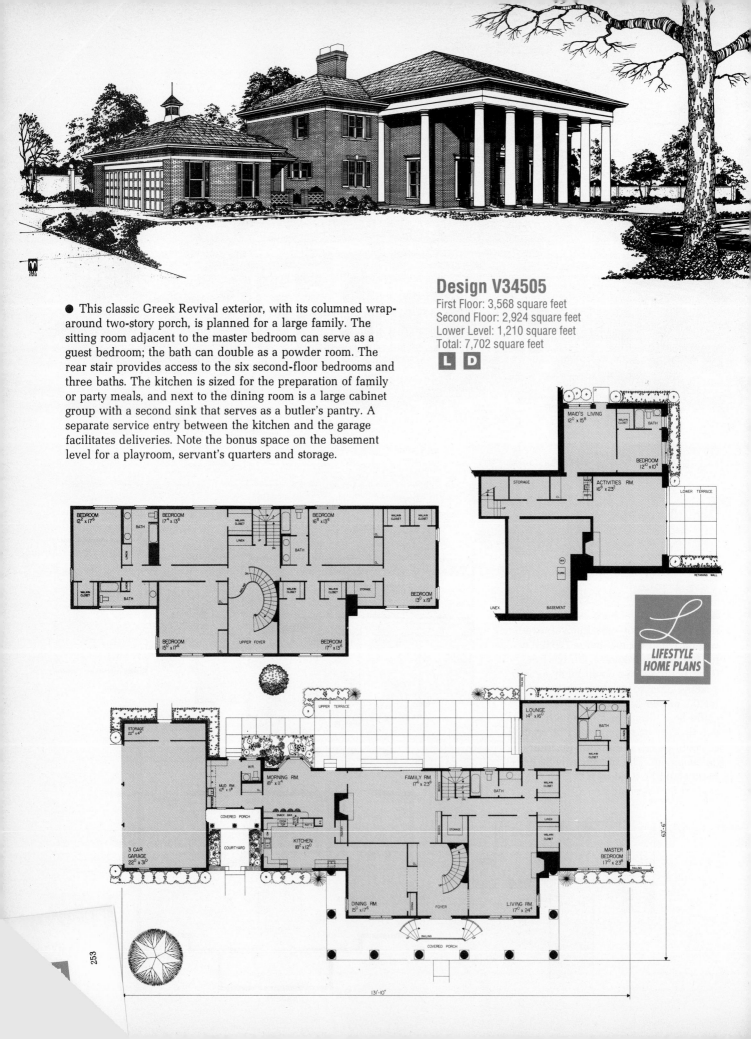

This classic Greek Revival exterior, with its columned wrap-around two-story porch, is planned for a large family. The sitting room adjacent to the master bedroom can serve as a guest bedroom; the bath can double as a powder room. The rear stair provides access to the six second-floor bedrooms and three baths. The kitchen is sized for the preparation of family or party meals, and next to the dining room is a large cabinet group with a second sink that serves as a butler's pantry. A separate service entry between the kitchen and the garage facilitates deliveries. Note the bonus space on the basement level for a playroom, servant's quarters and storage.

Design V34505

First Floor: 3,568 square feet
Second Floor: 2,924 square feet
Lower Level: 1,210 square feet
Total: 7,702 square feet

L D

LIFESTYLE HOME PLANS

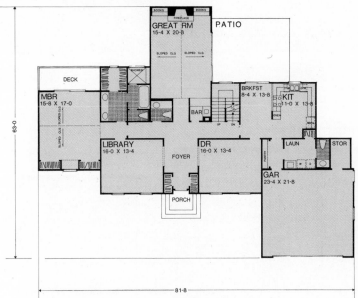

Design V34525

First Floor: 2,258 square feet
Second Floor: 1,169 square feet
Lower Level: 2,200 square feet
Total: 5,627 square feet

● This exterior is from New England Colonial days, but the interior is definitely modern. The library can be converted to a parlor or a living room. The view from the entrance doors goes back across the great room and its cathedral ceiling to the large fireplace at the back. The master bedroom has twenty-four feet of hanging space for clothes; its three-compartment bath has a spacious stall shower as well as an oversized whirlpool tub. The stairs at the back give access to the three upper-floor bedrooms. Stairs below lead to a basement that could hold a family activities area.

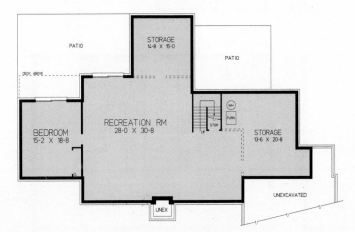

LIFESTYLE
HOME PLANS

Design V34520

First Floor: 1,914 square feet
Second Floor: 1,807 square feet
Lower Level: 1,425 square feet
Total: 5,146 square feet

● This handsome Georgian exterior features arched brick over the windows, double entrance doors with classic pedimented trim, and floor-length first-floor windows. The living room opens to the den through a short passage lined on both sides with shelves for collectors' items. The den has one full wall of built-in cabinets and bookshelves and is designed with raised panel oak walls in 18th-Century style. The upper floors have four bedrooms, one with a private bath, two with a compartmented bath. The master bedroom has two closets and a bath with stall shower and separate tub. The basement opens out at grade level to the back and has a large play room, a storage area, and a maid's bath and room.

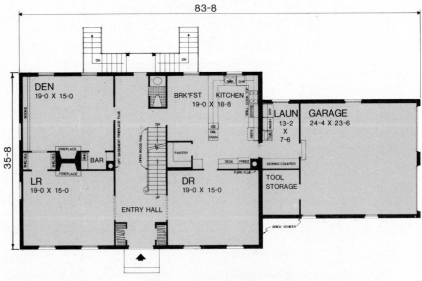

LIFESTYLE
HOME PLANS

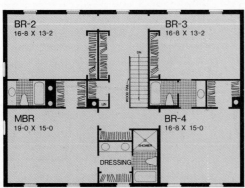

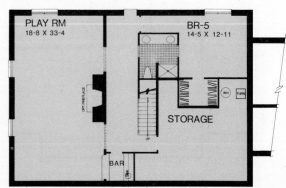

Design V34391

First Floor: 1,315 square feet
Second Floor: 1,312 square feet
Lower Level: 1,273 square feet
Total: 3,900 square feet

● Hillside living takes on elegant proportions in this thoughtful plan. Formal and informal living areas to the left of the central foyer complement the dining and cooking areas on the right. A large deck to the back adds outdoor enjoyment. The master bedroom, with full bath, upstairs misses nothing in the way of luxury and is joined by two family bedrooms and baths. Bonus space to the front makes a perfect office or computer room. Note recreation room with fireplace.

BAY WINDOWS

WHIRLPOOL

SHOWER

BEDROOM-2
13-8 X 12-10

W.I.C.   W.I.C.   W.I.C.

HALL

MASTER
BEDROOM
13-8 X 19-2

LINEN

DN

LINEN

BEDROOM-3
13-8 X 11-4

COMPUTER /
OFFICE
9-4 X 9-0

38-0

DECK

WET BAR

FAMILY ROOM
13-8 X 18-0

W
LAUNDRY

BREAKFAST
9-0 X 13-8

FIREPLACE

PANTRY

KITCHEN
11-0 X 13-8

D/W

SURF.
UNIT

REF. OVEN

33-0

DN.

COATS

LIVING ROOM
13-8 X 14-0

DINING ROOM
13-8 X 14-0

UP   FOYER

L
LIFESTYLE
HOME PLANS

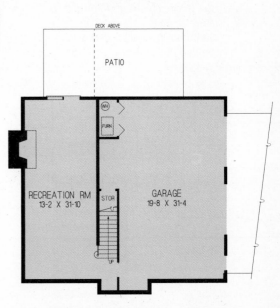

DECK ABOVE

PATIO

WH

FURN.

RECREATION RM
13-2 X 31-10

STOR

GARAGE
19-8 X 31-4

Design V34396

First Floor: 1,772 square feet
Second Floor: 674 square feet
Lower Level: 908 square feet
Total: 3,354 square feet

● Reminiscent of French country houses, this delightful two-story offers a wealth of extras. Two wood decks flank the great room on either side and are also accessed through the breakfast room and the master bedroom. Storage space abounds with walk-in closets in all three bedrooms (two in the master bedroom) and extra store rooms in the garage extension and off a second floor closet. Notice the built-ins, skylights, and wet bar.

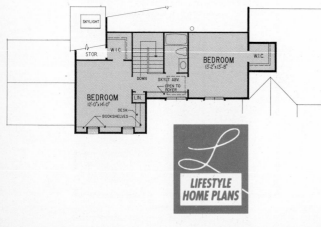

● By placing living areas to the back of this plan, a wide rear and side deck can be enjoyed in privacy away from street noise. The large central dining room has access to the deck and leads to the sunken living room (take note of built-ins and bay window). Sleeping accommodations on the second floor allow for a large master suite and two more bedrooms with full bath.

Design V34404

First Floor: 1,336 square feet
Second Floor: 1,210 square feet
Lower Level: 1,321 square feet
Total: 3,867 square feet

L

LIFESTYLE HOME PLANS

FAMILY ROOM
15-0 X 24-8

RECREATION ROOM
31-8 X 28-8

UNEX UNEX

DECK

BOOKS SLOPED CEILING FIREPLACE SLOPED CEILING

LIVING ROOM
15-8 X 23-4

BAY WINDOW

BOOKS

DECK

WET BAR CHINA

DN DINING DN
19-4 X 12-0

UP

OVEN D/W

KITCHEN

BREAKFAST
10-4 X 9-8 SURF. UNIT REF.

DN

W LAUNDRY
D

PANTRY POWDER ROOM

W/H FURN. FOYER

73-0

GARAGE
22-4 X 23-8

30-0

MASTER BEDROOM
13-8 X 16-4

SHOWER

WIC

BOOKS

DN

LINEN

LINEN

BALCONY

WIC HALL

OPEN TO FOYER

BEDROOM-2
11-0 X 14-8

BEDROOM-3
11-0 X 14-8

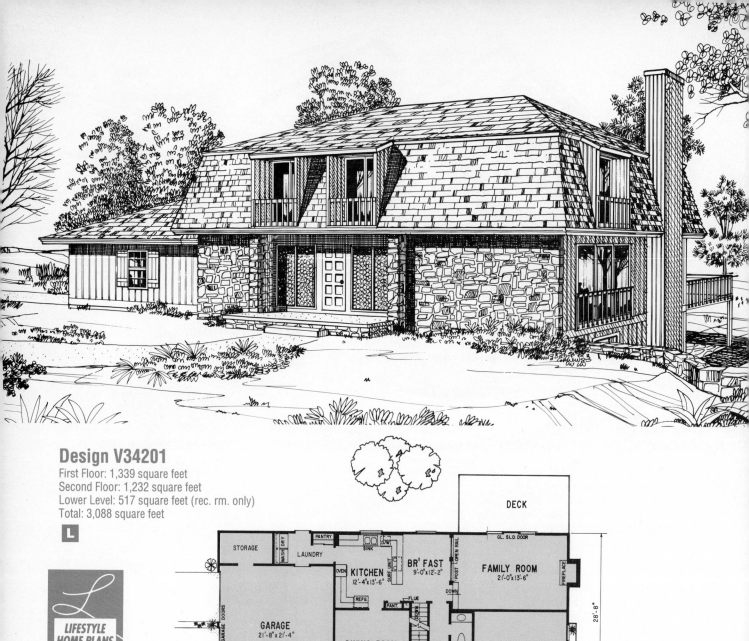

Design V34201

First Floor: 1,339 square feet
Second Floor: 1,232 square feet
Lower Level: 517 square feet (rec. rm. only)
Total: 3,088 square feet

L

LIFESTYLE
HOME PLANS

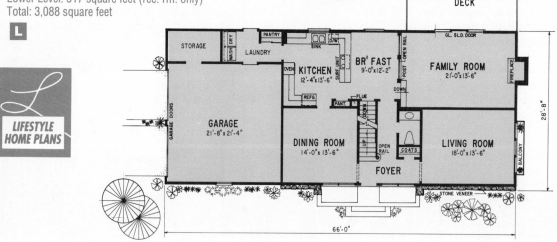

DECK

STORAGE | WASH DRY | PANTRY | SINK | D/W

LAUNDRY

KITCHEN
12'-4"x13'-6"

OVEN | SURF UNIT

REFG.

PANT

BR' FAST
9'-0"x12'-2"

GL. SLD. DOOR

FAMILY ROOM
21'-0"x13'-6"

FIREPLACE

POST | OPEN RAIL

DOWN

GARAGE DOORS

GARAGE
21'-8" x 21'-4"

DINING ROOM
14'-0"x 13'-6"

FLUE | DOWN

UP

OPEN RAIL

FOYER

COATS

LIVING ROOM
18'-0"x 13'-6"

BALCONY

STONE VENEER

28'-8"

66'-0"

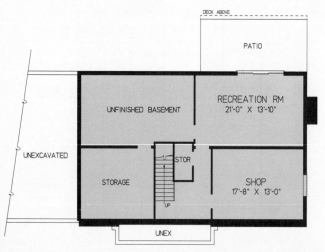

DECK ABOVE

PATIO

UNEXCAVATED

STORAGE

UNFINISHED BASEMENT

STOR

UP

RECREATION RM
21'-0" X 13'-10"

SHOP
17'-8" X 13'-0"

UNEX

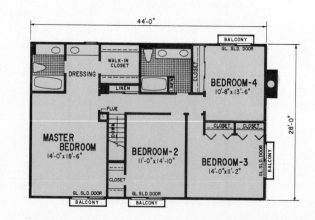

44'-0"

BALCONY

GL. SLD. DOOR

WALK-IN CLOSET

DRESSING

LINEN

CLOSET

BEDROOM-4
10'-8"x13'-6"

FLUE

MASTER BEDROOM
14'-0"x18'-6"

DOWN

CLOSET | CLOSET

BEDROOM-2
11'-0"x14'-10"

BEDROOM-3
14'-0"x11'-2"

GL. SLD. DOOR

CLOSET

GL. SLD. DOOR | GL. SLD. DOOR

BALCONY | BALCONY

28'-0"

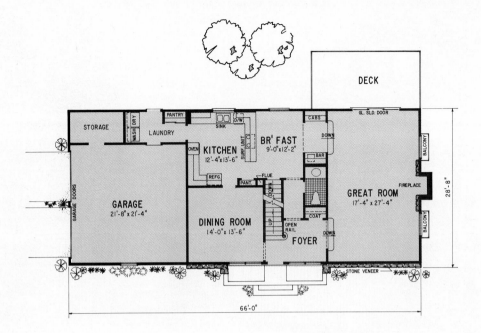

First Floor plan labels:
STORAGE · WASH · DRY · PANTRY · LAUNDRY · SINK · D/W · CABS · DOWN · GL. SLD. DOOR · DECK · BALCONY · OVEN · KITCHEN 12'-4" x 13'-6" · SURF. UNIT · BR' FAST 9'-0" x 12'-2" · BAR · REFG · PANT. · FLUE · DOWN · GREAT ROOM 17'-4" x 27'-4" · FIREPLACE · BALCONY · GARAGE DOORS · GARAGE 21'-8" x 21'-4" · DINING ROOM 14'-0" x 13'-6" · OPEN RAIL · COAT · FOYER · DOWN · STONE VENEER · 28'-8" · 66'-0"

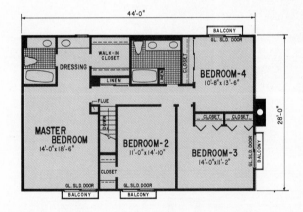

Second Floor plan labels:
44'-0" · BALCONY · GL. SLD. DOOR · WALK-IN CLOSET · DRESSING · CLOSET · CLOSET · BEDROOM-4 10'-8" x 13'-6" · LINEN · LINEN · FLUE · CLOSET · CLOSET · MASTER BEDROOM 14'-0" x 18'-6" · DOWN · BEDROOM-2 11'-0" x 14'-10" · BEDROOM-3 14'-0" x 11'-2" · GL. SLD. DOOR · BALCONY · CLOSET · GL. SLD. DOOR · GL. SLD. DOOR · BALCONY · BALCONY · 28'-0"

Design V34200

First Floor: 1,339 square feet
Second Floor: 1,232 square feet
Lower Level: 517 square feet (rec. rm. only)
Total: 3,088 square feet

● Choose floor plan V34201 or V34200 for this beautiful hipped-roof exterior. Either plan allows all the space you're looking for in living areas on the first floor and in the walk-out basement. Notice the fine kitchen layout with its attached breakfast room and nearby laundry. Its proximity to the dining room assures graceful dinner service. The sunken family room in V34201 will serve casual gatherings. It has sliding glass doors to a deck and complements the more formal living room. V34200 has a great room rather than the two separate living areas. It features two balconies and a centered fireplace. In both plans, each of the four upstairs bedrooms has its own balcony.

LIFESTYLE HOME PLANS

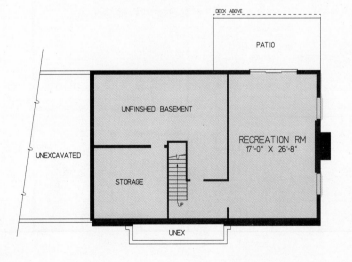

Lower Level plan labels:
DECK ABOVE · PATIO · UNFINISHED BASEMENT · UNEXCAVATED · STORAGE · RECREATION RM 17'-0" X 26'-8" · UP · UNEX

ONE-STORY OPEN-STAIRCASE PLANS . . .

show a wonderful innovation of design that brings two levels of living together in a graceful way. The open design allows an incorporation of basement-level recreation space into main-level living areas and creates dramatic balcony and overlook areas.

Design V34124
Square Footage: 1,772

● From the delightful bridged entry to the expansive rear deck, this home will provide great livability in limited square footage. An open staircase to the basement allows the potential for expansion at a later time. Living areas include a great room with fireplace, dining room with built-in shelves, and a spacious L-shaped kitchen. The master bedroom is truly fit for a king: notice the huge walk-in closet, dressing area and sliding glass doors to the deck. Two family bedrooms share a full bath.

LIFESTYLE HOME PLANS

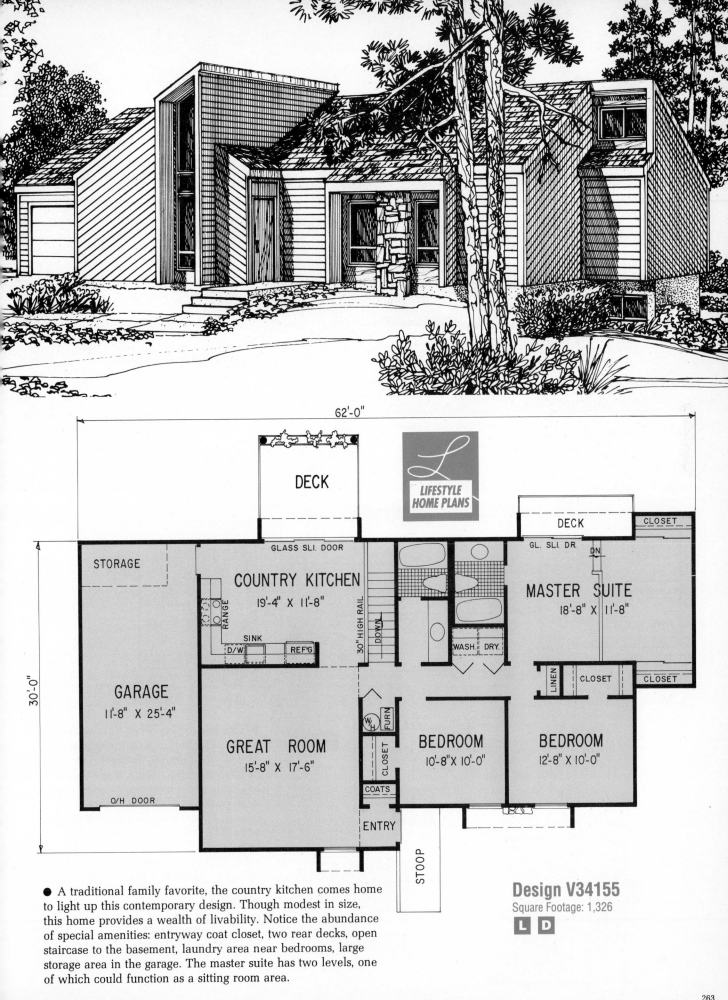

DECK

LIFESTYLE
HOME PLANS

DECK

CLOSET

STORAGE

GLASS SLI. DOOR

GL. SLI. DR.

DN

COUNTRY KITCHEN
19'-4" X 11'-8"

MASTER SUITE
18'-8" X 11'-8"

RANGE

SINK

D/W

REF'G

30" HIGH RAIL

DOWN

WASH.

DRY.

GARAGE
11'-8" X 25'-4"

LINEN

CLOSET

CLOSET

GREAT ROOM
15'-8" X 17'-6"

W
H

FURN

CLOSET

BEDROOM
10'-8" X 10'-0"

BEDROOM
12'-8" X 10'-0"

COATS

O/H DOOR

ENTRY

STOOP

62'-0"

30'-0"

● A traditional family favorite, the country kitchen comes home to light up this contemporary design. Though modest in size, this home provides a wealth of livability. Notice the abundance of special amenities: entryway coat closet, two rear decks, open staircase to the basement, laundry area near bedrooms, large storage area in the garage. The master suite has two levels, one of which could function as a sitting room area.

Design V34155
Square Footage: 1,326

L D

263

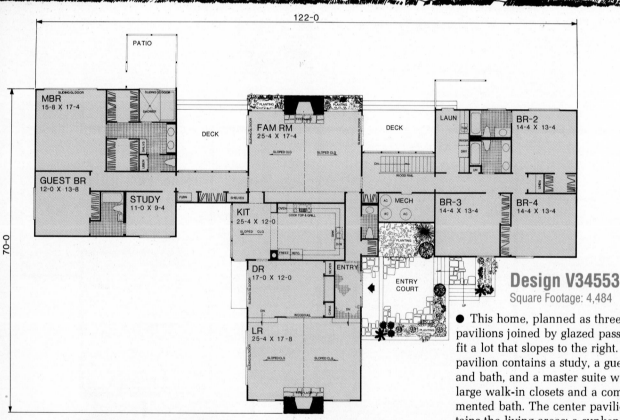

PATIO

MBR
15-8 X 17-4

SLIDING GL DOOR   SLIDING GL DOOR

SHOWER

DECK

FAM RM
25-4 X 17-4

PLANTING   PLANTING

FIREPLACE

SLOPED CLG   SLOPED CLG

DECK

LAUN

BR-2
14-4 X 13-4

TUB

WASH

DRY

GUEST BR
12-0 X 13-8

STUDY
11-0 X 9-4

FURN   SHELVES

KIT
25-4 X 12-0

SLOPED CLG

OVEN

COOK TOP & GRILL

SINK

FREEZ   REFG

DN   WOOD RAIL

LN

AC   MECH
AC   AC

BR-3
14-4 X 13-4

BR-4
14-4 X 13-4

PLANTING

DR
17-0 X 12-0

ENTRY

ENTRY
COURT

LR
25-4 X 17-8

DN   WOOD RAIL   CHINA

DN

SLOPED CLG   SLOPED CLG

FIREPLACE

PLANTING

UP

70-0

122-0

Design V34553
Square Footage: 4,484

● This home, planned as three separate
pavilions joined by glazed passages, will
fit a lot that slopes to the right. The left
pavilion contains a study, a guest room
and bath, and a master suite with two
large walk-in closets and a compartmented bath. The center pavilion contains the living areas: a sunken living
room with a stone fireplace, a dining
room with built-in buffet and lock-up
closets for china and silver, a big
U-shaped kitchen and breakfast area
with bay windows, and in the rear a
family room with its own fireplace and
two decks for outdoor living. In the right
wing is a laundry and three children's
rooms with two baths. An open staircase
leads to the basement.

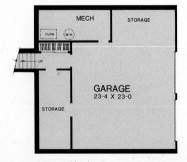

MECH   STORAGE

FURN   W/H   UP

GARAGE
23-4 X 23-0

STORAGE

LIFESTYLE
HOME PLANS

● A gorgeous garden court introduces the entry to this lovely traditional home. The court idea is echoed to the rear and side in expansive terrace areas that can be reached from the dining room, breakfast room and family room. Notice that these areas are a few steps down from the living room, making the design great for a sloping lot. On the upper level are four bedrooms. The master is contained by itself. It is ornamented with two window planters.

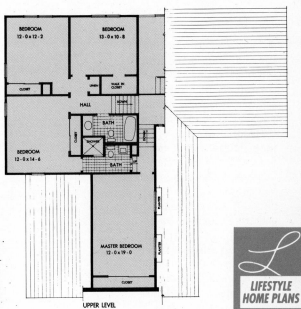

UPPER LEVEL

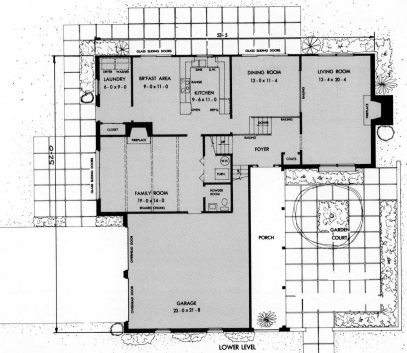

LOWER LEVEL

Design V34023

Lower Level: 1,371 square feet
Upper Level: 1,112 square feet
Total: 2,483 square feet

L LIFESTYLE HOME PLANS

Design V32917
Square Footage: 1,813

● Here's a smart-looking Contemporary home with lots of carefully packaged comfort on the inside. All three bedrooms, including a master bedroom suite, are isolated on one side of the house, away from household traffic. The master bedroom includes a private bath, vanity and walk-in closet. A spacious rear gathering room enjoys its own fireplace and sloped ceiling. An efficient kitchen features pass-thru to an adjoining breakfast room. There's also a formal dining room just steps away, with view of a front trellis area. A mud room with washroom is conveniently located between garage and kitchen. Note also the covered rear porch and built-in planter off the spacious two-car garage. Includes plans for optional basement.

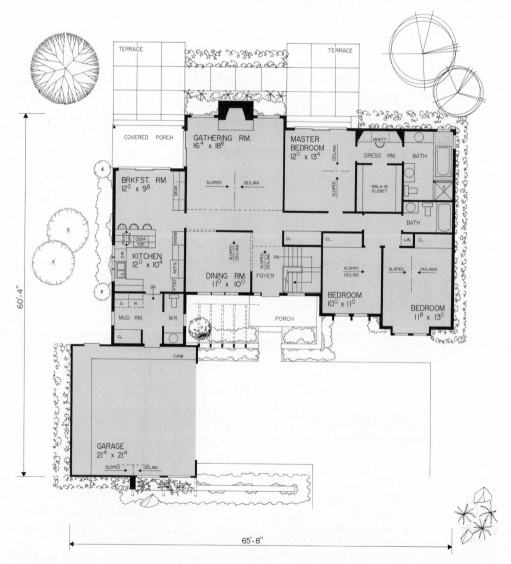

Design V32913
Square Footage: 1,835

D

● This smart design features multi-gabled ends, varied roof lines, and vertical windows. It also offers efficient zoning by room functions and plenty of modern comforts for Contemporary family lifestyle. A covered porch leads through a foyer to a large central gathering room with fireplace, sloped ceiling, and its own special view of a rear terrace. A modern kitchen with snack bar has a pass-thru to a breakfast room with view of the terrace. There's also an adjacent dining room. A media room isolated along with bedrooms from the rest of the house offers a quiet private area for listening to stereos or VCRs. A master bedroom suite includes its own whirlpool. A large garage includes extra storage.

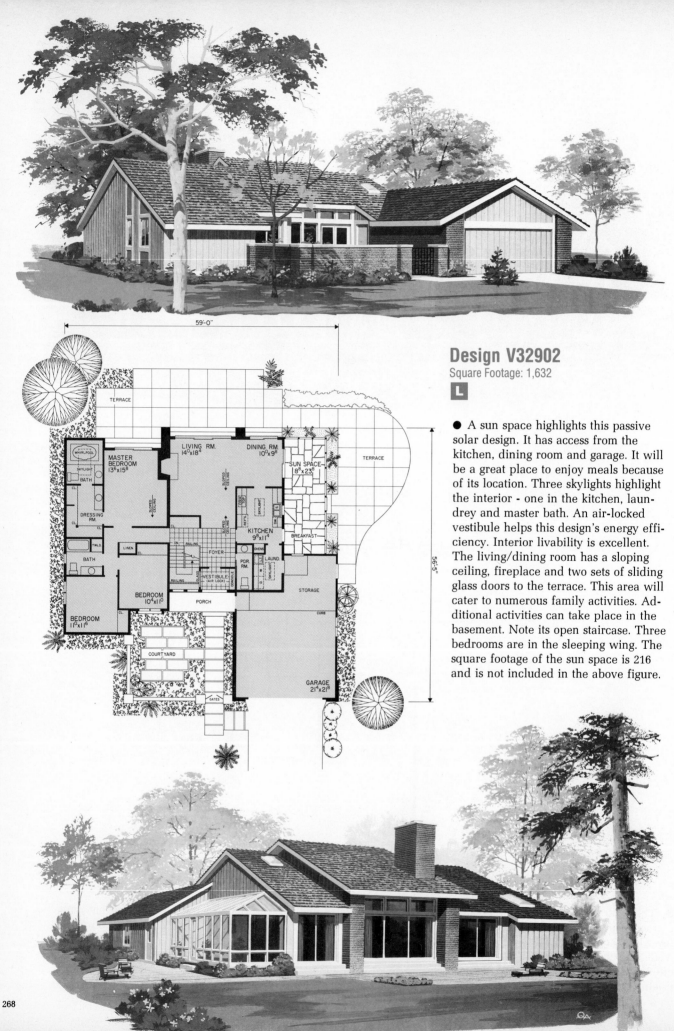

Design V32902

Square Footage: 1,632

L

● A sun space highlights this passive solar design. It has access from the kitchen, dining room and garage. It will be a great place to enjoy meals because of its location. Three skylights highlight the interior - one in the kitchen, laundrey and master bath. An air-locked vestibule helps this design's energy efficiency. Interior livability is excellent. The living/dining room has a sloping ceiling, fireplace and two sets of sliding glass doors to the terrace. This area will cater to numerous family activities. Additional activities can take place in the basement. Note its open staircase. Three bedrooms are in the sleeping wing. The square footage of the sun space is 216 and is not included in the above figure.

Design V32886
Square Footage: 1,733

● This one-story house is attractive with its contemporary exterior. It has many excellent features to keep you and your family happy for many years. For example, notice the spacious gathering room with sliding glass doors that allow easy access to the greenhouse. Another exciting feature of this room is that you will receive an abundance of sunshine through the clerestory windows. Also, this plan offers you two nice sized bedrooms. The master suite is not only roomy but also unique because through both the bedroom and the bath you can enter a greenhouse with a hot tub. The hot tub will be greatly appreciated after a long, hard day at work. Don't forget to note the breakfast room with access to the terrace. You will enjoy the efficient kitchen that will make preparing meals a breeze. A greenhouse window here is charming. An appealing, open staircase leads to the basement. The square footage of the greenhouses is 394 and is not included in the above figure.

Design V32941

Square Footage: 1,842

D

● Here is a basic floor plan which goes with each of the differently styled exteriors. The Early American version above is charming, indeed. Horizontal siding, stone, window boxes, a dovecote, a picket fence and a garden court enhance its appeal. Note the covered entrance.

Design V32942

Square Footage: 1,834

D

● The Tudor exterior above will be the favorite of many. Stucco, simulated timber work and diamond-lite windows set its unique character. Each of the delightful exteriors features eye-catching roof lines. Inside, there is an outstanding plan to cater to the living patterns of the small family, empty nesters, or retirees.

Design V32943

Square Footage: 1,834

D

● The Contemporary optional exterior above features vertical siding and a wide-overhanging roof with exposed rafter ends. The foyer is spacious with sloped ceiling and a dramatic open staircase to the basement recreation area. Other ceilings in the house are also sloped. The breakfast, dining and media rooms are highlights, along with the laundry, the efficient kitchen, the snack bar and the master bath.

Floor plan (58'-2" × 57'-5"):

TERRACE — TERRACE

WHIRLPOOL — MASTER BEDROOM 12⁰ x 15⁰ — GATHERING RM. 18⁶ x 15⁰ — DINING RM. 10⁴ x 11⁰

SEAT — SLOPED CEILING — SLOPED CEILING — SLOPED CEILING — SLOPED CEILING

BATH — BRKFST. RM. 10⁰ x 9⁰ — BAR

LIN. — WALK-IN CLOSET — SHELVES

BATH — LIN. — SLOPED CEILING — SLOPED FOYER — RAILING — LAUND. — KITCHEN 10⁰ x 9⁸ — RANGE

CL. — BEDROOM 11⁰ x 11⁸ — MEDIA RM. 11⁰ x 12⁰ — COVERED PORCH

GARDEN COURT

GARAGE 21⁴ x 21⁸ + STOR.

STORAGE

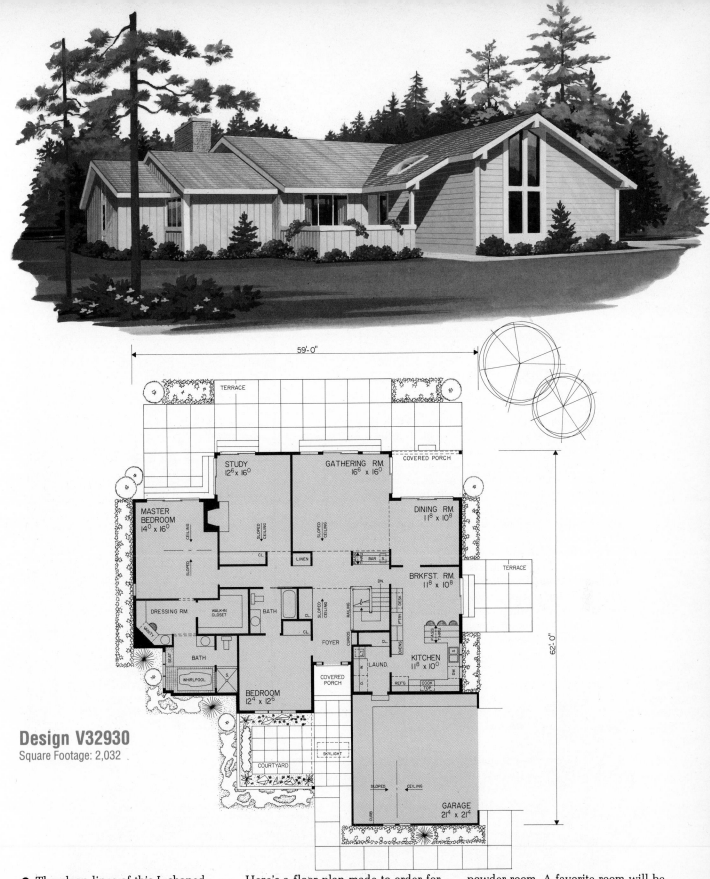

Design V32930
Square Footage: 2,032

● The clean lines of this L-shaped contemporary are enhanced by the interesting, wide overhanging roof planes. Horizontal and vertical siding compliment one another. The low privacy fence adds interest as it forms a delightful front courtyard adjacent to the covered walkway to the front door.

Here's a floor plan made to order for the active small family or empty-nesters. Sloping ceilings and fine glass areas foster a spacious interior. The master bedroom has an outstanding dressing room and bath layout. The guest room has its own full bath. Note how this bath can function as a handy

powder room. A favorite room will be the study with its fireplace and two sets of sliding glass doors. Don't miss the open-planned gathering and dining rooms, or the kitchen/laundry area. The breakfast room has its own terrace. Notice the rear covered porch. Fine indoor-outdoor relationships.

Design V32882

Square Footage: 2,832

● This contemporary, one-story design should be oriented on a west-facing site if it is built in the northern regions of the country. The result will be minimal exposure to the cold northern winds during the winter. Study the north side of this plan. There is only one small window and it will be protected by the privacy wall. This means that the rooms on the opposite side of the house will have the desirable southern exposure. A westerly exposure for the living room will be most beneficial in many areas of the country. This plan reflects interesting living patterns and excellent indoor/outdoor relationships. Wide overhanging roofs, skylights, glass gables, vented walkways, wind-buffering privacy fences and 2x6 construction are among this design's energy-oriented features.

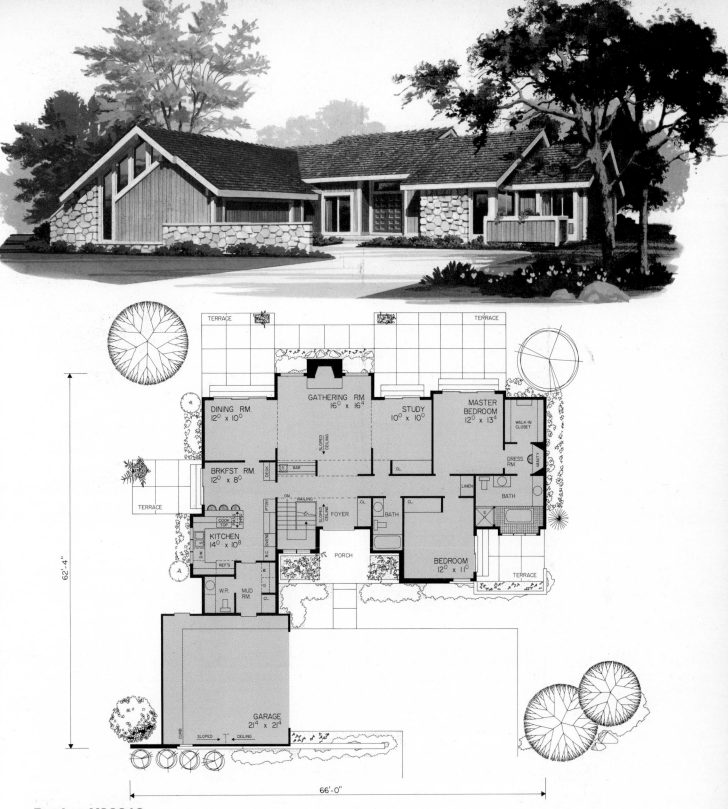

Design V32918
Square Footage: 1,693

D

● An exciting contemporary facade with fieldstone, vertical siding and interesting roof lines. The projecting garage creates a pleasing drive court as the impressive approach to this moderately-sized home. Double front doors open into a spacious foyer. Traffic is efficiently routed to all areas of the interior. Of particular interest is the open staircase to the lower level basement. Sloped ceilings in this area and the gathering room, along with the open planning reinforce the delightful feeling of spaciousness. The U-shaped kitchen is handy to the utility area and works well with the formal and infor-mal dining areas. Like the dining room, the study flanks the gathering room. Open planning makes this 38 foot wide area a cheerful one, indeed. The master bedroom suite features a big walk-in closet, a dressing area with vanity and an outstanding bath. Note the terraces.

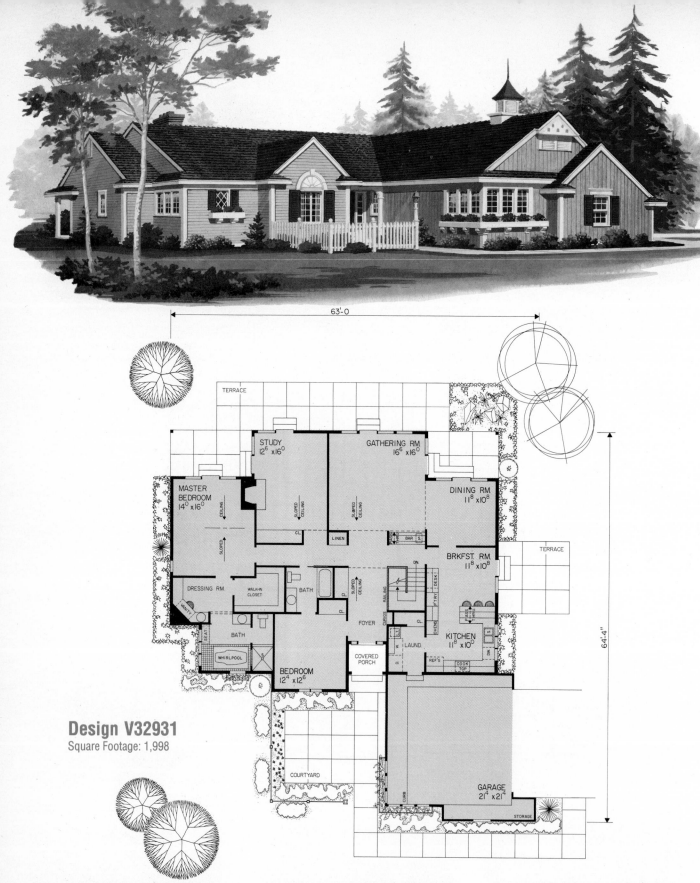

Design V32931
Square Footage: 1,998

● Little details make the difference. Consider these that make this such a charming showplace: Picket-fenced courtyard, carriage lamp, window boxes, shutters, muntined windows, multi-gabled roof, cornice returns, vertical and horizontal siding with corner

boards, front door with glass side lites, etc. Inside this appealing exterior there is a truly outstanding floor plan for the small family or empty-nesters. The master bedroom suite is long on luxury, with a separate dressing room, private vanities, and whirlpool bath. An

adjacent study is just the right retreat. There's room to move and — what a warm touch! — it has its own fireplace. Other attractions: roomy kitchen and breakfast area, spacious gathering room, rear and side terraces, and an attached two-car garage with storage.

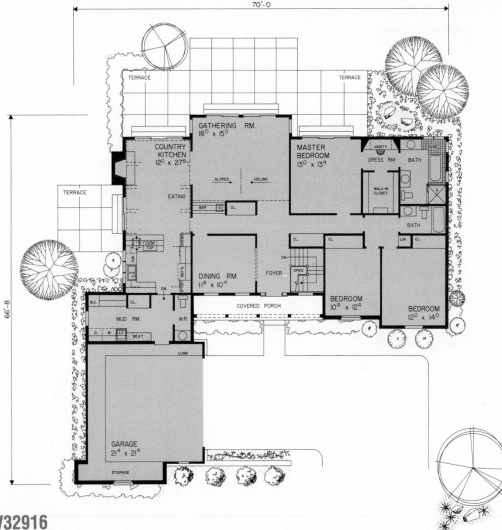

Design V32916
Square Footage: 2,129

● Pride of ownership will be forever yours as the occupant of this Early American styled one-story house. The covered front porch provides a shelter for the inviting panelled front door with its flanking side lites. Designed for fine family living, this three-bedroom, 2½-bath home offers wonderful formal and informal living patterns. The 27-foot country kitchen has a beamed ceiling and a fireplace. The U-shaped work center is efficient. It is but a step from the mud room area with its laundry equipment, closets, cupboards, counter space and washroom. There are two dining areas — an informal eating space and a formal separate dining room. The more formal gathering room is spacious with a sloping ceiling and two sets of sliding glass doors to the rear terrace.

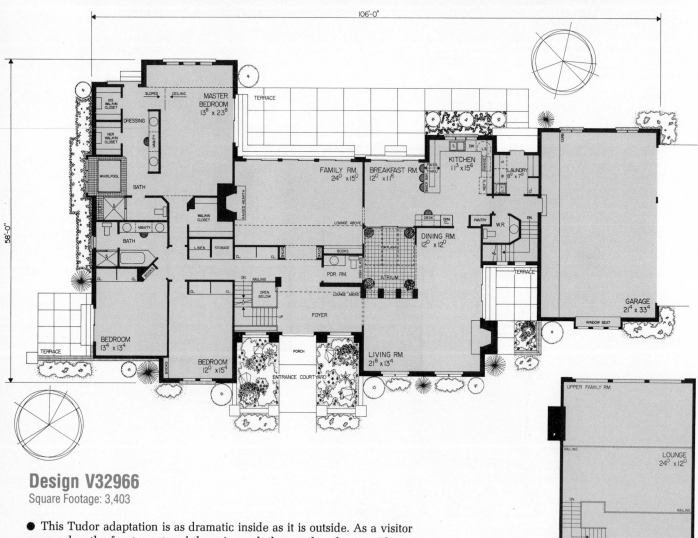

Design V32966
Square Footage: 3,403

● This Tudor adaptation is as dramatic inside as it is outside. As a visitor approaches the front courtyard there is much that catches the eye. The interesting roof lines, the appealing window treatment, the contrasting exterior materials and their textures, the inviting panelled front door and the massive twin chimneys with their protruding clay pots. Inside, the spacious foyer with its sloping ceiling looks up into the balcony-type lounge. It also looks down the open stairwell to the lower level area. From the foyer, traffic flows conveniently to other areas. The focal point of the living zone is the delightful atrium. Both the formal living room and the informal family room feature a fireplace. Each of the full baths highlights a tub and shower, a vanity and twin lavatories. Note the secondary access to the basement adjacent to the door to three car garage. Lounge adds an additional 284 sq. ft.

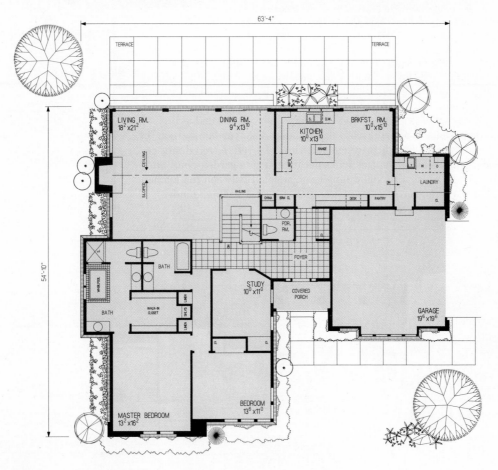

Design V32962
Square Footage: 2,112

● A Tudor exterior with an efficient floor plan favored by many. Each of the three main living zones — the sleeping zone, living zone, and the working zone — are but a couple steps from the foyer. This spells easy, efficient traffic patterns. Open planning, sloping ceiling and plenty of glass create a nice environment for the living-dining area. Its appeal is further enhanced by the open staircase to the lower level recreation/hobby area. The L-shaped kitchen with its island range and work surface is delightfully opened to the large breakfast room. Again, plenty of glass area adds to the feeling of spaciousness. Nearby is the step-saving first floor laundry. The sleeping zone has the flexibility of functioning as a two or three bedroom area. Notice the economical back-to-back plumbing.

Design V32879 Living Area including Atrium: 3,173 square feet
Upper Lounge/Balcony: 267 square feet; Total: 3,440 square feet

● This plush modern design seems to have it all, including an upper lounge, upper family room, and upper foyer. There's also an atrium with skylight centrally located downstairs. A modern kitchen with snack bar service to a breakfast room also enjoys its own greenhouse window. A deluxe master bedroom includes its own whirlpool and bay window. Three other bedrooms also are isolated at one end of the house downstairs to allow privacy and quiet. A spacious family room in the rear enjoys its own raised-hearth fireplace and view of a rear covered terrace. A front living room with its own fireplace looks out upon a side garden court and the central atrium. There's also a formal dining room situated between the kitchen and living room, plus a three-car garage, covered porches, and sizable laundry with washroom just off the garage.

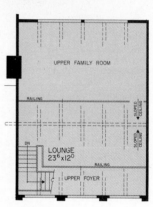

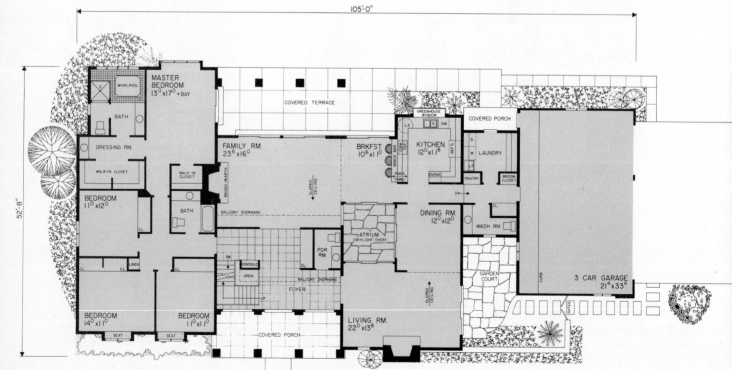

TWO-STORY OPEN-STAIRCASE PLANS . . .

present their levels of living in open, expansive floor plans. Open staircases to an upper or lower level (sometimes both) provide unobstructed living patterns and dramatic use of indoor and outdoor balconies, two-story gathering rooms and lounge overlooks. Both traditional and contemporary plans are offered here.

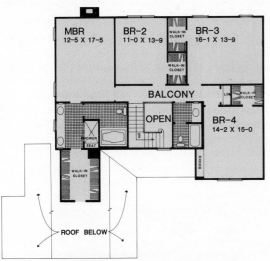

● Tradition takes over the exterior of this fine Tudor home, while the floor plan inside is made for today's family. First-floor rooms bow to casual as well as formal gatherings. The kitchen is centrally located between family and dining rooms. Special amenities include a pass-through wet bar, pantry cabinet, and huge walk-in coat closet. An open, railed staircase leads to the second floor where there are four bedrooms and two baths. All bedrooms have spacious walk-in closets.

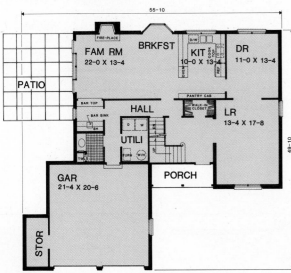

OPTIONAL FOR CRAWL FOUND.

LIFESTYLE
HOME PLANS

Design V34277
First Floor: 1,329 square feet
Second Floor: 1,437 square feet
Total: 2,766 square feet

D

Design V34214

First Floor: 1,152 square feet
Second Floor: 1,144 square feet
Total: 2,296 square feet

D

● Combining some of the best features of both contemporary and traditional design, this home is comfortable as either a country or city dweller. Beyond its rustic covered front porch is a classic of a floor plan. Because the open staircase to the second floor is located in the entry foyer, it contributes to the feeling of space and height throughout the home. A grand-sized family room blends in with the U-shaped kitchen, sharing a pass-through snack bar with it. Formal entertaining is handled easily in the living room and dining room on the right side of the home. Upstairs there's plenty of sleeping room in four bedrooms. Two full baths here serve the family's needs.

MASTER BEDROOM
15'-4"x13'-4"

BEDROOM - 2
10'-4"x11'-0"

BEDROOM - 3
14'-8" x 11'- 0"

CLOSET

FLUE

DRESSING

POWDER

LINEN

RAILING

UPPER FOYER

BEDROOM - 4
11'-0"x11'-8"

CLOSET

FLUE

LIFESTYLE HOME PLANS

PANTRY · REFG.

LINEN · W/H · FURN.

COATS · MECH.

FOYER

RAILING · UP

OPTION OMITTING BASEMENT

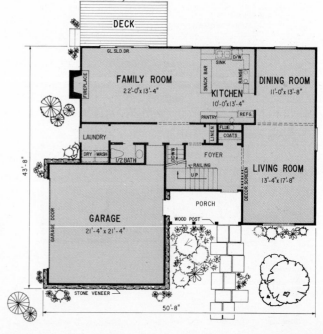

RAILING

DECK

GL. SLD. DR.

FIREPLACE

FAMILY ROOM
22'-0"x13'-4"

SNACK BAR

SINK · D/W

KITCHEN
10'-0"x13'-4"

RANGE

DINING ROOM
11'-0" x 13'-8"

PANTRY

REFG.

LAUNDRY

DRY · WASH

1/2 BATH

FLUE

LINEN

COATS

DOWN

FOYER

UP

RAILING

LIVING ROOM
13'-4" x 17'-8"

DECOR SCREEN

PORCH

WOOD POST

GARAGE DOOR

GARAGE
21'-4" x 21'-4"

STONE VENEER

43'-8"

50'-8"

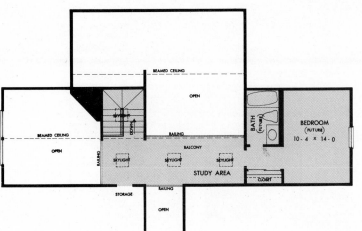

● This seemingly low-slung ranch home holds some delightful surprises on the inside. There's an open staircase to a second floor! The main living area on the first floor is highlighted with a large living room and dining room, both with beamed ceilings. The L-shaped kitchen is found nearby and connects conveniently to the family room (notice the corner fireplace here). Three bedrooms and two full baths occupy the right wing of the home. Upstairs is space for expansion to another bedroom and full bath. A study area here is skylit and has a balcony overlook to the living room.

Design V34036

First Floor: 1,833 square feet
Second Floor: 409 square feet
Total: 2,242 square feet

D

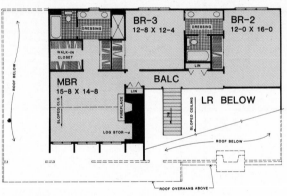

Design V34264

First Floor: 1,406 square feet
Second Floor: 1,067 square feet
Total: 2,473 square feet

D

● Contemporary configuration makes a dramatic statement in this lovely two-story home. The list of special features is quite impressive: two fireplaces (one in the living room, one in the master suite), large storage room and tool room off the garage, walk-in pantry and island cook top in the kitchen, dressing areas in both full baths. The second floor has a balcony overlook to the living room below.

LIFESTYLE
HOME PLANS

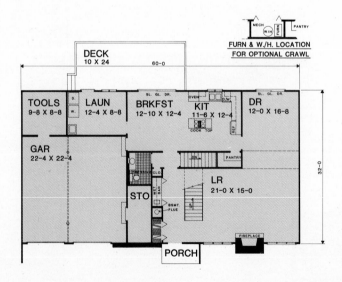

BEDROOM
13-0 x 11-0

OPEN TO
LIVING ROOM

DOWN TO
FIRST
FLOOR

RAIL

BEDROOM
13-0 x 14-8

OPEN TO
FOYER

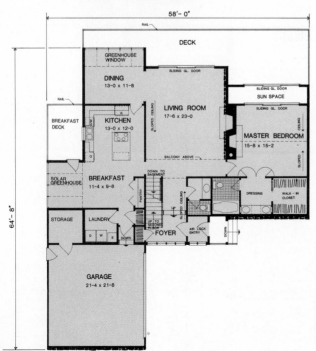

58'- 0"

RAIL

DECK

GREENHOUSE
WINDOW

DINING
13-0 x 11-8

SLIDING GL. DOOR

SLIDING GL. DOOR

SUN SPACE

SLIDING GL. DOOR

LIVING ROOM
17-6 x 23-0

BREAKFAST
DECK

KITCHEN
13-0 x 12-0

MASTER BEDROOM
15-8 x 15-2

BALCONY ABOVE

64'- 8"

SOLAR
GREENHOUSE

BREAKFAST
11-4 9-8

DOWN TO
BASEMENT

DRESSING

WALK- IN
CLOSET.

PANTRY

STORAGE

LAUNDRY

D W S

DOWN

UP TO
SECOND
FLOOR

FOYER

AIR LOCK
ENTRY

DOWN

GARAGE
21-4 x 21-8

Design V34334

First Floor: 1,838 square feet
Second Floor: 640 square feet
Total: 2,478 square feet

● Grand sloping rooflines and a design created for southern orientation are the unique features of this contemporary home. Outdoor living is enhanced by a solar greenhouse off the breakfast room, a sun space off the master bedroom, a greenhouse window in the dining room, a casual breakfast deck, and full-width deck to the rear. The split-bedroom plan allows for the master suite (with fireplace, and huge walk-in closet) to be situated on the first floor and two family bedrooms and a full bath to find space on the second floor. Be sure to notice the balcony overlook to the sloped-ceiling living room below.

LIFESTYLE
HOME PLANS

● If you like a contemporary plan with plenty of windows, this is the home for you. It offers a wealth of glass area throughout. Besides well-planned living areas on the first floor, there are four bedrooms and two full baths upstairs. The garage supplies a large storage area and is uniquely camouflaged as a wing of the house. Look also for abundant closet space, the screened porch and attached deck, and two-story foyer with open staircase to the second floor. All four bedrooms feature sloped ceilings.

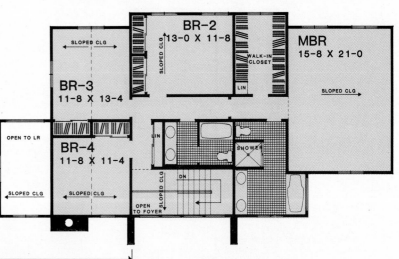

BR-2
13-0 X 11-8
SLOPED CLG
WALK-IN CLOSET
MBR
15-8 X 21-0
SLOPED CLG
BR-3
11-8 X 13-4
OPEN TO LR
BR-4
11-8 X 11-4
SHOWER
DN
SLOPED CLG
SLOPED CLG
OPEN TO FOYER

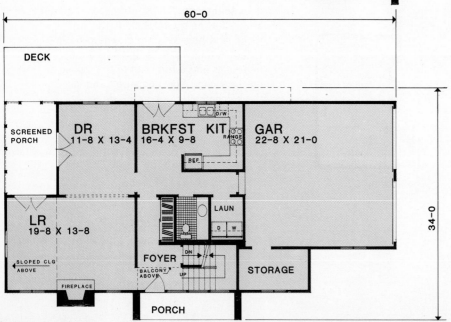

60-0

DECK

SCREENED PORCH

DR
11-8 X 13-4

BRKFST KIT
16-4 X 9-8

GAR
22-8 X 21-0

REF

LR
19-8 X 13-8

LAUN
D W

FOYER
DN
UP
BALCONY ABOVE

STORAGE

SLOPED CLG ABOVE

FIREPLACE

PORCH

34-0

Design V34287
First Floor: 930 square feet
Second Floor: 1,362 square feet
Total: 2,292 square feet

L D

L
LIFESTYLE
HOME PLANS

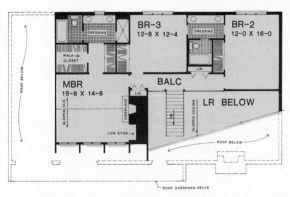

BR-3
12-8 X 12-4

BR-2
12-0 X 16-0

DRESSING · DRESSING

WALK-IN CLOSET

MBR
15-8 X 14-8

BALC

LR BELOW

SLOPED CLG · LIN · FIREPLACE · LOG STOR

SLOPED CEILING

ROOF BELOW

ROOF BELOW

ROOF OVERHANG ABOVE

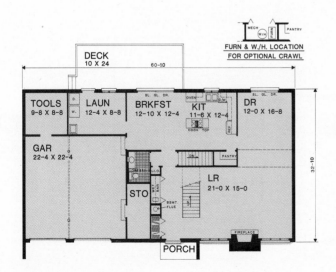

MECH W/H · FURN · PANTRY

FURN & W./H. LOCATION
FOR OPTIONAL CRAWL

DECK
10 X 24

60-10

TOOLS
9-8 X 8-8

LAUN
12-4 X 8-8

BRKFST
12-10 X 12-4

KIT
11-6 X 12-4

DR
12-0 X 16-8

SL. GL. DR. · OVEN · P/W · SL. GL. DR.

GAR
22-4 X 22-4

COOK TOP · REF

32-10

DN · PANTRY

STO

DRESSING/ULO · WET BAR

LR
21-0 X 15-0

BSMT FLUE

FIREPLACE

PORCH

Design V34281

First Floor: 1,454 square feet
Second Floor: 1,101 square feet
Total: 2,555 square feet

● A beautiful brick design, and one that will remain stylish and practical for many years. Its convenient floor plan includes living and working areas in a first-floor living room, dining room, kitchen with breakfast room and large laundry area. A powder room is found in the entry hall, as is a wet bar and open staircase to the second floor. Three bedrooms handle sleeping accommodations for the family. One of the bedrooms is a sumptuous master suite with walk-in closet, fireplace with log storage, and grand master bath. Don't miss the tool storage area in the garage.

LIFESTYLE
HOME PLANS

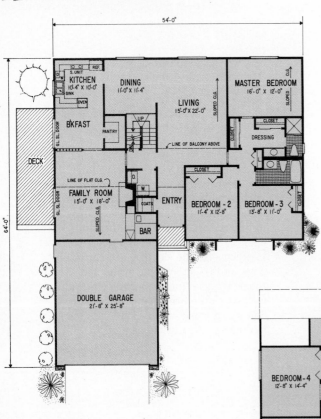

● It's hard to believe that this compact-looking plan houses five bedrooms, three baths, and room for casual and formal entertaining. Its unique design moves from front entry to living and dining rooms and U-shaped kitchen with breakfast room to the rear. The family room is oriented to the front and has a wet bar, a fireplace and sliding glass doors to the deck. Three bedrooms are found in the right wing of the first floor. One is the master suite. Upstairs are two more bedrooms and a full bath. The skylit balcony here overlooks the living and dining rooms.

Design V34328

First Floor: 2,035 square feet
Second Floor: 700 square feet
Total: 2,735 square feet

L D

L
LIFESTYLE
HOME PLANS

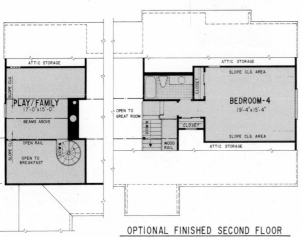

ATTIC STORAGE

PLAY/FAMILY
17'-0" x 15'-0"

BEAMS ABOVE

OPEN RAIL

OPEN TO
BREAKFAST

SLOPE CLG

SLOPE CLG

DOWN

ATTIC STORAGE

SLOPE CLG. AREA

BEDROOM-4
19'-4" x 15'-4"

OPEN TO
GREAT ROOM

CLOSET

CLOSET

WOOD
RAIL

DOWN

SLOPE CLG. AREA

ATTIC STORAGE

OPTIONAL FINISHED SECOND FLOOR

Design V34330

First Floor: 2,292 square feet
Second Floor: 714 square feet
Total: 3,006 square feet

LIFESTYLE HOME PLANS

● There's bonus space in this home that might easily be missed from a cursory glance at its wood-sided exterior. The first floor houses complete livability with the centralized great room, formal dining room, kitchen with island range and attached breakfast nook, three bedrooms and two full baths. Three decks (two partially covered) complement these rooms. But upstairs is the real treat — an optional fourth bedroom and full bath and playroom or family room with spiral staircase down to the first floor. Two storage areas in the garage and attic storage add to this home's practicality.

WOOD RAIL

OPEN

DECK

COVERED

GL. SLD. DR.

DINING ROOM
17'-0" x 12'-0"

GL. SLD. DR.

SLOPE CLG

WALK-IN CLOSET

PLANT DECK

GL. SLD. DR.

DRESSING

MASTER BEDROOM
19'-4" x 15'-4"

POWDER

BEAM ABOVE

WOOD RAIL

REFG.

KITCHEN
13'-4" x 11'-0"

CHINA SILVER

SINK

RANGE

PANTRY

RAISED HEARTH

GREAT ROOM
17'-4" x 26'-8"

BEAM ABOVE

LINEN

WALK-IN CLOSET

OPEN

DECK

COVERED

GL. SLD. DR.

3' HIGH WALL

BREAKFAST
13'-4" x 9'-4"

CLOSET

DOWN

UP

SLOPE CLG

WOOD RAIL

CLOSET

SEATS

BEDROOM-2
11'-0" x 13'-4"

BEDROOM-3
11'-4" x 13'-4"

FOYER

STORAGE

ENTRY

LAUNDRY

DRY WASH SHELVES

STONE PLANTER

ENTRY

DOUBLE GARAGE
21'-4" x 21'-4"

STOR.

OVERHEAD GARAGE DOOR

STONE

64'-4"

80'-0"

287

Design V34194

First Floor: 1,419 square feet
Second Floor: 1,087 square feet
Total: 2,506 square feet

● Sweeping rooflines and an impressive chimney stack make an elegant statement for this contemporary residence. Formal living takes place to the front of the floor plan with a sunken living room and dining room with small deck. To the rear is the large family room with its full-width deck. The L-shaped kitchen has a built-in shelf and large pantry. Three bedrooms on the second floor include a master with deck and two huge walk-in closets. Notice the lovely open staircase to this floor.

Design V34313

First Floor: 1,685 square feet
Second Floor: 818 square feet
Total: 2,503 square feet

● There are five decks to enjoy in this home, each strategically placed to accept full use. Begin with the front entry deck that leads to grand double doors. From the entry hall step down into the great room with corner fireplace. Dining takes place to either side of the galley kitchen in the formal dining room or casual breakfast room. The master bedroom is found on this floor also and has its own full bath. Upstairs there are three more bedrooms, one with a deck; the other two have walk-in closets.

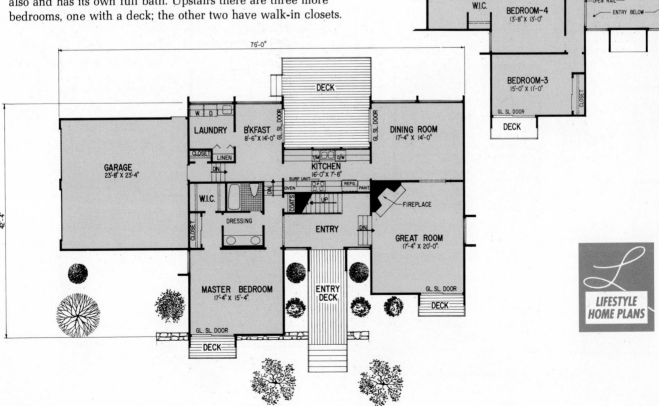

● Drama is a key element in the attraction of this bold contemporary. Though compact in size, it offers great living potential. The front entry opens directly to the great room/dining room combination. Close by is an L-shaped kitchen with a laundry area. The master bedroom upstairs has a balcony overlook to the great room below. It shares the second floor with two family bedrooms. Note that the carport has two large storage areas for tools or gardening equipment.

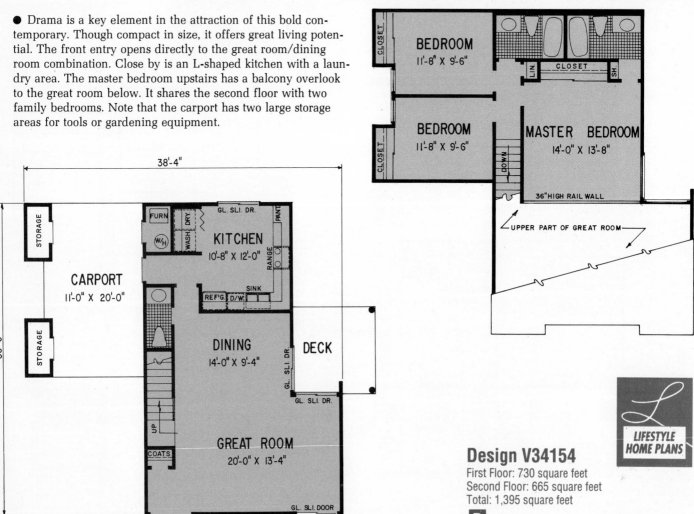

BEDROOM
11'-8" X 9'-6"

CLOSET

BEDROOM
11'-8" X 9'-6"

MASTER BEDROOM
14'-0" X 13'-8"

CLOSET

LIN   CLOSET   SH

DOWN

36" HIGH RAIL WALL

← UPPER PART OF GREAT ROOM →

38'-4"

36'-0"

STORAGE

STORAGE

CARPORT
11'-0" X 20'-0"

FURN

W/H   WASH   DRY

GL. SLI. DR.   PANT'Y

KITCHEN
10'-8" X 12'-0"

RANGE

REF'G.   D/W   SINK

DINING
14'-0" X 9'-4"

DECK

GL. SLI. DR.

GL. SLI. DR.

UP

COATS

GREAT ROOM
20'-0" X 13'-4"

GL. SLI. DOOR

STOOP

L LIFESTYLE HOME PLANS

Design V34154
First Floor: 730 square feet
Second Floor: 665 square feet
Total: 1,395 square feet

D

Design V32831

First Floor: 1,758 square feet
Second Floor: 1,247 square feet
Total: 3,005 square feet

D

Floor plan — First Floor

59'-8"
58'-4"

TERRACE

COVERED PORCH
(ALT SOLARIUM WHEN
REAR FACES SOUTH)

FAMILY RM.
13⁸ x 15⁰

BREAKFAST RM.
9⁴ x 9⁶

KITCHEN
12⁰ x 11⁶

DINING RM.
15² x 11⁰

OPTIONAL
GREENHOUSE

LOUNGE
13² x 11⁶

LAUND.

PDR. RM.

LINE OF SECOND FLR.

ATRIUM

POOL

LIVING RM.
15² x 22⁰

GARAGE
21⁸ x 21⁸

Floor plan — Second Floor

BED RM.
10⁴ x 12⁴

BED RM.
11⁰ x 13⁶

BATH

DRESSING

ROOF

UPPER PORCH

MASTER BED RM.
11⁰ - 15⁴ x 17⁴

BED RM.
13⁸ x 10⁰

LOUNGE
10⁸ x 11⁶

WALK-IN CLOSET

UPPER GARAGE

UPPER ATRIUM

UPPER LIVING RM.

Expandable Cape Ann Cottage

Design V32983 First Floor (Basic Plan): 776 square feet
First Floor (Expanded Plan): 1,072 square feet; Second Floor (Both Plans): 652 square feet
Total: 1,428 square feet of (Basic Plan); 1,724 square feet of (Expanded Plan)

● This charming gambrel-roofed Colonial cottage is reminiscent of the simple houses built and occupied by seafarers on Cape Ann, Mass. in the 17th and 18th Centuries. However, this adaptation offers a new twist. It is designed to expand as your need and/or budget grows. Of course, building the expanded version first will deliver the bonus livability promised by the formal dining room and quiet study, plus the convenience of the attached garage.

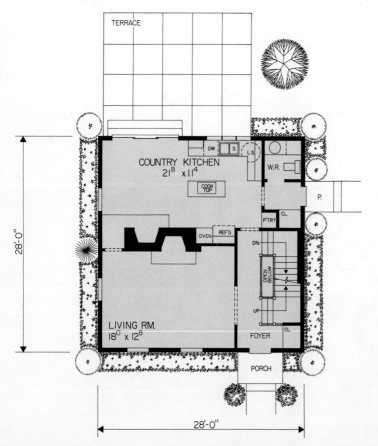

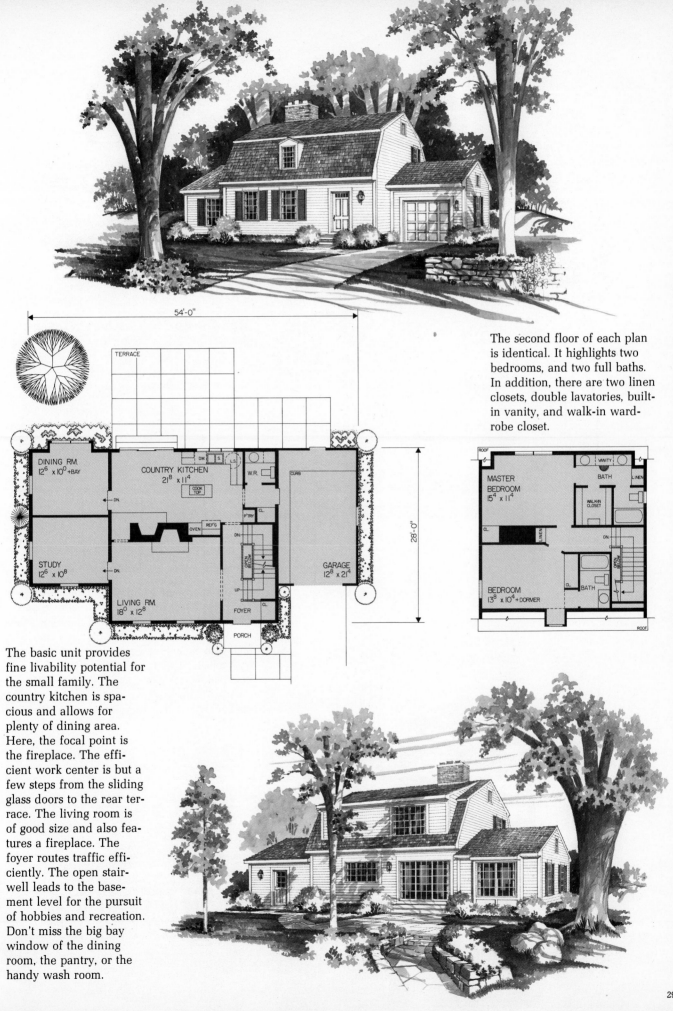

54'-0"

TERRACE

DINING RM.
12⁶ x 10⁰ +BAY

COUNTRY KITCHEN
21⁸ x 11⁴

COOK TOP

DW. S. L.S.

W.R.

CURB

DN.

OVEN REF'G

P'TRY CL.

STUDY
12⁶ x 10⁸

DN.

OPEN BELOW

DN.

GARAGE
12⁸ x 21⁴

LIVING RM.
18⁰ x 12⁸

UP

CL.

FOYER

PORCH

28'-0"

The second floor of each plan is identical. It highlights two bedrooms, and two full baths. In addition, there are two linen closets, double lavatories, built-in vanity, and walk-in wardrobe closet.

ROOF

VANITY

MASTER BEDROOM
15⁴ x 11⁴

BATH

LINEN

WALK-IN CLOSET

CL.

LINEN

DN.

BEDROOM
13⁸ x 10⁴ +DORMER

BATH

OPEN BELOW

ROOF

The basic unit provides fine livability potential for the small family. The country kitchen is spacious and allows for plenty of dining area. Here, the focal point is the fireplace. The efficient work center is but a few steps from the sliding glass doors to the rear terrace. The living room is of good size and also features a fireplace. The foyer routes traffic efficiently. The open stairwell leads to the basement level for the pursuit of hobbies and recreation. Don't miss the big bay window of the dining room, the pantry, or the handy wash room.

Design V32928 First Floor: 1,917 square feet
Second Floor: 918 square feet; Total: 2,835 square feet

● This handsome gambrel-roof design with Early American front window treatment and contemporary view windows in the rear is certain to turn heads wherever built! Its many highlights include a second-floor lounge, country kitchen, 74-sq. ft. greenhouse (not included in above total footage), and large gathering room with music alcove. Note fireplaces in both the country kitchen and gathering room!

Design V32883 First Floor: 1,919 square feet
Second Floor: 895 square feet; Total: 2,814 square feet

● A country-style home is part of America's fascination with the rural past. This home's emphasis of the traditional home is in its gambrel roof, dormers and fanlight windows. Having a traditional exterior from the street view, this home has window walls and a greenhouse, which opens the house to the outdoors in a thoroughly contemporary manner. The interior meets the requirements of today's active family. Like the country houses of the past, it has a gathering room for family get-togethers or entertaining. The adjacent two-story greenhouse doubles as the dining room. There is a pass-thru snack bar to the country kitchen here. This country kitchen just might be the heart of the house with its two areas - work zone and sitting room. There are four bedrooms on the two floors - the master bedroom suite on the first floor; three more on the second floor. A lounge, overlooking the gathering room and front foyer, is also on the second floor.

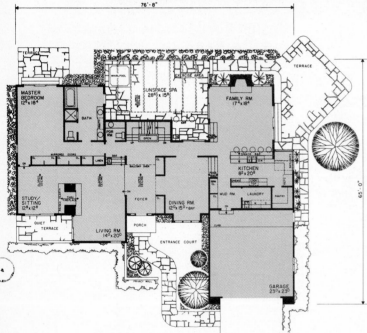

Design V32900 First Floor: 2,332 square feet
Second Floor: 953 square feet; Total: 3,285 square feet

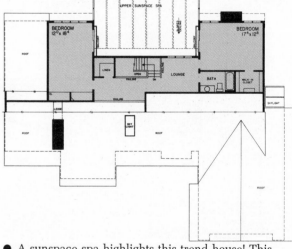

● A sunspace spa highlights this trend house! This energy-efficient contemporary design calls for 2 x 6 exterior wall construction with placement on a north-facing lot. Traffic flows efficiently, too, by way of a spectacular foyer. Study the spacious master bath with direct access to the sunspace spa. Note also the second-floor balcony with skylight, spacious sunken living room with thru-fireplace and second-floor lounge.

● This contemporary design also has a great deal to offer. Study the living areas. A fireplace opens up to both the living room and country kitchen. Privacy is the key word when describing the sleeping areas. the first floor master bedroom is away from the traffic of the house and features a dressing/exercise room, whirlpool tub and shower and a spacious walk-in closet. Two more bedrooms and a full bath are on the second floor. The three car garage is arranged so that the owners have use of a double-garage with an attached single on reserve for guests. The cheerful sun room adds 296 sq. ft. to the total.

Design V32920
First Floor: 3,067 square feet
Second Floor: 648 square feet; Total: 3,715 square feet

L D

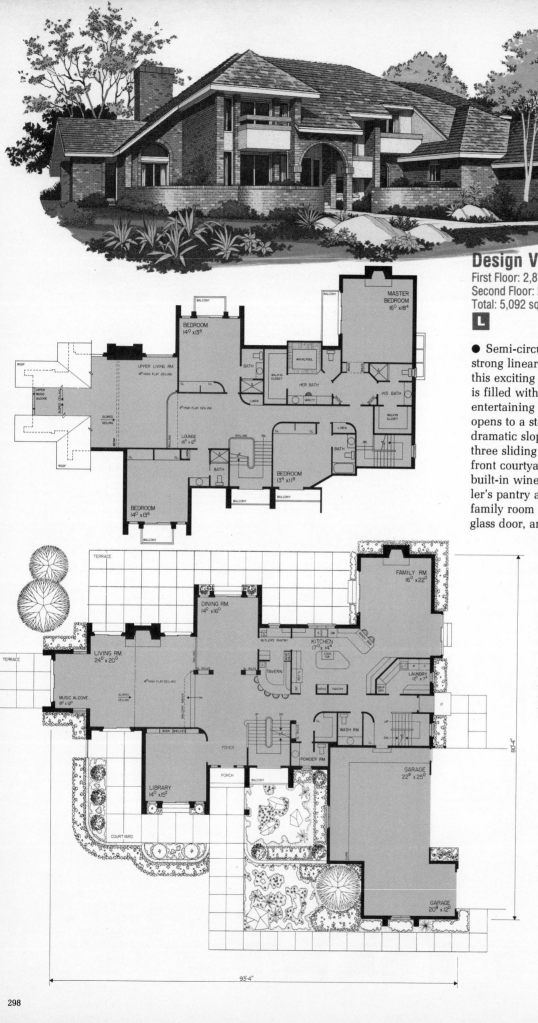

Design V32952

First Floor: 2,870 square feet
Second Floor: 2,222 square feet
Total: 5,092 square feet

L

● Semi-circular arches complement the strong linear roof lines and balconies of this exciting contemporary. The first floor is filled with well-planned amenities for entertaining and relaxing. The foyer opens to a step-down living room with a dramatic sloped ceiling, fireplace, and three sliding glass doors that access the front courtyard and terrace. A tavern with built-in wine rack and an adjacent butler's pantry are ideal for entertaining. The family room features a fireplace, sliding glass door, and a handy snack bar. The kitchen allows meal preparation, cooking and storage within a step of the central work island. Three second-floor bedrooms, each with a private bath and balcony, are reached by either of two staircases. The master suite, with His and Hers baths and walk-in closets, whirlpool, and fireplace, adds the finishing touch to this memorable home.

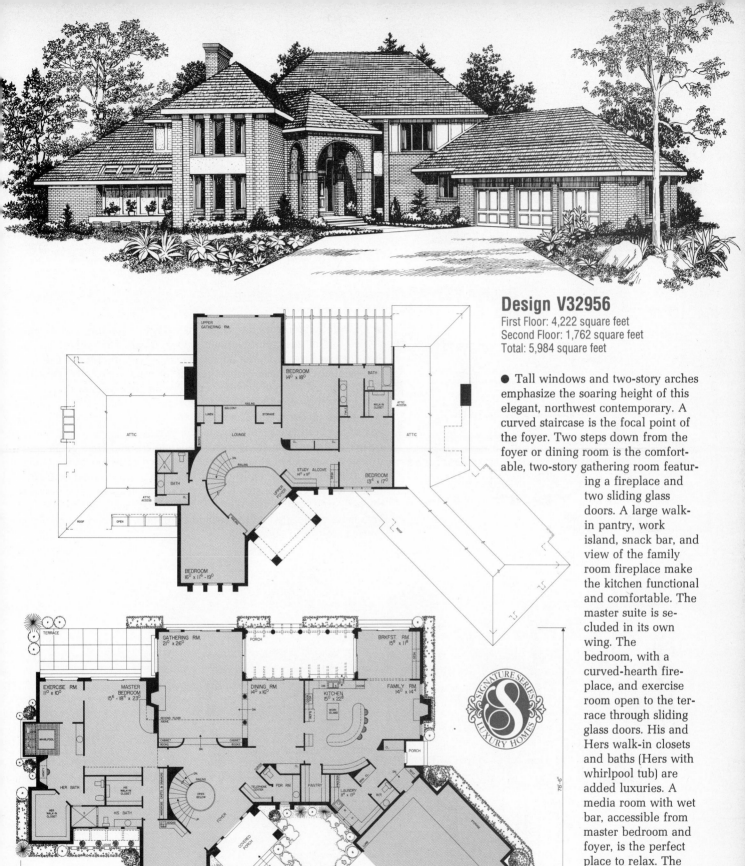

Design V32956

First Floor: 4,222 square feet
Second Floor: 1,762 square feet
Total: 5,984 square feet

● Tall windows and two-story arches emphasize the soaring height of this elegant, northwest contemporary. A curved staircase is the focal point of the foyer. Two steps down from the foyer or dining room is the comfortable, two-story gathering room featuring a fireplace and two sliding glass doors. A large walk-in pantry, work island, snack bar, and view of the family room fireplace make the kitchen functional and comfortable. The master suite is secluded in its own wing. The bedroom, with a curved-hearth fireplace, and exercise room open to the terrace through sliding glass doors. His and Hers walk-in closets and baths (Hers with whirlpool tub) are added luxuries. A media room with wet bar, accessible from master bedroom and foyer, is the perfect place to relax. The second floor stairs open to a lounge which overlooks the gathering room. Three additional bedrooms and a quiet study alcove on the second floor round out the living area of this gracious and functional home.

299

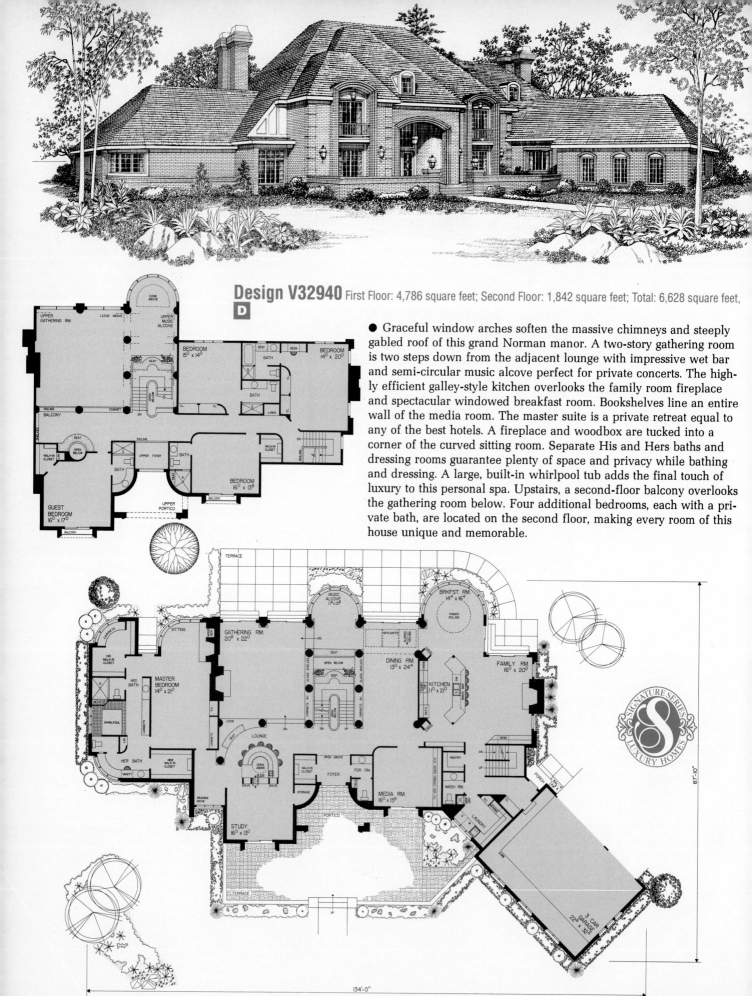

Design V32940 First Floor: 4,786 square feet; Second Floor: 1,842 square feet; Total: 6,628 square feet,

● Graceful window arches soften the massive chimneys and steeply gabled roof of this grand Norman manor. A two-story gathering room is two steps down from the adjacent lounge with impressive wet bar and semi-circular music alcove perfect for private concerts. The highly efficient galley-style kitchen overlooks the family room fireplace and spectacular windowed breakfast room. Bookshelves line an entire wall of the media room. The master suite is a private retreat equal to any of the best hotels. A fireplace and woodbox are tucked into a corner of the curved sitting room. Separate His and Hers baths and dressing rooms guarantee plenty of space and privacy while bathing and dressing. A large, built-in whirlpool tub adds the final touch of luxury to this personal spa. Upstairs, a second-floor balcony overlooks the gathering room below. Four additional bedrooms, each with a private bath, are located on the second floor, making every room of this house unique and memorable.

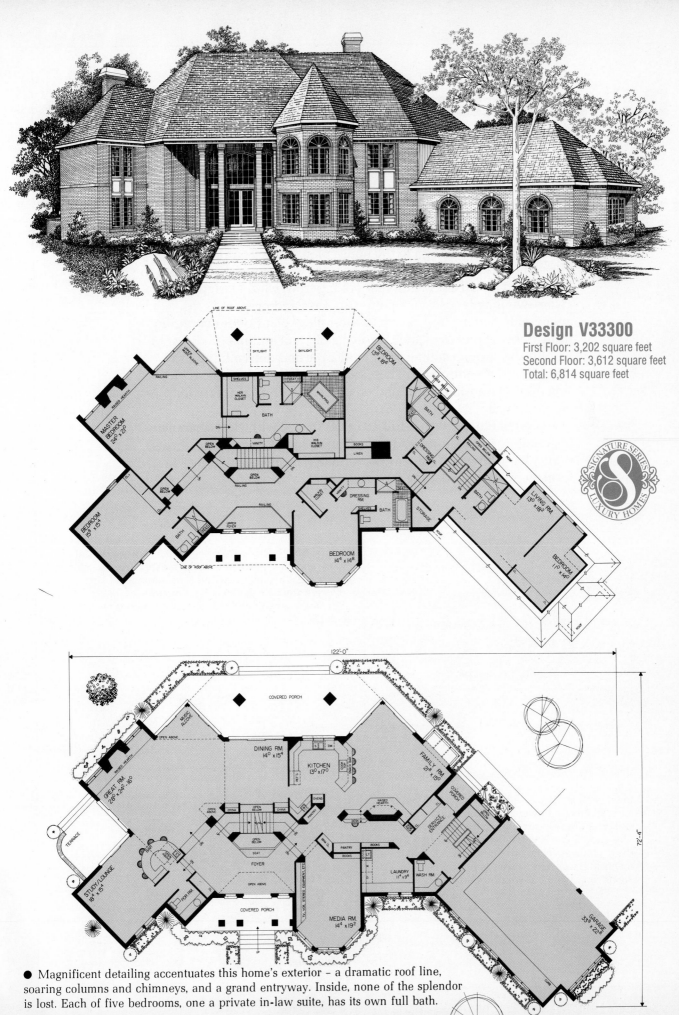

Design V33300

First Floor: 3,202 square feet
Second Floor: 3,612 square feet
Total: 6,814 square feet

● Magnificent detailing accentuates this home's exterior – a dramatic roof line, soaring columns and chimneys, and a grand entryway. Inside, none of the splendor is lost. Each of five bedrooms, one a private in-law suite, has its own full bath.

◤ The Landscape Blueprint Package

For the home plans marked with an ◤ in this book, Home Planners has created a front-yard landscape plan that matches or is complementary in design to the house plan. These comprehensive blueprint packages include all the necessary information you need to lay out and install a professional-looking front yard. Designed by an award-winning landscape architecture firm and prepared with attention to detail, these clear, easy-to-follow plans offer everything from a precise plot plan and regionalized plant and materials list to helpful sheets on installing your landscape and determining the mature size of your plants. These plans will help you achieve professional results, adding value and enjoyment to your property for years to come.

Each set of blueprints is a full 18" x 24" in size with clear, complete instructions and easy-to-read type. Consisting of six detailed sheets, these plans show how all plants and materials are put together to form an exciting landscape for your home.

Frontal Sheet. This artist's line sketch shows a typical house and all the elements of the finished front-yard landscape when plants are at or near maturity. This will give you a visual image or "picture" of the design and what you might expect your property to look like when fully landscaped.

Plan View. Drawn at 1/8" equals 1'-0", this is an aerial view of the property showing the exact placement of all landscape elements, including symbols and callouts for flowers, shrubs, ground covers, walkways, walls, gates, and other garden amenities. This sheet is the key to the design and shows you the contour, spacing, flow, and balance of all the elements in the design, as well as providing an exact "map" for laying out your property.

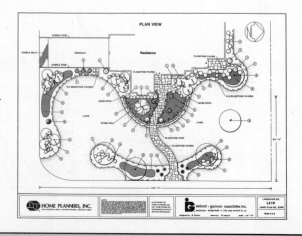

Regionalized Plant & Materials List. Keyed to the Plan View sheet, this page lists all of the plants and materials necessary to execute the design. It gives the quantity, botanical name, common name, flower color, season of bloom, and hardiness zone for each plant specified, as well as the amount and type of materials for all driveways, walks, walls, gates, and other structures. This becomes your "shopping list" for dealing with contractors or buying the plants and materials yourself. Most importantly, the plants shown on this page have been chosen by a team of professional horticulturalists for their adaptability, availability, and performance in your specific part of the country.

Planting and Maintaining Your Landscape. This valuable sheet gives handy information and illustrations on purchasing plant materials, preparing your site, and caring for your landscape after installation. Includes quick, helpful advice on planting trees, shrubs and ground covers, staking trees, establishing a lawn, watering, weed control, and pruning.

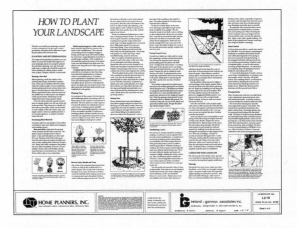

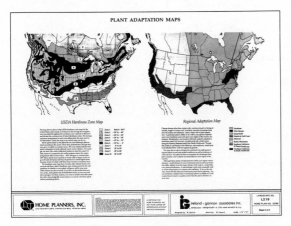

Zone Maps. These two informative maps offer detailed information to help you better select and judge the performance of your plants. Map One is a United States Department of Agriculture Hardiness Zone Map that shows the average low temperatures by zones in various part of the United States and Canada. The "Zone" listing for plants on Sheet 3 of your Plant and Materials List is keyed to this map. Map Two is a Regional Adaptation Map which takes into account other factors beyond low temperatures, such as rainfall, humidity, extremes of temperature, and soil acidity or alkalinity. This map is the key to plant adaptability and is used for the selection of plant lists in your plans.

Plant Size & Description Guide. Because people often have trouble visualizing plants, this handy regionalized guide provides a scale and silhouettes to determine the final height and shape of various trees and shrubs in your landscape plan. It also provides a quick means of choosing alternate plants in case you do not wish to install a certain tree or shrub or if you cannot find the plant at local nurseries.

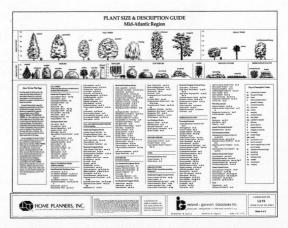

To order, see page 305.

Landscape Plans Index

A complete Landscape Blueprint Package is available for each of the house plans listed below. The Plant Availability column indicates regions of the country where plant lists are available for the plan. See Regional Order Map below.

House Plan	Landscape Plan	Page	Price	Available For Regions:
V31981	V3-L228	83	Y	All
V32171	V3-L228	84	Y	All
V32502	V3-L212	196	Z	All
V32511	V3-L229	186	Y	All
V32608	V3-L228	58	Y	All
V32624	V3-L228	75	Y	All
V32716	V3-L229	187	Y	All
V32761	V3-L229	194	Y	All
V32787	V3-L228	69	Y	All
V32827	V3-L229	138	Y	All
V32843	V3-L228	118	Y	All
V32847	V3-L220	206	Y	1-3, 5, 6, 8
V32850	V3-L236	77	Z	3, 4, 7
V32901	V3-L229	38	Y	All
V32902	V3-L234	268	Y	All
V32920	V3-L212	297	Z	All
V32937	V3-L229	185	Y	All
V32952	V3-L235	298	Z	1-3, 5, 6, 8
V34334	V3-L231	283	Z	All

Landscape Plans Price Schedule

Price Group	X	Y	Z
1 set	$35	$45	$55
3 sets	$50	$60	$70
6 sets	$65	$75	$85
Additional identical sets $10 each			
Reverse sets (mirror image) $10 each			

Regional Order Map

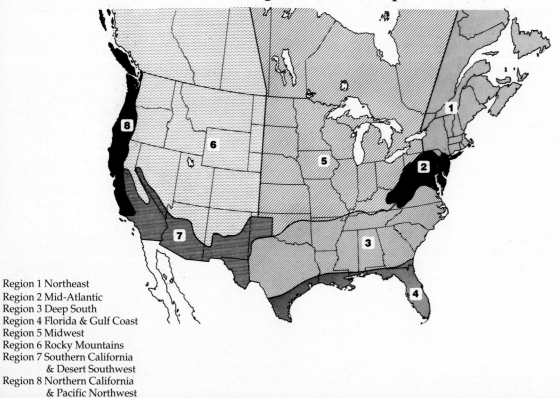

Region 1 Northeast
Region 2 Mid-Atlantic
Region 3 Deep South
Region 4 Florida & Gulf Coast
Region 5 Midwest
Region 6 Rocky Mountains
Region 7 Southern California
    & Desert Southwest
Region 8 Northern California
    & Pacific Northwest

■ Landscape Blueprint Order Form

Landscape Plans Price Schedule

Price Group	X	Y	Z
1 set	$35	$45	$55
3 sets	$50	$60	$70
6 sets	$65	$75	$85
Additional identical sets $10 each			
Reverse sets (mirror image) $10 each			

TO ORDER: Find the number of the House Plan in the Plans Index and note the corresponding Landscape Plan Number. Consult the Price Schedule (above) to determine the price of your plans, choosing the 1-, 3- or 6-set package and any additional or reverse sets you desire. To make sure your Plant and Materials List contains the best selection for your area, refer to the Regional Order Map (opposite) and specify the region in which you reside.

Complete the Order Coupon on this page and mail with your check or money order. If you prefer, you can also use a credit card or order C.O.D. (Sorry, no C.O.D. shipments to foreign countries including Canada.) Please include the correct postage and handling fees.

Our Exchange Policy
Because we produce and ship plans in response to individual orders, we cannot honor requests for refunds. However, you can exchange your entire order of blueprints, including a single set if you order just one, for a set of another landscape design. All exchanges carry an additional fee of $15.00, plus $5.00 for postage and handling if they're sent via surface mail; $7.00 for priority air mail.

About Reverse Blueprints
If you want to install your landscape in reverse of the plan as shown, we will include an extra set of blueprints with the Frontal Sheet and Plan View reversed for an additional fee of $10.00. Although callouts and lettering appear backwards, reverses will prove useful as a visual aid if you decide to flop the plan.

How Many Blueprints Do You Need?
To study your favorite landscape plan or make alterations of the plan to fit your site, one set of Landscape Blueprints may be sufficient. On the other hand, if you plan to install the landscape yourself using subcontractors or have a general contractor do the work for you, you will probably need more sets. Because you save money on 3-set or 6-set packages, you should consider ordering all the sets at one time. Use the checklist below to estimate the number you'll need:

Blueprint Checklist
- _____ **Owner**
- _____ **Landscape Contractor or Subcontractor**
- _____ **Nursery or Plant Materials Supplier**
- _____ **Building Materials Supplier**
- _____ **Lender or Mortgage Source, if applicable**
- _____ **Community Building Department for Permits** (sometimes requires 2 sets)
- _____ **Subdivision Committee, if any**
- _____ **Total Number of Sets**

Blueprint Hotline
Call Toll-Free 1-800-521-6797. We'll ship your order the following business day if you call us by 5:00 p.m. Eastern Time. When you order by phone, please be prepared to give us the Order Form Key Number shown in the box at the bottom of the Order Form.

CANADIAN CUSTOMERS: For faster, more economical service, Canadian customers should add 20% to all prices and mail in Canadian funds to:

Home Planners, Inc.
20 Cedar Street North
Kitchener, Ontario N2H 2WB
Phone (519) 743-4169

HOME PLANNERS, INC.
3275 WEST INA ROAD, SUITE 110
TUCSON, ARIZONA 85741

Please rush me the following Landscape Blueprints:

_____ Set(s) of Landscape Plan _____
(See Index and Price Schedule) $ _____

_____ Additional identical blueprints
in the same order @ $10.00 per set $ _____

_____ Reverse blueprints @ $10.00 per set $ _____

Please indicate the appropriate region of the country for Plant & Material List (See Map on opposite page):
- [ ] Region 1   Northeast
- [ ] Region 2   Mid-Atlantic
- [ ] Region 3   Deep South
- [ ] Region 4   Florida & Gulf Coast
- [ ] Region 5   Midwest
- [ ] Region 6   Rocky Mountains
- [ ] Region 7   Southern California & Desert Southwest
- [ ] Region 8   Northern California & Pacific Northwest

SUBTOTAL: (Arizona residents add 5% sales tax; Michigan residents add 4% sales tax) $ _____

POSTAGE AND HANDLING

UPS DELIVERY-Must have street address — No P.O. Boxes		
•UPS Regular Service Allow 4-5 days delivery	☐ $5.00	$ _____
•UPS 2nd Day Air Allow 2-3 days delivery	☐ $7.00	$ _____
•UPS Next Day Air Allow 1-2 days delivery	☐ $16.00	$ _____
POST OFFICE DELIVERY — If no street address		
•Priority Air Mail Allow 4-5 days delivery	☐ $7.00	$ _____
C.O.D. (Pay mail carrier; Available in U.S. only)	☐	

TOTAL IN U.S. FUNDS $ _____

YOUR ADDRESS (please print)

Name _____

Street _____

City _____ State _____ Zip _____

Daytime telephone number (____) _____

CREDIT CARD ORDERS ONLY

Fill in the boxes below

☐☐☐☐☐☐☐☐☐☐☐☐☐☐☐☐

Credit card number

☐☐☐☐

Exp. Date: Month/Year

Check one   ☐ Visa   ☐ MasterCard

_____
Signature

Order Form Key
V3LP

◧ The Deck Blueprint Package

Many of the homes in this book can be enhanced with a professionally designed Home Planners' Deck Plan. Those home plans highlighted with a ◧ have a matching or corresponding deck plan available which includes all the information you need in order to plan, lay out, and build a beautiful outdoor addition to the home. Our plans and details are carefully prepared in an easy-to-understand format that will guide you through every stage of your deck-building project. The Deck Blueprint Package contains four sheets outlining information pertinent to the specific Deck Plan you have chosen. A separate package — Deck Construction Details — provides the how-to data for building any deck, including instructions for adaptations and conversions.

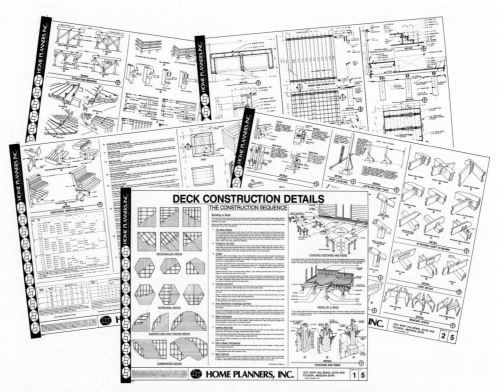

In five information-packed sheets, these standard details provide all the general data necessary for building, adapting, and converting any deck. Included are layout examples, framing patterns, and foundation variations; details for ledgers, columns, and beams; schedules and charts; handrail, stair, and ramp details; and special options like spa platforms, planters, bars, benches and overhead trellises. This is a must-have package for the first-time deck builder and a useful addition to the custom deck plans shown on the next pages.

Custom Deck Plans

Each house plan in this book displaying a **D** has a matching or corresponding Deck Plan that has been custom-designed by a professional architect. With each Custom Deck Plan, you receive the following:

Deck Plan Frontal Sheet. An artist's line drawing shows the deck as it connects to its matching or corresponding house. This drawing provides a visual image of what the deck will look like when completed, highlighting the livability factors.

Deck Framing and Floor Plans. In clear, easy-to-read drawings, this sheet shows all component parts of the deck from an aerial viewpoint with dimensions, notes, and references. Drawn at 1/4" = 1' - 0", the floor plan provides a finished overhead view of the deck including rails, stairs, benches, and ramps. The framing plan gives complete details on how the deck is to be built, including the position and spacing of footings, joists, beams, posts, and decking materials. Where necessary, the sheet also includes sections and closeups to further explain structural details.

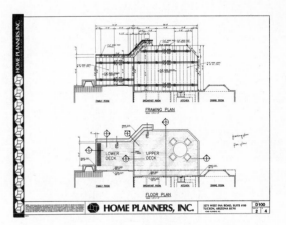

Deck Elevations. Large-scale front and side elevations of the deck complete the visual picture of the deck. Drawn at 3/8" = 1' - 0", the elevations show the height of rails, balusters, stair risers, benches and other deck accessories.

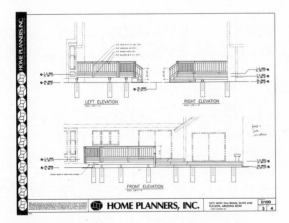

Deck Materials List. This is a complete shopping list of all the materials needed (including sizes and amounts) to build your deck. The Materials List is complemented by section drawings showing placement of hardware such as thru-bolts, screws, nuts, washers, and nails and how these items are used to secure deck flooring, rails, posts, and joists. Scale is 3/4" = 1' - 0".

QUANTITY	SIZE	DESCRIPTION
23	4"x4"-4'	TREATED LUMBER
12	4"X4"-5'	TREATED LUMBER
52 L.F.	2"x2"	TREATED BALUSTERS 30" LG.
300 L.F.	2"x4"	TREATED LUMBER
1850 L.F.	2"x6"	TREATED LUMBER
600 L.F.	2"x8"	TREATED LUMBER
10 L.F.	2"x10"	TREATED LUMBER
8 L.F.	2"x12"	TREATED LUMBER
70 L.F.		LANDSCAPE EDGE
550 S.F.		FILTER FABRIC
550 S.F.		2" DEEP PEA GRAVEL
60	3/8"øx8" LG.	THRU-BOLTS W/ NUTS & WASHERS
30	3/8"øx6" LG.	THRU-BOLTS W/ NUTS & WASHERS
4		1 1/2"x1 1/2"x1/8"-7" LG. STEEL ANGLES
16	3/16"øx2"	LAG SCREWS
2 LBS.	8d	FOR RAILINGS
5 LBS.	16d	FOR POSTS & JOISTS
25 LBS.	10d	FOR DECKING
		NOTE: ALL NAILS TO BE HOT DIPPED GALVANIZED SCREW NAILS
		•QUANTITY OF NAILS MAY VARY DEPENDING ON TYPE OF CONNECTIONS USED.

To order, call Toll Free 1-800-521-6797, or see page 309.

Deck Plans Index

Deck Plans Price Schedule

PRICE GROUP	Q	R	S
1 set	$25.00	$30.00	$35.00
3 sets	$40.00	$45.00	$50.00
6 sets	$55.00	$60.00	$65.00

Additional identical sets: $10 each.
Reverse sets (mirror image): $10 each.

House Plan	Deck Plan	Price	Page
V31981	V3-D117	S	83
V32171	V3-D112	R	84
V32366	V3-D112	R	90
V32511	V3-D108	R	186
V32608	V3-D112	R	58
V32624	V3-D112	R	75
V32628	V3-D105	R	58
V32758	V3-D120	R	66
V32761	V3-D105	R	194
V32787	V3-D105	R	69
V32831	V3-D113	R	291
V32841	V3-D108	R	64
V32842	V3-D114	R	65
V32847	V3-D112	R	206
V32850	V3-D122	S	77
V32893	V3-D120	R	52
V32913	V3-D124	S	267
V32918	V3-D124	S	273
V32920	V3-D104	S	297
V32934	V3-D109	S	192
V32940	V3-D114	R	300
V32941	V3-D112	R	270
V32942	V3-D112	R	270
V32943	V3-D112	R	270
V34128	V3-D112	R	15

◨ Deck Blueprint Order Form

TO ORDER: Find the Deck Plan number in the Plans Index (opposite). Consult the Price Schedule (opposite) to determine the price of your plan, choosing the 1-, 3-, or 6-set package and any additional or reverse sets you desire. Complete the Order Coupon on this page and mail with your check or money order. If you prefer, you can also use a credit card or order C.O.D. (Sorry, no C.O.D shipments to foreign countries, including Canada.) Please include the correct postage and handling fees.

Our Service Policy
We try to process and ship every order from our office within 48 hours. For this reason, we won't send a formal notice acknowledging receipt of your order.

Our Exchange Policy
Because we produce and ship plans in response to individual orders, we cannot honor requests for refunds. However, you can exchange your entire order of blueprints, including a single set if you order just one, for a set of another deck design. All exchanges carry an additional fee of $15.00, plus $5.00 for postage and handling if they're sent via surface mail; $7.00 for priority air mail.

About Reverse Blueprints
If you want to install your deck in reverse of the plan as shown, we will include an extra set of blueprints with the Frontal Sheet, Framing and Floor Plans, and Elevations reversed for an additonal fee of $10.00. Although callouts and lettering appear backwards, reverses will prove useful as a visual aid if you decide to flop the plan.

How Many Blueprints Do You Need?
To study your favorite deck plan or make alterations of the plan to fit your home, one set of Deck Blueprints may be sufficient. On the other hand, if you plan to install the deck yourself using subcontractors or have a general contractor do the work for you, you will probably need more sets. Because you save money on 3-set or 6-set packages, you should consider ordering all the sets at one time. Use the checklist below to estimate the number you'll need:

Blueprint Checklist
_____ **Owner**
_____ **Deck Contractor or Subcontractor**
_____ **Building Materials Supplier**
_____ **Lender or Mortgage Source, if applicable**
_____ **Community Building Department for Permits**
_____ **(sometimes requires 2 sets)**
         Subdivision Committee, if any
_____ **Total Number of Sets**

 Blueprint Hotline
Call Toll-Free 1-800-521-6797. We'll ship your order the following business day if you call us by 5:00 p.m. Eastern Time. When you order by phone, please be prepared to give us the Order Form Key Number shown in the box at the bottom of the Order Form.

CANADIAN CUSTOMERS: For faster, more economical service, Canadian customers should add 20% to all prices and mail in Canadian funds to:

Home Planners, Inc.
20 Cedar Street North
Kitchener, Ontario N2H 2W8
(519) 743-4169

HOME PLANNERS, INC.
3275 WEST INA ROAD, SUITE 110
TUCSON, ARIZONA 85741

Please rush me the following Deck Blueprints:

_____ Set(s) of Custom Deck Plan _____
         (See Index and Price Schedule) $ _____
_____ Additional identical blueprints
         in the same order @ $10.00 per set $ _____

_____ Reverse blueprints @ $10.00 per set $ _____

_____ Sets of Standard Deck
         Details @ $14.95 per set $ _____

SUBTOTAL: (Arizona residents add 5% sales tax; Michigan residents add 4% sales tax) $ _____

POSTAGE AND HANDLING			
UPS DELIVERY—Must have street address — No PO Boxes			
•UPS Regular Service Allow 4-5 days delivery	☐ $5.00	$ _____
•UPS 2nd Day Air Allow 2-3 days delivery	☐ $7.00	$ _____
•UPS Next Dair Air Allow 1-2 days delivery	☐ $16.00	$ _____
POST OFFICE DELIVERY If no street address			
•Priority Air Mail Allow 4-5 days delivery	☐ $7.00	$ _____
C.O.D. (Pay mail carrier; Available in U.S. only)	☐	

TOTAL IN U.S. FUNDS $ _____

YOUR ADDRESS (please print)
Name _____
Street _____
City _____ State ____ Zip _____
Daytime telephone number (____) _____

CREDIT CARD ORDERS ONLY
Fill in the boxes below

☐☐☐☐☐☐☐☐☐☐☐☐☐☐
Credit card number

☐☐☐☐
Exp. Date: Month/Year

Check one ☐Visa   ☐ MasterCard

_____
Signature

Order Form Key
V3DP

When You're Ready To Order...

Let Us Show You Our Blueprint Package.

Building a home? Planning a home? The Blueprint Package from Home Planners, Inc. contains nearly everything you need to get the job done right, whether you're working on your own or with help from an architect, designer, builder or subcontractors. Each Blueprint Package is the result of many hours of work by licensed architects or professional designers.

QUALITY

Hundreds of hours of painstaking effort have gone into the development of your blueprint set. Each home has been quality-checked by professionals to insure accuracy and buildability.

VALUE

Because we sell in volume, you can buy professional-quality blueprints at a fraction of their development cost. With Home Planners, your dream home design costs only a few hundred dollars, not the thousands of dollars that custom architects charge.

SERVICE

Once you've chosen your favorite home plan, we stand ready to serve you with knowledgeable sales people and prompt, efficient service. We ship most orders within 48 hours of receipt and stand behind every set of blueprints we sell.

SATISFACTION

We have been in business since 1946 and have shipped over 1 million blueprints to home builders just like you. Nearly 50 years of service and hundreds of thousands of satisfied customers are your guarantee that Home Planners can do the job for you.

ORDER TOLL FREE 1-800-521-6797

After you've studied our Blueprint Package and Important Extras on the following pages, simply mail the accompanying order form on page 317 or call toll free on our Blueprint Hotline: 1-800-521-6797. We're ready and eager to serve you.

Each set of blueprints is an interrelated collection of floor plans, interior and exterior elevations, dimensions, cross-sections, diagrams and notations showing precisely how your house is to be constructed.

Here's what you get:

Frontal Sheet

This artist's sketch of the exterior of the house, done in two-point perspective, gives you an idea of how the house will look when built and landscaped. Large ink-line floor plans show all levels of the house and provide a quick overview of your new home's livability, as well as a handy reference for studying furniture placement.

Foundation Plan

Drawn to 1/4-inch scale, this sheet shows the complete foundation layout, including support

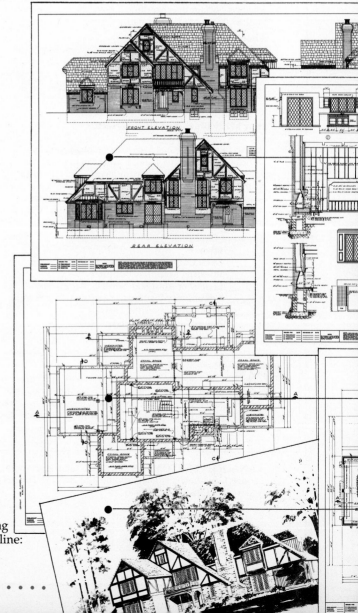

walls, excavated and unexcavated areas, if any and foundation notes. If slab construction rather than basement, the plan shows footings and details for a monolithic slab. This page, or another in the set, also includes a sample plot plan for locating your house on a building site.

Detailed Floor Plans

Complete in 1/4-inch scale, these plans show the layout of each floor of the house. All rooms and interior spaces are carefully dimensioned and keys are provided for cross-section details given later in the plans. The position of all electrical outlets and switches are clearly shown.

House Cross-Sections

Large-scale views, normally drawn at 3/8-inch equals 1 foot, show sections or cut-aways of the foundation, interior walls, exterior walls, floors, stairways and roof details. Additional cross-sections are given to show important changes in floor, ceiling or roof heights or the relationship of one level to another. Extremely valuable for construction, these sections show exactly how the various parts of the house fit together.

Interior Elevations

These large-scale drawings show the design and placement of kitchen and bathroom cabinets, laundry areas, fireplaces, bookcases and other built-ins. Little "extras," such as mantelpiece and wainscoting drawings, plus moulding sections, provide details that give your home that custom touch.

Exterior Elevations

Drawings in 1/4-inch scale show the front, rear and sides of your house and give necessary notes on exterior materials and finishes. Particular attention is given to cornice detail, brick and stone accents or other finish items that make your home distinctive.

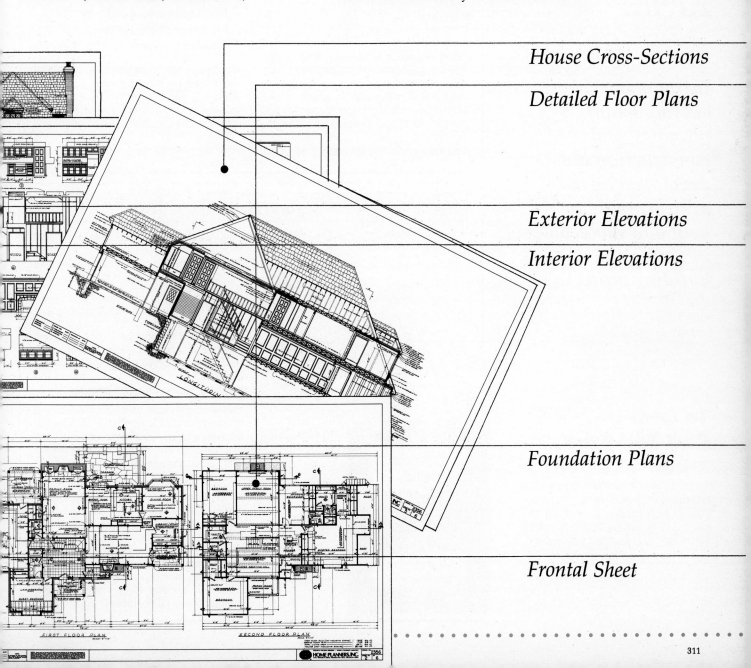

House Cross-Sections

Detailed Floor Plans

Exterior Elevations

Interior Elevations

Foundation Plans

Frontal Sheet

Important Extras To Do The Job Right!

Introducing six important planning and construction aids developed by our professionals to help you succeed in your home-building project.

To Order, Call Toll Free 1-800-521-6797

To add these important extras to your Blueprint Package, simply indicate your choices on the order form on page 317 or call us Toll Free 1-800-521-6797 and we'll tell you more about these exciting products.

MATERIALS LIST

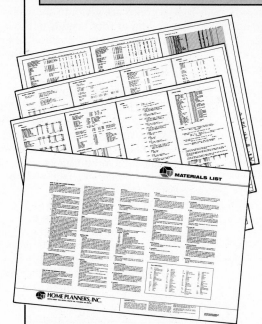

For each design in our portfolio, we offer a customized materials take-off that is invaluable in planning and estimating the cost of your new home. This comprehensive list outlines the quantity, type and size of material needed to build your house (with the exception of mechanical system items). Included are:

- framing lumber
- roofing and sheet metal
- windows and doors
- exterior sheathing material and trim
- masonry, veneer and fireplace materials
- tile and flooring materials
- kitchen and bath cabinetry
- interior sheathing and trim
- rough and finish hardware
- many more items

This handy list helps you or your builder cost out materials and serves as a ready reference sheet when you're compiling bids. It also provides a cross-check against the materials specified by your builder and helps coordinate the substitution of items you may need to meet local codes.

(Note: Because of differing local codes, building methods, and availability of materials, our Materials Lists do not include mechanical materials. To obtain necessary take-offs and recommendations, consult heating, plumbing and electrical contractors. Materials Lists are not sold separately from the Blueprint Package.)

SPECIFICATION OUTLINE

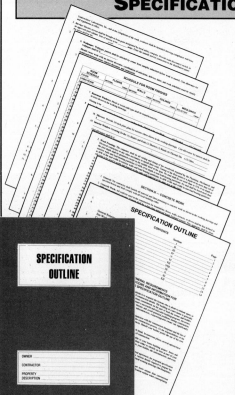

This valuable 16-page document is critical to building your house correctly. Designed to be filled in by you or your builder, this booklet lists 166 stages or items crucial to the building process.

For the layman, it provides a comprehensive review of the construction process and helps in making the specific choices of materials, models and processes. For the builder, it serves as a guide to preparing a building quotation and forms the basis for the construction program.

Designed primarily as a reference for the homeowner, this Specification Outline can become a legally binding document. Once it is filled out and agreed upon by owner and builder, it becomes a complete Project Specification.

When combined with the blueprints, a signed contract and schedule, the Specification Outline becomes a legal document and record for the building of your home. Many home builders find it useful to order two of these outlines—one as a worksheet in formulating the specifications and another to be carefully completed as a legal document.

<table>
<tr><td>

DETAIL SHEETS
</td><td>

Because local codes and requirements vary greatly, we recommend that you obtain drawings and bids from licensed contractors to do your mechanical plans. However, if you want to know more about techniques – and deal more confidently with subcontractors – we offer these remarkably useful detail sheets. Each is an excellent tool that will enhance your understanding of these technical subjects.
</td></tr>
</table>

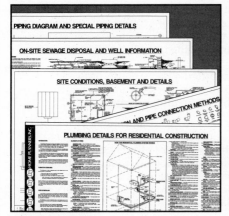

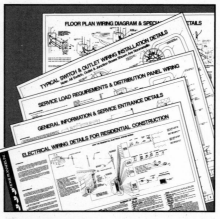

PLUMBING

The Blueprint Package includes locations for all the plumbing fixtures in your new house, including sinks, lavatories, tubs, showers, toilets, laundry trays and water heaters. However, if you want to know more about the complete plumbing system, these 24x36-inch detail sheets will prove very useful. Prepared to meet requirements of the National Plumbing Code, these six fact-filled sheets give general information on pipe schedules, fittings, sump-pump details, water-softener hookups, septic system details and much more. Color-coded sheets include a glossary of terms.

ELECTRICAL

The locations for every electrical switch, plug and outlet are shown in your Blueprint Package. However, these Electrical Details go further to take the mystery out of household electrical systems. Prepared to meet requirements of the National Electrical Code, these comprehensive 24x36-inch drawings come packed with helpful information, including wire sizing, switch-installation schematics, cable-routing details, appliance wattage, door-bell hook-ups, typical service panel circuitry and much more. Six sheets are bound together and color-coded for easy reference. A glossary of terms is also included.

CONSTRUCTION

The Blueprint Package contains everything an experienced builder needs to construct a particular house. However, it doesn't show all the ways that houses can be built, nor does it explain alternate construction methods. To help you understand how your house will be built – and offer additional techniques – this set of drawings depicts the materials and methods used to build foundations, fireplaces, walls, floors and roofs. Where appropriate, the drawings show acceptable alternatives. These six sheets will answer questions for the advanced do-it-yourselfer or home planner.

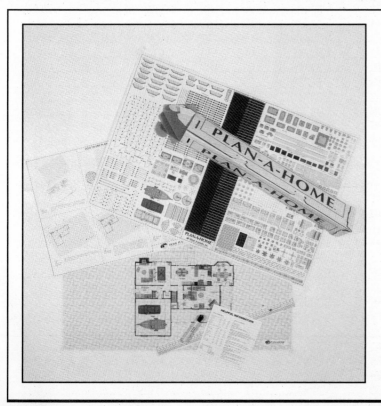

Plan-A-Home®

Plan-A-Home® is an easy-to-use tool that helps you design a new home, arrange furniture in a new or existing home, or plan a remodeling project. Each package contains:

- More than *700 peel-off planning symbols* on a self-stick vinyl sheet, including walls, windows, doors, all types of furniture, kitchen components, bath fixtures and many more. All are made of durable, peel-and-stick vinyl you can use over and over.
- A reusable, transparent, *1/4-inch scale planning grid* made of tough mylar that matches the scale of actual working drawings (1/4-inch equals 1 foot). This grid provides the basis for house layouts of up to 140x92 feet.
- *Tracing paper* and a protective sheet for copying or transferring your completed plan.
- A *felt-tip pen*, with water-soluble ink that wipes away quickly.

With Plan-A-Home®, you can make basic planning decisions for a new house or make modifications to an existing house. Use with your Blueprint Package to test modifications to rooms or to plan furniture arrangements before you build. Plan-A-Home® lets you lay out areas as large as a 7,500 square foot, six-bedroom, seven-bath house.

House Blueprint Price Schedule and Plans Index

These pages contain all the information you need to price your blueprints. In general, the larger and more complicated the house, the more it costs to design and thus the higher the price we must charge for the blueprints. Remember, however, that these prices are far less than you would normally pay for the services of a licensed architect or professional designer. Custom home designs and related architectural services often cost thousands of dollars, ranging from 5% to 15% of the cost of construction. By ordering our blueprints you are potentially saving enough money to afford a larger house, or to add those "extra" amenities such as a patio, deck, swimming pool or even an upgraded kitchen or luxurious master suite.

To use the index below, refer to the design number listed in chronological order (a helpful page reference is also given). Note the price index letter and refer to the House Blueprint Price Schedule at right for the cost of one, four or eight sets of blueprints or the cost of a reproducible sepia. Additional prices are shown for identical and reverse blueprint sets, as well as a very useful Materials List to accompany your plans.

House Plan	Price	Page
V31093	A	48
V31210	A	123
V31220	B	120
V31230	A	91
V31265	C	99
V31267	B	100
V31270	D	71
V31292	A	93
V31298	C	209
V31308	A	83
V31324	B	92
V31341	A	125
V31347	B	97
V31348	B	95
V31353	A	59
V31358	A	81
V31375	B	126
V31376	A	127
V31377	A	126
V31378	B	127
V31386	A	123
V31391	A	93
V31705	B	87
V31717	A	97
V31739	C	213
V31768	B	83
V31770	A	81
V31822	C	129
V31842	B	120
V31850	B	122
V31882	B	81
V31927	C	70
V31930	B	94
V31935	B	98
V31961	C	86
V31963	D	203
V31974	C	208
V31976	C	212
V31977	B	88

House Plan	Price	Page
V31978	B	59
V31981	B	83
V31985	C	89
V32111	C	60
V32125	B	89
V32137	B	85
V32143	B	76
V32169	D	199
V32171	B	84
V32173	D	44
V32205	B	195
V32213	C	201
V32216	C	86
V32218	C	63
V32243	C	72
V32247	C	43
V32248	C	45
V32254	C	72
V32291	B	98
V32331	C	85
V32334	C	124
V32354	C	74
V32361	B	92
V32366	A	90
V32373	B	91
V32375	B	49
V32377	A	51
V32392	D	191
V32393	B	50
V32502	C	196
V32504	C	197
V32511	B	186
V32512	C	78
V32514	B	128
V32536	C	42
V32547	C	128
V32548	C	193
V32549	C	200
V32552	C	182

House Plan	Price	Page
V32560	C	204
V32574	C	79
V32576	C	205
V32579	D	133
V32580	C	132
V32583	C	210
V32584	C	46
V32588	C	47
V32589	C	121
V32608	A	58
V32624	B	75
V32628	A	58
V32669	B	131
V32679	C	41
V32715	C	130
V32716	C	187
V32735	C	55
V32758	C	66
V32759	C	135
V32761	B	194
V32763	C	40
V32769	C	211
V32770	B	192
V32773	C	67
V32786	B	68
V32787	B	69
V32788	B	121
V32827	C	138
V32828	B	53
V32831	C	291
V32835	C	184
V32836	C	56
V32837	C	57
V32841	B	64
V32842	B	65
V32843	C	118
V32844	C	119
V32845	B	49
V32846	C	207

House Plan	Price	Page
V32847	C	206
V32848	C	188
V32849	C	94
V32850	C	77
V32856	C	136
V32868	B	137
V32879	D	278
V32882	C	272
V32883	C	295
V32886	B	269
V32893	C	52
V32894	C	134
V32895	D	180
V32896	C	181
V32900	C	296
V32901	C	38
V32902	B	268
V32913	B	267
V32916	B	275
V32917	B	266
V32918	B	273
V32920	D	297
V32926	D	54
V32928	C	294
V32930	B	271
V32931	B	274
V32932	C	39
V32934	D	192
V32936	C	183
V32937	C	185
V32940	E	300
V32941	B	270
V32942	B	270
V32943	B	270
V32944	C	62
V32951	E	302
V32952	E	298
V32955	E	303
V32956	E	299

House Blueprint Price Schedule
(Prices are subject to change without notice)

	1-set Study Package	4-set Building Package	8-set Building Package	1-set Reproducible Sepias
Schedule A	$150	$210	$270	$300
Schedule B	$180	$240	$300	$360
Schedule C	$210	$270	$330	$420
Schedule D	$240	$300	$360	$480
Schedule E	$360	$420	$480	$600

Additional Identical Blueprints in same order ....$40 per set
Reverse Blueprints (Mirror Image) ....$40 per set
Specification Outlines ....$5 each
Materials Lists
    Schedule A-D $35
    Schedule E $45

To Order: Fill in and send the Order Form on page 317 – or call us Toll Free 1-800-521-6797.

House Plan	Price	Page
V32962	B	277
V32966	D	276
V32983	A	292
V33148	B	97
V33151	C	61
V33198	B	124
V33300	E	301
V33311	D	179
V33360	D	214
V33361	D	178
V33362	D	177
V34019	A	101
V34023	B	265
V34036	B	281
V34052	B	215
V34074	C	16
V34084	B	224
V34090	B	151
V34091	B	155
V34092	C	154
V34095	A	104
V34096	A	175
V34099	A	173
V34101	B	225
V34102	B	172
V34103	B	23
V34104	B	105
V34105	A	17
V34106	A	163
V34107	A	31
V34115	B	167
V34117	A	20
V34121	B	106
V34122	B	232
V34124	B	262
V34127	C	142
V34128	B	15
V34130	D	28
V34133	A	160
V34136	B	26
V34139	A	168
V34141	C	166
V34143	B	107
V34146	A	102
V34147	B	139
V34149	B	162
V34152	A	37
V34154	A	290
V34155	A	263
V34159	A	113
V34160	B	156
V34162	B	157
V34163	A	33
V34165	C	149
V34168	A	32
V34171	C	29
V34174	A	230
V34175	A	231
V34179	B	112
V34180	B	171
V34181	B	115
V34182	A	114
V34184	C	22
V34185	D	170
V34188	B	176
V34189	B	169
V34190	B	153
V34191	B	150
V34192	B	174
V34193	B	143
V34194	B	288
V34195	A	35
V34196	B	141
V34197	B	145
V34198	A	34
V34199	B	27
V34200	B	261
V34201	B	260
V34202	B	233
V34203	A	140
V34207	B	36
V34209	A	30
V34212	A	18
V34213	A	21
V34214	B	280
V34215	C	152
V34240	C	108
V34241	C	159
V34247	B	111
V34248	A	110
V34249	B	161
V34250	C	164
V34254	B	165
V34257	B	244
V34264	B	282
V34268	B	250
V34270	C	251
V34277	C	279
V34278	B	245
V34281	B	285
V34283	C	24
V34287	B	284
V34288	C	25
V34289	C	116
V34290	C	239
V34291	C	148
V34295	B	103
V34298	C	229
V34300	B	228
V34308	C	109
V34309	C	144
V34313	B	289
V34325	C	147
V34326	C	146
V34327	C	19
V34328	C	286
V34330	C	287
V34331	C	158
V34334	B	283
V34350	C	217
V34354	C	227
V34361	C	217
V34365	C	227
V34372	C	217
V34376	C	227
V34389	C	117
V34391	B	257
V34396	B	258
V34397	B	238
V34404	B	259
V34405	B	243
V34406	B	242
V34408	C	246
V34503	C	240
V34505	E	254
V34506	D	253
V34513	C	241
V34520	D	256
V34525	C	255
V34527	C	252
V34530	D	249
V34531	C	248
V34534	C	223
V34535	D	220
V34537	C	236
V34538	D	221
V34543	C	218
V34547	D	234
V34548	E	235
V34551	D	222
V34553	D	264
V34554	D	247

Before You Order . . .

Before completing the coupon at right or calling us on our Toll-Free Blueprint Hotline, you may be interested to learn more about our service and products. Here's some information you will find helpful.

Quick Turnaround
We process and ship every blueprint order from our office within 48 hours. On most orders, we do even better. Normally, if we receive your order by 5 p.m. Eastern Time, we'll process it the same day and ship it the following day. Because of this quick turnaround, we won't send a formal notice acknowledging receipt of your order.

Our Exchange Policy
Since blueprints are printed in response to your order, we cannot honor requests for refunds. However, we will exchange your entire first order for an equal number of blueprints at a price of $20.00 for the first set and $10.00 for each additional set, plus the difference in cost if exchanging for a design in a higher price bracket. (Sepias are not exchangeable.) All sets from the first order must be returned before the exchange can take place. Please add $7.00 for postage and handling via UPS regular service; $10.00 via UPS 2nd Day Air.

About Reverse Blueprints
If you want to build in reverse of the plan as shown, we will include an extra set of reversed blueprints (mirror image) for an additional fee of $40. Although lettering and dimensions appear backward, reverses will be a useful visual aid if you decide to flop the plan.

Modifying or Customizing Our Plans
With over 2,500 different plans from which to choose, you are bound to find a Home Planners' design that suits your lifestyle, budget and building site. In addition, our plans can be customized to your taste by your choice of siding, decorative detail, trim, color and other non-structural alterations.

If you do need to make minor modifications to the plans, these can normally be accomplished by your builder without the need for expensive blueprint modifications. However, if you decide to revise the plans significantly, we strongly suggest that you order our reproducible sepias and consult a licensed architect or professional designer to help you redraw the plans to your particular needs.

Architectural and Engineering Seals
Some cities and states are now requiring that a licensed architect or engineer review and "seal" your blueprints prior to construction. This is often due to local or regional concerns over energy consumption, safety codes, seismic ratings, etc. For this reason, you may find it necessary to consult with a local professional to have your plans reviewed. This can normally be accomplished with minimum delays, for a nominal fee.

Compliance with Local Codes and Regulations
At the time of creation, our plans are drawn to specifications published by Building Officials Code Administrators (BOCA), the Southern Standard Building Code, or the Uniform Building Code and are designed to meet or exceed national building standards.

Some states, counties and municipalities have their own codes, zoning requirements and building regulations. Before starting construction, consult with local building authorities and make sure you comply with local ordinances and codes, including obtaining any necessary permits or inspections as building progresses. In some cases, minor modifications to your plans by your builder, local architect or designer may be required to meet local conditions and requirements.

Foundation and Exterior Wall Changes
Most of our plans are drawn with either a full or partial basement foundation. Depending upon your specific climate or regional building practices, you may wish to convert this basement to a slab or crawlspace. Most professional contractors and builders can easily adapt your plans to alternate foundation types. Likewise, most can easily convert 2x4 wall construction to 2x6, or vice versa. If you need more guidance on these conversions, our handy Construction Detail Sheets, shown on page 313, describe how such conversions can be made.

How Many Blueprints Do You Need?
A single set of blueprints is sufficient to study a home in greater detail. However, if you are planning to obtain cost estimates from a contractor or subcontractors - or if you are planning to build immediately - you will need more sets. Because additional sets are cheaper when ordered in quantity with the original order, make sure you order enough blueprints to satisfy all requirements. The following checklist will help you determine how many you need:

_____ Owner

_____ Builder (generally requires at least three sets; one as a legal document, one to use during inspections, and at least one to give to subcontractors)

_____ Local Building Department (often requires two sets)

_____ Mortgage Lender (usually one set for a conventional loan; three sets for FHA or VA loans)

_____ TOTAL NUMBER OF SETS

 Toll Free 1-800-521-6797

Normal Office Hours:
8:00 a.m. to 8:00 p.m. - Eastern Time
Monday through Friday
Our staff will gladly answer any questions during normal office hours. Our answering service can place orders after hours or on weekends.

If we receive your order by 5:00 p.m. Eastern Time, we'll process it the same day and ship it the following day. When ordering by phone, please have your charge card ready. We'll also ask you for the Order Form Key Number on the opposite page. Please use our Toll-Free number for blueprint and book orders only.

By FAX: Copy the Order Form on the next page and send it on our International FAX line: 1-602-297-6219.

Canadian Customers

For faster, more economical service, Canadian customers should add 20% to all prices and mail in Canadian funds to:

Home Planners, Inc.
20 Cedar Street North
Kitchener, Ontario N2H 2W8
Phone (519) 743-4169

HOME PLANNERS, INC., 3275 WEST INA ROAD
SUITE 110, TUCSON, ARIZONA 85741

THE BASIC BLUEPRINT PACKAGE

Rush me the following (please refer to the Plans Index and Price Schedule in this section):

_____ Set(s) of blueprints for
plan number(s) _____. $_____

_____ Set(s) of sepias for
plan number(s) _____. $_____

_____ Additional identical blueprints in same
order @ $40.00 per set. $_____

_____ Reverse blueprints @ $40.00 per set. $_____

IMPORTANT EXTRAS

Rush me the following:

_____ Materials List @ $35.00 Schedule A-D;
$45.00 Schedule E $_____

_____ Specification Outlines @ $5.00 each. $_____

_____ Detail Sets @ $14.95 each; any two for $22.95;
all three for $29.95 (save $14.90). $_____

☐ Plumbing ☐ Electrical ☐ Construction

(These helpful details provide general
construction advice and are not
specific to any single plan.)

_____ Plan-A-Home® @ $29.95 each. $_____

_____ SUB-TOTAL $_____

SALES TAX (Arizona residents add 5% sales tax;
Michigan residents add 4% sales tax.) $_____

POSTAGE AND HANDLING	1-3 sets	4 or more sets	
UPS DELIVERY (Requires street address - No P.O. Boxes)			
•UPS Regular Service Allow 4-5 days delivery	☐ $5.00	☐ $7.00	$_____
•UPS 2nd Day Air Allow 2-3 days delivery	☐ $7.00	☐ $10.00	$_____
•UPS Next Day Air Allow 1-2 days delivery	☐ $16.50	☐ $20.00	$_____
POST OFFICE DELIVERY If no street address available. Allow 4-5 days delivery	☐ $7.00	☐ $10.00	$_____
OVERSEAS AIR MAIL DELIVERY Note: All delivery times are from date Blueprint Package is shipped.	☐ $30.00	☐ $50.00	$_____
	☐ Send C.O.D.		

TOTAL (Subtotal, tax, and postage) $_____

YOUR ADDRESS (please print)

Name_____

Street_____

City_____ State_____ Zip_____

Daytime telephone number (_____)_____

FOR CREDIT CARD ORDERS ONLY

Please fill in the boxes below:

Credit card number_____

Exp. Date: Month/Year_____

Check one ☐ Visa   ☐ MasterCard

Signature_____

Order Form Key   Please check appropriate box:
[V3BP]   ☐ Licensed Builder-Contractor
          ☐ Home Owner

H O M E   O R D E R   F O R M

HOME PLANNERS, INC., 3275 WEST INA ROAD
SUITE 110, TUCSON, ARIZONA 85741

THE BASIC BLUEPRINT PACKAGE

Rush me the following (please refer to the Plans Index and Price Schedule in this section):

_____ Set(s) of blueprints for
plan number(s) _____. $_____

_____ Set(s) of sepias for
plan number(s) _____. $_____

_____ Additional identical blueprints in same
order @ $40.00 per set. $_____

_____ Reverse blueprints @ $40.00 per set. $_____

IMPORTANT EXTRAS

Rush me the following:

_____ Materials List @ $35.00 Schedule A-D;
$45.00 Schedule E $_____

_____ Specification Outlines @ $5.00 each. $_____

_____ Detail Sets @ $14.95 each; any two for $22.95;
all three for $29.95 (save $14.90). $_____

☐ Plumbing ☐ Electrical ☐ Construction

(These helpful details provide general
construction advice and are not
specific to any single plan.)

_____ Plan-A-Home® @ $29.95 each. $_____

_____ SUB-TOTAL $_____

SALES TAX (Arizona residents add 5% sales tax;
Michigan residents add 4% sales tax.) $_____

POSTAGE AND HANDLING	1-3 sets	4 or more sets	
UPS DELIVERY (Requires street address - No P.O. Boxes)			
•UPS Regular Service Allow 4-5 days delivery	☐ $5.00	☐ $7.00	$_____
•UPS 2nd Day Air Allow 2-3 days delivery	☐ $7.00	☐ $10.00	$_____
•UPS Next Day Air Allow 1-2 days delivery	☐ $16.50	☐ $20.00	$_____
POST OFFICE DELIVERY If no street address available. Allow 4-5 days delivery	☐ $7.00	☐ $10.00	$_____
OVERSEAS AIR MAIL DELIVERY Note: All delivery times are from date Blueprint Package is shipped.	☐ $30.00	☐ $50.00	$_____
	☐ Send C.O.D.		

TOTAL (Subtotal, tax, and postage) $_____

YOUR ADDRESS (please print)

Name_____

Street_____

City_____ State_____ Zip_____

Daytime telephone number (_____)_____

FOR CREDIT CARD ORDERS ONLY

Please fill in the boxes below:

Credit card number_____

Exp. Date: Month/Year_____

Check one ☐ Visa   ☐ MasterCard

Signature_____

Order Form Key   Please check appropriate box:
[V3BP]   ☐ Licensed Builder-Contractor
          ☐ Home Owner

Additional Plans Books

The Design Category Series

1.

2.

3.

4.

ONE-STORY HOMES
A collection of 470 homes to suit a range of budgets in one-story living. All popular styles, including Cape Cod, Southwestern, Tudor and French. **384 pages. $8.95 ($10.95 Canada)**

TWO-STORY HOMES
478 plans for all budgets in a wealth of styles: Tudors, Saltboxes, Farmhouses, Victorians, Georgians, Contemporaries and more. **416 pages. $8.95 ($10.95 Canada)**

MULTI-LEVEL AND HILL-SIDE HOMES 312 distinctive styles for both flat and sloping sites. Includes exposed lower levels, open staircases, balconies, decks and terraces. **320 pages. $6.95 ($8.95 Canada)**

VACATION AND SECOND HOMES 258 ideal plans for a favorite vacation spot or perfect retirement or starter home. Includes cottages, chalets, and 1-, 1 1/2-, 2-, and multi-levels. **256 pages. $5.95 ($7.50 Canada)**

The Exterior Style Series

9.

10.

11.

12.

330 EARLY AMERICAN HOME PLANS A heartwarming collection of the best in Early American architecture. Traces the style from Colonial structures to popular traditional versions. Includes a history of different styles. **304 pages. $9.95 ($11.95 Canada)**

335 CONTEMPORARY HOME PLANS Required reading for anyone interested in the clean-lined elegance of Contemporary design. Features plans of all sizes and types, as well as a history of this style. **304 pages. $9.95 ($11.95 Canada)**

TUDOR HOUSES The stuff that dreams are made of! A superb portfolio of 80 enchanting Tudor-style homes, from cozy Cotswold cottages to impressive Baronial manors. Includes a decorating section with colorful photographs and illustrations. **208 pages. $10.95 ($12.95 Canada)**

COUNTRY HOUSES Shows off 80 country homes in three eye-catching styles: Cape Cods, Farmhouses and Center-Hall Colonials. Each features an architect's exterior rendering, artist's depiction of a furnished interior room, large floor plans, and planning tips. **208 pages. $10.95 ($12.95 Canada)**

Plan Portfolios

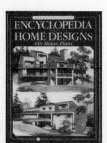

ENCYCLOPEDIA OF HOME DESIGNS
The largest book of its kind — 450 plans in a complete range of housing types, styles and sizes. Includes plans for all building budgets, families and styles of living.

14. 320 pages. $9.95 ($11.95 Canada)

MOST POPULAR HOME DESIGNS
Our customers' favorite plans, including one-story, 1 1/2-story, two-story, and multi-level homes in a variety of styles. Designs feature many of today's most popular amenities: lounges, clutter rooms, media rooms and more.

15. 272 pages. $8.95 ($10.95 Canada)

HOME PLANNERS' STYLE PORTFOLIO
A superb collection of today's most popular styles from Colonials to cool Contemporaries. Incorporates detailed renderings and floor plans with a Chronology of Styles and Glossary of Architectural Terms.

16. 320 pages. $9.95 ($11.95 Canada)

New From Home Planners

5.

AFFORDABLE HOME PLANS For the prospective home builder with a modest or medium budget. Features 430 one-, 1 1/2-, two-story and multi-level homes in a wealth of styles. Included are cost-saving ideas for the budget-conscious. **320 pages. $8.95 ($10.95 Canada)**

6.

DECK PLANNER 25 practical plans and details for decks the do-it-yourselfer can actually build. How-to data and project starters for a variety of decks. Construction details available separately. **112 pages. $7.95 ($9.95 Canada)**

7.

THE HOME LANDSCAPER 55 fabulous front- and back-yard plans that even the do-it-yourselfer can master. Complete construction blueprints and regionalized plant lists available for each design. **208 pages. $12.95 ($15.95 Canada)**

8.

HOME PLANS FOR OUT-DOOR LIVING More than 100 plans to bring the outdoors in. Features terraces, balconies, courtyards, atriums, and sunspaces for homes of all types and styles. Color photography of homes built. **192 pages. $10.95 ($12.95 Canada)**

13.

COLONIAL HOUSES 161 history-inspired homes with up-to-date plans are featured along with 2-color interior illustrations and 4-color photographs. Included are many plans developed for *Colonial Homes'* History House Series. **208 pages. $10.95 ($12.95 Canada)**

17.

LUXURY DREAM HOMES At last, the home you've waited for! A collection of 150 of the best luxury home plans from seven of the most highly regarded designers and architects in the United States. A dream come true for anyone interested in designing, building or remodeling a luxury home. **192 pages. $14.95 ($17.95 Canada)**

Please fill out the coupon below. We will process your order and ship it from our office within 48 hours. Send coupon and check for the total to:

 HOME PLANNERS, INC.
3275 West Ina Road, Suite 110, Dept. BK
Tucson, Arizona 85741

THE DESIGN CATEGORY SERIES – A great series of books edited by design type. Complete collection features 1376 pages and 1273 home plans.

1. ____ One-Story Homes @ $8.95 ($10.95 Canada)	$____
2. ____ Two-Story Homes @ $8.95 ($10.95 Canada)	$____
3. ____ Multi-Level & Hillside Homes @ $6.95 ($8.95 Canada)	$____
4. ____ Vacation & Second Homes @ $5.95 ($7.50 Canada)	$____

NEW FROM HOME PLANNERS

5. ____ Affordable Home Plans @ $8.95 ($10.95 Canada)	$____
6. ____ Deck Planner @ $7.95 ($9.95 Canada)	$____
7. ____ The Home Landscaper @ $12.95 ($15.95 Canada)	$____
8. ____ Home Plans for Outdoor Living @ $10.95 ($12.95 Canada)	$____

THE EXTERIOR STYLE SERIES

9. ____ 330 Early American Home Plans @ $9.95 ($11.95 Canada)	$____
10. ____ 335 Contemporary Home Plans @ $9.95 ($11.95 Canada)	$____
11. ____ Tudor Houses @ $10.95 ($12.95 Canada)	$____
12. ____ Country Houses @ $10.95 ($12.95 Canada)	$____
13. ____ Colonial Houses @ $10.95 ($12.95 Canada)	$____

PLAN PORTFOLIOS

14. ____ Encyclopedia of Home Designs @ $9.95 ($11.95 Canada)	$____
15. ____ Most Popular Home Designs @ $8.95 ($10.95 Canada)	$____
16. ____ Home Planners' Style Portfolio @ $9.95 ($11.95 Canada)	$____
17. ____ Luxury Dream Homes @ $14.95 ($17.95 Canada)	$____
Sub Total	$____
Arizona residents add 5% sales tax; Michigan residents add 4% sales tax	$____
ADD Postage and Handling	$ 2.50
TOTAL (Please enclose check)	$____

Name (please print) _____

Address _____

City _____ State _____ Zip _____

CANADIAN CUSTOMERS: Use Canadian prices and remit in Canadian funds to: Home Planners, Inc., 20 Cedar St. North Kitchener, Ontario N2H 2W8 Phone: (519) 743-4169

TO ORDER BOOKS BY PHONE CALL TOLL FREE 1-800-322-6797

V3BK

REAR ELEVATION

OVER 2½ MILLION BLUEPRINTS SOLD

"We instructed our builder to follow the plans including all of the many details which make this house so elegant... Our home is a fine example of the results one can achieve by purchasing and following the plans which you offer... Everyone who has seen it has assured us that it belongs in 'a picture book.' I truly mean it when I say that my home 'is a DREAM HOUSE.'"

S.P.
Anderson, SC

"We have had a steady stream of visitors, many of whom tell us this is the most beautiful home they've seen. Everyone is amazed at the layout and remark on how unique it is. Our real estate attorney, who is a Chicago dweller and who deals with highly valued properties, told me this is the only suburban home he has seen that he would want to live in."

W. & P.S.
Flossmoor, IL

"Home Planners' blueprints saved us a great deal of money. I acted as the general contractor and we did a lot of the work ourselves. We probably built it for half the cost! We are thinking about more plans for another home. I purchased a competitor's book but my husband only wants your plans!"

K.M.
Grovetown, GA

"We are very happy with the product of our efforts. The neighbors and passersby appreciate what we have created. We have had many people stop by to discuss our house and kindly praise it as being the nicest house in our area of new construction. We have even had one person stop and make us an unsolicited offer to buy the house for much more than we have invested in it."

K. & L.S.
Bolingbrook, IL

"The traffic going past our house is unbelievable. On several occasions, we have heard that it is the 'prettiest house in Batavia.' Also, when meeting someone new and mentioning what street we live on, quite often we're told, 'Oh, you're the one in the yellow house with the wrap-around porch! I love it!'"

A.W.
Batavia, NY

"I have been involved in the building trades my entire life... Since building our home we have built two other homes for other families. Their plans from local professional architects were not nearly as good as yours. For that reason we are ordering additional plan books from you."

T.F.
Kingston, WA

"The blueprints we received from Home Planners were of excellent quality and provided us with exactly what we needed to get our successful home-building project underway. We appreciate Home Planners' invaluable role in our home-building effort."

T.A.
Concord, TN